Return of
THE STRAIGHT DOPE

Have a good
summer.

Your friend,
Alec

Return of
THE STRAIGHT DOPE

Cecil Adams

Edited and with an Introduction by
Ed Zotti

Illustrated by Slug Signorino

BALLANTINE BOOKS / NEW YORK

Library of Congress Catalog Card Number: 93-90463

ISBN: 0-345-38111-4

Illustrations by Slug Signorino
Three-dimensional box on the cover created by George C. Morrissey
Text design by Mary A. Wirth

Manufactured in the United States of America

First Edition: April 1994

10 9 8 7 6 5 4 3 2 1

To Mary, still a fox after all these years, and to Ryan, Annie, and a third party to be named later, who give their father not the strength to go on, God knows, but certainly, in view of the bills, the desperate need.

Contents

Introduction

We had every expectation of getting this volume out a couple years ago but, as you can see, didn't. Sorry. Our dog ate it. Besides, you don't know what those cops in Barbados are like. We know the delay resulted in a great void in the lives of many of you and has led to considerable social unrest. Los Angeles, Somalia, Bosnia. It is all our fault. (We are *never* going to procrastinate on the Serbo-Croatian translation again.) Then again, the worldwide rise in national frustration levels owing to the drought of quality reading material . . . well, I'm not saying it was the *only* factor in the overthrow of Communism. You can't underestimate the role played by bad shoes. But we feel a warm glow of satisfaction just the same.

Tell you one thing. Cecil and I are going to quit making these damn books so fat. Three volumes in ten years, and in that time some of our competitors have filled half a shelf. Of course it is all wide margins and pictures, whereas each Straight Dope book embodies a lifetime of intellectual sustenance. But Lordy, they're charging $14.95 a pop, while we nick you for a lousy $10.00! No wonder we can't afford new linoleum for the chalet. We have therefore decided to adhere to a strict limit of 135,000 jewellike words per volume, which is all the brilliance the ordinary human mind can tolerate at one sitting anyway. The result will be a more frequent supply of Straight Dope books for you, and even vaster—if assuredly deserved—wealth for us.

But enough kvetching. The truth is it has been a satisfying six years. The write-ups in national newspapers, the talk-show appearances, the intimate little dinners with Hillary and Bill . . . FOCs (Friends of Cecil) we were going to call them, but the acronym has an unfortunate ring to it. Being a font of terrestrial wisdom is such a solace. Not that we're getting soft, mind you. Nobody can say a column that deals frankly with placenta stew isn't pushing the envelope.

We could ramble on a bit more here, but heaven knows enough of the Amazon rain forest has been pulped in our behalf already (although I guess if you are going to lay waste to the planet, the Straight Dope is as good a cause as any*). In conclusion we wish to thank Clarence Petersen of the *Chicago Tribune*, who fulfilled the dream of a lifetime by describing our last book as a "mammoth blockbuster" per our detailed instructions in the intro to *More of the Straight Dope*. Good job, Clarence, but try not to be so conspicuous with the cigars. Also, plea though we might, we could not convince Ballantine to put mam. blb. in big letters in a starburst on the cover. (They also nixed our idea about putting the title and, more important, the author's name in embossed gold letters, which always seemed to work for Dean Koontz.) These people have no sense of humor at all. Then again, they always spell our name right on the checks.

And so to the book. We hope you noticed that the SAT scores have finally started to inch up, proof positive that our long, lonely struggle is starting to pay off at last.

—Ed Zotti

Questions, flowers, and expressions of regard to:

Cecil Adams
c/o Chicago Reader
11 E. Illinois St.
Chicago, IL 60611

---

*My, we *are* laying it on a bit thick, aren't we?

Return of
THE STRAIGHT DOPE

In the Beginning

What is the origin of Uncle Sam, the cartoon character symbolizing the United States? Any relation to Sam Hill, as in what the S.H.?
—Anonymous, Denver

Hill, no. Sam Hill is just a soundalike euphemism for "hell" once used by macho American frontiersmen in the presence of women, children, and other sensitive souls. Uncle Sam is a whole different story.

A widely held belief, reported as fact in supposedly reliable reference books, is that the original Uncle Sam was one Sam Wilson, a meat packer in Troy, New York, who supplied rations to the U.S. military during the War of 1812. Wilson was a subcontractor to one Elbert Anderson, and the letters *E.A.—U.S.* were stamped on all the pair's army-bound grub. On being asked what the letters stood for (the abbreviation *U.S.* supposedly was unfamiliar at the time), one of Sam's workers joshed that it stood for "Elbert Anderson and Uncle Sam," meaning the jovial Wilson himself.

The joke was quickly picked up by Wilson's other employees. Many of these men later served in the army during the war, and the story spread from there. This tale appears to have first found its way into print in 1842.

Very neat, but is it true? On the surface it might seem so. Researchers have established that Elbert Anderson and Sam Wilson did exist and did supply meat to the government during the War of 1812.

What's more, the earliest known reference to Uncle Sam in the sense of the U.S. government appeared in 1813 in the Troy *Post*.

But there are reasons to doubt. For one thing, the Uncle Sam = Sam Wilson story didn't see print until thirty years after the event, which seems suspiciously tardy. Second, the notion that someone in 1812 would have to ask what "U.S." stood for is hard to swallow; the available evidence shows that the initials were then in common use.

Third, there's something odd about the newspaper evidence. Sam Wilson was a leading citizen of Troy, New York. Yet none of the newspapers in his hometown seem to have had any knowledge of his connection to Uncle Sam until very late in the day. The 1813 reference in the Troy *Post* says nothing about Wilson, noting merely that "the letters 'U.S.' on the government waggons, &c are supposed to have given rise to [Uncle Sam]."

In 1816 the *Post* reprinted a story from Philadelphia claiming that Uncle Sam originated in the initials *USLD*, meaning United States Light Dragoons, a regiment of which had been formed in 1807. The account said that on being asked what the USLD on their caps stood for, the soldiers said "Uncle Sam's Lazy Dogs." In 1817 the *Post* took up the matter again, this time reverting to the original explanation that Uncle Sam was simply a jocular expansion of the letters *U.S.*

When Sam Wilson died in 1854, none of the newspaper obituaries by Troy writers mentioned the Uncle Sam connection. Significantly, however, two obituaries reprinted from Albany newspapers did talk about Uncle Sam. This suggests that the legend was concocted by out-of-towners with no firsthand knowledge of the facts.

So where did Uncle Sam originate? Nobody knows for sure, but it's likely the original explanation in the Troy *Post* was correct: there was never an actual Uncle Sam; instead, the name was just a wiseguy expansion of the initials *U.S.*

It's worth noting that all the early references to Uncle Sam appeared in "peace" newspapers—that is, papers opposed to the War of 1812—and in every case the usage was derisive. This suggests Uncle Sam was dreamed up by critics of the government who simply wanted to personify the object of their scorn.

I don't doubt, however, that the Sam Wilson story will live on. All the dissenting facts above were set down by antiquarian Albert Matthews in 1908, for God's sake, and you see what headway they've made. Pit truth against a plausible legend and the truth hits the mat every time.

Is there any significance to Italian last names beginning with de, del, or della ("of," "of the")? Do they indicate nobility? Someone told me that della is the highest rank.—Thomas Della Fave, Irving, Texas

Don't get your hopes up, your lordship. Once in a while *de, della,* and the like mean the family was, if not noble, at least a cut above the common herd. But more often the prefix is merely the equivalent of the Irish *Mac* or *O,* the English suffix *-son* (e.g., Johnson), or the Norman-French *Fitz*—that is, it indicates descent, as in de Stefano, "son of Steven." Or it may indicate place of origin, as in del Corso, "dweller near the highway." Roughly the same holds true of French and Spanish names. I've been told that if the initial *D* is capitalized, it signifies noble origin, but knowing how much immigrant names got scrambled en route to the New World, I wouldn't place too much faith in this.

Della has nothing to do with rank; quite the contrary. The surname of New York ad man Jerry Della Femina means "of the

SLUGO de la SIGNORINO ✦ di RATTO di PIGGI CECILIO ADAMSI

woman"; this can mean the original Della Femina was illegitimate, though not necessarily.

The rarely seen prefix *degli*, as in degli Alberti, is one of the few semireliable indications that an Italian family was once part of the gentry, if not the nobility. Degli Alberti means "of the Alberts," and was used in central and northern Italy to mean a family that had become sufficiently grand to refer to itself in the plural.

The situation is clearer with German names. The prefix *von* means "of" and was originally appended to all sorts of names, most of them pretty humble. But at some point over the centuries *von* came to mean that the family had been ennobled—or at least they'd like you to think so. For example, the architect Ludwig Mies van der Rohe, from the West German city of Aachen, was originally Ludwig Mies; he added the rest (Rohe was his mom's maiden name) to give himself a little more status when pitching impressionable clients. Quoth a biographer: "He would not have dared to assume a designation of real German nobility, like 'von,' but 'van der' was permissible; it sounded faintly elegant to the German ear though it was common enough to the Dutch."

Some folks, happily, are above all this faux nobility jive. The writer Sanche de Gramont came from a noble French family, but on moving to the United States changed his name to Ted Morgan, an anagram of his old last name, to celebrate his embrace of democracy. I trust you'll take his example to heart.

Mc Attack

You goofed in your column on surname prefixes. Mac is a Scottish prefix, not Irish. The Irish use Mc instead.—Lisa Files, Chicago

A common belief, but wrong. As Edward MacLysaght writes in *A Guide to Irish Surnames*, "Reference should again be made to one popular misconception, often held outside Ireland, viz. that all Mac names are Scottish—with such well-known Irish names as MacCarthy, MacNamara, MacMahon and MacGuinness prominent all over the world this should not be necessary, yet the illusion seems to persist."

A Failure to Communicate

In a recent column you stated (correctly) that in Italian surnames del, della, and the like are not an indication of noble lineage. You erred, however, when you said plurals such as degli and dei do indicate nobility. In Italian there are seven definite articles: the singular il, lo, la, and l' and the plural i, gli and le. When an article follows the preposition di ("of"), the two words combine to create del, dello, della, dell', dei, degli, or delle. All mean "of the."

Dei and degli simply indicate the plural. The name dei Corsi means "of the highways," just as del Corso means "of the highway." Use of dei, degli, etc., in no way implies that one family was nobler than another.—David Bowie, Greenbelt, Maryland

As so often happens in this wicked world, Cecil has been misunderstood. I did not mean to suggest that use of the plural necessarily meant nobility, only that it sometimes did, especially when used with a proper name (e.g., degli Alberti). You can see why. If you were to introduce yourself rather grandly as David of the Bowies (and by the way, Dave, what's a rock legend such as yourself doing in Greenbelt, Maryland?), people would definitely get the idea that you considered yourself one of the swells.

For similar reasons the would-be big bananas of the Italian Renaissance referred to themselves in the plural; thus Lorenzo de' (short for *dei*) Medici, Lorenzo of the Medicis. In short, a plural could well mean you're descended from the quality, especially if your family came from central or northern Italy.

But it's just as likely you're an ordinary shlub. Another of Cecil's correspondents points out that Thomas Della Fave, the name of the guy who originally wanted to know if he came from nobility, translates as "Thomas of the Beans." What's more, it's misspelled—it should properly be Delle Fave. One more reason to think twice before putting on airs.

The Truth Comes Out

You are absolutely right about my name being spelled wrong. When my father died in 1973, I saw for the first time his naturalization papers. I was shocked that it read "Delle Fave."—Thomas G. Della Fave, Irving, Texas

Everywhere I go these days I see yellow ribbons tied around oak trees, light poles, small animals, etc. These supposedly are to show concern for our troops in the Middle East. However, as I recall, in the song (you know, "tie a yellow ribbon round the old oak tree," blah blah blah) the guy in question is returning from jail. Presumably he went to jail for a reason. Do the troops really appreciate being compared to a criminal? A friend tells me that the song is based on a true story, and that the fellow's crime was something along the lines of stealing bread to feed orphans. True? And why yellow?—Steve Langer, Chicago

After a heroic research effort involving New Jersey talent agents, Iran-hostage spouses, and the Library of Congress, I think I've finally pieced together the whole story. Here are the highlights:

Yellow ribbons first emerged as a national symbol in January 1981, when they sprouted like weeds to welcome home the Americans held hostage in Iran. The whole thing was started by Penelope (Penne) Laingen, wife of Bruce Laingen, U.S. charge d'affaires in Teheran. Ms. Laingen says she was inspired by two things: (1) the song "Tie a Yellow Ribbon Round the Ole Oak Tree," written in 1972 by Irwin Levine and Larry Brown and made famous by Tony Orlando and Dawn, and (2) the prior example of one Gail Magruder. Ms. Laingen writes:

> Gail Magruder, wife of Jeb Stuart Magruder of Watergate fame, put yellow ribbons on her front porch to welcome her husband home from jail. This event was televised on the evening news.
>
> At this point ... I stepped in to change the legend and song from the return of a forgiven prodigal to the return of

an imprisoned hero. Interestingly, I had remembered the Gail Magruder ribbons, but I had only a vague understanding of the Levine-Brown song lyrics, although I knew it involved a "prisoner," which my husband surely was in Iran.

Penne's aim, and that of the other hostage families she was in contact with, was to keep public attention focused on the prisoners. Various ideas had been proposed or tried early on, including asking people to turn on their porch and car lights, honk their horns, ring church bells, display the flag, wear Vietnam-type POW bracelets, etc.

The only idea to catch on was yellow ribbons. Penne hung one made from yellow oilcloth on an oak tree in her front yard in December 1979 and mentioned it to a *Washington Post* reporter who was doing a story on how hostage families were dealing with stress. The reporter described what Penne had done in her article and the yellow ribbon phenomenon took off from there.

Okay, but where did the song "Tie a Yellow Ribbon Round the Ole Oak Tree" come from? At this point the thread starts to get a little tangled.

Larry Brown claimed he heard the returning-convict story on which the song was based in the army. Apparently it was a widely circulated urban legend—so widely, in fact, that it got the songwriters into a bit of hot water. *New York Post* writer Pete Hamill had related the story in a 1971 column with a few different details—for one thing, the convict told his story not to a bus driver but to some college students headed for Fort Lauderdale.

Hamill claimed he'd heard the story from one of the students, a woman he'd met in Greenwich Village. He sued Brown and Levine for stealing his work, but the defense turned up still earlier versions of the tale (Penne Laingen quotes a version from a book published in 1959) and the suit was dropped.

A big difference in many of the earlier stories was that the centerpiece wasn't a yellow ribbon, it was a *white* ribbon or kerchief. But Levine claimed "white kerchief" wouldn't fit the meter, so yellow ribbon it became. In addition to being trochaic, yellow seemed "musical and romantic," he reportedly said.

But there was more to it than that. The 1949 John Wayne movie

She Wore a Yellow Ribbon featured a hit song of the same name, and the line appears in a 1961 Mitch Miller songbook. A source who knows Brown and Levine says they (or at least Levine) privately admit they got the concept of yellow ribbons from the 1949 song.

The movie tune was a rewrite of a song copyrighted in 1917 by George A. Norton titled "Round Her Neck She Wears a Yellow Ribbon (For Her Lover Who Is Fur, Fur Away)." This in turn was apparently based on the popular 1838 minstrel-show song "All Round My Hat" (surely you remember it), which sported the line, "All round my hat I [w]ears a green willow [because] my true love is far, far away." Doesn't scan (or parse) very well, which no doubt explains the switch to yellow ribbons in the twentieth century. Songs with green willows and distant lovers go back at least to 1578.

It's interesting that the ribbons and willows in these songs simply serve as a reminder of a distant loved one, since that's pretty much the only significance of yellow ribbons today. There is no suggestion of the returning prodigal such as we find in the Levine-Brown song, or even of imprisonment, as was the case during the Iran hostage crisis. So I guess we can say that yellow ribbons do have some grounding in tradition, although it's ribbons rather than green willows chiefly as a metrical convenience.

Contrary to popular belief, there is no indication that yellow ribbons had any symbolic value during the American Civil War. The notion that they did stems from the aforementioned John Wayne movie, which featured soldiers in Civil War–era uniforms.

Ribbons Revisited

The first widespread "yellow ribbon fever" was not in 1981 but rather 1973, when the POWs were released from Vietnam. I distinctly remember newsreels of wives, daughters, and sweethearts wearing or displaying this emblem when greeting their loved ones. In fact, I believe the song's massive popularity at the time was due to popular belief that the "prison" mentioned in the lyrics was the Hanoi Hilton.

The "white kerchief" you mention as a precursor of the yellow ribbon is alluded to in medieval and renaissance literature as a token of affection from a fair lady to her noble knight as he goes into battle. In fact, one of the pieces of "evidence" in the trial of Anne Boleyn was a hand-kerchief she allegedly gave to one of Henry VIII's soldiers. (Henry, en-raged at this "proof" of adultery, had her executed.)—N.G., Chicago

It's possible yellow ribbons were displayed here and there in 1973, but they weren't the national phenomenon they became in 1979–1981. I found no references to ribbons in contemporary press accounts of the POW release. That's not surprising, because most of the POWs were home before the song became a hit. The first POWs were released February 12, most were home by the middle of March, and the last was out April 1. Dawn's version of "Tie a Yellow Ribbon" debuted on the *Cash Box* singles chart on February 2 at number eighty-eight and didn't reach number one until May.

Rumor has it that the melody of "The Star Spangled Banner" was taken from an old colonial drinking song. If so, what were the orig-inal, pre–Francis Scott Key words? Can you print them uncut and complete so I can get a singalong going in the clubs?—Reena Pearl, West Hollywood, California

Coming right up, my sweet, but in most nightspots I think you'd have a better luck organizing a singalong of "Onward Christian Sol-diers," for reasons that will become clear. The tune for "The Star Spangled Banner" was taken from "To Anacreon in Heaven," a pop-ular English drinking song written around 1770. Originally it was the theme song of the Anacreontic Society, an organization of up-scale London boozers. (Anacreon was an ancient Greek poet known for his songs of wine and women.)

You probably have the idea that "To Anacreon in Heaven" is some raucous footstomper, and by comparison to the national anthem I suppose it is. However, a generation raised on "99 Bottles of Beer on the Wall" may find it pretty heavy going. Here's the first verse:

> *To Anacreon, in heav'n, where he sat in full glee,*
> *A few sons of harmony sent a petition*
> *That he their inspirer and patron would be;*
> *When this answer arriv'd from the jolly old Grecian—*

Voice, fiddle, and flute,
No longer be mute;
I'll lend ye my name, and inspire ye to boot:
And, besides, I'll instruct ye, like me, to intwine
The myrtle of Venus with Bacchus's vine.

There are five more verses in the same vein. Passable for a bunch of eighteenth-century frat rats, I suppose, but not in the same league as, "Oh Anna, my Delta Gamma, she's got legs like a baby grand pianuh."

Why do women shave their legs and underarms? When did this cus-
tom begin? If it's for hygienic reasons, why don't men do it too? Is it all
a big conspiracy by the razor companies? I've heard some European
women don't shave. Please clarify this mystery.—A., Chicago

I knew if I procrastinated long enough on this often-asked question somebody would eventually do the legwork for me. Sure enough, Pete Cook of Chicago has sent me a 1982 article from the *Journal of American Culture* by Christine Hope bearing the grand title "Caucasian Female Body Hair and American Culture." The gist

of it is that U.S. women were browbeaten into shaving underarm hair by a sustained marketing assault that began in 1915. (Leg hair came later.)

The aim of what Hope calls the Great Underarm Campaign was to inform American womanhood of a problem that till then it didn't know it had, namely unsightly underarm hair. To be sure, women had been concerned about the appearance of their hair since time immemorial, but (sensibly) only the stuff you could see. Prior to World War I this meant scalp, and, for an unlucky few, facial hair. Around 1915, however, sleeveless dresses became popular, opening up a whole new field of female vulnerability for marketers to exploit.

According to Hope, the underarm campaign began in May, 1915, in *Harper's Bazaar*, a magazine aimed at the upper crust. The first ad "featured a waist-up photograph of a young woman who appears to be dressed in a slip with a toga-like outfit covering one shoulder. Her arms are arched over her head revealing perfectly clear armpits. The first part of the ad read 'Summer Dress and Modern Dancing combine to make necessary the removal of objectionable hair.' "

Within three months, Hope tells us, the once-shocking term "underarm" was being used. A few ads mentioned hygiene as a motive for getting rid of hair but most appealed strictly to the ancient yearning to be hip. "The Woman of Fashion says the underarm must be as smooth as the face," read a typical pitch.

The budding obsession with underarm hair drifted down to the proles fairly slowly, roughly matching the widening popularity of sheer and sleeveless dresses. Anti–arm hair ads began appearing in middlebrow *McCall's* in 1917. Women's razors and depilatories didn't show up in the Sears Roebuck catalog until 1922, the same year the company began offering dresses with sheer sleeves. By then the underarm battle was largely won. Advertisers no longer felt compelled to explain the need for their products but could concentrate simply on distinguishing themselves from their competitors.

The anti–leg hair campaign was more fitful. The volume of leg ads never reached the proportions of the underarm campaign. Women were apparently more ambivalent about calling attention to their lower chassis, perhaps out of the well-founded fear that doing so would give the male of the species ideas in a way that naked underarms did not. After rising in the 1920s, hemlines dropped in the thirties, and many women were content to leave their leg hair alone.

Still, some advertisers, as well as an increasing number of fashion and beauty writers, harped on the idea that female leg hair was a curse. Though Hope doesn't say so, what may have put the issue over the top was the famous World War II pinup of Betty Grable displaying her awesome gams. Showing off one's legs became a patriotic act. That plus shorter skirts and sheer stockings, which looked dorky with leg hair beneath, made the antihair pitch an easy sell.

Some argue that there's more to this than short skirts and sleeveless dresses. Cecil's colleague Marg Meikle (*Dear Answer Lady*, 1992) notes that Greek statues of women in antiquity had no pubic hair, suggesting that hairlessness was some sort of ideal of feminine beauty embedded in Western culture. If so, a lot of Western culture never got the message. Greek women today (and Mediterranean women generally) do not shave their hair. The practice has been confined largely to English-speaking women of North America and Great Britain, although one hears that it's slowly spreading elsewhere.

So what's the deal with Anglo-Saxons? Some lingering vestige of Victorian prudery? Good question, but what with world unrest, the comet crisis, and Cecil's research assistants having missed their naps, not high on my priority list. Here's hoping some all-but-thesis Ph.D. candidate will pick up the trail.

During the recent Christmas season I saw references everywhere to "Victorian" Christmas celebrations—house tours, store windows, magazine advertisements, etc. I can understand people pining for a simpler time, provided we overlook such details as child labor, Jim Crow laws, and women not having the right to vote. What I wonder is whether people in Victorian times waxed nostalgic about prior eras. Did they have "Federalist" Christmases idealizing the late 1700s? For that matter, did the Federalists have "colonial" Christmases idealizing the late 1600s? Or did prior generations have enough sense to appreciate their own time?—Stella-Rondo Whitaker, Washington, D.C.

Sense has nothing to do with it. It's just that, to paraphrase musical philosopher Dan Hicks, you can't miss it if it won't go away.

Nostalgia, like Rice Chex, antacid tablets, and Dan Rather, is a product of modern urban industrial society, which is continually assaulted by change (a.k.a. progress, for the optimists among us) and where most people have lost their sense of connection to the land. In a traditional agricultural society there's nothing to get nostalgic about, since you're still living on the land and yesterday was pretty much the same as today.

Longing for the past dates from the early nineteenth century, not long after the start of the industrial revolution in England. (The word nostalgia wasn't widely applied to said longing until after World War I, having previously signified a pathological case of homesickness.) Early promoters of nostalgia included the poet William Wordsworth and the novelist Sir Walter Scott, whose novel *Ivanhoe* (1819) launched a fad for chivalry. Romantic literature appealed to city folk, now a bit disenchanted with urban life (as the philosophes of a previous generation had not been) and thus inclined to a sentimental view of the lost joys of nature, childhood, and the past.

Not coincidentally, our modern idea of Christmas also dates from the early nineteenth century. Prior to that time celebrations of Christmas varied widely among regions. (In Puritan New England, Christmas wasn't even a legal holiday until 1856.) Several things changed that, among them Charles Dickens's *A Christmas Carol* (1843). The success of this book and the many other Christmas books and articles Dickens wrote later was greatly amplified by the rise of large-scale commercial publishing and helped fix the Victorian era as the classic Christmas setting throughout the English-speaking world. Other contributors to the Victorian Christmas tradition include Prince Albert, husband of Victoria, who popularized the Christmas tree, previously a German custom.

Merchandised sentiment eventually replaced pre-industrial holiday traditions. Victorian celebrations had some inherent charm, of course. But it was only by dint of constant repetition in the media that frosted windowpanes, carolers, top hats and long dresses, and (in America) fat guys in red suits became "iconic" of Christmas, as we pop-culturati say. Harmless enough, I suppose. But next time you get the warm fuzzies watching some Victorian Xmas special on TV, remember you feel that way in part because you've been trained to.

How did we arrive at our standardized sizes of 8½ × 11 inches for letter paper and 8½ × 14 for "legal paper"? Was it totally random or was there some practical reason?—Phillip Raskin, Plantation, Florida

Random, mostly, although you'll hear lots of crackpot theories and lame jokes. Sample: lawyers use legal size because they need 14 inches to say what honest folks can fit in 11 (snort). Some say legal paper is used because when you're taking notes in a courtroom you don't have to make noise changing sheets as often. A likely story, you may say, but we don't really have a better one.

As for letter paper, it's cut from a 17 × 22 sheet, the mold for which, legend has it, was the largest a papermaker could conveniently carry in days of yore. It's claimed Henry VIII standardized this size, called *foolscap*, to prevent chiseling by the trade. Nice try, but the truth is that: (1) much larger molds were routinely used; (2) foolscap was anywhere from 12 × 15 to 14 × 18, depending on the grade, not 17 × 22; and (3) there is no evidence English paper sizes were standardized until long after Henry VIII.

For the facts, such as they are, we turn to paper historian John Bidwell, who writes, "I believe our standard 8½ × 11 typing paper is a quarter sheet of what eighteenth- and nineteenth-century papermakers would call 'writing medium.' Printers used a medium sheet of 18 × 23 inches but stationers preferred a smaller version of medium measuring 17 × 22 inches. . . . In 1923 a joint panel of manufacturers, distributors, and consumers drafted guidelines for standard paper sizes, which were revised in 1932 and eventually adopted, in a simplified form, by the Bureau of Standards, which is or was part of the Department of Commerce. These standards define writing medium as 17 × 22 inches."

Okay, but why 17 × 22? I say it was a random shot—you know how we Heisenbergians loathe causation—abetted somewhat by the fact that 8½ × 11 makes a nice-sized sheet.

The situation with legal size (8½ × 14) is equally murky. It arguably does derive from foolscap, a traditional paper size. The type of foolscap used for writing was typically 16¾ × 13½ inches and was often folded to make a page 8⅜ × 13½ that among other things was used for writing official documents. At this point we are required to make something of a stab, but we note that by the 1870s a paper size called legal cap or legal blank had emerged that was 8½ inches wide and anywhere from 13 to 16 inches long. It seems reasonable to suppose that somebody just started cutting foolscap pages in half and selling them to lawyers, who'd buy anything.

Eight-and-a-half-by-whatever is not a world standard. Letter paper in Europe is a size called A4, which is 210 × 297 millimeters—about 8¼ × 11½ inches. The basic A-series sheet, A0, is one square meter in area, 841 × 1189 millimeters. You fold that in half to get A1, you fold *that* in half to get A2, till eventually you get down to A4, A5, A6, etc. All A sizes are in the proportion 1 wide by the square root of 2 deep (1:1.414 . . .). It's a bit compulsive and you will not be surprised to learn it was thought up by the Germans. A-series paper became an international standard, though not an American one, in 1930.

What was the Spanish Main? Was there a Spanish Backup?—Aleck Smart, Chicago

Quiet, rodent. Apparently the Spanish Main originally meant the Spanish-controlled mainland, meaning the north coast of South America and later the Caribbean coast of Central America as well. English pirates, never punctilious in matters of usage, eventually began slinging the term around casually to denote the Caribbean itself.

Prior to the invention of the flying machine, did people fold paper into the traditional paper airplane shape and let 'er fly? Or did the airplane inspire the invention of the paper airplane?—Michael Anstead, Montreal, Quebec

One of your more piquant questions, ain't it? Presumably you didn't have model railroads until you had railroads. But not only did model (including paper) airplanes precede airplanes, the former were an essential step in the development of the latter, and the histories of the two are inextricably linked.

Unfortunately, that's about all we can definitively say about paper airplanes, a subject that is shrouded in obscurity—deservedly, the cretins may say, but what do they know? Credit for the first paper

airplane is generally given to Leonardo da Vinci, prompting *Scientific American* magazine to name the prize awarded in its 1967–1968 paper airplane contest the Leonardo. But while Cecil does not want to take anything away from the ultimate Renaissance man, close examination suggests he may not deserve the honor.

Leonardo, or Len, as I like to think of him, was interested in flight and designed a parachute (square, perversely enough) and a primitive helicopter. (One of his model choppers, using feathers for rotors, is thought to have gotten airborne, although scoffers downplay this accomplishment, saying it was simply based on a then-popular kid's toy that was also capable of flight.) He made reference in one of his notebooks to building a model airplane out of parchment, the paper of the day, and there is a tradition, undoubtedly false, that he actually flew.

But it's debatable whether Leonardo had any clue about airfoils, which of course are the heart and soul of paper airplanes and indeed of virtually all aircraft. Paper airplane aficionados, no doubt hoping to drag in a big name and thus lend a cloak of respectability to their craft, say Leonardo did understand airfoils and so may legitimately be said to be the father of the fold-'em-and-fly-'em school of aeronautics. But his notes and drawings make it pretty obvious that flying as he understood it was a brute force proposition—the way you stayed aloft was by flapping your wings, forcing air down, and clawing your way into the sky. This has little to do with the paper airplanes of today, whose charm lies in their ability to stay aloft simply by gliding, with minimal exertion on the part of the thrower.

One can argue that the true father of the paper airplane—at least the one true father of whom we have any detailed knowledge—was an English squire named George Cayley, who built gliders around 1800. Cayley constructed several of these from kites (linen rather than paper, but close enough) fastened to poles, which he flung like a javelin from a hillside near his home. After a little fine-tuning he found he could get up considerable distance, and a new form of recreation for sixth-grade recess was born.

Experimentalists by that time had a rough knowledge of airfoils, based in part on efforts to improve the efficiency of windmills. Cayley greatly expanded on this during his own research and later, when he wrote a detailed and fairly accurate treatise on aircraft design. It attracted little notice, but it's not Cayley's fault if he was surrounded by dopes.

As for who designed the classic paper "dart" known to every schoolchild—well, we don't know for sure. We do know that in 1867 J. W. Butler and E. Edwards of Great Britain proposed a human-sized dart that was virtually identical in design, if not in scale, to the modern paper variety. (The propellant was not to have been a giant hand, however, but rather a solid fuel.) The plane was never built and it was a long time before practical delta-winged aircraft emerged. But some bored grade-schooler either ripped off Butler-Edwards or had a remarkably similar inspiration, because the design has been the foundation of 90 percent of paper aircraft constructed since.

Why do we call polka dots "polka" dots when all they really are, are dots?—Curious, But Not Losing Too Much Sleep, a.k.a. Don Bogen, Dallas

Glad to see you're keeping a sense of perspective about this, Don. Polka dots are a by-product of the immense popularity of polka dancing in the nineteenth century. There were polka jackets, polka hats, even polka gauze. Whether you were originally supposed to use these while engaged in polka-ing is not clear; more probably it was like the "radio" in Radio Flyer wagons—the inventor just wanted to bask in the penumbra of with-itness the word suggested. "Polka dots" does have the advantage of suggesting a *pattern* of dots, which the word "dots" alone does not.

Has anyone ever actually been tarred and feathered, or is this just some kind of bizarro fable? Who engaged in this practice and against whom? Wouldn't being covered with boiling tar usually prove fatal? How would you get the tar and feathers off, if in fact you ever could? The topic is neglected in "Hints from Heloise."—Sherman Pothole, Somerville, Massachusetts

Tarring and feathering may have been bizarro, Sherm, but it's no fable. One of the stranger manifestations of the American propensity for mob violence, the practice dates back to at least 1740 and didn't die out until after World War I. It was especially popular just prior to the Revolutionary War, when many customs officials and British sympathizers got daubed. Moonshiners later tarred and feathered revenooers, and during World War I the same fate befell persons thought to be insufficiently patriotic.

Unlike its close cousin, lynching, tarring and feathering usually wasn't fatal. One historian says it was employed chiefly when a mob was feeling "playful." But the victim usually had a lot less fun than his tormentors. A Tory assaulted by a mob in 1775 was stripped naked and daubed with hot pitch, blistering his skin. He was then covered with hog dung, feathers being momentarily in short supply. In 1912 Ben Reitman, companion of the radical agitator Emma Goldman, was beaten by a mob in San Diego, then tarred and covered with sagebrush. Afterward he spent two hours cleaning off the worst of the gunk with turpentine and tar soap— just the kind of helpful household tip we at the Straight Dope pride ourselves in providing. Hope you don't have occasion to use it.

What is the origin of the design known as "paisley"? Most patterns have some basis in nature, such as flower patterns, leaves, etc. A paisley looks like some sort of amoeba. What is a paisley supposed to be and how did it get that way?—Rob Marchant, Carrollton, Texas

You probably think paisley originated at the same time as the Beatles, Peter Max, and the Summer of Love. Not so. Paisley is actually an ornate pattern that was commonly used for nineteenth-century shawls manufactured in the town of Paisley, a textile center in Scotland. The Scots stole the idea from similarly patterned cashmere shawls made in Kashmir from goat fleece (cashmere-Kashmir, get it?), which began to be imported from India around 1800. The traditional explanation for the commalike paisley motif is that it's a pine cone, but if so it's the damnedest pine cone I ever saw. Textile historian Martin Hardingham has a better idea; he says it's "more directly identifiable with the cashew fruit and seed pod which has been a symbol of fertility for thousands of years." Ergo, sex is at the bottom of it. My mother always suspected as much.

Why do people in Britain and some of their former colonies drive on the left side of the road? Is it just a case of clinging stubbornly to an outdated tradition, such as the confusing English system of measures?—Billy Bob, Memphis

Try to be tolerant, Bilbo. Seven hundred years ago everybody used the English system, and if distressing numbers of us have proven fickle in the centuries since, that's no reason to dump on the Brits. In the Middle Ages you kept to the left for the simple reason that you never knew who you'd meet on the road in those days; you wanted to make sure that a stranger passed on the right so you could go for your sword in case he proved unfriendly. This custom was given official sanction in 1300 A.D., when Pope Boniface VIII invented the modern science of traffic control by declaring that pilgrims headed to Rome should keep left.

The papal system prevailed until the late 1700s, when teamsters in the United States and France began hauling farm products in big wagons pulled by several pairs of horses. These wagons had no driver's seat; instead the driver sat on the left rear horse, so he could keep his right arm free to lash the team. Since you were sitting on the left, naturally you wanted everybody to pass on the left so you could look down and make sure you kept clear of the other guy's wheels. Ergo, you kept to the right side of the road. The first known keep-right law in the United States was enacted in Pennsylvania in 1792, and in the ensuing years many states and Canadian provinces followed suit.

In France the keep-right custom was established in much the same way. An added impetus was that, this being the era of the French Revolution and all, people figured, hey, no pope gonna tell *me* what to do. (See above.) Later Napoleon enforced the keep-right rule in all countries occupied by his armies, and the custom endured long after the empire was destroyed.

In small-is-beautiful England, though, they didn't use monster wagons that required the driver to ride a horse; instead the guy sat on a seat mounted on the wagon. What's more, he usually sat on the right side of the seat so the whip wouldn't hang up on the load behind him when he flogged the horses. (Then, as now, most people did their flogging right-handed.) So the English continued to drive on the left, not realizing that the tide of history was running against them and that they would wind up being ridiculed by folks like you with no appreciation of life's little ironies. Keeping left first entered English law in 1756, with the enactment of an ordinance governing traffic on the London Bridge, and ultimately became the rule throughout the British Empire.

The trend among nations over the years has been toward driving on the right, but Britain has done its best to stave off global homogenization. Its former colony India remains a hotbed of leftist sentiment, as does Indonesia, which was occupied by the British in the early nineteenth century. The English minister to Japan achieved the coup of his career in 1859 when he persuaded his hosts to make keep-left the law in the future home of Toyota and Mitsubishi.

Nonetheless, the power of the right has been growing steadily. When Germany annexed Austria in 1938, it brutally suppressed the latter's keep-left rights, and much the same happened in Czechoslovakia in 1939. The last holdouts in mainland Europe, the Swedes, finally switched to the right in 1967 because most of the countries they sold Saabs and Volvos to were righties and they got tired of having to make different versions for domestic use and export.

The current battleground is the island of Timor. The Indonesians, who own west Timor, have been whiling away the hours exterminating the native culture of the east Timorese. The issue? Some say it's religion, some say it's language, but I know the truth: in east Timor they drive on the right, in west Timor they drive on the left.

Why do men and women's shirts button on different sides?—Laury Hutt, Baltimore

I thought everybody knew this, but then again you're from Baltimore, the city from another dimension. Buttoning left over right—the man's way—is supposedly easiest for right-handed people. According to legend, women button right over left because in medieval times they were dressed by their right-handed maids. Don't buy it? Can't say as I blame you, but the alternative explanation is no improvement: men had to keep their right hand tucked into their coats so as to be ready for cold-weather swordplay, whereas women always breastfed with the left breast (hey, that's what it says here) and protected their babies by covering them with the right side of the dress or coat.

I've heard the fabric we know as denim originated in a French town called Neise but pronounced Nen, hence "de Nen," or denim. True?—George Manaras, Baltimore

No, but you're in the ballpark, which is about all we can hope for these days. Denim was originally known as *serge de Nîmes*, pronounced "neem," Nîmes being the French town where the stuff was first made.

I understand a few of the reasons behind our complicated English measurements. For instance, an acre was the area plowable in one day using draft animals. But where, pray tell, did the mile and, while we're at it, the yard come from? I mean, 1,760 yards or 5,280 feet can't possibly hold any mystical significance, even to the Illuminati.
—*Michael Hollinger, Herndon, Virginia*

Never underestimate the Illuminati, chum—I'm still stumped by the 17/23 correlation. (See *More of the Straight Dope*, page 297.) The mile, though, is more the result of congenital British half-arsedness than conspiracy. It originated in the Roman *mille passuum*, a thousand paces, or more precisely, a thousand strides. Each pace consisted of five Roman feet, giving us a mile of five thousand feet. Since the Roman foot (the *pes*) was smaller than to-day's foot, the Roman mile was about nine-tenths the length of our mile.

The English got the concept of the mile from the Romans, and though its actual length fluctuated over the centuries, up till the time of the Tudors the mile consisted of five thousand feet. Unfortu-nately, the English also had the idea, for reasons we needn't go into here, that a mile consisted of eight furlongs. The furlong, short for "furrow-long," is said to have been the distance a horse could pull a plow before having to rest. Its length was a matter of confusion for quite a spell, but by the sixteenth century folks generally agreed that it consisted of 40 rods of 16½ feet each, or 660 feet in all—and of course eight furlongs was 5,280 feet.

Having bumbled along with this contradiction for quite a while, Parliament decided to settle matters once and for all in 1593. It would have simplified things for us if they'd decided to whittle the furlong down a bit so the mile could still be five thousand feet, but no dice. Rods and furlongs were commonly used in surveying and changing them would have thrown land titles and such into confu-sion. Miles were used mainly to measure the distance between towns, a matter of no great consequence at the time, so what the hey, the Brits reasoned, who cares how long they are? Today furlongs are of interest only to horse racing buffs, but 5,280 feet to a mile lives on.

As for the yard, no one is quite sure how it originated. One twelfth-century historian said it was the length of Henry the First's outstretched arm as measured from the tip of his nose, a contention that causes most modern historians to roll their eyes. Others think it was a double cubit, originally a Roman measure used in surveying. Still others say it was the measurement of a man's waist. Whatever the case, the name has no relation to that place out back where the crabgrass grows but rather comes from old English *gierd*, meaning wand or stick.

Cumbersome though the present English system of measures is, it's a miracle of simplicity compared to what it was a thousand years ago. One distance then was defined as three miles, three furlongs, nine acres' breadths, three perches, nine feet, nine shaftments, nine handsbreadths, and nine barleycorns, which sounds more like the inventory of a chicken farm than a measurement. Give me a kilometer any day.

Not one of the burning issues of the day, but something I've wondered about on occasion at your fancy restaurants. Why do master chefs wear those tall white hats? Something so silly must have a logical reason for being.—John Rawls, Atlanta

Here's the story I've heard, which sounds so absurd you know it's got to be the truth. Lay scholars who took refuge in seventh-century Byzantine monasteries during persecutions adopted headgear based on that of their clerical hosts. You've seen pictures of Greek Orthodox priests with those crowned black hats with the high band, right? Well, that's what the lay scholars wore, only their version was white, so as not to confuse the faithful.

Exactly how the scholar's cap came to be the chef's cap is a little murky, but we know many of the scholars were Greeks, the Greeks were among the first gastronomes, the scholar's cap was a mark of distinction, cooks wanted a mark of distinction . . . okay, it's not going to get me an award from the historian's association but it's enough to fill out the bottom of a column. The top of the cap got progressively poufier over the years as master chefs sought ways to indicate that they outranked the pot washers.

But didn't you say something about a logical reason for being? The purpose of the cap, as opposed to its origin, is the same as for the caps worn by all food workers: it keeps your hair out of the soup.

Chapter 2

The Human Animal

Can you explain why placing a sleeping person's hand in a pan of warm water makes them piddle in their pants? In my adolescence I was quite a prankster and this particular trick seemed infallible.
—Dave Halonski, Brooklyn
P.S.: Nobody sleeps over at my house anymore.

Lord knows I hate expounding on these loathsome subjects, but as a journalist I feel it is my holy duty. Insofar as it works at all, the pan trick depends on the power of suggestion—simply thinking about water, or in this case dreaming about it, makes you want to go to the bathroom.

The effectiveness of the stunt is a matter of debate. Some urologists scoff at the idea. But other medical types have been known to tell patients having a tough time urinating after rectal surgery to put their hands in warm water. Merely letting the water run in a nearby sink sometimes works, too. I tried it once without success, perhaps because my richly deserving would-be victim was dead drunk. But I've gotten too many testimonials from satisfied perpetrators to think the whole thing's a fraud.

The suggestion need not be tactile. Recently I heard a talk by an architect who was trying to deal with the problem of men unable to perform in public restrooms. His solution: mount pictures of waterfalls over the urinals.

Audio stimuli work, too. I recall a meal I ate once on the upstairs veranda of a popular restaurant. It was delightful except for one thing: underneath the veranda a spigot tinkled steadily into a puddle. I could think of only one thing the entire time. My choices basically were to run to the bathroom every ten minutes or eat dinner with my legs crossed.

All of this makes me think it's lucky you and I never went to the same summer camp, Dave. How embarrassing if I had whizzed in my sleep. How tragic if you'd been strangled in yours.

I have often heard it said humans "use only 10 percent of our brains." (Why people make a point of saying this to me I'm not sure.) But for all the times I've run across this statement, no one has ever cited a source nor explained precisely what it means. Does it mean only 10 percent of the neurons ever fire at all, leaving the other 90 percent to atrophy? This would explain quite a bit about politics and college athletics, but it doesn't seem appropriate for most functioning adults. As someone with an above-average number of active brain cells, perhaps you can unravel these mysteries.—Eugene Dillenburg, Chicago

The 10 percent statistic has been attributed to the pioneering psychologist and philosopher William James (1842–1910). I haven't been

RODENT BRAIN

MORAL MAJORITY POLITICIAN BRAIN

PLASTIC SNAP-ON WITHERED LOBE COVER

able to confirm that he gave a specific percentage, but he did s.
"We are making use of only a small part of our possible mental and
physical resources" (*The Energies of Men*, 1908). The anthropologist
Margaret Mead supposedly said we used 6 percent, and similar
numbers have been mentioned by various lesser known parties.

Whatever the source, such figures have no scientific basis except
in the most limited sense. Serious brain researchers say that while
we perhaps don't use our brains as efficiently as we might, there's no
evidence we have vast unused abilities.

Admittedly no one has ever tested all the tens of billions of neurons in a given brain. You've certainly got a few spares; otherwise no
one would recover from a stroke. But attempts to map out the cerebral cortex, the center of the higher mental functions, have not
found large areas that don't do anything. The general view is that the
brain is too small (just three pounds), uses too many resources (20
percent of body oxygen utilization, though it accounts for just 2 percent of weight), and has too much to do for 90 percent of it to be
completely comatose.

Obviously not all the brain is in use at once. At any given time
about 5 percent of the neurons are active, the only sense in which
the old saw is even close to true. (Good thing, too, or you'd have the
equivalent of a grand mal seizure, a mental electrical storm in which
all the neurons fire continually.) The parts of the brain are highly
specialized, and some areas are more active than others depending
on the task at hand. But all the parts do something, and it seems safe
to say that over time you use pretty much all your brain, just as most
people use all their muscles to some degree.

In fact, muscles are a useful analogy. While we probably don't
have much extra capacity in the sense of unused neurons, it's possible we have untapped potential. Studies with rats suggest that just
as muscles grow stronger with exercise, so does the brain. Rats
raised in stimulating environments had thicker cerebral cortexes,
larger neurons, more connections between neurons, more glial (support) cells, and so on. In other words, good books, snappy conversation, and a regular dose of the Straight Dope may make you smarter.
But don't get your hopes up. Skeptics say what the rat studies prove
is not that an enriched environment will make you smarter, only that
a deprived one will make you dumber.

say. What about memory? Obviously we accumulate ꞏsly also the brain is finite and has some limit to its rcentage of memory capacity do we use? We don't ꞏven to hazard a guess. Old people find it harder to .arn, but that's probably more due to deterioration and rigidity (which may or may not have some neurological basis) than a lack of capacity.

Some popular beliefs about brains do have a basis in fact. Though the question is still disputed, it's possible that after age thirty you do lose 100,000 brain cells a day (or at least some large number). Studies suggest that between early adulthood and age ninety the cortex loses between 10 and 30 percent of its neurons. The remaining neurons develop more cross-connections with other cells, presumably to help pick up the load. Booze probably snuffs a few brain cells, too—at any rate it kills nerve cells in rats. All in all, not very encouraging. Not only do you not have great neural reserves, what you do have is drifting away like the clouds.

I recently read in Life *magazine about people who have had near-death experiences. These people report walking toward a being of light, feeling totally loved, etc. Do near-death experiences prove there is some type of existence after death?—Jeff Collier, Falls Church, Virginia*

If you doubt there's some type of existence after death, Jeff, you've never been to the suburbs. Whether it's anything akin to *personal* existence (that is, the kind of existence you have now) is another question. Unfortunately, near-death experiences (NDEs) don't offer much clue one way or the other.

A surprisingly large number of people have had an NDE—maybe a third to a half of those who almost die but don't—and their accounts of the experience are sufficiently similar to have intrigued scientists. The typical NDE has five stages: (1) you experience a sense of peace, (2) you have the sense of leaving your body and observing it from afar—in other words, you have an out-of-body experience (OBE), (3) you enter a tunnel or "darkness," (4) you see a light at the end of the tunnel, and finally (5) you enter the light. Often at some point during the process you see your life pass before your eyes.

All of this seems absolutely real. People who have had NDEs say there is nothing hallucinatory or dreamlike about them. Research has shown that many who have had NDEs permanently improve their behavior, presumably because they are convinced of the reality of an afterlife.

What really happens during an NDE? British psychologist Susan Blackmore, writing in *The Skeptical Inquirer*, reviews several theories: (1) *Astral projection*—the soul or "astral body" exits the physical body and departs for another world. Not as antiscientific a view as you might think, Blackmore opines, but not supported by any evidence either. (2) *Reliving the birth experience*, that is, traveling down the birth canal. Carl Sagan likes this idea, but Blackmore ridicules it, pointing out that the infant brain is too immature to retain any memory of birth. What's more, getting extruded through Mom's pelvis cannot by any stretch of the imagination be equated with floating blissfully toward the light. (3) *Just a hallucination*. Fine, but why does everybody have the same hallucination?

Blackmore points out that you don't have to be near death to feel you are floating through a tunnel. It's common "in epilepsy and migraine, when falling asleep, meditating, or just relaxing, with pressure on both eyeballs, and with certain drugs, such as LSD, psilocybin, and mescaline."

Why? Blackmore guesses it has to do with the structure of the visual cortex, the part of the brain that contains a "map" of what the eyes see. "There are lots of [cortical] cells representing the center of the visual field but very few for the edges," she says. As the brain begins to lose control, whether due to oxygen loss, drugs, or fatigue, random neural firing apparently begins to occur, which the mind interprets as light. Since there are more cells in the center of the visual field than at the edge, you get the impression of a light at the end of a tunnel. As random firing increases, the "light" takes up a larger portion of the visual field, making you think you are floating toward the light source.

You also don't have to be near death to have an out-of-body experience. We know that surgical stimulation of the brain can trigger extremely realistic re-creations from memory, and something similar probably occurs during an OBE or NDE. Subjects see themselves from afar because many people habitually use a bird's-eye view when dreaming or remembering. (If you're one of them, research suggests you may be more likely to have an OBE.) In short, Blackmore thinks that while the near-death experience is real, it can be explained on neurological grounds. Disillusioning, but in keeping with science's role as party pooper to the human race.

More Tales from the Crypt

Your explanation of the near-death experience was a fair one. I'd just like to add one fact and one question for pondering. Emanuel Swedenborg wrote all about this phenomenon two hundred years ago in his book Heaven and Hell. *He talks about the out-of-body experience, the being of light, meeting friends and relatives, the beauty of the spiritual world—everything those who have had the near-death experience speak of and more!*

My question to you (actually to Susan Blackmore, whom you quote) is if the NDE phenomenon is biological, why are people meeting their dead relatives—quite a peculiar biological reaction, don't you think? Isn't it easier (and even more scientific) to believe in life after death in light of such evidence?—Rev. Grant R. Schnarr, Chicago New Church (Swedenborgian)

Professor Blackmore doesn't specifically address the issue of meeting dead relatives, but I don't see that it presents any great challenge to the it's-all-in-your-head theory. People occasionally dream about the dead during ordinary sleep, but no one regards that as proof of an afterlife. Why should similar dreams during a near-death experience be viewed any differently? On the other hand, if Grandma tells you next week's winning lottery number, I'd be inclined to take the phenomenon a little more seriously.

How do astronauts perform their bodily functions in space? I've seen mentions of "collection systems," but that's about it. By the way,

*do you pay a reward for good questions? It would help to stimulate
my thinking.—Anxiously Awaiting Book 3, Calgary, Alberta*

A *reward*? You mosquito, the search for knowledge is its own reward. Besides, we're out of T-shirts this week.

Up until Skylab, "waste management systems" aboard spacecraft
were primitive. The "device that collected the feces was a plastic bag
that was stuck to the posterior [with adhesive] during defecation,"
NASA bluntly reports. "The system used for urination was a version
of the time-honored 'motorman's friend,' so called because the hose-
and-bag unit was worn by the streetcar motorman, whose job gave
him little opportunity for a rest stop." Cecil frankly is appalled—not
that the astronauts were subjected to this indignity (there wasn't
much choice), but that the motormen were. Gives new poignance to
the term "labor unrest."

Things improved dramatically with the advent of Skylab and later
the space shuttle, both of which were equipped with what is recognizably a toilet, though admittedly of the George Jetson variety. The
problem is the lack of gravity, which plays such a vital role in
earthbound elimination. Instead we substitute what amounts to a
vacuum cleaner. Sure, it's a little drastic, but there are times when
only drastic measures will do.

Besides, it's not so bad. Let's suppose you propose to cleanse yourself fore and aft, so to speak. First you seat yourself firmly on the commode. (Bear in mind that you wear civvies aboard the space shuttle, not a space suit.)

Various ingenious restraining devices are provided so you don't drift off at an untoward moment. In front of you is a urinal—essentially a funnel with a hose. It can be moved around if you later want to do your business standing up. The commode seat is cushioned so as to make a good seal with your bottom, thereby ensuring good suction and preventing the escape of undesirable substances.

Then you turn on a fan inside the commode and do your business. The fan pulls the nasties into a sort of mesh bag that traps solids but allows liquids to pass through. The water is pumped to a storage tank, which is later emptied into space. When you're done, you seal up the top of the commode and open the bowl to the vacuum of space. The moisture in the solids boils away instantly, considerably reducing their bulk. (NASA folks cheerfully refer to this process as "freeze-drying.") A special device compacts what's left and it's stored in the commode until you get back down to the ground.

Doesn't sound all that complicated in principle, but I'm skipping a lot of the fine points. (You don't really want to know about the wastewater cross-tie quick disconnect, do you?) Here's how astronaut Woody Spring described the experience in an interview with the *Journal of the Water Pollution Control Federation*:

During some of our training in the weightlessness environment, we practiced "potty training," which is unlike any seat one is accustomed to. It involves placing yourself over a special 4-inch hole seat, and sitting just right in order to maintain a vacuum seal. Naturally, this seat must accommodate people of all different sizes. To help practice placing ourselves correctly we used a closed circuit TV with a bull's-eye target from which we practiced; it wasn't easy.

I'll bet. Worse, there's always the chance that all the high-tech stuff may fail, forcing you to fall back on the good old "Apollo bag," already described. Worst of all, there's the danger you could leave the seat up while flushing, as it were, thus sucking out all the spacecraft's air. All in all, Cecil thinks he'd just as soon hold it till he got home.

Truth: Still Stranger Than Fiction

Cecil was kidding about leaving the potty seat up after flushing aboard the space shuttle, but evidently NASA doesn't think it's so funny. In early 1993 ground control radioed the crew of the *Endeavour* to tell them to put the seat down. Granted the air wasn't being sucked out of the cabin, but the fan was still going and might have run down the batteries, which could have been just as bad.

Please end the anxiety I've suffered over this question. What are those white spots that appear on my fingernails and where do they come from?—Katina Uribe, Flower Mound, Texas

Sorry to lay this on you, kid, but I figure if you're going to be anxious, you might as well be anxious big-time. What you've got is what's known as *punctate leukonychia* (medicalese for "white spots"). Extreme cases of leukonychia, in which the nails turn entirely white (*leukonychia totalis*) or develop white bands (*striate leukonychia*), can indicate anything from arsenic poisoning to leprosy. Leukonychia has also been linked to typhoid fever, frostbite, trichinosis, gout, diphtheria, cholera, acute rheumatism, myocardial infarction, colitis, and any number of other ghastly ailments.

But don't sweat, you probably don't have any of them. Mere spots are extremely common and undoubtedly harmless. The folklore about them goes back for centuries; they've been called "gift spots," "fortune spots," and for some reason "sweethearts." As with many other minor medical curiosities, little research has been done on punctate leukonychia in recent years. The white color has been variously attributed to trapped air and to defective keratinization, keratinization being the process by which nails are formed. The air bubbles and/or opaque, imperfectly keratinized granules within the nail cells refract light and the spot appears white.

The precise cause of leukonychia is a mystery. It's said to be more common in the young and in women and often shows up when the body undergoes stress or trauma, such as a blow to the fingertips. Excessive manicuring can make things worse; so can working in a pickle factory, of all things. So pitch the nail file (a bit too forties anyway, don't you think?), quit packing those kosher dills, and those damn spots will be out in no time.

Zinc Spots

I enjoy your column but this time I'm afraid you've missed. White spots on the fingernails are often a sign of zinc deficiency. One source of documentation is Dr. Pfeiffer's Total Nutrition *by Carl C. Pfeiffer, Ph.D., M.D., former director of the Princeton Brain Bio Center (now deceased). He writes, "Remember that one of the easily recognized signs of a zinc deficiency is the appearance of white spots on the fingernails."*

The late Carleton Fredericks talked of this many years ago also. I had white spots for a long time, as did one of my sons. Fifty milligrams of zinc daily stopped the spots. Doctor Fredericks said some individuals either have a greater need for zinc than most people or else a lessened ability to utilize available zinc in the average diet. —*Marcia Bernstein, Brooklyn*

I'll amend my remarks to this extent: an abundance of large white spots or bands *may* be a sign of zinc deficiency. But it would be wrong to suggest that zinc deficiency is always, or even usually, the cause of spotting. As I said in my column, there's a long list of things that can cause leukonychia, or nail whitening. You think zinc deficiency is a bummer, try malaria, Hodgkin's disease, or sickle-cell anemia. However, "in the great majority of punctate [spotting] cases . . . , which are extremely common, no cause can be found" (*The Nails in Disease*, Samman and Fenton, 1986).

My friend Heather and her hubby just laid out some fairly big bucks to spend a weekend learning how to maximize their total personhood and all that. Highlight of the weekend was a scamper across hot coals. The idea was to impress you with the power of your mind—if you kept thoughts of cool moss in mind as you walked, your feet wouldn't burn. The coals were in a strip about a yard wide and ten feet long. Walkers, in bare feet, made it through with few problems. Heather made it, too, with no trouble and no sign of damage to her feet.

Heather's (and my) question is this: she believes that, via mind over matter or hypnosis, a person might lower his blood pressure or speed up his pulse or even will himself not to feel pain. But whether she felt it or not, shouldn't the coals have burned her feet? After all, if you throw a steak on the grill, it cooks regardless of the thoughts it happens to be entertaining.

What's the deal? Does psychology triumph over physics? Is it a con—aren't the coals hot? Do sweaty feet protect you with a layer of sizzle?—Ed Dolnick, Chevy Chase, Maryland

Cecil initially feared he was going to have to risk cherished portions of his being for the sake of the Teeming Millions (and what have you guys done for me lately?). Fortunately, a quick check of the Straight Dope's vast data resources reveals that lots of journalists have rushed in where more sensible people dared not tread. Firewalk therapy, God help us, is widespread these days.

There's some disagreement on why fire walking works, but this much is clear: it does work. There's no trickery involved, although modern fire-walk entrepreneurs do take a few precautions, about which more below. Mind over matter has nothing to do with it. Skeptics have tried it with no preparation whatsoever, or (worse) while murmuring "hot rocks, hot rocks." They got over just fine. There's not much margin for error, though. Blisters are fairly common, and a few people have been badly burned.

What protects the rest? Two phenomena get the credit:

(1) *The sizzle effect,* also known as the Leidenfrost effect: a thin layer of sweat protects you. As Peter Garrison put it in a 1985 article on the subject in *Omni* magazine, "A liquid exposed to intense heat will instantaneously form an insulating boundary layer of steam." That's what enables you to snuff a candle flame painlessly with your fingertips after you've moistened them with spit. The soles of the feet are well supplied with sweat glands, and Lord knows *I'd* per-

spire while waiting to hike through hell. In addition, sometimes you're directed to walk over a moist surface such as grass before stepping out on the coals. (Another trick: don't replenish the coals; they quickly cool.)

(2) *Not enough heat.* This one requires some thought. While glowing coals are plenty *hot* (typically 600 degrees Celsius), they don't contain all that much *heat*—that is, thermal energy. (To use a water analogy, you've got a lot of pressure but not much volume.) What's more, the coals aren't charcoal but, rather, ordinary wood, which is a poor conductor. When you walk on them, your feet absorb the surface layer of heat, but there's too little of it to burn you. The fresh heat from within the coals makes it to the surface too slowly to do you any damage.

But fire walking in some parking lot is for wimps. If you're hard core there are more challenging methods. I've just spoken to my bud Jearl Walker, the former *Scientific American* columnist and, it turns out, the G. Gordon Liddy of physics.

As a classroom demo of the Leidenfrost effect, Jearl not only walked on hot coals (he has since given it up after getting badly burned once—he was so cool his feet didn't get sufficiently damp), he also dips his bare hand in water and then plunges it momentarily into a vat of molten lead, 700 degrees Celsius. Says Jearl, who's even done this on Johnny Carson, "There is no classroom demonstration so riveting as one in which the teacher may die." It'd definitely penetrate *my* ennui. Just don't volunteer in Jearl's class when he asks someone to give him a hand.

More on Fire Walking

A friend of mine forwarded your column on fire walking to me. It was a good column, but as you'll see from the enclosed journal article, which I coauthored, the sizzle effect is not critical (and Jearl Walker agrees with me, but keeps forgetting).—Bernard J. Leikind, Encinitas, California

Bernie's article comes down foursquare behind the not-enough-heat theory and says in addition that the fire walker's feet may be insulated by dirt, calluses, or water. Bernie discounts the Leidenfrost effect, noting that a fire walker with a pair of rope-sole sandals gamboled through the coals without damage to the sandals. Since the ground was dry, the day was cold, and sandals don't sweat, there was no moisture, which is the key to the Leidenfrost effect. The sandals' survival therefore must be credited to something else.

I am pleased to set the record straight, naturally, and hope I have not seriously retarded the advance of science in the meantime. However, any time you've got a phenomenon that lets you work in a Jearl-Walker-tempts-death story, as was the case with the Leidenfrost effect, in my book you want to cut it a little slack.

One of the highlights of my year is an all-girl backpacking trip with a group of friends. I mentioned this at a party recently, only to have some (male) geek give me dire warnings about women camping while on their periods. He claimed bears are irresistibly attracted to the scent.

I checked with one of my more experienced camping buddies, who said she'd heard the same story but attributed it to another fiendish male plot to keep us in the kitchen. Since this year's trip is planned for Yosemite, which is known for its bear population, I thought I'd better get the Straight Dope. Should we be concerned? Or just more careful about whom we converse with at parties?—Kate Reneau, Santa Monica, California

Always wise to discriminate in re: party chitchat, Kate; you never know when you might bump into someone who's never heard of, well, me. Dubious as this business about bears being attracted to menstruating women may sound, however, it can't be entirely dismissed. Two menstruating women were killed by grizzly bears in Glacier National Park in 1967, and the authorities have been warning women to stay out of bear territory during their periods ever since. There's been a fair amount of research, some of it conducted by women, suggesting that omnivores and carnivores (e.g., bears) are inspired to attack by the smell of human blood, while herbivores (e.g., deer) are repelled by it.

The key here is blood, not necessarily menstrual blood. Research

shows that deer are repelled by male blood, too. It's just that over time many animal breeds have learned humans mean trouble, some researchers believe, and women have the characteristic scent of human blood on them more often than men do.

Some think the attraction/repulsion of animals by human blood is one of the main reasons behind the menstrual taboos found in many primitive societies—a menstruating woman could play havoc with the hunt on which the tribe depended and so was best kept out of sight during her period. For the same reason women often were not allowed on hunting trips.

This tidy theory has some flaws in it, though. Research has shown that deer, at least, aren't repelled by the equally pungent and far more abundant scent of human urine. What's more, while grizzly bears have been known to attack menstruating women, there have been no such attacks by black bears, which are much more common. Extensive research with black bears published in 1991 (the bears were given an opportunity to sniff bloody tampons, menstruating women played with wild but human-habituated bears, etc.) showed that black bears had virtually no reaction to menstrual blood.

The question is far from settled. Experiments in 1983 showed that polar bears were attracted to menstrual blood. And that 1967 attack does give one pause. I wouldn't cancel my camping trip if I were you, but if I were headed into grizzly country I might give some thought to timing.

I was intrigued by a recent news report that members of a formerly men-only club were upset now that women were being admitted because they could no longer engage in nude swimming. Now, it's true I've led a sheltered life, having gone to school at the convent and all, but what exactly is the deal with nude swimming? Wouldn't this "style" affect performance due to an uncontrollable "rudder effect," so to speak? Should we consult a sailing expert to gain additional insight? What are the implications of this new rule? Will lap times improve? Help me sort out the meaning of this change.—All Wet in Wilmette

Don't worry about the rudder effect, A.W. Most of the guys at those clubs have, how shall I say, a very low coefficient of drag. Myself, I prefer to wear trunks.

How can a person "see stars"? When you exert yourself physically and then stop, you have these hundreds of little BBs zooming in space in front of you. It makes me actually believe I could touch them. Try staring at the ground about ten feet in front of you and follow one of the lights out of the corner of your eye until it blinks out. It's kind of a kick. Explain how this physical change of sight and mind can occur as easily as doing a cartwheel.—Terry, Waunakee, Wisconsin

Not being one for cartwheels, Terry, Cecil has been trying to see what kind of business he could drum up doing somersaults. Things were a little slow, but I did manage to get a passel of zooming BBs on one occasion, along with a monster headache. The little spots of light, which are to be distinguished from the opaque spots or threads we've discussed in the past, persist for perhaps five or ten seconds and appear to swim around. But I only got them after a particularly crazed gymnastic exhibition. What do you do, finish your cartwheels by slamming into a wall?

BBs, "stars," and other "nonphotic" visual stimuli (i.e., those not actually produced by light) are called photopsia or phosphenes. They're believed to be caused by mechanical stimulation of the nerves of the eye. Another example is the sensation of light produced by pressure on the eye, a phenomenon once described by no less an authority than Aristotle.

Young people see stars every once in a while as a result of a blow to the head or some sudden exertion. But the little BBs don't really become common until retirement age. What happens is that the eyeball fluid, which is contained in a sort of sac, starts to pull away from the back of the eye. This is called "posterior vitreous detachment," and it usually occurs suddenly, often following a jolt to the head. You see stars and spots and your vision is blurred and distorted. The stars may persist for weeks or even years as fibers from your eyeball sac continue to tug on your retina.

Grim though it sounds, vitreous detachment is normal, occurring in maybe half the population. Apart from stars and spots, your vision usually winds up about the same. But stars and spots can also herald a detached retina, which is bad news indeed. If you're nearing retirement age, you definitely want to slack off on those cartwheels.

Forget cremation, forget embalming—when I go, I want to go in style. For some time now, I've been wondering how to get my mortal remains fossilized. I know that soft tissue doesn't normally fossilize, but there must be some exceptions: for example, the Petrified Forest in Arizona. What kind of conditions are necessary, and how long will it take? Our creationist friends are of the opinion that fossils are remains of animals that existed before the Flood; does that mean a man can become a fossil in a couple thousand years?—Forever Young, San Pedro, California

Oh, I dunno. In my experience, with the right fluids, you can get pretty fossilized in about two hours. But the effect isn't permanent. For long-lasting results you need more elaborate techniques.

Strictly speaking, a fossil is any vestige of past life embedded in the earth's crust. This includes the frozen mammoths of Siberia, whose bodies were preserved soft tissue and all. It just so happens I have here a slender volume entitled *How to Deep-Freeze a Mammoth*, by Björn Kurten. Though largely a whimsical meditation on archaeology, the book does offer a few practical hints for prospective fossilees:

1. Arrange to have your remains placed on a steep south-facing hillside during winter in the high arctic tundra.
2. See that said remains are protected from predators until frozen solid.
3. Wait.

In spring, when the topsoil thaws, your corpse will slide to the bottom of the hill and, with luck, get buried in mud. If the mud is thick enough, your body will remain frozen in subsequent years and thus be preserved indefinitely.

The problem, of course, is that your carcass has to *stay* frozen, lest decomposition resume. (As it is, most of your internal organs will likely have putrefied prior to initial freezing.) This is not ideal if your plan is to leave something your great-grandkids can display on the mantelpiece. One alternative is mummification, which requires an extremely dry climate, or else preservation in a peat bog. If neither of these sounds fossillike enough for you, you could try getting trapped in amber (fossilized tree sap), though this seems to work best with small Baltic insects, such as Roman Polanski.

If what you really want is to get *lithified* (i.e., stoned in the literal sense), your best bet is to chuck this bourgeois attachment to skin and have your corpse buried in sediment percolated by groundwater containing calcium carbonate, silica, or the like. Your (ahem) "soft parts" will soon decay but with luck your bones will get caulked up with minerals in . . . oh, I'd check back in a century or two.

If you absolutely *must* have soft tissue, you could conceivably have yourself mummified first and then . . . aw, who am I kidding? If you're that desperate, get yourself bronzed. My advice: resign yourself to enriching the biota with your decaying corpus. It's more than some people will have accomplished while alive.

Why does head hair (as well as beard hair, I think) grow indefinitely, whereas hair on the rest of the human body grows to a certain length and then stops?—Kim M., Washington, D.C.

What makes you think scalp hair grows indefinitely? Didn't you ever listen to the title song from *Hair* ("Don't never have to cut it 'cuz it stops by itself")? Each scalp and beard hair grows two to six years before stopping, attaining a typical maximum length of two to three feet. Then it becomes dormant for about three months, whereupon a new hair starts growing and pushes the old one out of the follicle from behind. That's why even someone who's not balding loses seventy to one hundred head hairs a day. By comparison, the growth cycle for other body hair is only a few weeks, so it doesn't get very long.

Maximum scalp-hair length varies greatly among individuals. The all-time champ had ten and a half feet, although Diane Witte of Worcester, Massachusetts, is said to be closing in fast. Diane, whose hair grows at the rate of a half inch per month, had ten and a quarter feet as of 1988 and by now has surely broken the record. Watch for it soon on "Wide World of Sports."

So why do we have to sleep, anyway? I hate spending almost a third of my life in a coma.—Bill Toman, Madison

Why? It helps you understand what it's like being president. Besides, what else are you going to do at 4:00 A.M.? The truth is, re-

searchers don't know why we have to sleep, although they have pots
of theories. For example:

1. *Sleep restores.* In other words, "sleep either allows or promotes
   physiological processes which rejuvenate the body and the mind,"
   as one researcher puts it. Studies suggest sleep restores neurons
   and increases production of brain proteins and certain hormones.
2. *Sleep conserves energy.* It takes a lot of energy to keep us warm-
   blooded critters warm-blooded. Since energy consumption drops
   during sleep, maybe we doze so we don't have to eat all day long.
   Supporting this theory is the fact that cold-blooded animals have
   a much less regular sleep-wake cycle.
3. *Sleep keeps you out of trouble.* No kidding. Says here, "According
   to this theoretical position, prehistoric mankind adapted the pattern of sleeping in caves at night, because it protected humans
   from species physiologically suited to function well in the dark,
   such as saber-toothed tigers."
4. *Sleep helps you remember.* In other words, it gives the brain a
   chance to process the day's experiences and file them away in the
   memory. Thus we remember things learned just before sleep better than things learned earlier.
5. *Sleep helps you forget.* Unlearning during sleep prevents the brain
   from becoming overloaded with knowledge. Not, in my observation, a critical problem for most folks, but perhaps sleeping simply
   works all too well.

Complicating matters is the fact that some people thrive on virtually no sleep. In 1973 British researchers reported on a seventy-year-
old woman who claimed she slept only an hour a night with no
daytime naps. In one seventy-two-hour test, during which she was
under constant watch, the woman stayed awake fifty-six hours, then
slept only an hour and a half. Yet she remained alert and in good
spirits.

According to one study, short sleepers (six hours or less per night)
are well-organized, efficient, ambitious, decisive, and self-
confident—in other words, totally obnoxious. Not to encourage paranoia, but next time your lids get heavy, consider: the short sleepers
are out there, gaining on you.

Has there ever been a human raised entirely by (other) animals?
We are particularly interested in wolves here à la Kipling.—Hanna L.
and J.P., New York

It wouldn't surprise me. One look at Axl Rose and you know
the guy wasn't raised by Ozzie and Harriet. But nobody knows for
sure.

The idea of children raised by wolves definitely stirs the
imagination—it's inspired stories ranging from Romulus and Remus
to Tarzan of the Apes. There are a lot of claims of actual sightings,
too, many from India, where keeping a pet human is apparently de
rigeur for the wolf with everything. But the flake factor in these tales
is pretty high.

On the other hand, the experts generally accept the possibility of
so-called feral children—that is, kids living like (if not necessarily
with) animals in the wild. More than fifty cases of feral children have
been reported, wolf children included.

The best-documented case of wolf children involves two girls
found in 1920 by an Indian missionary named J. A. L. Singh. The
two, later named Amala and Kamala, were supposedly found hud-
dled with a couple wolf pups in an old ant mound in the jungle near
a remote village. They'd earlier been seen with adult wolves; two of
these ran off at the time of capture and a third (apparently the mama
wolf) was killed.

The children were unkempt, were incapable of speech apart from
some inarticulate howling, and in general exhibited animallike behavior. Typical teenagers, you may think. But no. They also walked
on all fours, were indifferent to heat and cold, and lapped up their
food like dogs.

Singh and his wife cared for the pair in the orphanage they ran.
Amala, who appeared to be about eighteen months old when found,
died after a year, but Kamala, who was about eight, survived until
1929. It was years before she learned to walk or speak, and her vocabulary never exceeded some fifty words.

The credibility of this story has taken a few nicks. In a book published after Kamala's death Singh said he found the children himself,
but in earlier newspaper accounts he was quoted as saying they were
brought to him—clearly a pivotal difference. Even if the children in

fact were found in a wolf's lair, that doesn't necessarily mean they were raised by wolves, merely befriended—no small thing in itself, I suppose. Since even the most hardened anthropologist won't leave a child in the wild for purposes of observation, whether beasts have actually raised humans may never be definitely settled.

Stories of feral children, as opposed to wolf children, have gained wider acceptance. One of the best authenticated cases is the Wild Boy of Aveyron. Discovered at about age twelve digging in a garden in the Aveyron district of France in 1800, the Wild Boy was mute, naked, and seemingly retarded. (Unlike most feral children, he did walk upright.) It was learned he'd been roaming the hills on his own for at least two years, living on handouts from obliging farmers and whatever he could steal. The boy was turned over to a determined doctor named Jean Itard who taught him to dress himself and perform simple chores. But he never learned to speak more than a couple words.

Feral children have long fascinated scientists. Apart from the sheer pathos of their stories, they raise some gut issues: how do we become human? If we fail to learn critical skills as children, is it impossible to do so later?

Most feral children have been severely stunted and remained so all their lives, suggesting that early human contact is essential to normal development. But others believe the children were retarded to start with. The child psychologist Bruno Bettelheim, perhaps not the best of sources, argued that the children were autistic—that is, severely withdrawn. Those unconvinced say no autistic or otherwise incapacitated child could survive in the wild for long.

A 1970 California case suggests the deprivation theory is closer to the mark. "Genie," a more or less normal two-year-old, was locked up by her demented father for eleven years, reducing her to a state of whimpering imbecility. Despite later training, her language development never exceeded that of a five-year-old. Being a wild child may conjure up visions of some *Blue Lagoon*–type idyll, but the reality is unspeakably cruel.

Are human beings still evolving? Or are we devolving? Are our genes, when passed on to our kids, copied faithfully like a digital re-

cording? Or is the process more like a photocopy of a photocopy, deteriorating more and more with each generation? I hope it's not the latter, because if the results are anything like those from the self-serve copy place down the street, we're in big trouble.—David Westwood, Santa Monica, California

David, it's obvious you not only slept through Intro to Biology, you were a little groggy during a couple key college bull sessions, too. We covered this topic a little after 2:00 A.M. the second month of freshman year. The prevailing view was that humans weren't evolving, because what with the welfare state and the miracle of modern medicine and all, natural selection (i.e., survival of the fittest) had ceased to operate.

Nonsense, I argued (correctly, of course, because even then I could see I was never wrong)—natural selection by definition is always at work. If nobody dies before reaching reproductive age, well, that merely meant that everybody got naturally selected.

You don't get it, said my opponents. If there aren't any differences in mortality among genotypes (isn't it great the way I sling these words around like you know what I'm talking about?), that means the gene pool is static and we aren't evolving.

Sure we are, sez I. The fundamental question isn't whether people die young, it's whether they fail to reproduce, or reproduce less abundantly than others. On this basis we can say that the genes for the following physical types or traits are slowly disappearing from the population:

1. People so lacking in sex appeal that nobody could stand to get close enough for long enough to beget children with them. We may thus anticipate that in the distant future people will be extremely good looking and sociable, but nobody will know how to operate the computers.
2. Yuppieness, since yuppies typically have fewer children later than other population groups. The people of the future, in all likelihood, will drink Bud, eat jalapeños, and believe that Cleopatra was . . . well, let's not get into it. But you won't have your parking space stolen by some sphincter in a Beamer, either.

3. Certain other well-known spiritual and physical callings, shall we say. You know who you are.

Okay, so maybe Cecil is kidding around a little. We can't assume any of the alleged traits above have a genetic basis. What's more, widespread interbreeding among population groups has a leveling effect. You generally only see noticeable changes when a group is reproductively isolated and key genes get passed around by inbreeding, as with sickle-cell anemia in blacks and Tay-Sachs disease in Jews. But you get the idea: as long as some folks reproduce more than others for reasons related however tenuously to their genes, the gene pool isn't completely static.

As for whether our genes are accurately reproduced, you silly goose, the genes *always* accurately reproduce. Except sometimes. On the latter occasions one of several things results: one, monsters— that is, grossly malformed babies resulting from a genetic mistake. Years ago most monsters died, but now many can be saved. This has made possible the National Football League. Two, useful mutations increasing one's chances of reproductive success. Think of the first little mutant to discover he could comb his hair in a ducktail. Or, to bring up a more sober possibility, the first to become resistant to AIDS. Three, maladaptive but not immediately fatal mutations, such as those causing certain diseases.

So yes, we're still evolving. But not very quickly. Most students of the subject say we haven't changed much in the past thirty thousand to fifty thousand years, except that we're now willing to eat head-cheese. As for that sci-fi stuff about evolving giant brains . . . well, modesty prevents me from saying much about it. But it sure does make it a bitch to buy hats.

My girlfriend is half black and half white. While she was filling out a form recently I noticed when it came to the question of race she checked "black." I asked her why she didn't mark white since she is as much one as the other. She replied that in America one is considered black if the amount of black parentage is one eighth or greater. Is or was this true? Why? Since I am a Mexican male, what will the

white establishment consider our children? Not that it matters, but I'd
like to know what is in store for us.—An in-love but mixed-up couple,
Los Angeles

Lord knows. My advice is, if anybody asks, tell 'em the kids are
Phrygian. Nobody will have any idea what you're talking about, and
you'll be able to divert the conversation to some less stupid topic.

These days there's not much official guidance on who's black and
who's white. The census bureau has adopted the sensible policy of
letting you be whatever you mark down on the form. You can look
like Snow White and talk like George Plimpton, but if you want to
be a Fiji Islander, by God you're a Fiji Islander as far as the census
is concerned.

Things are only marginally more rigorous when it comes to stuff
like affirmative action. A spokesman for the Small Business Administration says they'll basically take your word for what race you are,
although conceivably they might ask for a birth certificate or pass-
port in the rare event there was some question.

Unofficial standards are a different story. Experts on race relations
agree that up until very recently, and to some extent even today,
white America held to the "one-drop" rule: if you had one drop of
black blood in you—any detectable African ancestry at all—you
were black. This is an extremely peculiar attitude that may well be
unique in the world; even South Africa acknowledges the existence
of people of mixed race.

The one-drop rule didn't reach its full flowering until after World
War I, but its roots go back to before the Civil War. Prior to 1850,
mulattoes—people of mixed race—were widely recognized as being
distinct from full-blooded African slaves. In fact, in some parts of the
south, notably South Carolina and Louisiana, free mulattoes were a
(relatively) privileged class, with money, prestige, and sometimes
slaves of their own.

After 1850, however, southern whites became obsessed with the idea
of racial purity and white superiority. If you had any black blood at all,
you were supposed to be out back choppin' cotton. White planters who
got female slaves pregnant willingly enslaved their own children. Far
from being scandalized, other southerners complained that some mulattoes remained free to pollute the gene pool.

Defeat in the Civil War only intensified these feelings. States not just in the south but throughout the Union passed increasingly strict antimiscegenation laws—laws that weren't struck down by the Supreme Court until 1967. The one-drop rule was actually enacted in only seven states (Virginia did so in 1930); more commonly the cutoff was one-eighth black. But according to historian Joel Williamson (*New People: Miscegenation and Mulattoes in the United States,* 1980), the one-drop rule was the de facto standard throughout the country.

Williamson relates an episode from the 1926 musical *Show Boat* in which a white boy in love with a mulatto actress is accused by a Mississippi sheriff of violating the state's antimiscegenation law. Thinking fast, the white guy pricks his beloved's finger with a knife, swallows a drop of the blood, and says, Hey, I'm no white man, I've got Negro blood in me. The sheriff lets him off.

So where does that leave you? Hard to say. No question the one-drop rule still prevails for a lot of white folks. But since even racists don't have the nerve to ask for proof of pedigree these days, what matters most is what you look like. The fact that you're Hispanic is the perfect smokescreen. Your kids probably won't pass for Swedish, but they'll be able to declare themselves black or Hispanic as the whim moves them. Better yet, have them say it's nobody's damn business.

Then Again, You Could Say the Kids are Albarazados

I found your column on racial designations interesting and thought I could help clarify or confuse the issue even more by sending you the Mexican list of names for the possible mixtures of races. These are the basis of the caste system in Mexico. There is also a series of paintings to accompany this so that those unable to read could at least get an idea of the racial features. The pictures also give an idea of the kind of work assigned to a person of that caste.—Brother Edward Loch, S.M., San Antonio, Texas

Holy cow. The list, which is from *Las Castas Mexicanas* (1989) by Maria Concepción Garcia Saiz, gives names for more than two dozen racial/ethnic combinations. These range from the well-known mulatto (white/black) and mestizo (white/Indian) to *zambo* (Indian/black or mulatto), *morisco* (white/mulatto), and *albino* (white/morisco). Then you get into *ahí te estás* (mulatto/mestizo coyote—don't ask), *albarazado*, *barcino*, *calpamulato*, *cambujo*, and on and on. Clearly Americans aren't the only ones obsessed with their neighbors' pedigrees.

Another Suggestion

In your column on racial designations, you omitted what was to me the most important alternative. For forty years the only response I have ever given to questions on my race put to me by anyone under any circumstances has been human. *There are no other races.*

Back in 1959, the D.C. Department of Motor Vehicles (or whatever it was called back then) sent me a questionnaire for renewal of my driver's license. In response to a question on race, I answered "human." They returned the form to me on the ground that I had provided an improper or unacceptable answer to the question.

I wrote back saying I was not about to be instructed on scientific matters by a bunch of two-bit bureaucrats; that I had given the only legitimate answer to the question; that they were suborning perjury by pressuring me to provide any other answer on an official government form.

They issued the license with a conventional racial designation on it. I erased the designation (licenses were then on heavy paper, not encased in plastic as now), and wrote them saying I had done so on the ground that I would not permit an official document relating to me to bear false information.

They wrote back telling me that altering an official document made me subject to criminal prosecution with a possible $300 fine and ten days in jail.

I wrote back and said, "I dare you," pointing out that the trial would be latched on to by the then-emergent civil rights struggle and could cause the department considerable embarrassment. Nothing further ensued, and a few years later they redesigned the whole li-

cense, deleting any references to race and introducing picture driver's licenses.

Recently a retired D.C. official involved in these matters said in an interview that "only four or five" people had objected to racial designation. I am proud to have been one of them.

After a respite of some years from racial questions they have again become widespread, ostensibly for the acquisition of demographic data. I continue to advise that such questions be answered "human." I strongly believe that if everyone were to respond in this fashion to questions on race, ours would be a far happier society.—Franklin E. Kameny, Washington, D.C.

Hear, hear, brother. For those who find "human" a bit too smart-ass, I advise just leaving the question blank. If anybody is dumb enough to come after you, Cecil will be pleased to contribute to your defense.

Is it true that Anne Boleyn, wife of Henry VIII, had a sixth finger and three breasts?—Anonymous, Chicago

Ooh, you're so *nasty*, A.—ordinarily a quality we prize in this department, but in this case disproportionate to the facts. Anne did have some physical defects that her many detractors interpreted as signs of the devil, but she was hardly the sideshow freak that some (e.g., *The Book of Lists*) have made her out to be.

Ms. Boleyn had a double nail and a bulge of flesh on the little finger of her right hand that was apparently the beginnings of a sixth digit, and she also had a strawberry-size mole on the front of her neck. Conceivably the latter was a vestigial nipple, a benign congenital defect occurring in about one percent of the population. Other than that she presented a reasonably attractive appearance, which, at the risk of sounding a little catty, is more than can be said for some of Henry VIII's other wives. In any case I'd say a little generosity is in order—who knows what they'll be saying about you after *you're* beheaded?

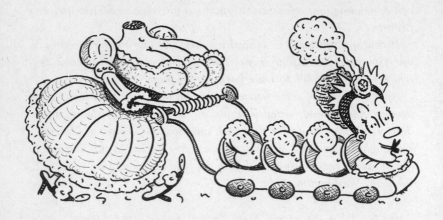

I was just reading about those boat people in Southeast Asia who had to resort to cannibalism to survive and it reminded me of something I heard once. Is it true that cannibalism was outlawed because people developed laughing sickness afterward and died by literally busting a gut?—Listener, Dick Whittington show, KIEV radio, Los Angeles

Let's take this step-by-step. Number one, forget about laughing sickness. It's possible to die laughing, a topic I have addressed in the past, but that's not the disease you allegedly get from people-eating. Most likely you're thinking of *kuru*, a fatal neurological ailment characterized by trembling. From 1957 to 1977 kuru was epidemic among certain New Guinea tribes and was suspected of being contracted by eating human flesh. But cannibalism had been outlawed long before.

The question you should have asked, if you don't mind my saying so, is whether cannibalism (or anthropophagy, as we intellectual snobs like to call it) occurs on a systematic basis at all. In a 1979 book called *The Man-Eating Myth*, anthropologist William Arens argues that cannibalism is the equivalent of an urban legend: lots of researchers say they've heard about it, but hardly anybody has actually seen it happen.

Arens does not deny the occurrence of cannibalism in survival situations, as with the boat people or those guys whose plane crashed in the Andes in 1972. But he says there is no proof it has ever taken place anywhere routinely. Most accounts by early explorers are so larded with patent nonsense that no credence can be placed in them. Reports by contemporary anthropologists, which rely heavily on hearsay, aren't much better.

What is common, Arens believes, is not cannibalism but *belief* in cannibalism, spurred by the mixture of horror and fascination maneating has always inspired. Many cultures have built up a considerable mythology around cannibalism—consider the Christian notion of consuming the body and blood of Christ. Explorers and anthropologists heard non-Western versions of such legends and made the mistake of taking them literally.

In some cases, I should point out, the mistake was no accident. Stories about cannibalism in the Caribbean spread in part because Spanish kings allowed only cannibal tribes to be enslaved. Naturally this inspired the conquistadors to declare just about every inhabitant of the New World guilty.

Cannibalism stories arise for a variety of reasons. A people may accuse its enemies of cannibalism (and often incest) to demonstrate its superiority: we're civilized, they're savages. One recalls accusations that Jews drank the blood of Christians; many Africans today believe Europeans drink blood. A tribe may confess to having practiced cannibalism in the indefinite past as a way of saying, Look how far we've come. In the African equivalent of witchcraft trials, a few unlucky souls might confess to cannibalism under torture just as women here and in Europe confessed to sorcery.

Even prehistoric cannibalism can't be regarded as a sure thing. A number of archaeologists have reported finding human bones showing the cut marks and breakage characteristic of food refuse, but these may represent isolated instances of survival cannibalism. There is little evidence to suggest that man-eating was customary in the Stone Age.

In the scientific community reaction to Arens's book has been sharply divided. A few people liken him to the nuts who claim the mass slaughter of Jews and others during World War II never happened. But the more common view is that while routine cannibalism may not be entirely unknown, its frequency has probably been greatly exaggerated. Many now believe, for instance, that New Guinea natives are not cannibals and that kuru is spread by contact with corpses during funeral preparations, although there is still some argument about this. Cannibalism may yet join witchcraft on the dustheap of history.

When a prisoner is put to death by lethal injection, does he or she still get their arm cleaned with an alcohol swab?—Mark Alonso, 101st Airborne Division

Does make you wonder. Here they are, about to snuff the guy, and they're worried he might get infected with germs? But according to a spokesman for the Texas Department of Corrections, which has carried out many executions by lethal injection, the technician (it's never a doctor) is in fact supposed to swab the prisoner's arm first. One presumes other states employing this method do likewise.

There are several reasons for this. Apart from its usefulness as an antiseptic, alcohol causes blood vessels to rise to the surface, making it easier to insert the needle. More important, there's a chance the prisoner's sentence might be delayed or commuted at the last minute.

It's happened before. In October 1983 condemned murderer James Autry was strapped to a gurney for an hour in a Texas prison with saline solution dripping into his arm. (He was awake the whole time, incidentally.) At about the time he was scheduled to die he was told he had received a stay of execution. He was returned to his cell and not executed until the following March. Whatever you think of the death penalty, you wouldn't want the guy to die of sheer carelessness.

Which brings us to what I think is the *real* reason for swabbing the arm—it allows the executioners to think of themselves as professionals doing a job rather than killers. Interviews with members of execution teams reveal that they place great stock in following proper procedures. We may be certain that if the prisoner were to choke on a chicken bone during his last meal, the authorities would spare no effort to save his life an hour prior to ending it. Nazi death camp guards observed no such niceties. Thus do we persuade ourselves that we are better than they.

Everybody has heard that in the early days of radio broadcasting, there were people who received broadcasts through their teeth. A psychologist who is writing about it in a forthcoming book told me that he could find no actual or authentic case. I recall the play Something for the Boys *in 1943 with Ethel Merman, and the movie of the play with Carmen Miranda, in which the actresses pretended they heard broadcasts. Indefatigable researcher that I am, I finally located an item in the 1934* New York Times *index, "Ukrainian complains his ears register broadcast sounds." Is there anything to such stories or are the human receiving sets candidates for the loony bin?—David Shulman, New York*

Hey, sometimes *my* ears register broadcast sounds. But usually I just yell to turn the damn thing down. Apparently that wasn't an option for the Ukrainian (no name given) mentioned in the two-paragraph *Times* item you cited. A resident of the Brazilian state of Paraná, he was seeking medical help because "his ears, radio-like, register broadcast sounds; in fact, he is a walking antenna."

One of the famous Brazil nuts, right? The *Times* evidently thought so. The item continues, "In these hard times, when many would like to own but cannot afford to buy a radio, it is held that this Ukrainian should feel highly elated in owning an irremovable receiving-set. On the contrary, however, he wishes to be rid of this gift or to be at least provided with means of shutting it off. He asserts it is injuring his health because the noises keep him awake at all hours of the night."

That's the story with most "human antennae"—no one takes them seriously. I went through the medical journals from 1928 to the present and found only a few brief mentions. "In most cases, where the [radio-generated] hearing phenomena were accessible to controlled experimentation, the effects could be explained as artifacts," one article notes. But no references or other information were given. I'd write the whole thing off as folklore except for one thing: one of Cecil's associates got to talking about this on (fittingly) the radio and within minutes got leads on two people who said it happened to them.

Case #1. George, of suburban Chicago, lost a front tooth at age twelve. A year or so later, in about 1961, he was fitted with a cap that was attached to the tooth stump with what George recalls as a brass wire. Thereafter he began hearing music in his head, generally popular tunes of the day, usually while he was outdoors. The music was soft but distinct. He never heard an announcer's voice or commercials and was unable to identify what radio station, if any, he was hearing. After a year or two of this a new dentist put in a cap without a wire and the tunes stopped.

Case #2. Lois, also of suburban Chicago, says it happened just once, in 1947, while she was riding a train from her home in Cleveland to college in Rhode Island at about age eighteen. The experience lasted maybe ten minutes. She couldn't tell what station she was listening to but recalls hearing commercials and an announcer's voice. She has silver tooth fillings but doesn't recall if she'd had one put in just before the event.

Delusions? Maybe, but both George and Lois seemed perfectly sane. Neurologist Oliver Sacks, confronted with several similar cases, has suggested epileptic hallucinations, but his patients with experiences like this were elderly and the music was loud, whereas George and Lois were young at the time and the sounds were soft.

We do know that (1) radiators, faucets, etc. (but not, it is generally thought, silver tooth fillings), can act as radio receivers under certain conditions, (2) people can be made to "hear" (poorly) through stimulation with electrodes and via bone conduction from the teeth, and (3) test subjects hear buzzing when irradiated with UHF and VHF radio pulses from one hundred feet. (Shielding the subjects' teeth didn't stop the buzzing, but shielding their temples did.) Granted, it's a long leap from all this to say folks can hear radio broadcasts in their heads. But the American Dental Association says it gets an inquiry on this topic roughly every six weeks. The whole business deserves more thorough investigation than it apparently got.

If the average body temperature is 98.6 degrees F, why is it that when the air temperature reaches 85 or 90 we feel uncomfortable?
—Scott Hadley, Santa Barbara, California

One of Cecil's competitors once wrote that it was because we wore clothes—as though all you had to do to be comfortable in 98-degree heat was walk around naked. Clearly what we have here is a failure to grasp the scientific essence of the thing, namely, that the air temperature has to be lower than body temperature if you're to cool yourself efficiently.

Your body is a little fuel-burning engine and like all engines generates waste heat. That heat has to go somewhere, lest you pop a gasket. The easiest place to put it is someplace cooler, such as the air around you. However, if the ambient air temperature is the same as your body temperature, you have to go to great lengths to shove the waste heat out into it, e.g., sweating like a pig or going out to K mart to buy an air conditioner.

What we want, therefore, is an ambient temperature that lets us dump waste heat with the least strain. From experience we know this temperature is 68 to 72 degrees F. If you're very lightly dressed you may prefer 80. But even if you're starkers there's no way you'll be happy when it's 98 in the shade.

What's the deal with the historical hiring of Native American Indians to work on skyscrapers? Have they all truly been blessed with a lack of fear for heights?—Robert Wallman, New York

Nah, it's the warrior ethic. Really. But first a little background. It's not just any American Indian who goes into ironwork, it's mostly Iroquois, specifically Mohawks from the Kahnawake Reservation near Montreal.

The Mohawks got into the business by happenstance. In 1886 a Canadian company was building a railroad bridge over the St. Lawrence river near the Kahnawake reservation. The company hired a number of Mohawks as day laborers and found that they loved to climb around on the ironwork without any apparent fear of heights. Since it was difficult to find men with the moxie for high work, the company decided to try an Indian crew. "We picked out some and gave them a little training, and it turned out that putting riveting tools in their hands was like putting ham with eggs," a company official later wrote. Mohawks helped build bridges from then on.

In 1907 ninety-six men were killed when a span of the Quebec Bridge collapsed during construction; thirty-five of them were Indians from Kahnawake. The dead were buried in the Kahnawake cemetery under crosses made of steel beams. Your average construction worker might have decided it was time to go into a safer line of work, but not the Mohawks. From that day forward every young male on the reservation was convinced that risking your neck on high steel was the coolest calling this world could offer.

The Mohawks eventually branched out from bridges into general steel construction, including office buildings. During the late 1920s a number of Kahnawake crews started working on skyscrapers in New York, and they've been a fixture of the city's construction scene ever since. Some crews—the members are often related to one another—spend the weekends on the reservation and drive down to New York for the week; others live in Brooklyn. But they'll travel anywhere if there's steel to climb.

Do the Mohawks really have no fear of heights? Their employers think so, and the Indians themselves like to make out as though dancing on some I-beam six hundred feet in the air is no more disruptive to their peace of mind than stepping off a curb. Edmund Wilson, who wrote several essays about the Iroquois for *The New Yorker* in the 1950s, quoted one modest steel jockey's claim that he had "an uncanny sense of balance," and attributed their skill to "their earlier life, from threading forests and scaling mountains, from canoeing in streams rough with rapids. A very important factor is undoubtedly their habit, in walking, of putting one foot in front of the other, instead of straddling, as we seem to them to do. They do not need to make an effort in walking a narrow beam."

Far be it from me to make light of this portrait of the noble red man, but there may be a simpler explanation: they do it because it's macho. Evidence on this point comes to us from anthropologist Morris Freilich, who published a solemn academic study on the subject in 1958. Ordinarily Cecil doesn't take this kind of thing too seriously, but in this instance he was impressed by Freilich's impeccable research methodology: he spent his nights getting shnockered with the Mohawks at their favorite bar in Brooklyn.

One night when they were all drunk the Indians admitted they were scared fecal matter–less while iron hopping; they just didn't admit it because of the above-mentioned warrior ethic. (They didn't actually say "warrior ethic," of course; that was Freilich's take on it.) Freilich pointed out in his article that the Iroquois warrior tradition boiled down to going off with the boys to perform insane feats of bravery and raise hell, then coming home and boasting about your exploits. The warpath being no longer socially acceptable, steelwork was the next best thing. Sure, it's one of those silly male things. But I'd say it beats joining the men's movement and pounding a drum.

Chapter 3

Strange Beliefs

How did Uri Geller bend spoons?—Ms. Tified, Hollywood, California

By sheer force of his powerful mind—powerful, that is, compared to those of the dopes who bought his line of baloney. Geller, who recently began making appearances again after a long hiatus, was able to convince millions he had psychic powers when he was really just a talented showman using a few simple tricks. He even fooled a team of scientists at the Stanford Research Institute, which just shows you can have an M.A. and a Ph.D. and still fall for the same old B.S.

Geller's best-known stunt was making a spoon or key bend by merely rubbing it. In reality he'd surreptitiously bend the spoon or key beforehand, then keep the bent part concealed in his hand. When showtime came around, he'd display the spoon or key to the audience with the bowl or flat side facing out, from which angle it looked straight. Then he'd commence rubbing, all the while keeping up a furious line of chatter. By and by he'd extrude the bent part of the spoon or key from his fingers, if you follow me, giving the appearance that it was bending before the audience's eyes.

It sounds like there's nothing to it, but that's like saying the Sistine Chapel is just paint on plaster. Execution is everything to a magician, and Geller is a master of the art. Witnesses would claim they'd never taken their eyes off him, but videotapes would later show he'd distracted them just long enough to make whatever preparations he needed. Occasionally somebody would slip him a key or spoon too stiff to bend, in which case he'd claim his powers just weren't up to snuff that day. Paradoxically, these failures reinforced the idea that Geller was for real—if it was a trick, it'd always work, right?

Other tricks were even more simpleminded. To "see" a drawing inside a sealed envelope, Geller would secretly hold it up to the light. An assistant would signal the right answers to him when he was doing mind-reading demonstrations. He'd copy down license plates and makes of cars in the parking lot to dazzle audiences with his uncanny knowledge of their private lives. A child could do it. *You* could do it. For more details, see *The Truth About Uri Geller*, by James Randi, or *Gellerism Revealed*, by Ben Harris.

He's a Believer

Ouch! I found the way you dispensed with Uri Geller uncharacteristically simplistic. I personally witnessed two examples of Geller's powers, and I can't believe I was taken in by sleight of hand.

I and two colleagues interviewed Geller in 1975. We met in a small, well-lit office we had borrowed for the occasion. Geller was dressed simply in a long-sleeve shirt. We saw no wires, tools, unusual paraphernalia or bulges in his clothes.

During the interview we tried various drawing tricks that didn't amount to much. Then Geller asked if we had any metal. He rejected various things we had brought, so my colleagues offered a heavy silver ring off his finger that he had bought in Spain. Geller liked that. My colleague gave the ring to me since I sat closest. Geller asked that I not give the ring to him but instead hold it between my thumb and index finger. As I did so, he stroked it gently. It slowly warped and collapsed until it was unwearable. The ring never left my hand from the time it was handed to me till the time I passed it around, bent. We set it on the desk, and it continued to change perceptibly for another minute. No substitutions (my colleague recognized it as his own ring). No heat or acid. No physical force.

Later we went outside. Geller asked again if I had any metal. I produced my car key. He placed it on the sidewalk and covered it with his outstretched hand. When he removed his hand the key was found broken in half. It was my key, identifiable by its serial number. We had the key examined under an electron microscope. This revealed a crystalline alignment typical of a thermal break (meaning it had melted) rather than a flexion break. To confirm this, the folks at the lab broke another Volkswagen key by flexion and examined it. There was no similarity.

I think it is right to call Geller a showman. But a magician? I think not. His repertoire is too narrow, boring, and undependable. I found both your explanation and other lengthier exposés shallow, unconvincing, and objectively less believable than what I experienced. Give it another shot, would you?—David T., Washington, D.C.

Honestly, David, aluminum-siding salesmen must love you. Think about what you've just said. All of us have seen convincing examples of table (i.e., close-up) magic. The difference with Geller, according to you, is that his repertoire is "narrow, boring, and undependable." In other words, he's not good enough to be a fake, so he must be real. Puh-leeze.

I've consulted with Geller debunkers Ben Harris and James Randi, both professional magicians and the latter a winner of a MacArthur "genius" grant. Given the lapse of time, here's the best we can offer on the tricks you saw:

(1) You say the ring never left your hand. That's what many of Geller's victims say. Careful questioning or video analysis afterward usually reveals otherwise. A common ploy in magic is to take an object from someone and then hand it back, saying, "Whatever you do, I want you to hang on to this the whole time I'm talking to you." If you're as suggestible as most people—and I'm not saying I'd do any better—you'll forget the magician was holding it to begin with.

Similarly, the magician can drop the ring on the table and say, "Look! It's still bending!" It's not, of course, but you're so caught up in the moment you think it is. Silver is easily bent by hand; that's why Geller rejected the other items. In *Gellerism Revealed*, Ben Harris explains several tricks in which items seem to bend while a spectator is holding onto them.

(2) Geller could easily have stuck your car key in a crack in the

sidewalk and snapped it off with his foot. A hasty electron micro-scope test proves little. A tragic demonstration of this occurred in 1972, when Will Franklin, a professor at Kent State University, re-ported that a ring Geller had allegedly bent psychically showed "unusual fracture surfaces" when examined under an electron micro-scope. These "provided evidence that a paranormal influence function was probably operative." Five years later Franklin publicly confessed he'd misinterpreted the test results; in fact, the fracture surfaces were easily explained. He later committed suicide. Don't think you're any less susceptible to illusion.

Questions about UFOs may be unanswerable, but on the chance you may be even better connected than I thought, here goes. Why are UFO sightings always at night? And why do they seem to appear mostly to stranded motorists or farmers in the middle of Montana or Kansas? Are our friends from afar allergic to light, or do they just prefer the late-night specials at Denny's? And what is it with their ships? They always seem to be illuminated in colorful lights that either impair the victim's vision or provide him with an incredible light show. Do our space visitors have some arrangement to buy out the contents of defunct discos?—Eleanor T., San Antonio, Texas

I detect a certain lack of reverence here, Eleanor, which is typical of the younger generation. Whatever happened to the paranoia that made this country great? Actually, UFO sightings aren't always at night, and they aren't always in rural areas. They do tend to involve suspiciously few witnesses, however.

Flying-saucer debunker Robert Sheaffer calls UFO encounters "jealous phenomena," meaning that UFOs are finicky about letting themselves be seen. In *The UFO Verdict* he writes, "It is a well-known fact that UFOs are supposed to be extremely wary of showing themselves openly. . . . They will not . . . under any circum-stances fly low over a crowded vacation site in broad daylight or hover conspicuously over a major city, because the photographic rec-ord they would presumably leave behind would be clear and unmis-takable. . . . In short, one must conclude that the UFOs' reported behavior is principally determined by an overriding concern with human thoughts and emotions."

Similar behavior was attributed years ago to—don't laugh—fairies. In 1920 Sir Arthur Conan Doyle, the creator of Sherlock Holmes and a sucker for tales from the unknown, proclaimed in all serious-ness that fairies existed. He even published photos of them taken by a young woman, inspiring a rash of sighting reports by others. But Doyle never saw the fairies himself—like UFOs, they were a jealous phenomenon that would only reveal itself to those with the Right Stuff. It was later learned that the fairies' poses had probably been copied from an illustration in a children's book.

The moral of this story, of course, is that jealous phenomena al-most always turn out to be illusions or hoaxes. In the case of UFOs it's easy to see how this happens. The typical sighting occurs at night, when you can readily mistake a planet, satellite, aircraft, etc., for an alien visitor. (The planet Venus, which is quite bright, is no-torious in this regard.)

Adding to the illusion is the fact that our ability to gauge the size and distance of airborne objects is laughably poor. (Example: When asked to judge the size of the image of the moon in the sky, most people say it's about the size of a dinner plate. In reality it's smaller than the nail on your little finger held at arm's length.)

Another factor is the natural human tendency to "fill in" (i.e., make up) missing details when we get a hasty glimpse of something. This is often what accounts for reports of blinking and/or colored lights, spacecraft windows with aliens visible inside, and so on.

A good example of this is the rash of UFO sightings that occurred the evening of March 3, 1968. Three people in Tennessee saw a large cigar-shaped craft zip overhead at about one thousand feet with orange flame shooting out the tail. One person said the craft had ten large square windows illuminated from within. Six people in Indiana saw a similar UFO at about the same time. It had windows, was 150 to 200 feet long, and flew at treetop level. A woman in Ohio saw *three* UFOs at 1,500 feet that frightened her dog. Another Ohioan also saw three fast-moving objects, which executed various turns and thus appeared to be under intelligent control.

What the witnesses actually saw were the flaming remnants of a cluster of Russian booster rockets that burned up over the central

U.S. after launching a Zond spacecraft. The rockets were many miles overhead, did not have windows, and were not under intelligent control. Neither were the humans, from the sound of it, but let's be kind and just say you shouldn't always believe what you think you see.

Has anyone vanished in the Bermuda Triangle lately? There were many reports of mysterious incidents back in the seventies, but since then the whole subject has simply dropped out of sight (grin). Is the mystery any closer to being solved? I'm thinking of sending my in-laws on a permanent vacation.—K.T., Saint Louis, Missouri

Better stick to cyanide or blunt instruments, K.; the lethality of the Bermuda Triangle has been greatly exaggerated. The only reason I bring up the subject at all, in fact, is to bestow some belated publicity on a fine example of the debunker's art. But more on this in a moment.

In case anybody's forgotten, the Bermuda Triangle is a region in the Atlantic Ocean where scores of ships and planes allegedly have vanished—usually without a trace, in good weather, and without sending distress calls. Two typical cases:

- In December 1945, five Navy planes took off from Fort Lauderdale on a routine training mission. After reporting that their compasses were acting up and everything looked "strange," the five lost contact with their base and were never seen again. Another plane sent out to look for them vanished as well. No wreckage from any of the planes was ever found.
- On December 28, 1948, a DC-3 carrying thirty-six persons disappeared while en route from San Juan, Puerto Rico, to Miami. In their last radio message around 4:00 A.M. the plane's crew reported they were only fifty miles south of Miami and within sight of the city's lights. The plane was never heard from again. A massive search turned up no wreckage, despite the shallowness of the waters south of Miami.

These and many other incidents were blamed on everything from UFOs to electromagnetic fluctuations in the space-time continuum. Fortunately a few levelheaded folk also looked into the matter, among them Lawrence David Kusche, who wrote a book entitled *The Bermuda Triangle Mystery—Solved* in 1975.

In an analysis of some fifty cases, Kusche found that overeager BT buffs had been playing fast and loose with the facts. In many cases the disappearance *had* taken place in bad weather, involving craft known to have been experiencing trouble. Wreckage was found in many cases; in others, darkness or delay in starting the search provided ample time for debris to disperse. Many of the cases hadn't even taken place in the Bermuda Triangle, but rather in other sites near Ireland, in the Gulf of Mexico, off the coast of Africa or South America, or, in one case, in the Pacific Ocean. Here's what Kusche found out about the cases cited above:

- The five Navy planes were piloted by four student pilots and one instructor. The instructor's compasses failed, and he became disoriented, thinking he was over the Florida Keys when he was really near the Bahamas. Radio interference from ground stations hindered efforts to help him. After flying aimlessly for several hours, the planes ran out of gas and were presumably ditched in the ocean shortly after nightfall. By this time the seas were extremely rough. Darkness, delay, and equipment failures hampered search efforts. One of the planes sent up to search for the missing flight apparently blew up in midair; the explosion was spotted by a nearby ship.

· While in San Juan the crew of the DC-3 found the plane's batteries were dead but decided to take off without adequately recharging them. Because of the lack of power, the radio was operational only intermittently. An investigating panel speculated that additional electrical problems might have rendered the plane's navigation equipment inoperable. The crew never said they were within sight of Miami; these reports were the work of Triangle buffs who jumped to conclusions. The waters fifty miles due south of Miami are shallow, but those fifty miles along the flight path to San Juan (i.e., southeast) are approximately five thousand feet deep.

In short, both disappearances could be plausibly explained without reference to UFOs or mysterious vortexes or any other paranormal phenomenon. The same could be said for almost all the other cases Kusche looked into. Conclusion: the Bermuda Triangle "mystery" is a figment of a lot of overactive imaginations.

What is Kirlian photography? How is it that it captures on film an object that is no longer present?   J. Ramirez, Chicago

Let's not jump to conclusions, friend. The "phantom object" effect isn't what it's cracked up to be.

But first some facts. On second thought, bag the facts. Let's start with the fiction, which is more interesting. A common feature of your typical New Age mystic's understanding of the cosmos is that every living thing is surrounded by an *aura*, a cloud of energy radiated by your inner being, also known as your "life force," "bioplasma," etc.

A psychic supposedly can scope out your aura and diagnose the state of your soul. Unfortunately, not all of us have the gift, and that's where Kirlian photography comes in handy. The Kirlian effect enables the aura to be photographed. Presumably the photos can then be interpreted by any skilled aura analyst, psychic or not.

The apparatus used to make Kirlian photographs is a little complicated, but typically you start off with a device called a Tesla coil, which emits a high-voltage (fifteen thousand to sixty thousand volts) but low-current (and hence harmless) electrical discharge. If you hook the Tesla coil to a big metal sphere set up on a stand, the discharge will be visible as lightninglike blue streamers radiating off into space.

If, however, you instead hook the coil up to a piece of photographic paper and place an object in contact therewith (e.g., your finger, a leaf), you'll notice a faint Saint Elmo's fire–like effect known as "airglow" around the object. Develop the photographic paper and you'll have a permanent record of the airglow. That's a Kirlian photograph. Typically the airglow/aura appears as a dark cloud outlining the thing photographed.

At this point you're probably thinking, What the hey, shoot a jillion volts into *anything* and it'll have an aura, whether it's living or not. Just so—people have made K-photos of the auras of pennies, paper clips, and so on. Nonetheless the belief persists that Kirlian photos depict a purely biological essence.

Scientists, trying to be nice guys about it, note that the size of a human's aura is dependent on his skin moisture, among other things, so maybe a Kirlian photo does tell you something about a person, much as a lie detector does. But the whole thing seems too dumb to waste much time on.

"Phantom object" claims are more interesting. Some Kirlian researchers assert that if you K-P a broken leaf, the resultant photo will show the missing portion of the leaf, supposedly proving that the aura lingers on even after the reality is gone. But most attempts to duplicate this in the lab have failed. The best guess is that phantom leaves are dust, sap, and whatnot from previously photographed leaves that oozed onto the photographic equipment and got onto subsequent photos. All in all, nothing to lose sleep over.

Out here in the northwest, it's becoming increasingly common to put gallon milk jugs half filled with water on the perimeter of your lawn. Supposedly this discourages dogs from relieving themselves and they move along to a jugless lawn. Can this possibly be true? Or is this the pink flamingo of the nineties?—Ralph Goldstein, Oregon City, Oregon

And Oregonians think people from *California* are flakes? This silly stunt has been floating around since the late 1970s and by now has spread all over the world. Folklorist Jan Brunvand, who tells the whole story in his book *Curses! Broiled Again!*, says he saw plastic bottles on lawns everywhere during a trip to New Zealand, and apparently they were common in Australia, too. Where the idea started nobody knows, but numerous early instances have been reported from California.

"Explanations" for it include (1) dogs won't foul their own drinking water, (2) they get spooked seeing their reflections and/or the glitter of the water, (3) it ain't the water, it's the bottles—the water just keeps the jugs from blowing over, (4) it only works when you put ammonia or mothballs in the water—the *smell* is what repels the dogs.

With the possible exception of (4), all are unlikely. As one of Brunvand's correspondents notes: "I was not completely convinced of the efficacy of such a system [upon first hearing of it]. My skepticism proved justified when, a block later, my dog backed directly onto one of the plastic bottles and left one large turd delicately balanced on top of it." Next case.

I trust you can settle a matter that threatens to create a vast rift between my love and I. What is the absolute, unequivocal Straight Dope on astrology? My girl maintains that while horoscopes in newspapers may be rubbish, astrology as a whole is not. She believes that a person's traits are dictated by their astrological chart (i.e., time of birth, position of planets, etc.) and that a person's zodiac sign may be guessed by simply observing them. In fact, she has done this on occasion. I say astrology is completely illogical and that her predictions are the result of a twelve-to-one shot paying off. Cece, set my lady straight.—B. Hayes, Chicago

Couple problems you got here, B. Number one, it's "between my love and *me*," not I. (For that matter, it's "couple problems you've*

got," not you got, but when I massacre the language it's art.)
Number two, don't count on me to get your girlfriend turned
around. My powers of persuasion are awesome, but experience
shows these people are immune to argument.

The usual objections to astrology boil down to: how the hell could
it possibly work? After all, the stars are unthinkably distant, and the
planets, an essential part of astrology, revolve around the sun, not
the earth. Besides, what's so magical about the time of your birth—
wouldn't it make more sense if your personality were determined by
the time of your *conception*? On top of everything else, astrologists
don't even agree on how to do charts—check out the difference between tropical and sidereal zodiacs sometime.

But this is not what astrology buffs want to hear. To them it
doesn't matter that there's no plausible basis for astrology; they claim
it just "works." By this they mean a skilled astrologer can give you
genuine insights into your personality. In this they're undoubtedly
correct—but the credit goes not to astrology per se but to the prac-
titioner.

Many experienced astrologers are pretty fair amateur shrinks. In
the course of a one- or two-hour consultation they can usually get a
good fix on your problems. Back this up with a lot of B.S. about
Mars conjunct Uranus and the effect is convincing—and what the
heck, it may even do you some good.

But to say astrology can be helpful doesn't mean it has any objective validity. Studies have shown that (1) astrologers trying to deduce
someone's personality from his chart do no better than chance, (2)
different astrologers studying the same chart come to opposite conclusions as often as not, (3) the birth dates of people with occupa-
tions linked to certain signs (e.g., politicians, scientists, soldiers) are
in fact randomly distributed throughout the zodiac; and (4) couples
with "incompatible" signs get married and divorced at the same rate
as compatible couples.

The fact is, people who want to believe in astrology will convince
themselves it works no matter what. In one study of twenty-two astrology buffs, half were presented with their real horoscopes and half
were presented with fake charts saying the exact opposite. Both
groups said their horoscopes were 96 to 97 percent accurate.

So maybe you'd better give this relationship some thought. If your girlfriend's not rational now, what's she going to be like when you're arguing about who's supposed to feed the cat?

I've always cast a jaundiced eye on the shenanigans of scientific fringe groups. But my eye is a little less yellow when I look at Wilhelm Reich. Reich claimed to have discovered a life energy he called "orgone" back in the 1930s. He made a device that supposedly accumulated the energy, the "orgone accumulator" (ORAC), and another that allegedly could manipulate it in the atmosphere called a "cloudbuster."

Some M.D.'s who still subscribe to Reich's theories publish the Journal of Orgonomy. *I remember one article claiming tomato plants grown inside an ORAC produce more and larger tomatoes. There's a meteorologist named James DeMeo who does research on the cloudbuster. Plus (and this is the ultimate evidence) Kate Bush sang a song about the cloudbuster on her* Hounds of Love *album. Seeing*

as you're the last word on subjects like this, what's the last word on orgone? Yes, no, or maybe?—Steven Stocker, Baltimore

No. Reich was a nut—an unjustly persecuted nut, it should be said, but still a nut. He claimed that (1) he had done battle with alien spaceships, (2) he could produce clouds and create rain with his cloudbuster, and (3) his orgone boxes could cure (or at least ameliorate) everything from cancer to the common cold. He believed living cells arose spontaneously from inorganic matter, that cancer cells are actually protozoalike critters that have tails and can swim like fish, and that orgone energy is what makes the sky blue and causes heat shimmer.

Even his terminology was like something out of a bad science-fiction movie. UFOs he called EAs, for Energy Alpha. The alien spaceships gave off DOR, for Deadly Orgone. The aliens themselves he called CORE men, for Cosmic Orgone Engineering.

Still, you have to give Reich some credit. He was an intelligent, charismatic man who had his share of admirers. He was a cherished associate of Freud's in his early years and made some useful contributions to psychoanalytic theory.

But he seems to have had only the most tenuous grasp of reality. His ideas became more and more eccentric over time and he was eventually expelled from the International Psychoanalytic Association. He wound up in the United States and from then on devoted all his time to the mad pursuit of the orgone.

Reich convinced a great many people, including a few scientists like the aforementioned DeMeo, who claims he ended a drought with a cloudbuster. To this day there are are several orgonomic societies. But the mainstream view has always been that Reich was a quack and that his ideas have no scientific basis.

Loony though Reich was, he did not deserve the shameful treatment he received at the hands of the government. From the early 1950s onward he was hounded by federal agents. His laboratory in Maine was raided, his equipment destroyed, and his books confiscated and burned. Reich did make exaggerated claims for the medicinal powers of his orgone boxes, but he was hardly a major threat to the republic and there was no excuse for the ferocity of the campaign that was raised against him.

In 1956 Reich was convicted of shipping orgone boxes across state lines in defiance of a court order obtained by the Food and Drug Administration. He was sent to prison, where he died of a heart attack in 1957. But his ideas, both good and bad, live on.

What's this I hear about "crop circles" being mysteriously flattened in the corn and wheat fields in the English countryside around Stonehenge? I heard that attempts have been made to duplicate these circles without success. What's the Straight Dope?—Kimberly Moon, Dallas

Oh, please, not crop circles. According to *The New York Review of Books*, nearly one thousand of the flattened circles (and other more elaborate designs called pictograms) had been reported as of 1990, some up to 150 feet in diameter. The stalks aren't broken, just bent over. Although a few circles were reported in the sixties and seventies, they've only become common since 1980. Numerous explanations have been offered: snared animals running in circles, helicopters flying upside down, giant mushrooms, and, just to show you even crackpots read the newspapers, a hole in the ozone layer that allows ultraviolet radiation to fry the alfalfa.

A physicist blames the circles on "small, stationary wind vortices"; others predictably chalk them up to an unknown intelligence. The *Economist* magazine a couple years ago gave a respectful write-up to a Japanese researcher who thinks the circles are caused by ball lightning, known in some quarters as plasma vortices.

Whatever may be said for these notions, at least some (and in my opinion, probably all) of the circles are hoaxes. The circles are almost invariably made under cover of darkness; the few claimed eyewitness accounts are highly suspect. The number of circles increases dramatically after each new round of publicity. The circles are almost always located astride tractor tracks, down which hoaxers can easily walk undetected. The designs have gotten increasingly (and absurdly) elaborate; one pictogram spelled out WEARENOTALONE. Sometimes the patterns are decked out with Ouija boards and crosses. The vast majority are located in a couple counties in southern England, presumably because the hoaxers don't care to travel too far from home.

On one occasion the BBC, in the course of doing a report on the phenomenon, snuck a crew of wise guys into the middle of a field, making sure everybody walked there in the tractor tracks so as not to leave footprints. The pranksters then formed a line, linked arms, and did a slo-mo shuffle somewhat reminiscent of a marching band on Valium. The result was pronounced a genuine crop circle by a leading "cereologist," or crop circle investigator. Gotcha, said the BBC people, it's fake! I knew that, said the cereologist. It was too perfect. Sure.

In 1991 two men named Bower and Chorley appeared on the scene claiming they'd spent the last thirteen years making circles as a lark. They even demonstrated their technique on TV, using boards to flatten the crops. Crop circle buffs were thrown into momentary disarray. Some refused to believe Bower and Chorley; others, while conceding that hoaxes may account for as many as half the circles, continue to maintain the rest are real.

I doubt it. Crushing the corn in order to sucker the feebleminded clearly has gotten to be a popular sport among the young bloods of southern England. While the buffs may profess to be baffled by this so-called mystery, there's no need for the rest of us to play the same game.

Proof That the Aliens Have Landed!

Aliens do create "crop circles." Specifically, to give indications of their presence here, according to my reliable sources (several, mostly channeled independently). Despite massive official denials and cover-ups, this planet's been crawling in ETs since we shook up this sector of the galaxy splitting atoms. Why "answer" questions to which you don't know the answers?—J. Jones, New York City

The Earth is crawling with space aliens? The more letters I get like this, J., the more I start to think you're right.

A little over a year ago I was doing my coachly duty at a high school speech tournament when a fellow coach announced that she wanted the pull tabs from our empty soda cans. She said she was saving them for a woman who could turn them in to get cancer treatment. It sounded like an urban legend to me, but I kept my mouth shut, since it's uncool to dis one's fellow coaches.

Not surprisingly, the story had legs. At the start of this school year my students started mentioning that we should be saving pull tabs to help someone get kidney dialysis. As it is okay to dis one's students, I told them they were nuts and pressed them for evidence. None could name the generous hospital or even the needy kidney patient. I hoped I'd put an end to this goofy tale.

Sadly, the story has now appeared again, with the added authority endowed by the school public address system. Every day an announcement is read urging students to place their pull tabs in collection containers so they can be given to some poor nameless kidney patient. The kids are now convinced there must be some substance to this, and my insistence to the contrary is losing credibility. Please, Cecil, find out what you can and restore my reputation.—Lexy A. Green, Oakland, California

Don't get your hopes up, teach. So-called redemption rumors have been floating around at least since the 1950s and probably earlier. Before kidney dialysis came along you typically were told to save cigarette packs to buy somebody time on an iron lung—one of your classic sick bargains.

Most such stories were false, but not all. For example, from 1948 till 1979 the makers of Vets dog food would make a one- to two-cent donation to an outfit that trained Seeing Eye dogs for each Vets label redeemed. Today Heinz baby food labels can be redeemed to benefit children's hospitals and Campbell's soup labels can be used to buy school equipment.

The kidney dialysis legend may have started with the Betty Crocker coupon program run by General Mills. Most folks redeemed the coupons for kitchen utensils and stuff, but beginning in 1969 General Mills okayed several fund-raising campaigns in which coupons were used to purchase some three hundred kidney dialysis machines. The company soon stopped dialysis drives due partly to complaints that it was "trading in human misery." But the idea evidently survived in the public mind, with one twist: the medium of exchange was somehow switched to pop-can pull tabs.

The story was so persistent that in 1988 the kidney and pop-can people decided to play along. Today if you walk into a Reynolds Aluminum recycling center with a pile of pull tabs and say they're for "kidney dialysis," the staff will nod knowingly, exchange winks, and send a donation equal to the salvage value of the aluminum to the National Kidney Foundation. However, the donation will *not* pay for dialysis, because there's no need. Medicare picks up 80 percent of the cost of dialysis and state programs or private insurance typically covers the rest. Instead, the donation goes to kidney research, education/prevention programs, and patient services.

So saving pull tabs isn't a complete waste of time. But let's make one thing clear: *there's nothing special about pull tabs*. You'd save yourself a heap o' trouble and make a lot more money if you recycled the whole can. The Reynolds and kidney foundation people have tried to get that point across with a poster showing a red *Ghostbuster*-type slash through a cartoon of someone trying to detach a pull tab from a can. The headline says, KEEP TABS ON YOUR CANS.

But the public hasn't gotten the message. Supposedly responsible people—e.g., the honchos at your school—will organize pull tab collection drives without ever bothering to get the whole story. Urban legends expert Jan Brunvand reports that in 1989 a Minneapolis VFW post organized a pull tab collection drive for the local Ronald McDonald House. When Brunvand asked the organizers why they didn't tell people to save whole cans, they lamely replied that there were "hygiene problems" and that people liked mailing in the tabs, even though the postage often exceeded the value of the aluminum. In other words, it's not important to *do* good as long as people *feel* good. Excuse me while I grind my teeth.

A couple questions: (1) Is there any scientific evidence that crystals emit power or store energy? (2) Is it possible to create a comic book-

type flashlight so bright the briefest exposure would cause permanent blindness?—Xah L., Montreal, Quebec

(1) Sure, crystals emit power—the power to enrich gemshop owners beyond their wildest dreams. The wholesale price of quartz crystals, the kind most often mentioned as having mystic properties, has increased 1,000 percent since the crystal craze began. Claims of healing powers, however, are spurious and are a result largely of a misunderstanding of quartz's technical properties by addle-brained New Agers.

Quartz, also know as silicon dioxide or silica, is the earth's most abundant mineral, most often seen in the form of sand. Quartz crystals can be created in hot water under pressure, a process that may be readily duplicated in the lab. Though not as iridescent (or as hard) as diamonds, quartz crystals are undeniably pretty, and that plus their large size and easy availability has undoubtedly contributed to their popularity.

Quartz crystals are widely used in timepieces and radio tuners owing to two interesting properties: they don't expand much when heated, and they change shape slightly when subjected to an electric field, a phenomenon known as the *piezoelectric effect*. When the electric field in question is alternating, the crystal vibrates.

All crystals have a certain natural "pitch," or frequency of vibration, much as a glass of water has a characteristic tone when you tap it with a spoon. If you hook an alternating circuit to a crystal and tune the circuit's frequency to the crystal's natural frequency, the two will resonate. Thereafter the circuit will stay locked into the crystal's frequency through a process of mutual reinforcement. A crystal's pitch is determined by its size and shape, and since quartz expands only minimally when warm, quartz-tuned circuits are quite accurate.

Crystal buffs have used the fact that quartz crystals vibrate as the basis for a vast edifice of nonsense about "resonance," "harmonics," and "energy." The mildest claim is that crystals will "center your energies" and improve your life somehow, and if that's as far as you take it, using crystals is no worse than reading your horoscope or buying diet books. But a few extremists claim crystals can help cure cancer, AIDS, and other diseases. There is no scientific grounding for these claims, and anyone who uses crystals as a substitute for proven therapies is endangering his health and possibly his life.

(2) Certainly—in fact, such a flashlight was first demonstrated in 1945. It's called an atom bomb. In his book *Hiroshima* John Hersey describes some victims: "There were about twenty men, and they were all in exactly the same nightmarish state: their faces were wholly burned, their eyesockets were hollow, the fluid from their melted eyes had run down their cheeks. (They must have had their faces upturned when the bomb went off; perhaps they were anti-aircraft personnel.)" The bomb emitted a vast amount of thermal (i.e., nonnuclear) radiation, a mixture of ultraviolet, visible, and infrared rays. The invisible infrared rays, which we perceive as heat, caused most of the damage. I suppose one could argue infrared doesn't really qualify as "light" in the colloquial sense, but the distinction hardly seems worth making.

Currently 13 is considered to be an unlucky number. However, I am told it used to be—and in some earth-worshipping, i.e., pagan, religions still is—a lucky and magical number. Consequently there were 13 months and 13 zodiac signs (the Gemini twins had separate iden-

tities). Knowing how Christianity and other god-as-a-man–based religions were prone to say that what the pagans (Earth-and-god-as-a-woman) considered good was bad, I wonder if this was the case with the number 13. And why was 13 singled out of an infinity of numbers in the first place? Also, if the number 13 is so bad, why is it reflected so many times on the U.S. $1 bill—13 levels in the pyramid, 13 stars, 13 arrows, 13 stripes, 13 leaves, and 13 olives? Is it because of the original 13 colonies?—L. S. Thomas, Berkeley, California

With regard to your last question, L., of course not. It's just one of those crazy coincidences. The matter of how 13 came to be a numerological pariah, on the other hand, is an interesting story. While your rap about the pagans is a little off the wall (Thor the feminist?), you're right about one thing: 13 hasn't always been considered unlucky.

Though I wasn't able to do as thorough a study of cross-cultural number significance as I would have liked—the Straight Dope Field Survey Team preferred to be read to from *The Cat in the Hat*—what I've seen suggests that in ancient times 13 either was considered in a positive light or, more commonly, wasn't considered at all. I note, for example, that the Gnostics of the early Christian era totted up 13 Conformations of the Holy Beard. The significance of the Holy Beard is not entirely clear to me, but I gather it's something you wanted on your side. Thirteen was also once associated with the Epiphany by mainstream Christians, the Christ child having received the Magi on his thirteenth day of life.

But 13's stock dropped like a rock in the Middle Ages. The proximate cause of this apparently was the observation that Judas, the betrayer of Jesus, made 13 at the table. Other great medieval minds, I read here, pointed out that "the Jews murmured 13 times against God in the exodus from Egypt, that the thirteenth psalm concerns wickedness and corruption, that the circumcision of Israel occurred in the thirteenth year," and so on.

Pretty thin excuse for maligning a number that never meant any harm, you may think. I agree. We must inquire further, and if we do we conclude that while open hostility to 13 may be relatively recent, folks have had their suspicions about it for quite a while. Thirteen is a prime; primes have always attracted attention (compare 7).

What's worse, 13 is one past 12, the dozen, almost universally regarded as a perfect number, signifying harmony and all good things.
Thirteen, by contrast, is a number of transgression, taking matters
one step too far, turning harmony into discord.

A bit of a stretch? Maybe. But consider how often 13s seem to in-
trude on our tidy arrangements of 12. In many a twelvemonth, to
use an old term, there are 13 full moons, and a woman on a twenty-
eight-day menstrual cycle will be "unclean," as Leviticus has it, 13
times a year. The moon has long been a female symbol, and the full
moon, (male) chroniclers tell us, is when (female) witches fly. I hesitate on that evidence alone to ascribe triskaidekaphobia to the fell
hand of the patriarchy. But 13's bad reputation may have more to do
with fear of women, witchcraft, and disorder than is commonly supposed.

*Back in 1980 when Ronald Reagan was elected president I heard
several mentions of an American Indian curse, cast in the early nineteenth century, which foretold the death while in office of all presidents elected during years ending in a zero. Who placed this curse,
and what has been its success rate? Ronnie obviously survived.—
Kiazi Brown, Washington, D.C.*

If Reagan achieved nothing else while in office—and sometimes
you have to wonder—he broke the back of the "Tecumseh's curse"
legend by leaving office alive. The previous seven presidents elected
in years ending with zero weren't so lucky. Here's the grim roll
call:

- Harrison, elected in 1840, died of pneumonia after serving
  thirty-one days.
- Lincoln, elected in 1860, assassinated.
- Garfield, elected in 1880, assassinated.
- McKinley, elected to a second term in 1900, assassinated.
- Harding, elected in 1920, died of a stroke in 1923.
- Roosevelt, elected to a third term in 1940, died of a cerebral
  hemorrhage in 1945.
- Kennedy, elected in 1960, assassinated.

The "curse" was popularly attributed to the Indian chief Tecumseh, whose forces were defeated in 1811 at the battle of Tippecanoe by troops led by William Henry Harrison, who became the first of the seven presidents to die. Harrison also led soldiers against Tecumseh at another battle in 1813 during which the Indian leader was killed. An 1836 play had Tecumseh cursing the white man as he lay dying on the battlefield, but there is no evidence that he actually did so. The whole thing was pretty spooky just the same.

Please debunk the "missing day" theory described in the enclosed flyer.—Ross Rhone, Chicago

Debunk it? Hey, I want to *believe* in it. I also want to believe that Jimmy Hoffa and Elvis are running a 7-Eleven in Kalamazoo, Michigan. Unfortunately, we're out of luck on all counts.

The best-known version of the tale, a classic bit of "xeroxlore" that creationists have been passing around for more than twenty years, is attributed to one Harold Hill, supposedly a consultant to the NASA space program. It seems a bunch of "astronauts and space scientists" at the Goddard Space Flight Center in Greenbelt, Maryland, were using a computer to calculate the orbits of the sun, moon, and planets so that a satellite sent up today would not crash into something a hundred years from now. This entailed figuring the position of the heavenly bodies many centuries into the past. (Why I don't know; I'm just telling the story.)

After a while the computer halted and "put up a red signal, which meant that there was something wrong either with the information fed into it or with the results as compared to the standards." On investigating, the scientists found there was "a day missing in space in elapsed time." They were puzzled until a "religious fellow on the team" recalled a passage in the Bible (Joshua 10:12–13) where Joshua asked the Lord to make the sun stand still until he could defeat his enemies. The Lord obliged, and the sun stood still "about a whole day."

Damn, the missing day! shouted the scientists. Not quite. After further calculations they concluded that the missing "elapsed time" in Joshua's day was only twenty-three hours and twenty minutes, not a full day.

Then the religious fellow had another brainstorm. He recalled that in II Kings 20:9–11 Hezekiah prevailed upon the prophet Isaiah to ask the Lord to make the sun go backward ten degrees. No problemo, said the Lord.

"Ten degrees is exactly 40 minutes," the tale concludes. "Twenty-three hours and 20 minutes in Joshua, plus 40 minutes in II Kings make the missing 24 hours the space travelers had to log in the logbook as being the missing day in the universe. Isn't that amazing? Our God is rubbing their noses in His Truth!"

Well. The folks from NASA sensibly point out that they have no need to compute orbits thousands of years into the past and future because the typical satellite lasts only a dozen years. Nonetheless, there may be a germ of truth to the "missing day" story.

NASA spokesman Charles Redmond points out that in the early 1960s, when scientists were first using computers to figure out orbits for the manned space program, there was a discrepancy of about twenty seconds between Universal time (basically Greenwich Mean Time) and so-called ephemeris time, i.e., the "real" time based on astronomical observations. A twenty-second error when you're trying to bring a manned spacecraft down to earth is enough to put the astronauts in somebody's backyard in Orlando rather than in the ocean where they're supposed to be. So the scientists jiggered the numbers to get UT synchronized with real time. (This is handled today by throwing in leap seconds every few years.)

These adjustments may have provided the basis for Harold Hill's story. But there wasn't any missing day, and it certainly didn't have anything to do with the Book of Joshua. I should point out that Hill wasn't a NASA consultant; his firm did diesel engine maintenance and such for the space agency.

Creationists have been trying to work the "missing day" angle for a long time. Folklorist Jan Brunvand—Jan and I have gotten to be good buddies over the past few years—says he unearthed a story about an alleged confrontation between an unbelieving scientist and C. A. Totten, an eccentric military instructor at Yale in the 1890s.

Totten, who became notorious for his wild theories about science and religion, supposedly made a believer out of an agnostic astronomer by pointing out a "missing day" in the latter's calculations that could only be accounted for by the passages from Joshua and II Kings. It's the kind of story that only a true believer could love, since it makes no sense to anybody else.

Food, Glorious Food

Having seen Chinese restaurants with banners proclaiming NO MSG, I gather monosodium glutamate is bad for you. So how come you can't pick up a can or package of chicken soup or a TV dinner that doesn't contain MSG (or hydrolyzed vegetable protein, which contains MSG)? What does MSG do for manufacturers that makes it worth using? More important, what does it do to us?—Murdoch Matthew, Jersey City, New Jersey

MSG is a flavor enhancer that accentuates "meatiness." It's a component of the proteins found in many foods, but critics say in its purified form it can be a potent neurotoxin, causing nerve cells literally to excite themselves to death. An alleged example of this is "Chinese restaurant syndrome." A half hour after eating MSG-laden soup, once a staple of budget Chinese cuisine, some people say they experience headaches, tightness of the chest, and a burning sensation. Researchers have had difficulty reproducing this in the lab, but the feds got so many complaints from the field that they've issued tougher label requirements for MSG in meat and poultry and are thinking of doing the same for other foods.

MSG may also be harmful to babies, which is why it was yanked out of baby food twenty years ago. But MSG makers and some scientists hotly deny that MSG poses a threat to the average adult. If you want to avoid it, watch out for the term "natural flavoring" on ingredients labels. Until the rules are changed, that could be a camouflage for MSG.

Is man a meat eater or a vegetarian by nature? According to the enclosed clipping from a vegetarian magazine, "The intestinal length of carnivores (meat-eating animals) is three times the body length to allow for quick removal of flesh wastes that putrefy in the intestines. Man's intestine length, like other herbivores, is six times his body length and is designed for digesting vegetables, grains, and fruits." I'm not a meat eater but my girlfriend is, and she is not convinced man is a natural vegetarian. We decided to leave it up to you. (Why I agreed to this I don't know, it's obvious from your aggressive tone that you like your steak rare.) Please, don't embarrass yourself by quoting that garbage from the National Beef Council that meat is our best source of protein. Even high school kids know better than that.—L. Williams, Culver City, California

Listen, wimp—whoops, too aggressive. Gimme some of that tofu burger. Ah, I can feel the testosterone receding already. Now then, let us reason like gentlemen. There are some intelligent arguments for vegetarianism, but claiming that man is "naturally" herbivorous isn't one of them. The settled judgment of science is that man is an omnivore, capable of eating both meat and plant food.

Like the hard-core carnivores, we have fairly simple digestive systems well suited to the consumption of animal protein, which breaks down quickly. Contrary to what your magazine article says, the human small intestine, at twenty-three feet, is a little under eight times body length (assuming a mouth-to-anus "body length" of three feet). This is about midway between cats (three times body length), and dogs (three and a half times), and other well-known meat eaters on the one hand and plant eaters such as cattle (twenty to one) and horses (twelve to one) on the other. This tends to support the idea that we are omnivores.

Herbivores also have a variety of specialized digestive organs capable of breaking down cellulose, the main component of plant tissue. Humans find cellulose totally indigestible, and even plant eaters have to take their time with it. If you were a ruminant (cud eater), for instance, you might have a stomach with four compartments, enabling you to cough up last night's alfalfa and chew on it all over again.

Or you might have an enlarged cecum, a sac attached to the intestines, where rabbits and such store food until their intestinal bacteria have time to do their stuff. Digestion in such cases takes place by a process of fermentation—bacteria actually "eat" the cellulose and the host animal consumes what results, namely bacteria dung.

The story is roughly the same with our teeth. We're equipped with an all-purpose set of ivories equally suited to liver and onions.

Good thing, too. I won't claim meat is the ideal source of protein, but on the whole it's better than plants. Sure, soybeans and other products of modern agriculture are pretty nutritious. But in the wild, much of the plant menu consists of leaves and stems, which are low in food value. True herbivores have to spend much of the day scrounging for snacks just to keep their strength up.

So make no mistake: we were born to eat meat. That's not to say you *have* to. There's no question that strictly from a health standpoint we'd all be a lot better off eating less meat (red meat especially) and more fruits and vegetables. But vegetarians aren't going to advance their cause by making ridiculous claims.

Vegetarians Go Ape

Your statement that "we were born to eat meat" is nonsense. In using comparative anatomy to determine what man was "meant" to eat, we should look at the species most similar to man, namely, the anthropoid apes—chimpanzees, gibbons, gorillas, and orangutans. Of all animals, man's digestive organs and teeth most closely resemble these apes. In captivity, some of these animals will eat meat if forced to rather than starve to death. But in the wild, all eat a vegetarian diet.

Another strong clue that man is naturally a vegetarian is the fact that vegetarians in general are much healthier than omnivores. The

American Dietetic Association has acknowledged that vegetarians are less at risk for a number of chronic diseases, including heart disease, some types of cancer, obesity, high blood pressure, and adult-onset diabetes.

Eating a healthy diet goes far beyond cutting back a bit on red meat. In a recent study of 6,500 Chinese, Dr. T. Collin Campbell of Cornell found that even though the Chinese overall eat only a fraction of the animal protein Americans do, those who ate the least animal protein nonetheless had lower risk of disease than the average Chinese. Dr. Campbell concludes, "We're basically a vegetarian species and should be eating a wide variety of plant foods and minimizing our intake of animal foods."—Glen Kime, president, Vegetarian Society of Washington, D.C.

I feel like I'm arguing that the pope is Catholic. To clarify a point that eluded many who wrote me about this: the issue is not whether vegetarianism is healthier, better for the planet, etc., than the standard U.S. diet. I don't doubt it is. It's whether humans are *naturally* vegetarians.

Here it seems to me the best evidence is our history as a species. We have been happily eating meat for at least 2 million years, and probably much longer. The common view among anthropologists, in fact, is that increased meat consumption was a key element in the development of human culture, since getting and distributing the stuff requires cooperation.

Contrary to your statement, not all anthropoid apes are exclusively vegetarian. The primatologist Jane Goodall established more than twenty years ago that wild chimpanzees kill other animals once in a while and eat the meat with relish. Other primates (although apparently not gorillas) do so as well. It's true chimps and other apes eat a mostly veggie diet, but for that matter so do most humans. Hunter-gatherers today consume only about 35 percent meat to 65 percent vegetables (Lee and Devore, 1976). Anyway, we and the anthropoid apes diverged 6 to 14 million years ago—who cares what monkeys munch now?

Your argument that meat eaters are more prone to chronic disease is irrelevant. Chronic disease typically strikes the old, not those of prime child-rearing age. Till recently most folks never got chronic disease because they died of the acute kind first. It's had minimal impact on our ability to reproduce ourselves, which of course is the basis of natural selection. In short, as we evolved, chronic disease did not "select out" for vegetarianism.

There is much to be said for vegetarianism. I am at a loss to know why vegetarians cannot be content simply to say it without taking the argument over a cliff.

There's One in Every Crowd

In reading through your column "Vegetarians Go Ape," I noticed an unusual fact that you seemed to expose with great confidence. You stated that "Jane Goodall established more than twenty years ago that wild chimpanzees kill other animals once in a while and eat the meat with relish." I question the accuracy of this. Where would wild chimpanzees obtain relish?—Guru Singh Khalsa, Los Angeles

Make That *Two* in Every Crowd

You obviously know everything. Is it true Stanley and Livingston penetrated darkest Africa wearing pith helmets because they knew they would find no plumbing there?—Eugene B. Vest, Chicago

Oh, pith off.

Consider, if you will, that classic breakfast cereal, Raisin Bran. A Raisin Bran raisin is heavier than a Raisin Bran flake. Logic dictates that heavy things ought to fall to the bottom of the box. However, when we examine a box of Raisin Bran, we find to our surprise (and delight, of course, because we love raisins) that the raisins are evenly distributed throughout! How so? Are the raisins cunningly charged with mutually repellent magnetic forces so they space themselves uni-

formly? Or does Kellogg's just put the raisins in last, counting on the hamhandedness of the shipping clerks to jostle them evenly through the cereal by the time it gets to your breakfast table? —Ed, Los Angeles

An idle mind, Edward, is the devil's workshop. There's no great mystery. Bran flakes are fairly dense and they pack themselves close together in the package, thus preventing the raisins from moving. Kellogg's simply mixes the flakes and raisins together when filling each box and they stay that way during shipping without much internal migration.

A more interesting question along these lines, if you don't mind my saying so, is this: how come, if you've got half a jar of shelled peanuts that's been knocking around the kitchen for a while, the big pieces wind up on top and the little chunks and crumbs wind up on the bottom, contrary to expectation? Aristotle, I think, used to wonder about this. Actually, there are two reasons. First, while a crumb weighs less than a big piece, the crumbs and chunks *in aggregate* weigh more per unit of volume. That's because the big pieces have lots of space between them and the crumbs don't.

Then we have the mechanics of sifting to think about. It's easy for the crumbs to slip down past the big pieces to the bottom of the jar, but the big pieces don't make much headway sinking into the densely packed small stuff. So it's crumbs at the bottom, nuts on top. Maybe now you have some insight into modern corporate life.

I saw a chemist's demonstration where a bowl of Total cereal was soaked in hot water (to dissolve the cereal). Then a white magnet was placed in the solution. Upon removal, the magnet was covered with tiny specks of metal, apparently iron. A white magnet placed into a packet of "iron fortified" instant oatmeal and shaken around will also come out covered with tiny iron filings. Are these filings actually nutritious, or is this some terrible joke so these products can claim to be "iron fortified"?—William B. Stockton, Washington, D.C.

You thought when they said "iron added" they were kidding? Different iron compounds may be used in different products and the particles may be of different sizes, all of which affects how "biologically available" the stuff is. But yes, when a product says "iron fortified," that often means they put iron filings into it—tiny ones, let me hasten to add, on the order of a few dozen microns in diameter. The particles can range from straight powdered iron ("reduced iron") to compounds such as ferrous sulfate and ferric phosphate.

The stuff is "harmless and assimilable," it says here, and your body definitely needs it. Iron deficiency is very common in the United States, and at one time the Food and Drug Administration even considered asking that higher levels of iron be added to more foods. (The plan died because of fears that more iron might trigger certain rare diseases.) Just don't try walking through an airport metal detector after eating your cornflakes. For more information on iron and other food additives, read *The Complete Eater's Digest and Nutrition Scoreboard* by Michael Jacobson (1985).

Every now and then I hear someone complain about being slipped a "Mickey" in a bar. But none of my bartender friends has any idea

what a Mickey is or how to make one. How about some background and a recipe?—R.B., Las Vegas

Bartenders in Las Vegas don't know how to make a Mickey? Next you'll be telling me butchers in Brooklyn don't know how to put their thumbs on scales. Thank God there are still guys like me around to salvage these great national traditions.

That said, I'm obliged to note there's no agreement on what goes in a Mickey (a.k.a. a Mickey Finn or Mickey Flynn), how it got its name, or even what it's supposed to do. Most people think a Mickey is a dose of knockout drops, usually administered to some hapless barfly as a preamble to rolling him. But to some it means a purgative—an agent, as my dictionary drolly puts it, "tending to cause evacuation of the bowels." One source goes so far as to say the original Mickey was a laxative for horses. This kind of Mickey you'd feed to a drunk to get rid of him.

As for what's in it—well, take your pick. A 1931 magazine article says it's croton oil, a purgative, while a slang dictionary says it's chloral hydrate, a sedative/hypnotic. To further confuse things, you sometimes see references to "croton chloral hydrate," which from the sound of it accelerates business at one end of you while slowing it down at the other. Others say a Mickey is cigar ashes in a carbonated beverage, or merely an industrial-strength drink.

Most word books say the origin of "Mickey Finn" is obscure. But Cecil has come across one colorful if not necessarily reliable explanation in *Gem of the Prairie*, a 1940 history of the Chicago underworld by Herbert Asbury. Asbury claims the original Mickey Finn was a notorious Chicago tavern proprietor in the city's South Loop, then as now a nest of hardened desperadoes. In 1896 Finn opened a dive named the Lone Star Saloon and Palm Garden, where he fenced stolen goods, supervised pickpockets and B-girls, and engaged in other sleazy enterprises.

Around 1898 Finn obtained a supply of "white stuff" that may have been chloral hydrate. He made this the basis of two knockout drinks, the "Mickey Finn Special," consisting of raw alcohol, water in which snuff had been soaked, and a dollop of white stuff, and "Number Two," beer mixed with a jolt of white plus the aforementioned snuff water. Lone Star patrons who tried either of these concoctions soon found themselves facedown in the popcorn. At the end of the night they were dragged into a back room, stripped of their valuables and sometimes even their clothes, then dumped in an alley. When the victims awoke they could remember nothing.

Finn evidently paid off the cops but became such a nuisance even by Chicago standards that his joint was ordered shut down in 1903. He was never prosecuted, however, and after a brief hiatus returned to bartending, having sold the MF recipe to other tavern owners. Eventually "Mickey Finn" became the name for any sort of knockout punch. How lucky we are that no one sells things like that today.

I've been trying a high-fiber diet for three weeks and have experienced stomach irritation, cramps, and the sudden need to use the bathroom at inconvenient moments. Can you have too much fiber? Is there proof fiber really prevents cancer? Is long-term consumption of substances the body can't properly digest itself a health hazard?
—*Jennifer Nadell, Madison*

You can have too much of anything, fiber included. Surgeon James McClurken reported a while back on a fifty-year-old man who com-

plained of abdominal pain and constipation. McClurken sliced him open and found "a large amount of branlike material with a dry, thick, toothpaste-like consistency" in the lower small intestine. Seems the guy had eaten two large bowls of bran with minimal milk the day before. His intestines absorbed what liquid there was and his guts basically turned to concrete. After the blockage was removed the patient was put on a liquid diet for a few days and was soon okay.

Intestinal blockage is rare, but too much fiber and not enough liquid can cause abdominal distention, cramps, and flatulence. There was fear at one time that a very high fiber diet (fifty to sixty grams per day, twice what many dieticians recommend and four times what the average American gets) could prevent the body from absorbing certain minerals, but this has since been discounted. On the other hand, the link between *low* fiber and colon cancer is firmly established. Fiber is also thought to be useful in treating and/or preventing heart disease, diabetes, and various gastrointestinal disorders, such as constipation. The lesson? Eat fiber in moderation, wash it down with lots of liquids, and in general don't be an idiot—useful advice in any context.

I was sitting at the Montreal Pool Room eating my all-dressed hot dog and suddenly the question hit me: why is there no ketchup in an all-dressed? Is ketchup not as respectable a condiment as relish or mustard? Is there a conspiracy? Does Dirty Harry's remark about ketchup in a hot dog have anything to do with it? I would be so thankful if you could shine a light on this obscure bit of knowledge for a passionate and perplexed user of ketchup.—Paul Macneil, Dorval, Quebec

Paul, I know you don't *mean* to act like an alfalfa-chewing barbarian, but this is like asking why Leonardo didn't paint the Mona Lisa on black velvet. Ketchup is destructive of all that is right and just about a properly assembled hot dog—and we're talking about a pure beef hot dog, not one of those things you could serve with dressing on Thanksgiving.

Ketchup smothers the flavor of the hot dog because ketchup makers add sugar to their products. That takes the edge off the highly acidic tomatoes, but it takes the edge off everything else, too. Which is exactly why a lot of parents like it, according to Mel Plotsky, sales manager for the David Berg hot dog company in Chicago. (Chicago is one of the hot dog's holy cities.) Put ketchup on it and a kid will swallow anything—and from there it's a straight shot to Velveeta cheese, Franco-American spaghetti, and Deborah Norville.

For that matter, you want to watch the mustard, too. Plotsky says your mainstream brands like French's put in too much turmeric and whatnot. What you want is some unpretentious mustard like Plochman's that enhances, rather than competes with, the flavor of the beef. You should also steam or grill rather than boil your hot dogs—water leaches away the flavor and softens the wiener till it becomes non-tooth-resistant mush.

But—getting back to the original question—you say you like the taste of tomatoes. Fine, then *eat* tomatoes, as God meant them to be eaten: fresh sliced and piled on top of the hot dog. The recommended ingredients of a hot dog with everything, in order of application, are mustard, relish, chopped onion, sliced tomato, kosher pickle spear, optional peppers, and celery salt. (Many think you have to get kraut in there, too, but Cecil wants a hot dog, not Oktoberfest.)

People get pretty emotional over the ketchup question. Mel Plotsky opened our discussion by describing the condiment as a "catchall of garbage." Over at crosstown rival Vienna Sausage, they refer to ketchup as the "K-word." If you go into an authentic hot dog joint and ask for ketchup on your hot dog, the counterman will pause and look you in the eye. He may or may not say, "Ketchup?" with a tone of disbelief. But you may be certain what he's thinking: "Behold this creature that walks like a man. It wants *ketchup* on its *hot dog*."

But hey, if you want ketchup, by all means get it.

The label of almost any food package today will tell you the calorie content. But how are calories determined? Is it very technical?
—*Steven Weinstein, Brooklyn*

Oh, sure, you've got your beakers and test tubes and stuff like that. But when you get right down to it, they measure calories in food the old-fashioned way: they burn it. At least they did years ago, in a wonderful device known as a *bomb calorimeter*, presumably so called because the centerpiece of it was a thick-walled metal can with wires leading out of it that would send everyone running for the exits if it were found in an airport locker. To figure the food's calorie content, you put the food inside, torched it, and then measured the total heat output. You thought maybe "burning off calories" was just a figure of speech? Uh-uh. Your body burns food just as the calorimeter did, admittedly in a less dramatic manner.

Researchers don't use calorimeters much today because years of experiment have reduced calorie calculations to a simple formula: protein and carbohydrate each have four calories per gram and fat has nine, regardless (more or less) of what food it's found in. Aha, you're thinking, I know my times tables, I'm qualified to be a food scientist. Not so fast. The trick is figuring out the amount of protein, fat, and carbohydrate in each food. That's where the beakers and test tubes come in. You want to hear about the oxidation of sugars by an alkaline solution of trivalent bismuth in the presence of potassium-sodium-tartrate? I didn't think so. But the underlying premise of calorie computation is simplicity itself.

I have heard that McDonald's milkshakes contain seaweed. Can this be true?—J.M., Arlington Heights, Illinois

Absolutely. But the real shocker is that every McDonald's hamburger contains chopped-up pieces of—brace yourself—*dead cow.* So let's not get hung up on a little seaweed.

McDonald's milkshakes, along with a great many other products, contain a seaweed extract called carrageenan, which is used as a thickener and emulsifier. (It keeps the butterfat in the shake from separating out.) Carrageenan comes from Irish moss, a red, bushy seaweed that grows on coastal rocks near, among other places, Carragheen, Ireland, whence the name. (You can also find it in Maine, the Canadian Maritimes, and various European localities.)

You either collect the stuff on the beach by hand or use a special long-handled rake. Carrageenan is extracted from the moss with hot water and used in milk-based products, soft drinks (for "body"), gelatin (it's the part that jells), etc. Not all that carcinogenic and, what the hell, centuries ago they used it to treat ulcers. So hold your nose and swig away.

A Clarification

In your column on carrageenan, the thickener used in McDonald's shakes, you reminded the writer that the company's most famous product contains "pieces of . . . dead cow." I am sure you are aware most beef products come from dead steer.—Jonathan Milenko, New York

Jonathan, I have a shameful confession to make. Many years ago, in response to a particularly dimwitted letter, I wrote, "If ignorance were cornflakes, you'd be General Mills." Priceless, eh? Here's the confession: *General Mills doesn't make cornflakes.* However, it was funnier that way. Same deal in the present instance. Cow = funny. Steer = stupid. Just a little insight into the twisted world of the media, where you never want to let the facts get in the way of a good joke.

Hold On There

Regarding the reader who wrote claiming that McDonald's hamburgers are made of "dead steer" and not, as you stated in an earlier column, "dead cow": my source says you're both right, although you, Cecil, are righter, ounce for ounce.

Back in the late seventies my husband put himself through college by working at a factory that produced hamburgers solely for McDonald's. This was done by grinding together bovine flesh from two very

*different sources. The lean meat came from dairy cows who had out-
lived their ability to profitably produce milk.*

*Since dairy cows aren't fed the fattening-up diet beef steers get,
their flesh is exceptionally lean and thus exceptionally flavorless. To
compensate, the workers added fat from beef steers (in chunks that
were referred to around the factory as "plate") during the grinding to
achieve a fattier, tastier final product. Since these burgers contain
more lean meat than fat, they can be said to contain more cow than
steer. (If memory serves, the fat ratio they tried to maintain was 20
percent.)*

*This manufacturing process also sheds a little light on McDonald's
profitability. Since the steer fat is just scrap trimmed away during the
butchering process, and the lean cow meat is essentially a waste
byproduct of the dairy industry, they're getting both components
of their burgers cheaply. Ingenious, no?—Candi Strecker, San Francisco*

See? Even my *jokes* contain deep truths. I queried McDonald's
and got this response from spokesperson Jane Hulbert:

"McDonald's hamburgers are 100 percent pure domestic beef
without fillers or seasonings. To maintain our customers' expectations
and preference for lean, flavorful hamburgers, we carefully select
fine cuts of grain-fed beef and leaner cuts from dairy cattle. This is
a typical combination for quality ground beef. More importantly, we
have found that this combination results in a flavorful hamburger
that also has a significantly lower percentage of fat (20 percent) than
the government limits (30 percent).

"Contrary to your reader's letter, we *never* under any circumstances use waste or scraps. We use only select cuts of grain-fed
beef. Our ground beef suppliers are designated solely to McDonald's, and their facilities are considered the most modern in the industry. In addition to meeting USDA requirements, our suppliers
have worked closely with us to develop very strict, detailed specifi-
cations and requirements that are strictly enforced."

In sum, then: (1) yes, McDonald's does mix meat from dairy cows
and steers—girl cows and boy (okay, ex-boy) cows, if you'll permit
me to murder the terminology, (2) yes, the resultant product does
have about 20 percent fat, (3) yes, the boy cow part does contribute

much of the flavor, but (4) no, they don't use boy cow scraps, just standard cuts of beef.

To clear up the discrepancy in item #4, I spoke to your husband, the guy who worked in the hamburger factory. He said it wasn't really steer scrap they threw into the grinder, rather what he described as "beef bellies"—fatty cuts of meat having the appearance of bacon. Defending the honor of her company, Jane replied that the stuff didn't look like bacon and wasn't beef bellies (a term rarely used in the beef industry) but beef flank, the part below the ribcage—a fine distinction, you may say, but it sounds better. Still, give McDonald's some credit: what you wind up with is a low (well, lower) fat hamburger, no small thing in a fat-conscious age.

One Last Detail

What is the name of the animal that chews its cud and says "Moo"? There's a plural form, "cattle," but if we want to refer to just one, all we can say is which sex it is: "cow" or "bull." We know Jumbo is a bull elephant, but what is Ferdinand—a bull "mooing animal"? Please address this grave injustice.—Sue and Jim, Baltimore

Hmm. Guess "bovine mammal" won't cut it, will it? "Ox" might do, but usually suggests a castrated bull. Looks like we're stuck with "neat" or "beef" (plural beeves). The former is archaic and the latter, in this sense, might as well be. But use it if you want.

A Word from the Women's Mooovement

Admit it for once. In cattle the feminine is the universal term, perhaps due to the ancient association of the cow with milk production compared to the more recent use of the cow for meat. Ferdinand is a bull cow, however oxymoronic that may sound to our he-means-everyone ears. This may be the only remnant in English of the gender parity more common in archaic speech. Cow may be the last word left which means both "female animal" and "generic animal." Get used to it, guys, she's coming back!—Robin NiDana, Oakland, California

Whatever you say, Robin. Incidentally, folks in the far provinces of Canada have apparently come up with a satisfactory (to them) gender-neutral term: "cattlebeast."

As a longtime reader of ingredients labels, I beg you to clarify the ubiquitous phrase "partially hydrogenated." I assume it has something to do with hydrogen, but what does that highly flammable gas have to do with food? And why partially hydrogenated? Why not get down, go crazy, and hydrogenate to the max?—Mr. Sinister, Chicago

Ah, the mad impetuousness of youth. We dasn't totally hydrogenate, you silly thing, or we'd all die of heart failure inside of a year. At least that's the impression I get from the extremists on the subject.

Hydrogenation involves cramming hydrogen gas into vegetable oil under pressure. It's what you do to make the oil semisolid at room temperature rather than liquid, which is obviously useful in the case of products like margarine. Hydrogenation also retards spoilage and prevents baked goods from winding up too greasy. Worthy though these goals may be, they involve converting unsaturated (good) fats into saturated (bad) fats, which have been linked with heart disease.

The solution is partial hydrogenation, in which you create no more saturated fat than necessary to accomplish the task at hand. Done properly, partial hydrogenation results in only a minor increase in saturated fats. Margarine made from soybean oil, for example, starts out around 15 percent saturated and winds up 17 to 20 percent. Soft margarine, the kind that comes in tubs, is less saturated than the stick variety, but both compare quite favorably with butter, which is 66 percent saturated.

Still, there are those who consider margarine to be on a par with drain cleaner, mainly because hydrogenation also produces something known as "trans" fats, trans referring to a certain configuration of hydrogen atoms in the fat molecules. A vocal minority of writers and researchers consider trans fats a major cause of heart disease.

The research supporting this view is dubious, however. Even the Center for Science in the Public Interest, a D.C.-based nutrition advocacy group that usually pounces on stuff like this, says trans fats are nothing to worry about. Of course, that's what they used to say about one-night stands. I'll let you know if anything develops.

How come the bottled red stuff you see in stores is sometimes called ketchup and sometimes catsup? It all looks the same to me.
—George Steinfeld, Dallas

There is an interesting answer for this, George, and then there is the real answer. The interesting answer is that our word ketchup, which originally meant a spicy fish sauce, comes from the Malay *kechap*, which Dutch traders transliterated as *ketjap*. But it turns out the Malays had borrowed the word from the Chinese *ke-tsiap*, which I gather sounds more like catsup. So you could argue that European merchants called their spicy fish sauce ketchup or catsup depending on whether they'd bought it in Malaya or China.

Unfortunately, it appears the Chinese themselves had two versions of the word, *ke-tsiap* and *koe-chiap*. So the real answer, unless some seventeenth-century Chinese shows up to clarify things, is that we just don't know why there are two versions, there just are. As a kid I used to get mad when my father fed me that line, but I'm starting to understand how the old guy felt.

I'm enclosing a bag of salted-in-the-shell peanuts because I think it makes a statement, although I'm not sure by whom or about what. Please note the warning on the back of the bag: CAUTION—REMOVE SHELL BEFORE CONSUMING NUTMEATS.

I'm speechless. Is this some kind of joke? Is this an indication of what peanut distributors think of the mentality of the people who consume their product? Is it a reflection of the paranoia corporate America has been pushed into by the lawsuit-happy American public? Or have we really gotten to the point where it is now necessary to tell the Teeming Millions how to eat peanuts?—Bob Madel, Chicago

All of the above, Jake. I talked to the people responsible for the warning, Ace Pecan Company of suburban Chicago, and while they were guarded on the phone, it's clear they're dealing with some real losers out there.

They tell of one character who ate an entire eight-ounce package of sunflower seeds, shells and all, and suffered an obstructed colon as a result. (An obstructed colon, which can be caused by too much roughage, is basically the world's worst case of constipation. Fecal matter backs up inside of you, developing the consistency of a brick.) The victim, dismissing the possibility that she may have brought this on herself, demanded compensation from Ace, but gave up after the company pointed to the warning that appears on all its products with shells, sunflower seeds and peanuts included. Admittedly the line looks silly, but you can understand the problem.

How is gelatin made? A friend of mine said he visited a "gelatin factory" where he saw cow skins piled to the ceiling. The skins are left to putrefy or "cure" for about a month, during which time they're overrun by rats, mice, and insects. The stench, my friend said, is unforgettable. After the hides are ripe, a tractor pushes them into a vat of acid that disintegrates the cow hairs, skin, cartilage, rat excrement, etc., into a nice, tasty, homogenized gel. Can this be true? I've been fortunate

enough not to have had gelatin since childhood, but there are a lot of people out there trying to strengthen their nails.—Victor D.

Victor, what's the problem here? We're talking about a process that is the epitome of the waste-not-want-not postindustrial ethic, whose only drawback is that it happens to be a little disgusting. Setting aside a few gratuitous details, notably the bit about the rats, mice, and insects, your description of the gelatin-making process is reasonably close to the mark. But instead of being grossed out, you should thank God you live in a country where they've learned to harness even the humblest forms of protein for the good of . . . well, if not all mankind, at least the shareholders of General Foods.

Cowhides are used for gelatin because they contain a seminutritious substance called collagen. They don't molder in the open air, but instead are immersed for a month in vats of lime, then dumped in acid, washed in water, and finally cooked. Pig hides get an expedited version of this process, but the result is the same, namely a uniform proteinaceous goo. The gelatin is then filtered, dried, and shipped off for manufacture into Jell-O, marshmallows, candy, and what have you.

A considerable body of off-the-wall legend surrounds the gelatin biz. For example, I've been told that the factory where they make the gelatin for Jell-O is the only General Foods plant off-limits to the public, owing to the repulsiveness of what goes on inside. As a matter of fact, the plant, which is located just outside Boston, isn't open to the public, but then neither are a number of other General Foods sites. The place is inspected periodically by the feds and is said to be pretty sanitary.

As for the smell . . . well, the place does have a certain fragrance, the company admits. A spokesman loyally describes it as "not bad," which I suppose could mean "not bad compared to a Bolivian skunk ranch," but who knows. You want to make a midnight raid and check for yourself, be my guest.

Here's the story. My wife just got back from Berkeley, where she helped a friend give birth—and of course it all happened at home, in some kind of tub, underwater, with violins playing and midwives hov-

ering about. Here's what she says happened next. Out came the after-birth, which was carefully collected in a pot and put in the fridge to keep cool. Through the day, various vegetarians who dropped by to pay their respects asked about the placenta. My wife inquired, and was told that a certain stripe of high-minded vegetarian eagerly pre-pares and devours placenta stew, the placenta being the only form of meat that does not involve the slaughter of some innocent animal. Can this be true? And if it is, why isn't some shrewd entrepreneur bagging cow and ewe placenta and selling it at the Jewel?

I want to be told this was a tall story.—Rip Sewell, Chicago

Love to accommodate you, Ripster, but once again we find our-selves outgunned by reality. Having investigated the matter with my customary thoroughness, no small achievement under the circum-stances, I can report the following facts: (1) chowing down on pla-centa doesn't happen often, but (2) it happens. May God have mercy on us all.

My principal source on this is a physician who has attended roughly a thousand births in the San Francisco Bay area over the years, more than two thirds of them at home. In all this time he has encountered placenta stew exactly once, in Berkeley in the early 1970s. The father was a professional cook who concocted his own tasty recipe for placenta stew, complete with potatoes and onions, which he served to his hard-core veggie friends.

The doctor, suffering an embarrassing failure of nerve, did not sample the stew himself, but says it smelled something like liver. The veggies munched away gamely but didn't look very happy. One woman, in fact, became nauseated, which the doctor attributes to a lack of exposure to organ meats. Having seen a few miracle-of-childbirth movies in high school, however, I'd say there's a simpler explanation.

There are those who wax eloquent about the joy of placenta cui-sine. In *Hygieia: A Woman's Herbal* (1978), Jeannine Parvati de-scribes her experience: "[It] was after a very powerful birthing. The mother ate some raw first; and then let me take some into the kitchen for fixing. My experience of this slab of meat was amazing. I had never felt such life-force present in meat before. . . . This meat still felt very much alive to me as I began to slice it and sauté it in garlic and oil. . . . By the time the placenta was tender, the birthday party members were very hungry, and exhausted. After the supper, eaten in a glowing silence, everyone was energized, very much revitalized. . . . Notwithstanding, the first time I ate placenta has also been my last time. . . . Guess I just lost [the] taste."

I'll bet. She goes on: "When you first encounter the meat, remember to pause—placenta can be sacred food, if you let the meat tell you how to prepare it for the fire. . . . Chew slowly, till the placenta becomes a liquid, ambrosia. Placenta is a rare privilege for most of us."

The rationale for placenta eating, apart from the fact that it doesn't entail snuffing animals, is that since it nurtures the child during pregnancy it must contain all sorts of valuable nutrients. My medical informant knows of no research supporting this view, but it's not implausible. Mama cats and dogs eat their placentas, and some say that a chemical in the stuff stimulates contractions of the uterus. Luckily for humans, breast-feeding and the drug Pitocin do the same thing. Parvati says some American Indian tribes had placenta rituals, although none of them apparently went so far as to eat the stuff. Leave it to the white man to get ridiculous about it.

The supper table is only one potential destination for the postpartum placenta. Although few new mothers realize it, many hospitals save placentas for eventual pharmaceutical use. A driver for one placenta-collection firm, Bio-Med-Hu of Louisville, Kentucky, told me his firm ships placentas to Europe for use in cosmetics. A spokesman for Bio-Med-Hu denies this, but says he's heard there are companies that do it. Hot on the trail, I called up the makers of Placentique, a skin potion that's been advertised in the newspapers lately. They claimed to use only cow placentas. I am still pursuing the matter, however. We'll get to the bottom of this yet.

Placenta Stew: Another Helping

Sorry, but you've been scooped on the placenta story. The use of placenta in cosmetics was featured in the Chicago Tribune *in a 1980 article entitled "Beauty May Be Only Placenta Deep." The writer interviewed the owner of RITA Organics, a company in Crystal Lake,*

Illinois, that makes freeze-dried extract from human placenta. They get the frozen organs individually wrapped, packed forty to a box. The final product sells for $3,500 to $5,500 per pound.—Tom Lubomski, Chicago

The Straight Dope never gets scooped, Tom. However, we freely concede that the daily newspapers can provide a useful supplement to our work. The *Tribune* reported that RITA once upon a time purchased frozen placentas from hospitals (the going rate was fifty to seventy-five cents each), which it thawed, sliced, and filtered. The end product was a white powder that RITA sold to cosmetics companies. Products containing placenta supposedly accounted for 5 percent of all protein-based beauty aids. I've learned RITA has since gotten out of the business, but the Merieux Institute of Lyons, France, may still be at it.

In other placenta news, I have received a Stern Warning to Youth from Richard Reich, M.D., of Madison, Wisconsin. Reich warns that placentophagia—that's placenta eating for you rustics—can help spread AIDS and hepatitis. Cecil therefore solemnly advises his readers, next time they're invited to a placenta party, to thoroughly inspect mother and child for signs of transmissible disease. As for Dr. Reich: come on, doc, let's chill. The stuff kept *you* alive for nine months, didn't it?

Finally, David English of Somerville, Massachusetts, has thoughtfully sent me a copy of the script for a censored "Saturday Night Live" skit featuring—you'd better sit down for this—Placenta Helper. "Placenta Helper lets you stretch your placenta into a tasty casserole," it sez here. "Like Placenta Romanoff—a zesty blend of cheeses makes for the zingy sauce that Russian czars commanded at palace feasts," etc. The last line was supposed to have been a voice-over from Don Pardo: "Placenta Helper: make a rare occasion, a rare occasion." Very tasteful. Why it got cut we'll never know.

Placenta Recipes!

A friend has sent me recipes from the summer 1983 issue of *Mothering* magazine for the following mouth-watering dishes: Placenta cocktail (¼ raw placenta, 8 ounces of V-8 juice, 2 ice cubes, ½ carrot, blend for 10 seconds at high speed), placenta lasagna, placenta spaghetti sauce, placenta stew, and placenta pizza. The last one will definitely stop conversation at your next Super Bowl party, and since you're not likely to be able to order it from Domino's, here's what you have to do:

"Grind placenta. Saute in 2T olive oil w/4 garlic cloves, then add ¼ tsp. fennel, ¼ tsp. pepper, ¼ tsp. paprika, ¼ tsp. salt, ½ tsp. minced onion, ½ tsp. oregano, ¼ tsp. thyme and ¼ cup wine. Allow to stand 30 min., then use your favorite homemade pizza recipe. It's a fine placenta sausage topping!"

Be sure to let me know how it comes out.

What are sulfites, and why do all American wines seem to have them, and should I let this bother me?—James Ryo Kiyan, Chicago

It's not a question of letting anything bother you, Jim-san. If sulfites want to bother you, they will, possibly by triggering your untimely death. In fact, sulfites are the only additives now in use that are known to kill people. Fortunately, deaths are rare and result from what amounts to an extreme allergic reaction. If you've drunk your share of wine and you're still breathing, you're probably safe.

Sulfiting agents, which are used as preservatives in wine and other products, are mainly a problem for asthmatics, 5 to 10 percent of whom—perhaps 500,000 people in the United States—are sulfite-sensitive. Since 1982 at least six people have died from severe asthma attacks apparently caused by sulfite-treated foods. All six cases occurred in restaurants, where it's impossible to read ingredient labels and where the servers usually have no idea whether the food contains sulfites or not.

Sulfiting agents include sulfur dioxide (commonly used in wine), potassium metabisulfite, sodium sulfite, sodium bisulfite, and sodium metabisulfite. In wine they're used to prevent discoloration, bacterial growth, and fermentation. They're also used to prevent discoloration in shrimp, raisins and other dried fruit, potatoes, lettuce, and other vegetables. Restaurants like sulfites because they can keep an ancient salad looking fresh. Years ago crooked butchers used to use bisulfite, a sulfite derivative, to give spoiled meat a fresh red appearance, a practice that's now illegal.

The World Health Organization recommends a daily limit of forty-two milligrams of sulfites for a 132-pound person. It's estimated that half the U.S. population is over the limit, and it's not hard to see why: a four-ounce glass of wine contains about 40 milligrams of sulfur dioxide, a green salad 160, and three ounces of dried apricots 175. At the urging of consumer groups, the Food and Drug Administration has banned the use of sulfites in most fresh fruits and vegetables and requires labeling for sulfites used in packaged goods.

The feds now require labeling on all alcoholic beverages containing more than ten parts per million of sulfites (wine typically contains 125 to 250 PPM). I'm told it's possible to find sulfite-free wines—try health food stores—but if they're not available, sulfite-sensitive folk should probably stick to lemonade.

This morning when I ordered hot tea from the restaurant next door, I got a Styrofoam cup of steaming hot water and a tea bag. Soaking

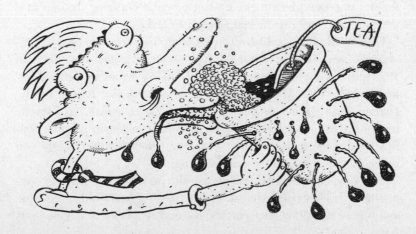

the bag in the water, I noticed the usual brownish-white foam floating up to the top of the cup. What is this foamy stuff—preservative from the bag, or is it just happy to see me? Also, after pouring the foamy stuff out, I noticed the cup had pits and craters in it. What happened? Am I drinking melted Styrofoam?—Steve Holmquist, Chicago

We will deal with this question in a moment, Steve. But first a word about your terminology. Since this column originally appeared in the newspaper I have received a friendly note from the Dow Chemical Company informing me that while you think what you've got there is a Styrofoam cup, it is really a "plastic foam" cup. "Styrofoam" is a brand name applied only to Dow Chemical's plastic foam products, none of which is cups. Clearly Dow wishes to distance itself pending the day when the melted cup scandal breaks.

Now then. Cecil always loves the thought of looming environmental disaster, so he hustled out to study this deadly phenomenon firsthand. First I got a jumbo pack of fifty-one foam cups, so as to do the job with the thoroughness it deserves. I also bought a lemon, a common tea additive, partly to give a splash of color to the lab (we're into nouvelle research), but also to test the corrosive effect of the juice. I know you didn't mention lemon in your letter, but over the years the Teeming Millions have shown a genius for omitting crucial details.

Sure enough, experiments indicated that while tea and hot water alone wouldn't do anything, tea, hot water, and lemon—for that matter, hot water and lemon alone—caused deep cratering. In one case the pits were so deep the cup began to leak.

Convinced of the reality of the foam-cup menace, I made a few inquiries. Turns out you're not the first person to notice the effect. In 1979 a doctor by the name of Michael Phillips wrote an alarmed letter about it to the *New England Journal of Medicine*. It seems polystyrene (plastic foam to you) is softened by limonene, an "acyclic terpene" that forms the principal constituent of lemon oil. Dr. Phillips cited some early research suggesting that polystyrene is—you probably saw this coming—carcinogenic.

The foam-cup industry, fearing that the jig was up, promptly counterattacked. They pointed to studies by the National Cancer Institute and others indicating that polystyrene and its chemical components were harmless, at least from the standpoint of causing tumors. They even dug up some tests showing that lemon tea drinkers really didn't swallow any dissolved foam—supposedly it just stuck to the side of the cup.

Suspiciously, however, nobody said anything about the "brownish-white foam" you mention, leading me to think maybe the researchers weren't patronizing the right restaurants. My advice: chuck the foam cups and stick to Mason jars. They're fun, they're funky, and you'll avoid getting your tonsils lined with plastic.

A while ago I read your column concerning the effects of hot tea on Styrofoam cups. Being an avid tea drinker myself, I was reminded of something. I work at the local public library where, in the staff lounge, there is an automatic dispenser for boiling water. When it broke recently, I had to start microwaving my water instead. But when I empty my packet of Sweet 'n Low into the mug after microwaving the water, it bubbles and fizzes as if some strange chemical reaction were going on. This never occurs when the water comes from the dispenser or is boiled in a kettle on the stove. What are the microwaves doing to my Sweet 'n Low? I'm worried!—Fred K., Evanston, Illinois

I never did trust that Sweet 'n Low stuff. For that matter, anything with " 'n" in the title has got to be on the suspicious list. But there's nothing special about Sweet 'n Low that causes it to effervesce, as we weens like to say. ("Bubble and fizz," indeed. How do you expect to get anywhere in science with a vocabulary like that?) Sugar and salt produce equally vigorous reactions, as will just about any powder except flour, which just sort of lies there.

Here's what happens. When you put a kettle on a conventional stove, some of the water at the bottom turns to steam, making bubbles that float to the surface. But the bubbles don't form just anywhere. At the outset they need to latch onto tiny crevices on the kettle's bottom or sides until they can get big enough to make it on their own. These crevices are called *nucleation sites*. A related phenomenon is the *condensation nuclei*—dust particles, usually—that water vapor needs in order to form raindrops.

In conventionally boiled water, there's a certain amount of internal motion called convection—the hot stuff at the bottom becomes less dense and rises while the cooler stuff sinks. Convection brings more water into contact with the nucleation sites, so the bubbles get bigger faster. Microwaved water, however, heats up uniformly. Since there's no convection, bubble formation is pretty limp. Without bubbles, the water heats as much as 7 or 8 degrees Celsius above boiling point without actually boiling, a process called *superheating*.

So what happens when you dump in the Sweet 'n Low? Instead of bringing water to the nucleation sites, you bring nucleation sites to the water. It's like seeding the clouds. All the superheated water that's been sitting around in frustration, unable to vaporize, suddenly gloms onto the nearest particle, forms bubbles, and rises to the surface. Result: fizz galore. Play your cards right—you want to get the water as superheated as possible without actually boiling—and you can get the water to erupt and scald everybody within a radius of three feet, providing numerous opportunities for lawsuits. (There have already been one or two cases, I'm told.) Another moneymaking opportunity from your friends at the Straight Dope.

Here's a deep one for you. How do they get the Ms on M&M's? My wife says they have a machine that stamps them one at a time, but I say that's too time-consuming. Can you give us the Straight Dope?
—G. Glenn Mahoney, Atlanta

I'm troubled by the expiration date on the enclosed M&M wrapper. As you can see, it says:

19 DEC 88

805 AM

My question is, what happens at 8:06?—Barry M., Chicago

You're on to something here, boys, although with luck and a little baking soda maybe you'll still pass the urine test. M&M's are definitely mysterious. I first tried to find out how they get the Ms on M&M's years ago, but was stymied by the company's total refusal to cooperate.

The culprit was M&M/Mars's parent company, Mars, Inc., whose paranoia is the stuff of legend. Mars's response to the most innocuous inquiry, even from schoolchildren, is that the information is "confidential." The $6 billion firm is privately held, publishes no annual report, and refuses all interview requests from the press. Interestingly, the main office is located in McLean, Virginia, a short distance from the headquarters of the CIA. I'm not saying there's a connection, but you have to wonder.

Now you might interject at this point, Hey, why does Cecil have to ask? Cecil just *knows*. Well, sure. But it's only polite to check. I bided my time. Eventually the spirit of glasnost reached Mars in the person of a guy named Hans, who took over the M&M PR department. A charming fellow with a German accent, Hans saw no reason to hide his company's achievements under a bushel basket. He cheerfully revealed the following facts:

(1) *M*s are applied to M&M's en masse using a process "akin to offset printing." (Actually, I would have guessed it was more like flexography, which involves a flexible printing plate, but Hans says no.) The "ink" is a simple vegetable dye. Blank M&M's are run through the printing press on a special conveyor belt with rows of dimples on it—indentations, actually—to hold the little guys in place. The real trick, Hans says, is calibrating the press so it won't smash those with peanuts. (Peanuts, being a natural product, are given to some variation of dimension.) As is my habit in these matters, I promised I wouldn't reveal the secret to the world, but believe me, you'd be amazed.

(2) "805 AM" doesn't mean what you think, sorry to say. Imagine an M&M route man making a mad lunge at 8:04—*give me that bag, you fool!*—lest a package of (shudder) expired M&M's remain on the shelf. Alas, Hans says, that's not the way it works. "805 AM" is a production code telling which factory, work shift, and wrapping machine filled the bag. The code might as easily have been "731 CP"; it's coincidence that it looks like the time of day. M&M/Mars, by the way, was a pioneer in putting freshness dates on its candy. They may be a little goofy about secrecy, but in their own odd way they're not such bad guys.

The Last Word on M&M's

While addressing a Mensa convention the other day (really), Cecil told the story of the letter about the M&M expiration date, concluding with the plaintive question, "What happens at 8:06?" From the back of the room someone promptly shot back the obvious answer: "They melt in your hand."

I see how they bottle beer, but how do they get beer into cans?
—Peter C., Madison

Peter, you must be the only person in Wisconsin who's never taken a brewery tour. First they put the beer in, then they put the top of the can on.

Reliable sources have informed me of the LSD-like properties of nutmeg. Eat sufficient quantities, they say, and you trip. One dude told me he washed down about fifteen grams with OJ and a Skor bar and when he woke up, he was high. I followed the formula dutifully and nothing happened. What's the dope?—James Como, Bronxville, New York

Elvis, Aerosmith, and now nutmeg. If you post–baby boomers are tired of this ancient history, don't blame me, you're the ones who keep bringing it up. According to Hal Morgan and Kerry Tucker, authors of a book called *Rumor!* (a splendid volume, if not quite as grand in scope as my own collected works), nutmeg *does* have hallucinogenic properties, if you eat enough. The high lasts about twenty-four hours. Unfortunately, the side effects include nausea, dehydration, and generalized body pain. Might as well stick to margaritas.

Why do all cereals have the same number of calories per serving, regardless of what's in them? I have scrutinized countless nutrition labels over the years and have yet to see a cereal that didn't have 110 calories to the ounce.—Listener, Dick Whittington show, KIEV radio, Los Angeles

Hold it right there, buddy. Not all cereals have 110 calories per one-ounce serving, as you'd know if you ever spent any time in a supermarket cereal section. (Believe me, it's a sure cure for writer's block.) Post Grape-Nuts, for one, has 100 calories (excluding milk), while Quaker Crunchy Bran has 90. Still, many cereals do have 110, ranging from Lucky Charms to Spoon Size Shredded Wheat. There are a couple of reasons for this. The simplest is that Food and Drug Administration guidelines for nutrition labeling require that when you have more than 50 calories, you have to round off to the nearest 10 in order to make things easier on the consumer. Cheerios, for instance, really have 106 calories per ounce, but they get rounded to 110.

Even so, it does seem suspicious that most cereals have 106 to 114 calories per serving regardless of what's in them. The explanation is that calorie count is more a function of weight than ingredients, at least when it comes to cereals. Protein and carbohydrates each provide about four calories per gram, regardless of the source, while fat provides nine calories. Fat content for most cereals is low—zero to two grams per ounce. You've got maybe a couple grams of noncaloric moisture and "ash," the food-tech term for minerals and stuff; with 28.35 grams per ounce, that leaves you 25, 26 grams of carbs and protein. Add it all up and round off and you get 110 calories.

Okay, but why is the calorie count for bran cereals typically only 90 per serving? Turns out you don't count fiber, which is abundant in bran. Even though fiber is a carbohydrate, it passes through the body undigested, hence no calories. Post Fruit & Fibre, for example, has 22 grams of carbs, but 5 of those are fiber. Taking the other 17, plus 3 grams of protein and 1 of fat, gives us 89 calories, 90 rounded. I suppose it'd be nice if they explained all this on the side of the cereal box, but considering how hard it is to focus at 7:00 A.M. anyway, we're probably better off leaving well enough alone.

When I read the ingredients of certain foods, I often see something of this sort: ". . . oil (may contain one or more of the following: soy

bean, safflower, palm, and/or lard) ..." Don't the food companies know what they're putting in their own products? Don't they care? I mean, they're either putting lard in the food or they're not.—Ben Schwalb, Laurel, Maryland

Your feelings are understandable. As many consumer advocates have pointed out, knowing exactly what's in a product is no trivial matter. For example, a Muslim or an Orthodox Jew obviously would object to eating lard, which comes from pigs, but wouldn't mind something like safflower oil. Of wider significance is the fact that animal fats and tropical oils like palm and coconut are much higher in saturated fat than ordinary vegetable oils such as soy, safflower, and cottonseed. Saturated fats, of course, have been associated with heart disease.

The reason the labels aren't more specific is that the food companies want to be able to substitute shortenings depending on availability and price without having to change labels at the same time. To date federal regulators haven't made an issue of it, pointing out that present labeling standards are actually stricter than they were in the early seventies, when all you had to say was "shortening."

Ah, but this is America. The free market has come to the rescue. In the last year or two the food companies have finally realized that by refusing to be more specific about their ingredients they were needlessly chasing away potential customers. General Mills is now phasing tropical oils out of all its products, and recently reformulated its Bisquick biscuit mix so it contains only cholesterol-free vegetable oils. The ingredients labels will be rewritten accordingly. To make sure you've got the new version, check the label or look for "No Cholesterol" on the front of the box.

I thought cholesterol came from animal fat. How can palm oil be as bad for us as I keep reading?—Marcia Wichorek, Coral Gables, Florida

Cholesterol as such is found only in animal products. But saturated fats, which (some feel) can produce high blood cholesterol levels in humans, can be found in many things, notably "tropical" oils such as palm and coconut.

Nontropical oils, such as corn, soy, and safflower, are high in poly unsaturated fats, which reduce blood cholesterol. Why are tropical oils different? Because they come from more forgiving climates. Vegetable oils are a major component of plant cell membranes. But they've got to stay liquid to work, and saturated fats congeal when cold. To avoid this, plants in northern climates have to produce unsaturated fats, which don't congeal. That takes extra energy. Tropical plants, though, can get by with the saturated stuff, which is easier to make.

One caution: discouraging the use of tropical oils may be potentially controversial. The following amazing letter to the editor appeared recently in a health journal:

"Have you thought about what happens to the Third World countries who rely heavily on tropical oil exports as a means of livelihood? The Philippines, for example, is beginning to suffer because of the sudden reduction in the U.S. market for their oil products. And where will these tropical oils go now that the United States is not consuming them? To other lesser developed countries, where the life span is actually going down now. Is there a difference in the value of a middle-class American life and the life of a poor Indonesian agricultural worker?"

In other words (as I understand it), Americans have an obligation to eat tropical oils to support third-world economies and keep the stuff out of the hands of poor people. Sort of like throwing ourselves on a slow-motion grenade. I've heard of liberal guilt, but this is absurd.

A friend recently told me that her boss, an Orthodox Jew, could not eat M&M's due to their shells being coated with beetle juice. Restricting bug intake doesn't seem extraordinary considering Talmudic law (which might *be more discerning than federal food regulations but who knows), but what about the accusation that insects are being used to make the candy coating that melts in your mouth, not in your hand?—Michael Chelm, Los Angeles*

You didn't get the whole story. The rumor is that the coating is made from a secretion of the lac beetle, the same insects used to make a well-known floor coating. Aha, you think, M&M's don't melt in your hand because they paint 'em with shellac! Worth a giggle (maybe), but untrue. The folks at M&M/Mars say the coating is actually a mixture of sugar and corn syrup that is buffed to a high sheen by tumbling the M&M's together during manufacture.

The story about the beetles has been circulating quite a while. It turned up in 1991 in a kid's book called *Kids Can Save the Animals*; after a little prodding from M&M/Mars, the publisher admitted hav-

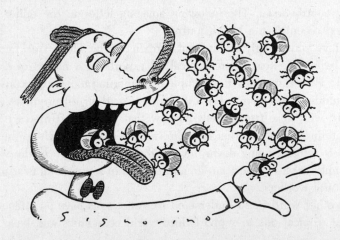

ing goofed. (Apparently some candies similar to M&M's do use a bug-based confectioner's glaze.) Although M&M's aren't certified as kosher, a company spokesman says, "To the best of our knowledge they would be accepted under kosher dietary laws." That probably wouldn't satisfy an Orthodox Jew, but for purposes of this question we can give Mars the benefit of the doubt.

The Truth Comes Out

I am enclosing for your interest a copy of a letter I received in 1984 from Nabisco outlining their use of shellac in Junior Mints. This makes it quite definite, and they weren't shy about saying it!
—*Rosemary Turpin, Montreal, Quebec*

I quote from the letter, which was written by Karen Gajda of Nabisco's consumer services department:

> The "shellac" listed as an ingredient on our Junior Mints box is more commonly recognized as confectioners' glaze. It is refined from the secretion of the lac insect and is free from all metallic and foreign matter contamination. This shellac glaze is guaranteed of food grade quality and is ... recognized as a safe edible ingredient. ... The reason that it is used in the manufacture of Junior Mints is that it provides excellent protection against dampness and ensures that the product you buy is of the highest freshness and quality possible.

One More for the Ick List

Pursuant to our recent disquisition on insect extracts in candy, a reader has sent us a newsletter from the Chicago Rabbinical Council, a kosher certifying agency. I quote: "Due to changes in government regulations, virtually every processor of fruit cocktail is using a non-kosher artificial coloring in the cherries. This coloring is called carmine and is derived from the dried bodies of the cochineal insect." (Actually cochineal is a red dye made from the bug *Dacty-lopius coccus*.)

Ooh, gross, some will say. But my attitude is, I'll swallow anything, as long as they don't make me eat it till it's dead.

Was spinach once considered the ultimate vegetable? Lately I've been spending a lot of time reading my daughter the classic children's story "The Little Engine That Could," which lists all the good things the circus train is carrying for the girls and boys on the other side of the mountain. In the food category, in addition to big golden oranges, red-cheeked apples, etc., we find "fresh spinach for their dinners." When called upon to read this line, needless to say, I gag and substitute something more palatable and nutritious, such as Fritos. But the mention of spinach has gotten me to thinking about the old Popeye the Sailor comic, where a timely can of spinach unfailingly endows Popeye with super strength. What magical qualities did people think spinach had that warranted such a shameless campaign of propaganda to get kids to eat it? As a child I regarded spinach as inedible mush and nothing I have learned about it since has made me change my mind.—Frank C., Chicago

Come on, spinach isn't so bad. If it were a choice between spinach and, say, radioactive pond slime, I'd definitely take spinach. But among things you're likely actually to be made to eat, I agree spinach rates pretty high on the yucky scale. Along with castor oil and mustard plasters, the stuff exemplifies the in-suffering-lieth-virtue school of child-rearing: if it's bad, it must be good for you.

In the early part of the century, when the study of micronutrients was in its infancy, spinach was regarded with something approaching awe. "When well cooked, it is about as health-giving an article as can be imagined," said Artemas Ward in the 1923 *Encyclopedia of Food*. Spinach was prized, at least by nutritionists, for its high concentration of iron and vitamins A and C. (Actually it contains a vitamin A precursor called carotene.) It was also considered a good source of roughage.

But its fans recognized that spinach was a tough sell and did what they could to hype it. "It is rendered sweeter and more delicate (and thus almost universally liked) by cooking with a fair proportion of lettuce," wrote Ward—but one suspects he had his fingers crossed when he did.

Writers aiming at the younger crowd felt compelled to do their bit, too. By far the champ in this line was Elzie Segar, the creator of Popeye, who first appeared in Segar's comic strip "Thimble Theater" in January 1929. (The main attraction previously, believe it or not, had been Olive Oyl.) The oddly built sailor was an immediate hit, and apparently so was his favorite vegetable. Whether Segar was in the pay of the spinach interests we do not know, but it seems significant that six years later a statue of Popeye was erected in the town square of Crystal City, Texas, the center of a major spinach-growing region.

Spinach's star dimmed once more research was done. It turned out the iron in it couldn't be readily absorbed by the body. Spinach also contained a substantial amount of oxalic acid, which inhibited the uptake of calcium from foods taken at the same meal. It wasn't an especially good source of fiber, and if you boiled the daylights out of the stuff, as was common for many years, most of the vitamin C leached away.

Spinach's reputation has recovered somewhat in recent years because some researchers think carotene will prevent cancer. Carotene can also be found in dark green, yellow, and orange foods such as broccoli, turnip greens, and kale. Like spinach, none of these is a vegetable to stir your columnist's soul. Still, you cross the carotene crowd at your peril. George Bush wouldn't eat broccoli, and you see what happened to him.

I have been told by someone who claims to know that you can preserve the carbonation in a half-consumed bottle of champagne by hanging a silver spoon upside down in the neck, with the handle suspended in the contents. As a none-too-convincing explanation for this miracle my source mumbled something about electrolysis. Any truth to this?—Joe Ryan, Chicago

Cecil hears a lot of weird theories like this. Sample: you can tell if someone has used LSD because an X ray of his jaw will show a glowing line. We decide what to check out on the basis of what sounds like the most laughs. Not having any great desire to have our jaw X-rayed (strictly as an experimental control, of course), we opted for champagne.

I asked the Champagne News and Information Bureau in New York and Paterno Imports, a champagne importer in Chicago, about the silver-spoon gambit. The responses from various parties: (1) never heard of this, (2) heard of it but think it's a crock, and (3) whatsamatter, these people never heard of stoppers? The folks at the CN&IB, in fact, were kind enough to send me a reusable stopper made of stainless steel.

We then moved to the experimental stage. Cecil obtained three standard (750 ml) bottles of champagne at the bargain price of two for $5—not stuff he would care to drink, frankly, but adequate for the purpose at hand.

We uncorked all three bottles and attempted to insert a silver spoon into one. Here we ran into our first complication: none of our silver spoons had a handle skinny enough to fit. In fact, the only spoon of any description that would fit into a bottle was a long-handled stainless steel baby-feeding spoon. Mighty suspicious and definitely inclining us to think that nobody promoting this theory had ever actually tried it.

Spurning the baby spoon on the ground that stainless steel was not sufficiently reactive, we accepted Mrs. Adams's offer of a silver chain. We noted that when we placed the chain in the bottle, suspending it from the neck with a paper clip, bubble production in the champagne greatly increased—mainly, we guessed, because the chain provided an abundance of nucleation sites where bubbles could form. We put the bottle with the chain in the fridge, along with a second opened but chainless bottle plus a third that had been opened and immediately capped with the CN&IB stopper.

Next morning we tested for carbonation. We did this by covering the mouth of each bottle with a, uh, condom. Okay, maybe they don't do it that way at the National Science Foundation, but when you're on a budget you take certain shortcuts. Condom in place, we gave the open-but-chainless bottle a couple of vigorous shakings. The condom inflated fully. After only a single shaking, the condom of the previously stoppered bottle not only inflated but champagne bubbled up into it and began leaking out the bottom. No amount of shaking, however, would cause the condom on the bottle with the chain to inflate more than partway.

Conclusion #1: not only does silver not preserve carbonation, if anything it will make the champagne go flatter faster. Conclusion #2: if you want *your* condom to inflate when things get shaking, keep the stopper on the alcoholic beverages.

Chapter 5

Getting Around

What does JCT stand for, as in "I-45—JCT 2 miles"? I almost had a wreck yesterday trying to figure it out, and I have yet to receive a satisfactory answer. Help please soon.—Dangerously Distracted Dallas Driver

That does it. Next time I wash the screwdriver *before* the lobotomy. JCT stands for "junction."

Can you solve a mystery for us? Why is it that every so often as you're driving along there's just one shoe lying there on the road? There's never the other shoe in the pair, just that one shoe. Does someone throw their shoe out the window in disgust? Do kids throw their parents' shoes out the back of the station wagon? Do they sprout from seeds sown by bird droppings in the pavement? This is a worldwide phenomenon: I've seen road shoes sit there, dusty and flattened, in India, Europe, and Mexico and on many highways and byways of North America. Any advice will be appreciated.—Emily Baumbach, San Rafael, California

Well, we can nix the sprout-from-seeds hypothesis right off the bat. You're undoubtedly thinking of shoe *trees*. (Haw!) Many great and not-so-great minds have wrestled with this phenomenon without arriving at any firm conclusions. I note, for instance, that fellow investigator David Feldman devotes *seven pages* to the topic in his

book *When Do Fish Sleep*, in the course of which he elucidates thirteen theories on lone-shoe origin. Clearly, what Dave needs is to meet a nice girl. It is high time I settled matters once and for all.

First a few observations from the field. As usual in the case of your more inscrutable questions, Cecil and his minions have been prospecting for tips on the radio. So far we have come up with the following:

- Peak shoe-spotting season is summer through fall.
- There is disagreement on how widespread the phenomenon is. Contrary to your report, some say it's confined to North America and that you never see shoes on, say, the German autobahn.
- There is no single explanation for the lone shoes. One woman said she placed an extra pair of shoes on the roof of the car while she loaded some stuff, then forgot about them and pulled off. When she checked a while later they were gone. Another said a passenger had his feet up on the dash when the car hit a pothole, whereupon he became unshoed. Unshod. You know what I mean. Yet another claimed he personally had gone around the country strategically depositing shoes in order to sow panic amongst the populace. There's one in every crowd.

None of this really gets at the heart of the matter, however. Cecil and his dedicated research team, including two short and irrepressible members who several times came perilously close to contributing personally to the lost-shoe population, recently conducted a 1,500-mile cross-country car trip, traveling on everything from interstates to gravel roads. En route we passed thousands of identifiable items of roadside debris, chiefly pieces of retread tire on the interstates (how anybody can stand to drive on those things I will never know) and food packaging (mostly cans and bottles) everywhere else. Total shoe count: four, including one each in Knoxville, Tennessee, and Louisville, Kentucky, and two on the road into Chicago.

Granted this was in May, not (to hear some tell it) the height of shoe season. And I probably missed a few, such as when one of the little researchers was screaming at the top of her lungs. Still, considering the vast quantity of roadside junk, we are talking about a tiny number of shoes.

I would venture to say people have the idea that the highways are littered with shoes simply because (1) a roadside shoe is an ineffably memorable sight, lending itself to many rude jokes about what the owner was doing or having done to him/her at the point of loss, and (2) virtually all other trash on the road is either anonymous or numbingly commonplace. As to why you always see one shoe, never a pair, what do you expect? Assuming most of the shoes are lost by accident, the chances of two randomly ejected shoes landing together is vanishingly small.

That's the way I see it, anyway. But I'll concede the topic has unplumbed depths. Further insight from the Teeming Millions is cordially solicited.

Testimony

At last you took on that great mystery of the universe, the single-shoe phenomenon, about which the scientific community has been suspiciously silent. As a lifelong observer of the one-shoe enigma, I can offer several observations:

(1) A few weeks ago while driving on the main Seattle freeway I

noticed that the passenger of the car in front of me was holding a shoe out the window. Accelerating to investigate, I saw that the shoe in question appeared to be covered with some foul substance (canine in origin, I suspect). As I continued to follow this car, the passenger lost his hold on the ill-fated Nike. They slowed down, but then appeared to give up and drove on, leaving the shoe to help carry on the legend.

(2) A neighbor of mine arrived home disgruntled. She had taken her children to the beach and had inadvertently left a pair of the kids' sandals on top of her car. Unlike the aforementioned owner of the befouled shoe, she tried to rescue them upon hearing them clump down the back of the Volvo, but the highway was too busy and the sandals had already been run over multiple times. During the next few days I traversed that stretch of road and saw Noel's sandals (in flattened state). Now the clincher: a week later I drove down that road once again, and ONLY ONE SHOE WAS LEFT.—Your faithful correspondent, Joyce Kehoe, Seattle

Regarding your recent column about the "one shoe in the road" mystery: I used to wonder about that, too, but now I know. It is a steamy night in August; you are wearing flip-flops; you are so drunk that you are crawling down Clark Street; you pass out, are picked up by an ambulance and taken to an emergency rehab facility; when you are released in the A.M., you have only one flip-flop, the other being somewhere on Clark Street.—Most sincerely and grateful to be alive, Jean, Evanston, Illinois

"Emergency rehab facility"? Man, I'm going to have to remember that one next time they toss me in the drunk tank. While we now have an explanation for the disgraceful situation on Clark Street, I stand by my view that the dimensions of the lone-shoe phenomenon have been greatly exaggerated.

More Testimony

Upon locating a parking place in the city this summer, I maneuvered into curbside position next to a bank of ice plant. Exiting the car, I could not help noticing what seemed to be a pair of shoes a couple feet up the bank. Imagine my bewilderment when on closer inspection these turned out to be almost identical, quite well-used, phosphorescent pink pumps—both left foot.—Jeste Trantwine, San Francisco

When I lived in Houston, I noticed a large number of (single) shoes on the highway, on gravel back roads, etc., and was driven to start a Roadside Shoe Collection. Often it was quite a feat, retrieving those worn-down items in traffic every day, but I did it—I was obsessed, I guess. I started taking Polaroids of the shoes, titling them and noting exactly where they were found. This went on for the better part of a year. I found that late summer through winter was the best time for adding to the collection. Eventually I accumulated nearly ten single shoes.

People thought I was weird, yes, but none thought so enough to make me abandon the hobby until a young lady came along, the friend of a friend—two friends removed—who discovered among my collection the missing mate to her favorite pair. She was really wasted when she lost the one I now had and couldn't identify from the photograph anytime she had been in the location noted. Reluctantly, I returned her shoe (she had kept the other one) and, either because of that turn of events or because a current love interest couldn't deal with such utter strangeness existing in the garage, I ceased my fetish. For the time being. Years later I moved to New York and for a short time collected single gloves. Should I seek help?—James Dean Jay Byrd, New York

Nah. Collecting gloves isn't that hard. In the interest of thoroughly beating the subject into the ground, I should mention that another reader has sent a column from *Denver Post* reporter Renate Robey, which reads in part:

"Denver street sweeping crews report that they find more single shoes in areas where there are more homeless people. In some neighborhoods, people leave boxes of clothes and shoes in the alley for homeless people who rummage through the alleys. They say a homeless person might be more likely to toss out one worn shoe, but keep the other half of the pair if the shoe is not worn out."

Breakthrough!

Noted friend of science Ken Grabowski of Chicago's Field Museum has sent me a clipping from the American Geophysical Union journal that may help unravel the why-you-always-see-one-shoe-by-the-side-of-the-road conundrum once and for all. It seems that on May 27, 1990, a storm struck the container ship *Hansa Carrier* in the North Pacific (48 degrees N, 161 W), resulting in—get ready for this—eighty thousand Nike-brand shoes being lost overboard. "Six months to a year later," the journal reports, "thousands of shoes washed ashore in North America from southern Oregon to the Queen Charlotte Islands."

Hmm, you're thinking, and you're not the only one. Ocean scientists immediately began investigating. So far, the report states, they have "gathered beachcomber reports and compared the inferred shoe drift with an oceanographic hindcast model and historical drift bottle returns." Such a joy to see professionals at work.

Yet to be explained is how one of the shoes got from the Pacific coast to Louisville, Kentucky, where it was transformed into the orange work boot spotted by the Straight Dope Field Survey Team last May. As Cecil's editor observed: "But Kentucky is landlocked!" You've put your finger on it, kid. Much obviously remains to be learned about ocean drift patterns. Maybe it was the seagulls. We'll keep you posted on further news.

How can there be interstate highways . . . in Hawaii? And why isn't a family-size pizza the size of a family?—Greg R., Incurable Smartypants, Greenbelt, Maryland

You're so immature, Greg. Back in the late 1950s Hawaiian officials had the same thought you did (about the interstates, I mean;

we'll ignore your divagation about pizzas), but they didn't think it was so funny. In fact, they were quite concerned that some literal-minded bureaucrat was going to say they weren't eligible for federal interstate highway money merely because there was this thing called an ocean separating them from the rest of the country.

They were probably right to worry. Early federal highway legislation said the interstate system "shall be designated within the continental United States," thereby excluding islands. But Hawaiians pointed out that one of the purposes of the interstate system was to strengthen national defense and that Hawaii (specifically, the island of Oahu) was crammed with military installations that needed to be connected by good roads.

Congress evidently saw the wisdom of this and dealt with the matter in the Hawaii Omnibus Act of 1960, which took care of various postadmission loose ends. Right after a section dealing with the Opium Poppy Control Act and shortly before a passage headed Purchases of Typewriters, they stuck in some language deleting the continental U.S. requirement and authorizing $12 million for Hawaiian roads.

Three routes were subsequently approved and built, with the result that Hawaii now has more miles of interstate than Delaware (48 versus 40.6). Meanwhile, Alaska, despite its unquestionable location on the mainland, has no miles of interstate at all and has to struggle along with dogsleds and snowshoes. One more illustration of Jimmy Carter's dictum that life ain't fair.

I'm looking at the road map. The main interstate route down the Atlantic coast is 95. In the New York City area there are spurs off it numbered 495, 295, and 895. Near Washington, D.C., it intersects with the beltway, Route 495. The bypass around Philadelphia is 295. This has got to be a pattern, right?—Eddie, Hoboken, New Jersey

You got it, Sherlock. Let me run through the whole numbering system, which was devised by the American Association of State Highway Officials (and I'll bet that's an acronym you don't hear pronounced too often). Even-numbered routes run mostly east-west, odd ones mostly north-south. Major routes have one- or two-digit numbers, and the really important routes, which form a more or less evenly spaced grid across the country, end in 5 or 0. The lowest route numbers are in the west and south, to avoid local duplication of the older U.S. route numbers, which are lowest in the northeast and Midwest.

Now, getting down to your question: three-digit numbers are reserved for adjuncts to the major routes. Circumferential roads and beltways have the main route number with an even-numbered prefix; radial and spur routes have an odd-numbered prefix (usually). It's simple. Just don't ever ask me to explain zip codes.

For a long time I've heard stories about a man who tied a bunch of balloons to a lawn chair and went soaring into the heavens. I even spent an afternoon searching at the library to see if it was true, but no luck. I gave up, thinking it must be someone's wild imagination. Then the other day a story in the paper made mention of a mad balloonist named Larry Walters. Can you tell me more?—Roger K., Dallas

How fleeting is fame. It's been a mere six years since Larry Walters made his legendary flight, and already people are starting to think he's a mythical being. Au contraire. Larry, an authentic working-class hero (at the time he was driving a truck), went aloft July 2, 1982, from his girlfriend's backyard in suburban Los Angeles. His craft: an aluminum lawn chair borne by forty-two helium-filled weather balloons.

Larry's original idea was that he would fly east to the Mojave Desert, but it didn't quite work out that way. As his girlfriend and his buddy were feeding out the tether, the line broke and he shot skyward. Eventually he reached sixteen thousand feet, where the pilots of at least two airliners saw him. Not wanting to cause a fuss, he began putting out calls on his portable CB radio. After a while his feet got cold, so he pulled out a pellet pistol and began shooting out balloons.

The descent was uneventful except for the fact that the balloons wrapped around some power lines at the end, knocking out the electricity in a Long Beach residential neighborhood for about twenty minutes. But Larry and his chair—stayed clear: he simply dropped a few feet to the ground, having spent about ninety minutes in the air.

Most people thought the whole thing was pretty funny, and Larry got to appear on Letterman and the *Today* show. But the FAA was not amused. "We know he broke some part of the Federal Aviation Act, and as soon as we decide which part it is, some type of charge will be filed," a spokesman said.

Sure enough, Walters was charged with reckless operation of an aircraft, failure to stay in communication with the tower, and flying a "civil aircraft for which there is not currently in effect an airworthiness certificate." He wound up paying a $1,500 fine. If you ask me, it was worth every penny.

Where is *Podunk?*—*Thomas G., Dallas*

You're not the first guy to wonder about this, Tomaso. As a matter of fact, the search for Podunk, the archetypal jerkwater town, is one of the great adventures of philology, which, as you can probably appreciate, is not a field that has great adventures in abundance.

Allow me to quote from a letter to the editors of the *Daily National Pilot*, Buffalo, New York, 1846: "I hear you ask, 'Where in the

world is Podunk?' It is in the world, sir; and more than that, is a little world of itself. It stands 'high up the big Pigeon [river],' a bright and shining light amid the surrounding darkness." There is a great deal more, all in a satirical vein, indicating that even then Podunk was thought to be a locality which, being imaginary, one might safely have a little fun with.

The idea that Podunk was purely mythical survived a long time. In 1925 philologist G. P. Krapp noted that no Podunk was to be found in the list of American post offices, which he took to be proof of the town's nonexistence—an alarming conclusion, given current opinions of the post office, but Krapp's was an innocent age. His one concession to the reality of Podunk was that it was an Indian word that had been applied to a few minor geographic features in New England.

In 1933 a *Boston Herald* columnist was simply restating the common wisdom when he observed that "Podunk, like Atlantis, has no locus." But even as Troy had its Schliemann, so did Podunk have its believers. One E. A. Plimpton promptly wrote to the *Herald* that there *was* a settlement called Podunk, that it might be found near Worcester, Massachusetts, and that he himself had a summer home there.

This was unsettling news, and as often happens with unsettling news, people chose to ignore it. But the truth could not be suppressed forever. A few years later the etymologist Allen Walker Read, who was later to earn everlasting glory for his explication of "OK" (see *More of the Straight Dope*) reported that the name Podunk had been applied to veritable heaps of places and persons throughout the northeast: to a brook flowing into the Connecticut River near Hartford, to a meadow near said brook, to a band of Indians living near the meadow, to a different meadow fifteen miles southwest of Worcester, to a pond near this latter meadow, and, under various spellings, to ponds, creeks, and meadows throughout New York State. Professor Read opined that Podunk derived from an Algonquin Indian word meaning "a boggy place."

In 1941 word of Read's work apparently found its way to the editors of the *Boston Herald*. They recalled that they had failed to follow up on a clue regarding Podunk that had appeared in their own pages years earlier. Filled with shame, they decided something needed to be done. Characteristically, however, they decided someone else should do it. They nominated the *Worcester Telegraph* to mount an expedition to establish once and for all whether a town called Podunk existed. The *Telegraph* accepted the challenge and assigned one William H. Moiles to the job.

"Early on a bright November morning," a later account of the expedition noted, "his safari shoved off from the *Telegraph* office, and by noon it had forded Seven-Mile River and was headed south into the rain forest along the East Brookfield River." Arriving in East Brookfield without further clues to Podunk's whereabouts, Moiles demonstrated the resourcefulness of a true journalist: he went into a tavern and asked the bartender. Driving in the indicated direction, he encountered a small boy with his thumb out.

" 'Where're you going?' we asked.

" 'Up by the old Podunk school,' he said.

" 'Where is Podunk?' we asked, failing entirely to suppress a quiver of anticipation.

" 'This is Podunk now,' said the small boy.

"He said it calmly, quietly, almost wearily. But we felt like Balboa."

It was later established that Podunk was an unincorporated area about six square miles in extent containing about one hundred families. It is located mostly within East Brookfield, a town about fifteen miles west of Worcester. Whether there is now a historical marker on the site I do not know, but if not, and the citizens of Massachusetts have any salt in them, they will see to it forthwith.

I've discovered that the world isn't what it appears to be. When National Geographic, for instance, publishes a map, they use Mercator projection, which distorts the physical size of many countries. Although it looks like Greenland and Africa are the same size on a Mercator map, Africa is actually nine times as large! This is due to the fact that they have placed the equator two thirds of the way down the page, elongating the Northern Hemisphere and shrinking the Southern. Is this a snide Western plot to diminish the physical impact

of continents like Africa and South
Quebec

Don't organize a hunger strike j
Geographic hasn't used Mercator
used mostly Van der Grinten projec.
projection, both of which are substantial,
Second, distortion in these maps isn't caused .
two thirds of the way down the page; on the co.
projections, the equator is a straight line in the exact
tion arises from the way all maps deal with the essential ..
problem, namely, trying to make a flat representation of a sp..
surface.

On a globe, the lines of longitude converge as they approach the
poles; on a Mercator map, to use the extreme example, the lines of
longitude are parallel. Making such a map means taking each
equator-to-pole globe segment, which is roughly triangular, and
stretching it into a rectangle. Obviously the stuff near the poles gets
stretched the most, greatly exaggerating its size. For that reason
Mercator projection isn't seen much anymore in general-purpose
maps of the world.

Still, Mercator maps are useful in navigation. If you draw a line
between you and your destination on a Mercator map and then calculate the angle relative to north, you'll get the compass bearing
needed to get you where you're going (though it won't necessarily be
the shortest route). Other methods of map projection such as the Van
der Grinten and Robinson reduce the distortion of land area but
aren't anywhere near as handy for charting a course.

A Word from the Bureau of Map Deviance

You recently discussed navigation with compass and Mercator map.
With this information in hand I plan my pilgrimage to the land of
Cecil. Since I live in Washington, D.C., I figure Chicago is approxi-
mately 292° off north on my map and about 695 miles away. I follow
my compass heading for that distance (ignoring the fact that roads

ght lines) and find myself near Normal, Illinois. As you
b hearing, this is one Teeming Millionth that doesn't want
where near Normal. (You take the jokes from there.) Why?
on a Mercator map north is true north. My compass shows
tic north. From my starting point there is a variance of about
ou must differentiate between true and magnetic bearings and
npensate, oh formerly perfect one, or you will be one lost bastion
wisdom. Having thus nailed you to the wall, I await your verbal
assault.—David Alexander, Washington, D.C.

If you don't mind, David, I'll save my ammo for a more worth-
while target. The difference between true north and magnetic north
is called declination. It varies from place to place and is routinely
corrected for in navigation.

*I've been hearing commercials for discount round-trip airfares that
have a peculiar requirement: you have to spend a Saturday night at
your destination before returning home. In other words, if you leave
Tuesday and come back the next day, you pay full fare, but if you
leave Tuesday and come back eight days later, you save big dough.
This makes no sense. Why do the airlines care where you spend your
Saturday nights? Do they get kickbacks from the owners of foreign
fleshpots? Rip the lid off this one, Cecil, I smell a rat.—Listener, Mike
McConnell show, WLW radio, Cincinnati*

Airline moguls are devious, tovarich, but not *that* devious. Deep-
discount airfares, the ones that usually involve a Saturday requirement, are aimed at pleasure travelers who otherwise couldn't afford
to fly. They're explicitly *not* aimed at business travelers, who constitute about half of all passenger traffic. Business travelers pay full fare
now without complaint; they're not going to fly appreciably more if
the fares are lower, and the airlines figure there's no sense sabotag-
ing the profit margin.

The problem, of course, is separating the business folk from the
tourists. Obviously it would be uncool to inquire into the motives of
prospective passengers when they bought tickets. ("Do you *always*
wear wingtips on vacation, Mr. Smith?") So the airlines came up

with what's called the "first Sunday return" requirement, meaning
you have to stay over Saturday night. The idea is that business travelers seldom stay at their destination over the weekend, but pleasure
travelers often do.

Sound like the poor business traveler is getting ripped off? Don't
lose any sleep over it. Business people can take advantage of
frequent-flier programs. These have been scaled back now, but at
one time they were the most incredible giveaway since triple Green
Stamps.

Cecil, whose wife often flies on business (she's in charge of
Straight Dope Inc.'s vast world holdings), was pleased some years
ago to participate in an unbelievably luxe junket to the Virgin Islands, courtesy of an up-and-coming carrier with plenty of ambition
and zero common sense. We got free air travel, a week's free resort
accommodations, and a free rental car. (Okay, it was a Suzuki Samurai, noted for its penchant for flipping over at untoward moments,
but we like living close to the edge.) Retail value: $2,500. Cost of the
previous two years' worth of air travel needed to qualify for the
freebies: $2,400. (Honest: there was a fare war on flights to Detroit.)

The airline that offered this deal has since gone bankrupt. When
Marx talked about capitalism collapsing of its own contradictions,
maybe this is what he had in mind.

*Why don't auto headlights go off when you turn off the ignition? Is
it a conspiracy to sell more car batteries? I can't think of a reason the
headlights need to be switched independently of the ignition except
possibly when you lose your keys at night in front of your car.*
—Curious in Marin County, California

Time for another adventure in industrial anthropology, which consists of getting the natives to ask themselves, Why do we do this,
anyway? Being a little vague on headlight theory (I was asleep when
they covered this in know-it-all school), I called up the car companies. Results: total double-talk.

The Ford guy pinned it on "cost and complexity"—as though making the headlights go off the same way the windshield wipers do
would be a spectacular feat of technology. The GM lady helpfully

noted that on pricey models you can get a high-tech option called a "twilight sentinel," which turns the headlights on and off automatically with the engine, depending on how dark it is out. A typically American example of a pile-driver solution for a thumbtack problem and certainly not an answer to the question.

The GM lady then threw up a smoke screen: it's because you want your emergency blinkers to operate independently of the ignition so you won't have to leave the key in the car when you go for help. No doubt, ma'am, but I wasn't asking about the emergency blinkers. Well, she said, sometimes you want the dome light on without having the key in, don't you? Uh-huh. Obviously we were getting nowhere.

The Ford guy, meanwhile, had come up with what I suspected was the real answer: we've always done it that way, and nobody ever complains. Jeez, I thought to myself, don't you guys ever respond to the inner muse? Where is our pride in getting the job done right, regardless of the madding crowd? But you can't expect these guys to understand poetry.

I called up Consumers Union. Surely, I said to myself, these flinty-eyed watchdogs will cut through the B.S. I learned the following: in some foreign makes, the ignition does shut off the lights, and anyway there are times when you want to be able to operate the radio or beep the horn with the ignition off. Cecil, of course, had not asked about the radio or the horn and did not care what foreign manufacturers did.

Finally the GM lady called back. She had been asking around, and the consensus was as follows: (1) it's a security measure—come on, we can all dream up some off-the-wall scenario in which you'd want to be able to turn the lights on with the ignition off; and (2) customers expect it to be that way, they're not complaining, so why rock the boat? Seems pretty silly, but if so, the fault, dear Curious, is in ourselves, that we sit still for it.

Why the Lights Don't Go Out: A Colloquium

By now millions of true geniuses must have let Cecil Adams know the real reason the ignition doesn't turn off the car lights. Because if *they turned off automatically they would turn on automatically. Everyone would drive all day with their lights on. Or there would be a turn-off switch for days and we would be back to square one. Or we would pay $50 or $100 for a sensor that would turn them off in daylight. Too simple for you?—Perry Lessin, Los Angeles*

Perry, my friend, you and Detroit were meant for each other.

I think it's great you can turn the headlights on when the ignition is off. I can think of countless times I used the headlights and wanted the ignition off. As a matter of fact, I had a VW Bug that automatically shut off the lights when you turned off the ignition and it drove me crazy!

It's obvious you are used to living in an area where there are lights on every corner. Didn't you ever have to work at night where there were no outside lights? How about trying to fix a car at night when nobody has a flashlight? It's usually more than a five-minute job, and you wouldn't want your car running the whole time.

Didn't you have any fun growing up? We used to park our cars in a field and dance in front of the headlights. On foggy nights we would plan to meet friends at an old graveyard, get there early, TURN OFF THE IGNITION, and wait. When our unsuspecting friends would arrive, WHAM, on went the headlights! It scared them to death! (Sixteen-year-olds in small towns have to find something to do!)

What about arriving at a campsite after dark and trying to set up camp? How much gas would you waste if you kept your car running while you were trying to figure out that "easy three-step tent"? You couldn't leave the campsite because you'd be out of gas!

I used to ride my horse at night and car headlights were perfect for lighting up my riding arena. My horse would not have put up with a running car.

There are lots of reasons to have your headlights on when the car is off. You just have to think about it.—One who grew up where there were few streetlights, Los Angeles

Keep reading, Einstein.

As a longtime fan I feel I must comment on your recent column about headlights. A couple years back we rented a GM car. When we started to get out with the headlights on, a sensor of some sort activated a buzzer. By contrast, on our Toyota, when I open the door with the headlights on, a sensor activates a shutoff switch. Thus I could never run down my battery by leaving the headlights on. For those rare occasions when I want my headlights on, I need only turn them off and on again; then they stay on. The common sense behind Toyota's approach, at what must be almost exactly the same production cost as GM's, is in my mind one of the major reasons why American car manufacturers are falling behind the Japanese.—Richard Aronson, Los Angeles

Agreed, but the buzzer is better than nothing. As of a few years ago I'm told you could buy a little gimmick for about five bucks at auto parts stores that, when installed, would beep if you shut off the ignition before dousing the lights. It's not as effortless as Toyota's approach, but it beats a dead battery.

Here is one I have been trying to find the answer to for years. I have asked flight attendants on airplanes all over the world. No one knows. No one even hazards a wild guess.

Why doesn't the plastic bag inflate? Since it doesn't, what is it for? I am speaking, of course, of the oxygen mask that will drop in case of emergency and that you are supposed to tie securely around your face before attending to infants or children. The plastic bag attached to the mask never inflates, and what's more, they make a point of telling you it won't inflate. This to me is more perplexing than some of the early undeciphered scripts I study.—Thomas P., Director, Program in Aegean Scripts and Prehistory, University of Texas at Austin

Doc, your prayers have been answered. First an inside secret: the bag does inflate, but only when you exhale.

Here's the deal. Passenger oxygen masks give you a continuous flow of oxygen (as opposed to oxygen on demand, which only flows when you inhale). The oxygen obviously can't flow into your lungs while you're exhaling, so if there weren't some way to store it tem-

porarily it would have to be vented wastefully. The bag makes this unnecessary. When you start exhaling, your breath plus the incoming O_2 flow into the bag. When a certain pressure is reached the bag stops filling and the rest of your exhaled breath is vented through a port in the mask.

The flight attendants make a point of telling you the bag won't inflate (right away, that is) because of an incident years ago. An airplane lost cabin pressure, the oxygen masks dropped down, and the passengers put them on—but when they noticed the bags didn't inflate, they figured the masks weren't working and took them off. Bad idea. Thus the warning. Simple, no? You want a hand with those Aegean scripts, just give me a call.

I sort of understand how an airplane wing works in terms of Bernoulli's principle (although I have only a vague idea why Bernoulli's principle is true). I know the wing is shaped to produce more air pressure on its lower surface than its upper surface and thus provide lift. If that's so, how can stunt planes fly upside down?—John K., Park Forest, Illinois

Simplissimo, chief. Airplane lift is the result of two things: (1) the shape of the wing, which has to do with the Bernoulli principle, and

(2) the angle at which the wing meets the wind, known as the "angle of attack." The most efficient wings make use of both factors, but in a pinch (or an air show) you can get by with just the latter.

The Bernoulli principle for now you're going to have to take on faith. Angle of attack is easier. You see a demonstration whenever you stick your palm out the window while driving down the highway: angle your palm upward and the wind forces your hand higher; angle your palm down and the wind forces your hand lower.

Same with planes. When you're zipping down the runway during takeoff, the Bernoulli principle generates a certain amount of lift, but to get that last crucial boost you pull up the plane's nose. This increases the angle of attack on the wings, popping the metal-fatigued welds on your starboard engine and sending you into a flaming cartwheel of . . . whoops, wrong index card. Actually, increased angle of attack provides the lift needed to get you flying.

Generating lift is easier at cruising speed, so stunt pilots can flip the thing over and rely on high angle of attack alone to keep them in the air (i.e., they keep the nose up and the tail down). This isn't a very efficient way to fly, since increasing your angle of attack also increases your aerodynamic drag. For that reason stunt planes need low-drag wings, heavy-duty construction (so they won't disintegrate in midair), and powerful engines that won't conk out when they're upside down. But in principle it's a piece of cake.

How do "night" rearview mirrors work? One flick of the switch and it seemingly dims all.—Chris G., Toronto

Here's the simple explanation: in a dimming rearview mirror you've got two reflecting surfaces—one with high reflectance, one with low. During the day you use the high reflector. At night the dimmer switch swings the low reflector into place, dimming glare from headlights behind you.

Now here's the trick: the two reflecting surfaces are the front and back of *the same piece of glass.* Said glass is specially ground so that the front and back surfaces are a few degrees out of parallel. (In other words, the glass looks wedge-shaped from the side.) The back surface is coated with silver, like a bathroom mirror, making it highly reflective. The front surface isn't coated, but it's still slightly reflective, just as all glass is.

Because the two surfaces aren't parallel, anytime you look at the rearview mirror, you're seeing two different reflections simultaneously. During the day with the mirror tilted into the normal position, the silvered surface shows you the road behind you. The nonsilvered surface, meanwhile, shows you the car's back seat (in GM cars, that is; other makes vary)—but it's so dim you don't notice.

At night the situation is reversed. When you flip the dim switch, the silvered surface tilts so it's showing you the car's ceiling, which is so dark you don't notice it. But now the nonsilvered surface is showing you the road. Because the headlights of the cars behind you are so bright, the nonsilvered surface reflects enough light to let you see what's behind you, but not so much that you're blinded.

The folks at GM tell me that on Cadillacs you can now get a high-tech "electrochromic" mirror that dims at night automatically, without having to flip a switch. The Caddy mirror has only one reflective surface, but there's a special film in front of it that gradually darkens at night through the magic of electronics. Very nice, but for sheer ingenuity the tilting surfaces are hard to beat.

If you're driving your car at the speed of light and put your headlights on, what happens?—Rob M., Sausalito, California

Man, what are you guys in Sausalito *on*, anyway? As anyone with even the most tenuous grasp of the theory of relativity knows, the speed of light is constant for any inertial observer. Does that answer your question? I didn't think so. Let me put it another way.

Suppose you're zipping down to the Dairy Queen in your Hyundai at $0.99c$—in other words, 99 percent of the speed of light. While en route you flip on the high beams and perform various subtle and ingenious experiments that I will not describe here. You discover that the light from the headlamps is traveling away from you at (surprise!) the speed of light. In other words, your headlights operate normally.

Now suppose a stationary observer at the side of the road performs the same experiment on the same beam of light. She (her name is Myra) discovers that the beam is moving away from *her* at speed *c* also. But how can this be, you ask? Since I'm going nearly the S. of L. to start with, shouldn't that give the photons emitted by the headlamps a running start, so to speak, enabling them to travel nearly *twice* the speed of light with respect to Myra?

Not to put too fine a point on it, no. The explanation for this is a little complicated, but the gist of it is this: when your speed approaches *c*, you and all your measuring sticks become foreshortened, i.e., squished like an accordion along your axis of travel. This throws off all your measurements, making the light beam appear to recede from you at the same speed *c* no matter how fast you're "really" going. Unfortunately, nobody knows how fast you're "really" going because in this morally permissive universe of ours, everything's relative. You think I'm moving and you're not? Hey, maybe the truth is you're moving and *I'm* not. Only God knows, and ip (see non-sexspecific pronouns, page 246) ain't saying.

No doubt this still leaves a few questions in your mind, but believe me, thousands have been over this ground before, and nobody's poked holes in the theory of relativity yet. For an excellent short treatment of the subject, see *Space and Time in Special Relativity* by N. David Mermin (1968).

Does an airplane have a lighter load after the passengers have consumed their rubber chicken and plastic vegetables?—R.C., Evanston, Illinois

Food doesn't cease to exist merely because somebody swallowed it, beanbrain. The only time a plane's mass decreases is if something gets dumped out or falls off, e.g., an engine. Ignoring the minor reduction in weight due to the loss of moisture and carbon dioxide to the outside atmosphere during air recirculation (which would occur whether the passengers ate anything or not), the plane's load stays the same. We'll also ignore—I hate to have to throw all these qualifications in here, but I'm surrounded by nitpickers—weight loss due to jet fuel consumption during the meal.

Next time ask something a little more challenging, like whether, if a passenger tosses a baseball into the air, the plane's weight decreases by the weight of the baseball (five to five and a half ounces, for you sticklers). Amazing answer on request.

The Teeming Millions Pounce

You recently answered "no" to the question, "Does an airplane have a lighter load after the passengers have consumed their food?" Have you forgotten the second law of thermodynamics? Matter cannot be converted into energy and vice versa without some loss. When the airplane passengers eat the food, some of it is broken down in the stomach and used as energy, which is dissipated as body heat through the plane's skin into the surrounding atmosphere. The amount involved may be insignificant—perhaps as little as one billionth of a gram—but yes, the plane does lose weight in flight when the passengers eat food aboard. Looks like the real beanbrain is you, not your reader!—Alex S., Lompoc, California

Oh, put a sock in it. The second law of thermodynamics, simply put, is as follows: left to themselves, things tend to go to hell in a handbasket. The truth of this assertion is irrefutable, but it has no bearing on the present discussion. What you're thinking of is Einstein's equation $E = mc^2$, which suggests that the extraction of energy from matter (e.g., during digestion) involves some loss of mass.

As you rightly note, however, in this case the amount of loss is insignificant. The average adult human requires about 2,700 kilocalories of energy per day. The potential energy of a kilogram of airline food (or of anything) is 21.5 trillion kilocalories. The loss of mass resulting from digestion is so small that it would fall within the range of error of any conceivable attempt at measurement. What we cannot reliably detect we are entitled to ignore. Ergo, the plane weighs the same after mealtime as before. Go and trouble me no more.

The Applicability of $E = mc^2$ to the Consumption of Airline Food, Continued

Regarding your recent column, in which you applied the equation $E = mc^2$ to the digestive process: not many of us have nuclear stomachs. We get our energy from chemical reactions, not nuclear reactions—that is, unless air food is even worse than I thought. It seems you're a beanbrain, too!—Rob Bonney, Lanham, Maryland

P.S.: I really enjoy your column!

Don't bandy words with *me*, you slime. Despite what many of the Teeming Millions apparently believe, $E = mc^2$ applies to *all* reactions, not just nuclear ones. Permit me to quote from *Space and Time in Special Relativity* by N. David Mermin, a book I read myself to sleep with every night: "A loss of mass occurs whenever internal energy (nuclear, electrical, chemical, etc.) is converted into energy of motion. Only in the nuclear case is the amount of energy so large that [it results] in an observable change in mass, but in principle $E = mc^2$ is as descriptive of a chemical explosive, a gasoline engine, or a flying bird [or, I might add, a flying human] as it is of a nuclear explosion." Case closed.

Finally, Somebody Takes the Bait

Pursuant to your recent column, I now ask you something a little more challenging. If a passenger on an airplane tosses a baseball into the air, does the plane's weight decrease by the weight of the baseball? I await your amazing answer.—Hayede F., Los Angeles

That's more like it. The amazing (if predictable) answer is that, although the plane experiences moment-to-moment fluctuations, on average it weighs exactly the same no matter what you do with the baseball, assuming it remains in the airplane. Bearing in mind that every action has an equal and opposite reaction, when you toss the ball upward, you simultaneously force the plane downward, increasing its weight. When the ball becomes airborne, the plane's weight decreases, then increases again when the ball lands.

Having performed various rites involving voodoo and integral calculus (one and the same, some may feel), we find that the weight of the plane during the tossing process is the same as its resting weight. This demonstrates ... well, I don't know what, but surely something profound.

But our restless intellectual curiosity won't allow us to leave it at that. (Well, maybe yours will, but I'm in charge here.) Suppose we're carrying a one-pound pigeon instead of a baseball. The pigeon takes off and flies around the cabin. What does the plane weigh? Exactly the same. On average, the pigeon must exert one pound of downward force on the cabin air to keep itself aloft, and the cabin air in turn presses down on the airplane.

Now suppose somebody opens a window. Does the weight of the plane change? Well, we do have the problem that everybody in the cabin will be sucked out and killed. But that's not the point I was trying to make. Let me think. Oh, yes. Antecedent to the loss of pay load, the plane weighs significantly less, if not necessarily a whole pound less, because it's no longer a closed system. Some of the downward force of the air being beat down by the pigeon's wings is dissipated to the exterior darkness. This may not seem like a big deal, and perhaps it isn't, but I have always thought an appreciation of the thermodynamic realities enhances one's quality of life.

After considerable debate and several fistfights in which I have been left friendless there remains a great "void" in my mind. What would happen if a person were thrown into the vacuum of space without protective clothing? Some bozos (e.g., my ex-friends) think you (the person thrown into space) would blow up. I, however, disagree. Please settle this festering wound.—Juan D. Montoya, Dallas

You sound like a man with a problem, Juan. Maybe a lot of problems. But this time the facts are on your side. There is such a thing as "explosive decompression," but that merely refers to the sudden loss of pressure in an air- or spacecraft, not the effect on the occupants. Though your chances of surviving such an experience are slim, your body would not explode (although see below). In fact, if you were able to scramble to safety quickly enough (as the

helmetless astronaut did in the famous scene from *2001: A Space Odyssey*), you might emerge virtually unscathed.

To be sure, there are a few troublemakers who will give Cecil an argument on this. Some flight surgeons at NASA, for instance, say death in a vacuum would be almost instantaneous. They offer the following Technicolor scenario: your blood would boil, your eyeballs would explode, and your lungs would turn to red slush.

But the medical literature suggests this view is exaggerated. For one thing, I have never seen anything indicating your eyeballs would explode (although your eardrums might burst). It's true that in the absence of ambient pressure your blood and other bodily fluids would boil, in the sense that they would turn to vapor. But that's not as drastic as it sounds. Your soft tissues would swell markedly, but they'd return to normal if you were recompressed within a short time.

It's conceivable your lungs might rupture, since in a vacuum the air in them would greatly expand. But experience suggests this is rare even if decompression is extremely rapid. The chances are much greater if your windpipe is closed, making it impossible for the expanding air to escape.

In any case, death would not be instantaneous. It's believed you'd have ten to fifteen seconds of "useful consciousness," and it'd be sev-

eral minutes before you'd die. If you were rescued within that time
there's a decent chance you'd survive. Research with chimps and
monkeys suggests that if you were exposed to a virtual vacuum for
less than 90 to 120 seconds you might not suffer permanent damage.

That said, there *are* circumstances involving explosive decompression in which your body might be torn to bits. This would result not
from the exposure to a vacuum per se, but from injuries caused by
the accompanying air blast. I have here a medical journal article
about a case of explosive decompression that killed four divers.
(They went from high pressure to normal rather than normal to vacuum, but same idea.)

The bodies of three of the dead men were outwardly normal. The
fourth man, however, was forced through a narrow hatch by the rush
of escaping air and his body, to be blunt, was reduced to pot roast.
Naturally, the authors of the article felt obliged to include pictures,
including a close-up of what was left of the face. You might show
them to your friends next time they're chattering about blown-up
bodies.

More on Explosive Decompression

*One of your recent columns dealt with the issue of explosive de-
compression. Although your information was good, you should have
mentioned the case history of near rapid decompression that killed
three astronauts in 1971. Below is an excerpt from my 1990 book,* Al-
manac of Soviet Manned Space Flight.

> *At 1:35* A.M., *June 30, the crew fired the* Soyuz *retro
> rockets to deorbit and twelve minutes later separated from
> the orbital and service modules. At this time, the orbital
> module was normally separated by 12 pyrotechnic devices
> which were supposed to fire sequentially, but they incor-
> rectly fired simultaneously, and this caused a ball joint in
> the capsule's pressure equalization valve to unseat, allowing
> air to escape. The valve normally opens at low altitude to
> equalize cabin air pressure to the outside air pressure. This
> caused the cabin to lose all its atmosphere in about 30 sec-*

onds while still at a height of 168 km. In seconds, Patsayev realized the problem and unstrapped from his seat to try and cover the valve inlet and shut off the valve but there was little time left. It would take 60 seconds to shut off the valve manually and Patsayev managed to half close it before passing out. Dobrovolsky and Volkov were virtually powerless to help since they were strapped in their seats, with little room to move in the small capsule and no real way to assist Patsayev. The men died shortly after passing out. Fifteen and a half minutes after retrofire, the pressure reached zero in the capsule and remained that way for eleven and a half minutes, at which point the cabin started to fill with air from the upper atmosphere. The rest of the descent was normal and the capsule landed at 2:17 A.M. The recovery forces located the capsule and opened the hatch only to find the cosmonauts motionless in their seats. On first glance they appeared to be asleep, but closer examination showed why there was no normal communication from the capsule during descent.

The Soviets had to give a detailed report on the accident to NASA in preparation for the Apollo-Soyuz Test Project, during which they said that the amount of tissue damage to the cosmonauts' bodies caused by the boiling of their blood during the 11.5 minutes of exposure to vacuum could at first have been misinterpreted as being the result of a catastrophic and instantaneous decompression. The cause of death was pulmonary embolism.

There has yet to be released any substantial data on the damage to their bodies, but from the descriptions commonly published the damage was not immediately recognizable.—Dennis Newkirk, Fairfax, Virginia

For years I've been hearing about fantastic carburetors that can give your car up to 200 MPG. But supposedly the automakers and Big Oil won't allow them to come to market because they'd wreck the industry. The people who tell you this are usually conspiracy buffs who offer it as an example of how the masses are duped by the Illuminati,

so you have to be skeptical. But still I wond
retor a complete fantasy, or does somethin'
you have one on your car?—Mike Wells,

Nah. My main energy-saving strateg'
from me, so I can just put it in neutral anu
limitations, but it works better than "200 MPG carb..
best are a fantasy and at worst a fraud.

Alleged high-mileage carbs are based on a beguilingly simp.
principle. Here's how one of my correspondents explains it:

> Detroit carbs put gas in the engine by spraying it in;
> much of the gas goes into the cylinder still in droplets and
> burns incompletely. High-mileage "vapor" carburetors pre-
> warm the gas using exhaust heat pumped through an in-
> line chamber. This enables the gas to evaporate quickly but
> thoroughly. More gas is burned and less goes out the
> tailpipe as pollution. Detroit seems to avoid these designs
> because they cost more. (Remember saving five cents per
> Pinto?) But better carbs are out there for the tinkering.

Someone also sent me a report that supposedly originated with
the Carb Research Center of Oklahoma, which promotes vapor
carbs. The report makes the astonishing claim that theoretical maximum fuel efficiency for a conventional auto is nearly 2,900 MPG. It
goes on to tell the story of the original 200-MPG vapor carb, invented
in the mid-1930s by one Charles N. Pogue. Another reader says vapor carbs work but they have a big drawback: backfiring.

While I don't want to belittle blue-collar ingenuity, the vapor
carb's inventors are trying to solve a nonexistent problem. According
to John Heywood, a professor of mechanical engineering at MIT and
an authority on internal-combustion engines, incomplete burning of
fuel is insignificant in modern cars. Fuel combustion today typically
exceeds 97 percent. While it's true cars aren't very efficient—only 20
to 35 percent of the fuel energy is converted to useful work—that's
mostly due to heat loss (through the engine block, out the exhaust
pipe) and unavoidable energy loss during burning itself.

The theoretical (and unobtainable) maximum efficiency for a small

Honda Civic is around 200 MPG; for your big beaters it's
ower. Claims to the contrary are fraudulent, and I gather Pro-
Heywood said as much in a report he wrote for the U.S. Postal
vice, which was investigating high-mileage carb vendors for fraud.

Carburetors in general are an obsolete technology now being replaced by electronic fuel injection, which offers superior emission
control. Truth is, vapor carbs are the equivalent of the improved
buggy whip. Forget 'em.

This is not to say super-high-mileage cars couldn't be built. On the
contrary, there are plenty of proven energy-efficient technologies
available, none of which has lacked for publicity or industry backing.

A recent survey in *Technology Review* listed ten experimental cars
developed by seven major automakers that got highway mileage
ranging from 71 to 110 MPG. A few years ago Renault trotted out a
rig that got 121 MPG on the run from Paris to Bordeaux. I'm told the
gas mileage record for motorcycles is about 400 MPG, and if you really want to go crazy, a GM subsidiary recently built a solar-powered
prototype called Sunraycer that doesn't use any gas at all. Weighing
only four hundred pounds, it completed a 1,800-mile race at an average speed of over forty MPH. On the downside, it seats only one,
has no trunk or luggage rack, and barely has room for a pair of fuzzy
dice. But hey, life is full of trade-offs.

High mileage is never the result of a single miraculous component, such as a carburetor. Rather it's the sum of numerous small im-
provements. Among these are lightweight materials, low-friction
tires, improved aerodynamics, flywheels to store and reuse energy
now lost during braking, and "ultra-lean-burn" engines for more efficient city driving (already available in certain Toyotas sold in Europe).

Another improvement used in some high-mileage prototypes is
the continuously variable transmission: instead of clumsily shifting
gears, the cars shift transmission ratios gradually, typically using an
ingenious (and conceptually quite simple) arrangement of belts and
cone-shaped pulleys. Soon to come, it's believed, are ceramic diesel
engines using turbochargers and perhaps stratified-charge engines
that combine the best features of gasoline and diesel technology.
While 200 MPG is pushing it, the experts think 100 MPG cars are
within range of current technology.

Sounds great, you say? Well, don't rush down to the auto show-room just yet. It may be years, if ever, before the new technology becomes widely available. That's not because the automakers are conspiring to withhold it, but rather because they doubt the public will buy it. People today are less concerned about energy efficiency and for good reason: corrected for inflation, gasoline today costs less than it did in 1973. Fuel-efficient cars tend to be little cars, and the size trend in recent years has gone the opposite way.

The only reason gas mileage has improved at all in recent years has been government-mandated fuel-economy standards, and God knows some recent administrations did everything they could to frustrate those. The superefficient cars now on the drawing boards don't figure to be cheap, and unless gas prices skyrocket, the fuel savings probably won't cover the higher cost. Barring a sudden burst of altruism on the part of the car-buying public, chances are you won't see ultra-high-mileage cars for sale until we're down to the last two gallons of Arab oil.

Why are there push buttons at intersections that say, "Push me and traffic will stop so you can cross quicker," or something like that? It doesn't work! I wouldn't say I'm neurotic about it, but about fifteen years ago I quit my job to hitchhike around the U S A to find a push-to-walk traffic signal that would actually stop traffic. After countless pairs of shoes and as many near-misses with cars, I can say that without a doubt none of these traffic signals provide the pedestrian with a quicker cross. What's going on? If I'm right maybe we can work some kind of lawsuit scam!—Markus T. Pellicori, Baltimore

I like a man who takes things seriously, Markus, but just the same I'm glad you weren't my partner in chem lab. The usual explanation for the apparent inertness of push-to-walk buttons is the foolish ex-pectations of users, who think the buttons will instantly bring traffic to a screeching halt. Satisfying though many hassled pedestrians would no doubt find this, it would also result in a lot of rear-end col-lisions. Instead, P-T-W buttons are set up so the "walk" signal lights at some nondisruptive point in the signal cycle, e.g., shortly after the previous signal up the street goes red. Since many suburban stoplights are on a two-minute-plus cycle, many impatient pedestrians erroneously conclude the button is broken.

Or so the engineers say. However, Cecil has been lied to before. I decided the only way to be sure was to stake out an actual P-T-W button, which happened to be at the crosswalk (no cross street) outside the traffic court building in downtown Chicago. During the Friday afternoon rush I spent half an hour pushing that damn button without any observable effect at all. It was twenty-five seconds "walk," fifty seconds "don't walk," button or no.

At 11:00 P.M. it was a different story. The "walk" signal didn't light *unless* you pushed the button, in which case the signal changed a second or two after the light went red at the previous signal up the street. Problem was, at that hour there were hardly any pedestrians, and the few there were didn't bother to push the button, no doubt having been burned by the signal's nonresponsiveness at five that afternoon.

Conclusion: push-to-walk buttons only work when there's nobody around to push them. To put it more charitably, the buttons generally are wired to insert a "walk" phase into an otherwise walkless signal cycle, not speed an existing "walk" phase up.

Every so often I see a car with a license plate holder that says "Los Angeles" above the plate and "KMA367" below it. The first time I encountered one of these things, I assumed it was a ham radio call sign. Having come across the same thing on dozens of other cars, however, I've discarded that interpretation. The most plausible explanation I've heard is that it is a license-plate dating service or a system for identifying the personal cars of law enforcement officers. Neither interpretation is diabolical enough for my tastes. I'm counting on you to spill the horrible secret.—Alan Levin, Los Angeles

Cecil hesitates to address these purely local issues, preferring to devote his attentions to questions that at a minimum affect an entire galactic sector. But I used to wonder about this myself, and besides, let's face it, the L.A. cop situation, which is in fact what we're talking about here, has achieved a certain global notoriety.

KMA367 is the call sign of the main L.A. police radio transmitter, something most cops know but most ordinary folks don't. So some shrewd entrepreneur began selling KMA367 license plate holders through the L.A. police academy store. An LAPD spokesman tells me the purpose of the plates is merely to identify your personal vehicle to fellow cops while not advertising it to the world at large. Similar license plate holders are used by other SoCal police orgs. But some cynics out there believe that at least one or two of the cops who bought the holders figured other cops might give them a pass next time they got a little heavy-footed on the freeway.

In time, word of the KMA367 code began leaking out to the civilian (i.e., noncop) population. Folks began buying used KMA license plate holders at garage sales and such, and you can always walk into the police academy store and pay full retail. Whether because the identificatory value of the holder is diminished or simply because all L.A. cops are virtuous, an LAPD spokesman says a KMA holder isn't going to do a damn bit of good preventing you from getting pulled over for traffic violations. Still, these days you'd be foolish not to take advantage of any break you can get. I bet Rodney King wishes he'd had a KMA license plate holder. I bet most of L.A. wishes he'd had one, too.

Chapter 6

High Finance

Since elementary school I have repeatedly heard the story of how Manhattan was bought from the Indians for a mere $24 worth of trinkets. Something about this has long troubled me. Assuming the value of the barter items was estimated at about the time of the famous transaction, shouldn't it be adjusted for all those years of inflation? Maybe Manhattan wasn't such a steal after all.—Charles R. McNeill II, Washington, D.C.

Sometimes this job is so joyously easy. In 1626 Peter Minuit bought Manhattan Island from the local Indians for a load of cloth, beads, hatchets, and other odds and ends then worth sixty Dutch guilders. According to my *Encyclopædia Britannica*, sixty guiders in 1626 would buy you one and a half pounds of silver. Naturally we assume this is troy weight, twelve ounces to the pound.

As of early 1993 silver was selling for a little more than $4 per troy ounce. Ergo—sorry, but a man in my position needs to say ergo once in a while—Minuit got the core of the Big A for $72 in today's money. (Lest you think the price of beads has increased remarkably slowly in the last 350 years, you should know that the $24 calculation was made in the nineteenth century.)

There are some who would contend that $72 or even $24 for Manhattan was not such a hot bargain. These people are mostly Republicans. But let's do a few calculations. According to the New York Public Library, the assessed value of taxable real estate in Manhattan for 1990–91 was $47 billion. Assuming the land alone accounts for 25 percent of this, land values have appreciated from a half cent per acre in 1626 to $827,000 per acre today, an increase of roughly 17 billion percent. Not bad, you are surely thinking, even by the stringent standards of the GOP.

But wait. I have a letter here from Andrew Johnston of N.Y.C inquiring whether maybe the Louisiana Purchase ($15 million for a quarter of the country) wasn't a better bargain. Now, the Louisiana Purchase was not the best land deal the U.S. ever got. It cost three cents per acre in 1803 (five cents when you figure in the interest), whereas Alaska cost two cents per acre in 1867. Just the same, it offers an interesting comparison.

According to Peter Wolf (*Land in America*, 1981), the total value of all land in the United States in 1975 was $1.3 trillion. Assuming an average annual appreciation of 5 percent per year, the land was worth $2.7 trillion as of 1991. The Louisiana Purchase accounts for about 23 percent of the present area of the United States, so figure it's worth $618 billion, or about $1,160 an acre.

Having performed prodigious feats of calculation, we find that since 1803 the heartland of America has appreciated at an average annual rate of 5.5 percent per year, whereas since 1626 Manhattan has appreciated at an average annual rate of . . . 5.3 percent. Conclusion: that dimbulb Minuit may have paid *too much!* Given the shaky assumptions behind some of the numbers above, I don't know that I'd go looking for an Indian asking for a refund. But compared to other historic U.S. land scams, Manhattan may not have been the steal everyone thinks.

The Purchase of Manhattan: Wuz We Robbed?

As a follow-up to your discussion of whether or not Peter Minuit got a bargain when he paid only $24 worth of trinkets for Manhattan, there is one added factor. I grew up in the Canarsie section of Brooklyn, New York. Named after the Canarsie Indians, it is the farthest point from Manhattan in Brooklyn.

When I was in high school, a history class published a research project in which they convincingly proved that Peter Minuit had purchased Manhattan from the Canarsie Indians. Since they did not live on Manhattan Island, it is unlikely that they had any ownership claim in the first place.

While $24 in trinkets might sound cheap for all of Manhattan, it is no bargain when you have paid it to a tribe that was just passing through. Rather than giving Mr. Minuit the bargain of the century, the Canarsie Indians may have actually sold him the proverbial Brooklyn Bridge.—Kevin W., Alexandria, Virginia

I didn't mention this because I figured Peter Minuit had suffered enough, but now that you bring it up, I may as well pile on. One popular history of Manhattan notes that the Canarsie Indians "dwelt on Long Island, merely trading on Manhattan, and their trickery [in selling what they didn't possess to the Dutch] made it necessary for the white man to buy part of the island over again from the tribes living near Washington Heights. Still more crafty were the Raritans of [Staten Island], for the records show that Staten Island was sold by these Indians no less than six times."

So okay, maybe Peter Minuit was no Donald Trump. (Then again, considering the current state of Mr. T.'s real estate empire, maybe he was.) But let's not be too quick to judge. The latest crop of New York historians has taken pains to point out that there is no evidence that either the Dutch or the Indians believed they had robbed or been robbed by the other party to the deal.

What is the true source of the wealth of the Kennedy family of Hyannis, Massachusetts? I have heard several stories about Joe Senior having made a killing in Prohibition rum, sleazy stock market practices, or the Boston construction industry. I heard the other day that he made the seed money for all this by selling opium to China, and that takes the cake. Also, what is the Kennedy money doing today? Besides the Democratic party, is there a family business? Do they have a foundation or something? Why don't I see the Kennedy Trust as a sponsor of quality public television?—Peter Greenberg, Jackson Heights, New York

Cecil doesn't ordinarily go in for this *People* magazine stuff, but Lord knows I like dishing the dirt as much as the next guy, and Joe Kennedy is a target the size of all outdoors.

J.P. was what we call an operator. He made his money by (1) pulling various hustles before it had occurred to anyone to make them illegal and (2) possibly pulling other hustles that were definitely illegal but generally winked at. His stock market shenanigans were an example of the former, his Prohibition liquor business (never proven, by the way) an example of the latter. That said, let's not get ridiculous. He didn't sell opium to the Chinese; the British did. Nineteenth century. Very famous. Trust me.

Joseph P. Kennedy was the ambitious son of a prosperous Boston saloonkeeper and ward boss. He married the mayor's daughter, went to Harvard, and generally made the most of his ample connections and talent. He ran a bank (admittedly two-bit) at twenty-five and was number two man at a shipyard with more than two thousand workers during World War I. At thirty he became a stockbroker and made a fortune through insider trading and stock manipulation. He was a master of the stock pool, a then-legal stunt in which a few traders conspired to inflate a stock's price, selling out just before the bubble burst.

Kennedy may also have traded in illegal booze, although the evidence is circumstantial. His father had been in the liquor business before Prohibition, and Joe himself got into it (publicly, that is) immediately after repeal. Some believe the family business simply went underground during the dry years. He may have been strictly a nickel-and-dimer; Harvard classmates say he supplied the illicit booze for alumni events.

But there might have been more to it than that. In 1973 mob boss Frank Costello said he and Kennedy had been bootlegging partners. Other underworld figures have also claimed Joe was in pretty deep. At least one writer (John Davis, 1984) thinks bootlegging enabled Joe to earn his initial financial stake, but that's hard to believe; he had plenty of chances to make money more or less legally.

Whatever the truth of the matter, Kennedy's real strength wasn't his alleged criminal ties but his business smarts, notably an exquisite sense of timing. In the mid-1920s he became a movie mogul (taking time out for a celebrated dalliance with Gloria Swanson), then organized a merger and sold out just when the industry was consolidating, clearing $5 to $6 million all told. He pulled out of stocks early in 1929 and sold short following the crash, actually making money while others got creamed. Just before Prohibition was repealed he lined up several lucrative liquor-importing deals.

By the 1930s Kennedy was rich, but he didn't make serious money by modern standards until he got into real estate in a big way during World War II, raking in an estimated $100 million. In 1945 he made the deal that remains the centerpiece of the Kennedy fortune: for a measly $12.5 million he bought the Merchandise Mart in Chicago, a huge wholesale emporium that had cost $30 million to build. Within a few years the annual gross in rent exceeded the purchase price. In 1957 *Fortune* declared Kennedy one of the richest men in America, with assets of 200 to 400 million bucks.

The Kennedy family's wide-ranging business affairs are now run by hirelings at Joseph P. Kennedy Enterprises in New York. Joe did establish a number of charitable ventures, several of which help retarded children (his daughter Rosemary was retarded). But he put most of his money in trust for his family. Being the odd combination of stud and monomaniacal family man that he was, he figured his real legacy to the country was the fruit of his loins.

When I was in an artillery unit in Vietnam, we were told that each shell we fired cost the taxpayers several thousand dollars to manufacture, disregarding the cost to develop the weapon itself or the cost of training the manpower to shoot it. We speculated that, considering the great number of rounds we fired, the United States instead could easily have built each Vietnamese a beautiful suburban house complete with swimming pool instead of spending the money trying to kill them. In that way we could have not only won the war but also the hearts and minds of the enemy. So I put it to you: if the cost in dollars of the Vietnam War were divided by the number of Vietnamese, how much could each have been paid to lay down their arms and live peacefully ever after?—Stephen Wilhelm, New York

Best damn question I've had in months. Let's take it step by step.

Estimates of the cost of the Vietnam War vary all over the place, with one analyst putting the figure as high as $900 billion. But that includes all kinds of indirect and future costs—twenty-first century veterans' benefits, the cost of inflation resulting from the war, you name it. A bit too blue-sky for our purposes.

The Defense Department in the 1970s came up with a much more conservative figure—$140 billion in direct military outlays between 1965 and 1974. This includes some Pentagon overhead, i.e., money that presumably would have been spent whether there was a war or not. However, other estimates of "incremental" costs run anywhere

from $112 billion to $155 billion, so we're probably safe in going with 140.

The combined population of North and South Vietnam in 1969, the midpoint of substantial U.S. involvement, was somewhere around 39 million. That means that over ten years we spent about $3,600 for every Vietnamese man, woman, and child. Today you could buy most of a Yugo with that kind of money. At first glance, hardly enough reason to abandon a war of national liberation.

But let's put this in perspective. Per capita annual income in South Vietnam in 1965 by one estimate was $113. At $3,600 per, we could have kept those guys in rice and fish sauce for pretty much the rest of their lives, with color TV and a Barcalounger thrown in. As an added bonus, the country would not have suffered incalculable war damage, and 1.8 million more Vietnamese would not be dead (or at least they would have died other than from being shot, blown up, etc.).

I know, I know: millions for defense but not one cent for bribes. But considering how things actually turned out, maybe we should have given it a try.

Thank you for your answer to my question on the cost of the Vietnam War. I was astounded to think we spent the equivalent of thirty-two years' worth of Vietnam's GNP trying to kill half the people who lived there. Now I have another question. Imagine that instead of the former Soviet Union rushing headlong toward capitalism, the rest of the world decided to become socialist. If all the world's wealth were divided up equally among all its inhabitants, how much would each of us have?—Stephen W., New York

What was once the Soviet Union is definitely rushing headlong toward something, Steve; would that it were only capitalism. Be that as it may, you do raise what seems like the obvious next question.

As before, the answer has to be larded with caveats. The numbers for world wealth are even shakier than those for the Vietnam War, where at least you had the benefit of unlimited M.B.A.'s to count the change. National bumbling aside, the figures reported by former Communist-bloc countries have to be regarded with skepticism because there's no free-market valuation of goods and services. Ditto for countries where a sizable portion of the population relies on sub-sistence agriculture.

Perhaps for these reasons, the numbers published by different sources don't mesh very well. Adding up the GNPs in the *Europa World Year Book 1990*, we get a gross world product for 1988 of $21.8 trillion, with a 1985 population of just over 5 billion, excluding some minor principalities. This works out to $4,339 per person. However, *The World in Figures*, compiled by *The Economist* of London, says "national income per person" in 1979 was only $2,130, and the *New Book of World Rankings* says worldwide GNP per capita in 1980 was $2,430. Either the 1980s were the most prosperous era in history—10 percent annual growth—or somebody's calculator needs new batteries. (To be fair, inflation and shifting exchange rates relative to the dollar have probably also helped boost the numbers.)

At any rate, extrapolating from *The Economist*'s conservative numbers, we come up with a current per capita world income of more than $3,100, or an average household income for a family of five of $15,500—a tidy sum. (Forgive me if I don't try to figure out per capita share of world resources, as opposed to income; life is short.) Pretty cold comfort for the average guy in Bhutan, where per capita GNP in 1980 was $80, the world low. But it does indicate that a more equitable distribution of resources wouldn't beggar everybody.

Other interesting numbers: according to various sources, the world has 1.2 billion cattle, 111 million turkeys, 43 million asses, and 1 billion sheep. Now you know where they get all the participants in the St. Patrick's Day Parade.

How much U.S. currency (cold cash) is in circulation around the world? Who decides how much to print? With the government continually borrowing money, shouldn't lenders be broke by now? Where do they get the money to keep lending out, especially when they know that none of it will ever be paid back?—F. Lucre, Dallas

Jumpin' Jehosaphat, Phil, this is the kind of stuff you cover in two semesters of freshman econ. Fortunately, through the miracle of

Newspaper College, we can boil it down to the following snappy observations, which will get you through five minutes' chat on the topic this weekend at the Hamptons.

- *Coins and paper currency are economic petty cash.* At the end of 1990 the total amount of *currency* in circulation was $246 billion. The total amount of *money*, by the strictest definition (what economists call M1), was $825 billion. M1 money is whatever you can spend right now—currency plus checking deposits. A more inclusive estimate of the money supply (M2—includes savings accounts) was $3.3 trillion.

  While currency is still the most popular method of payment, it accounts for only one percent of the value of all transactions. (The big money travels via "wire transfer" between banks—0.1 percent of the transactions, but 80 percent of the dollars.) People sometimes say inflation occurs when the government "prints too much money." Nonsense. The amount of money actually printed is inconsequential.

- *Nobody is in charge of deciding how much currency to issue.* The Treasury Department prints it, but the amount actually distributed to the public is purely a function of consumer demand. If people want more greenbacks, they draw down their checking accounts and get them. The government prints as much as people want.

· *The government doesn't create money, private banks do.* Banks create money by making loans. Suppose I put $100 in my checking account. The bank bets I won't draw it out for a while and lends $85 of my $100 to legendary cartoonist Slug Signorino. Slug blows the $85 on Captain Morgan and lottery tickets at McGinty's. Now McGinty's has $85 in folding green and I've got $100 in checking that theoretically I can draw out at any time. Behold, the local money supply has bloomed from $100 to $185.

It doesn't stop there. If McGinty's puts the $85 in its checking account, its bank will lend out most of it, increasing the money supply even more. That's how the banks find the cash to lend to Uncle Sam. They lend it out, the government spends it, the recipients put the money in the bank, and the banks lend out *that*. The total amount of money that banks can create is regulated by the Federal Reserve; too much money (not too much currency) = inflation.

· *The whole financial system is a house of cards.* Probably during that last example you were thinking, Jeez, what if Uncle Cecil drew out his $100, as he was legally entitled to do? It wouldn't be there! Righto. If everybody decided to take what they had coming out of their accounts and bury it in the garden, the financial system would collapse, civilization would end, and we'd all go back to being hunter-gatherers. The modern world is made possible by the trust and sheeplike predictability of millions of depositors. (Deposit insurance makes it less of a crapshoot than it once was.)

· *The Federal Reserve System is not part of the government and is answerable to no one.* (I know you didn't ask, but lots of other people have.) By "government" I mean the executive branch. The president does appoint the Fed's governing board, but the members serve for long terms and can do as they please, free of political interference (in theory). The Fed *is* a quasi-public agency created by Congress and as a practical matter does not lightly defy the president.

· *The government will never pay back the money it owes, and nobody expects it to.* The government borrows money by selling bonds. Each bond is a portable money machine, generating interest for its owner on a dependable schedule. Nobody wants these bonds to go away; indeed, in a time of worldwide financial instability, they are in great demand. To pay off old bonds the government simply issues new ones. The main concern is that the government not issue so many bonds that the interest payments get out of hand.

Strange business, eh? Strange as nuclear physics in its way, about as widely understood, and offering to its adherents the same attraction: the chance to yank the wires holding together the world.

Why do prices end in .99? My father says it started at Bill's Texaco in Waco, Texas, during a price war. I say it's a much older management technique to force employees to open cash register drawers for each transaction (making simply pocketing a bill more obvious). Since we're both inveterate bullshitters we've decided to leave it to you. —Richard H., San Francisco

The topic does lend itself to wielders of the big shovel, no question about it. The most elaborate explanation I've seen is in Scot Morris's *Book of Strange Facts & Useless Information* (1979):

In 1876, Melville E. Stone decided that what Chicago needed was a penny newspaper to compete with the nickel papers then on the stands. But there was a problem: with no sales tax, and with most goods priced for convenience at even-dollar figures, there weren't many pennies in general circulation. Stone understood the consumer mind, however, and convinced several Chicago merchants to drop their prices—slightly. Impulse buyers, he explained, would more readily purchase a $3.00 item if it cost "only" $2.99. Shopkeepers who tried the plan found that it worked, but soon they faced their own penny shortage. Undaunted, Stone journeyed to Philadelphia, bought several barrels of pennies from the mint, and brought them back to the

Windy City. Soon Chicagoans had pennies to spare and exchanged them for Stone's new paper.

Very interesting, maybe even true (up to a point), but probably not
the reason prices end in .99 today. The problem: Melville Stone ran
the *Daily News* for only a few months before selling out in 1876.
Judging from *Daily News* advertisements, prices ending in 9 (39
cents, 69 cents, etc.) were rare until well into the 1880s and weren't
all that common then. The practice didn't really become widespread
until the 1920s, and even then prices as often as not ended in .95,
not .99.

So what's the real explanation? Having spent two hours poring
over the microfilm—no guarantee that I'm not full of B.S., but at
least it's scientific B.S.—I'd say it was retail price competition in the
1880s. Advertising prices in the newspapers was rare before 1880,
but common after 1890. At first prices were usually rounded off to
the nickel, dime, or dollar, but it wasn't long before a few smaller operators, looking for an edge, began using what might be called "just
under" pricing (49 cents, $1.95, and so on), no doubt in an effort to
convince the gullible they were getting a bargain.

The idea caught on surprisingly slowly. Even in the 1920s some
large merchants still rounded prices off to the nearest dollar or, on
larger items, to the nearest $5 or sawbuck. Today's custom of having
nearly every price end in 99, 95, or 49 cents or dollars (or just a 9
for items under $5) is of fairly recent vintage. The practice bespeaks
a certain low cunning, but it's also pretty obvious and trying to
find out who invented it is like trying to find out who invented
the hat.

A few weeks ago I got a check for twenty-five cents from Illinois
Bell. The check was drawn on a bank in Lake Lillian, Minnesota. Do
you know how obscure Lake Lillian is? (Of course you do. You know
everything. I'm just asking rhetorically.) It's so obscure it's not in the
Minnesota key to my road-map book, which includes such metropo-
lises as Dundas, population 422. It's so obscure the person I talked to
at the Minnesota tourism office couldn't find it on her computer (she
said to call back when Jerry gets back from lunch). Why would a ma-

*jor corporation have its checking account in such an obscure bank
when there are lots of banks right in the neighborhood?—V.M., Chicago*

Maybe they want to head off the lunchtime rush of people cashing
their twenty-five-cent checks. Illinois Bell was not very forthcoming
on the subject. The company says it employs a contractor to handle
its refunds, and the contractor uses the Lake Lillian bank because
it's cheaper, somehow. I believe that, of course. I believe everything.
Let me merely speak in generalities, therefore, of what it *usually*
means when a big company uses a tiny boondock bank. I refer to the
arcane world of corporate cash management.

The idea behind managing cash is simple: speed it up coming in,
slow it down going out. The boondock bank stunt is an example of
the latter. It's called "remote disbursement," and it's so ridiculously
snaky it deserves some kind of award. You know how sometimes
you'll write a check to somebody when you haven't got any money
in your checking account, then rush to the bank the next morning to
put some money in before the check clears? Same idea.

Here's what happens. Let's suppose a large Chicago company—
the Flurgg Corporation—owes you some money. They mail you a
check drawn on a bank in, oh, Lake Henrietta, Minnesota. As soon
as you receive it you rush down to your local bank to get the twenty-
five cents, so you can invest it in thirty-day CDs. Your bank sends
the check to the Chicago branch of the Federal Reserve, which
sends it to the Fed's Minneapolis branch, which sends it to Lake
Henrietta for payment.

Since Lake Henrietta is so out of it that most deliveries are probably
handled by yak, this process takes a couple of days. But finally the
check arrives. Lo and behold, there is no money in the Flurgg Corporation's account. Not to worry. At a prearranged time, the Lake Henrietta bank tells Flurgg how much it needs to cover all the Flurgg
checks that have arrived that day for payment. Flurgg promptly wires
the money. The net result: you've officially been "paid," but Flurgg
gets a two-day grace period (also known as the "float") before it actually has to come up with the cash to cover your check.

Who gets screwed in this arrangement? Probably you. Banks are
wise to the check-float game, so they put a hold on any out-of-state

checks presented for payment. You can deposit the money in your account, but you won't be permitted to walk out of the bank with it for several days, thus giving the check time to clear Lake Henrietta or wherever.

If the whole thing sounds like a bit of a scam, that's because it is. To eliminate the worst abuses the Federal Reserve has greatly accelerated its check-clearing schedules so that a check that might have taken five days to clear years ago now takes only a couple of days.

As a result, remote disbursement has been giving way to something called "controlled" disbursement. In controlled disbursement, you select a bank that isn't necessarily in Irkutsk but is still small and far away enough that the only checks of yours it's going to have to cash are going to come by way of the Federal Reserve (as opposed to some mope walking in off the street, say).

Since the Fed typically makes its last delivery of checks by 9:00 A.M., you know early on exactly how much cash you're going to have to put in your account to cover that day's debits without leaving extra cash for checks dribbling in later. So you get maybe an extra day of float and you don't have money sitting around in non-interest-bearing accounts. A small thing, seemingly, but in the world of corporate finance, it's a big deal.

News from Lake Lillian

Recently I heard one of your readers was concerned about the existence of my hometown of Lake Lillian, Minnesota. It's there, all right, all 300-plus people (350-plus if you count the cats and dogs). Lake Lillian is on Highway 7 about twelve miles north of Bird Island, in case you can't find it on the map.

One more thing. There are no yaks in town. Harold Olson does have a llama, but its purpose is to keep his donkey company, not to make deliveries. Whoever told you there were yaks in Lake Lillian was obviously misinformed.—John S., Bloomingdale, Illinois

John has kindly enclosed an informative booklet published by an affiliate of First State Bank of Lake Lillian, no doubt the same outfit that sent our original correspondent that twenty-five-cent check.

Lake Lillian, we learn, is the "Gateway to the Little Crow Lake Region from the South." Despite this, the brochure says, "Finding Lake Lillian has always frustrated many folks. That must have started when recent Rand McNally road maps didn't show Lake Lillian even existed. And yet a small hamlet named Thorpe, Minnesota, did make the map. Thorpe, located a few miles east of Lake Lillian, consists of a few houses and a grain elevator, which is owned by the family of one of the bank's employees who lives there now. Unfortunately, he constantly rubs the map incident in our face."

The history of Lake Lillian is filled with Keilloresque poignance. For example, "Government land records show that claims had been made by a Peter Furdeen and a Peter France on the shore of Lake Lillian as early as the fall of 1858. They must not have stayed any length of time as none of the early settlers ever heard of them."

There are many tales of ventures that started out strong, then just sort of petered out. For instance: "HOTELS—Mr. and Mrs. Rudolph Vath built a hotel in 1923 called the Lake Lillian Hotel, but in 1944 sold it to Mr. and Mrs. Aug. Junkermier, who used it as a residence. In 1963 the K. M. Funeral Home purchased the lot and building which was torn down so they could construct an addition to the mortuary."

Finally we learn about First State Bank. First State, it seems, "is one of a handful of banks with expertise in processing high-volume, low-dollar rebate checks—the checks that companies send to consumers in return for buying a product being promoted or introduced. First State was the clearing bank for 55 million rebate checks [in 1985] alone. The little bank has won the loyalty of 120 corporate clients [including] General Electric, GM, Pillsbury, R. J. Reynolds, AT&T, and Procter & Gamble"—and evidently Illinois Bell as well.

How'd the bank get into this line of work? The booklet's answer is refreshingly candid. "About a decade ago, a fulfillment house—a company that makes sure people who send in rebate applications meet all the requirements—was looking for a bank to use as an endpoint for returned checks. The person in charge of the project happened to be a relative of First State Bank's president."

Why rebate checks? "For one thing, it's cheaper to mail out the checks than to transport, count, monitor, and mail cash. Also, by issuing bearer draft checks, which do not require endorsement, a company qualifies for bulk-mailing postage rates. . . . Most important of all . . . when checks are mailed, there's always some 'slippage.' Some people who send for rebate checks will not cash them before the expiration date. Because these checks are payable 'to the bearer,' any uncollected money is returned to the company that issued the checks. This avoids the 'escheat' laws—state laws that require companies to pay taxes on uncollected funds."

One more thing. Bank president Duane Lindgren "denies that corporations issuing rebate checks choose banks situated in out-of-the-way places to maximize float. 'One reason we're chosen is that we're centrally located. We also try to provide a comprehensive service at a competitive price. That's the name of the game.' " Whatever you say, Duane. Regards to all the folks in Lake Lillian.

Uh-oh

As president of the Lake Lillian Civic and Commerce organization, I am writing in response to, as you phrased it, "your brilliant disquisition on corporate cash management and boondock banking." On behalf of the city of Lake Lillian, I would like to take issue with the comments contained in the article.

Yes, Mr. Adams, there is a Lake Lillian. Lake Lillian is located in the south central part of the State of Minnesota. We are approximately ninety miles west of the Twin Cities. Edwin Whitefield, an artist and land promoter, visited the Kandiyohi Lakes in 1856 and gave his wife's name, Lillian, to one of the lakes.

Recreation and relaxation can be enjoyed at Big Kandiyohi Lake, four miles northwest of Lake Lillian on County Highway #8. Two resorts—County Park #1 and #2—have camping available, as well as resort services and public beaches.

From the article that was written I will guesstimate that your Chicagoan reader is a "city-slicker," just as I was before moving here approximately four years ago. I was under the impression a "farmer" had a tractor, two or more cows, and had a barn. You have not seen farmers, I'll assure you. The tractors our farmers use are huge, and they do not plow only ten acres—that probably would be a good-size garden for them! They do not raise a "couple" cows, or pigs, or tur-keys; they raise them by the hundreds or thousands.

It is unfortunate, to say the least, that a person from Chicago should automatically equate being from a small town with being ob-scure or make innuendos about both the town and the townspeople being backward. I cannot help but wonder, since this whole incident seems to have begun over our local bank's processing of a twenty-five-cent rebate check, what would have been said if there had been a whole dollar rebate check at stake! No doubt this person would have really believed our deliveries are handled by yaks!

In conclusion, while I know it is your job to print the news, I also know that being the dedicated writer that I'm sure you are, you feel a duty to also inform your readers. Therefore, I'm sure you'll pass all this information along to the particular reader in question. If you're ever in our area, please stop in to see us. The coffee is always on, it's free, and we'll even treat you to a free "yak-ride"!—Lynda L. Peart, Lake Lillian Civic and Commerce organization

Madam, I shall never say a mocking word about Lake Lillian or its yaks again.

My friend Dave is trying to organize a tontine. He says it's very simple. We each put an equal sum of money into an investment pool. Whoever outlives everybody else gets the money plus the accumu-lated earnings. What a strange concept! Put up your money, then hope for the ultimate misfortune to visit the other members of the group. I'm fascinated by the idea of it. What other chance do you have to gain from the deaths of your friends and acquaintances? It's the ultimate lottery. Who came up with this idea? Was it the forerun-ner of our current life insurance system? Have there been any famous tontines? Has anybody really raked in big bucks by winning a ton-tine? Should I join?—Barry Gardner, Washington, D.C.

This guy Dave—he doesn't have an odd gleam in his eye, does he? Tontines (pronounced TON-teens) are strange, but not as strange as he makes out. You don't have to wait until only one guy (presum-ably Dave) remains alive before they start paying off. On the con-

trary, they start paying off right away—the classic tontine basically is a weird annuity. You pay a specified nonreturnable sum of money and receive an annual interest payment for the rest of your life.

The twist is that the annual proceeds of the investment pool are divided among a smaller and smaller number of people as the participants die off. The last few people alive do very well indeed, and the last guy makes out like a bandit. The last survivor of one French tontine received an annual income of 73,000 livres from an original investment of 300 livres. She was ninety-six.

Tontines were dreamed up by a seventeenth-century schemer named Lorenzo Tonti and were adopted by the perennially cash-strapped French court as a way to raise money. Tontine subscriptions were sold to the public, with the participants divided into age groups to make it more sporting. After everybody died off, the original investment was turned over to the crown.

Ten tontines were raised in pre-Revolutionary France; the most successful raised 47 million livres. But they were a nightmare to administer and the big pot of cash was an invitation to steal, leading the crown to partially repudiate the last tontine in 1770. The resultant uproar, some argue, helped pave the way for the revolution of 1789.

The idea behind tontines was the same as that behind today's state lotteries: the government was trying to raise money by appealing to people's gambling instincts. The disadvantages for investors were pretty obvious. Even if the tontine were properly run, by the time the number of surviving investors shrank to the point that they were raking in big money, most were too creaky to enjoy it.

What's more, since payments halted on the investor's demise, a tontine left you with nothing to pass on to your children, the major selling point of ordinary life insurance. On the other hand, tontines did offer the benefit that the older and more decrepit you got, and thus the more in need of expensive care, the higher your income usually climbed.

Though tontines are usually associated with the excesses of monarchy, a modified version was tried by life insurance companies in the United States after the Civil War. In tontine life insurance, part of each participant's premiums bought conventional life insurance and the other part went into a tontine investment pool. After a predetermined period (usually twenty years), the tontine fund plus earnings was divided among the survivors.

The scheme proved wildly popular and is often credited with the life insurance industry's rapid early growth. But it was made illegal in New York in 1905 and later in other states, mainly because of corruption and fraud. Still, some historians say the fundamental idea was sound. I'll admit it sounds like a lot more fun than conventional life insurance; who knows, it might even have encouraged flabby Americans to watch out for their health to ensure they survived long enough to get a share. On the other hand, it does put you in the macabre position of rooting for your contemporaries to die—and of course some might be inclined to do more than root. My feeling is that if you do join Dave's little club, be sure you don't attend any reunions at isolated sites.

How much is "all the tea in China" worth? And why are so many people not willing to do things for it?—Charlie, Palm Beach via Madison

What do you mean, what is it worth? Who cares what it's worth? The impressive commodity here isn't supposed to be the money, it's the awesome acreage of tea. This bottom-line mentality sorely vexes my sensitive soul.

I regret to say that my most recent tea statistics are from 1983. However, the Chinese have not been very cooperative since that column about having the whole population jump off chairs at the same time (see "Earth: threats to orbital stability of," in my first book). Besides, my subscription to the *UN Food and Agriculture Organization Bulletin of Statistics* ran out. Be that as it may, in 1983 China produced 401,000 metric tons of tea out of a total world production of 2.06 million tons.

This is a pretty fair mess of tea, all right, and if you caved in and took it after all, there's no question you wouldn't have to go to the grocery store (for tea, anyway) for quite a while. In the scheme of things agricultural, however, it is not so much. In the same year China produced 169 million tons of rice, 4.3 million tons of rapeseed, and 1 million tons of jute, ambary, and hemp. Granted, "I wouldn't do that for all the jute, ambary, and hemp in China" does not stir the emotions the way tea does, but we have to keep things in perspective.

Also, I should point out that while all the tea in China might not tempt you, if somebody offered you all the tea in India, you might want to give it some thought. Indian production in 1983 was 588,000 tons, the largest output of any country. (China was #2.)

As for why so many people aren't willing to do things for all the tea in China, I don't know. Maybe they're still bugged about that little fracas in Tiananmen Square. But probably they just don't like tea.

What is the difference between MasterCard and Visa?—Jay, Evanston, Illinois

Precious little. In fact, some think the two cards ought to be merged—and it might be a good thing for consumers if they were. If the somewhat misleading "competing brands" business were stripped away, people might begin to understand what bank credit cards really were and learn to take better advantage of them.

Don't get me wrong. Visa and MasterCard are separate firms, and they do compete after a fashion. But they're not like Pepsi and Coke. One Pepsi is pretty much the same as any other Pepsi, but a Visa card is not necessarily the same as any other Visa card. Interest rates, fees, and other terms vary considerably. Though the Visa/MC split tends to disguise it, the real competition isn't between brands, it's among the thousands of banks who issue one or both of the cards.

Visa and MasterCard are not the multibillion-dollar conglomerates many people imagine, but actually are fairly small "membership associations" controlled by the banks that own them. They're a little like the American and National leagues. Fay Vincent may have thought he was in charge, but when you get right down to it, it's really the team owners (read: issuing banks) who call the shots.

A little history may clarify this. Visa started out in the 1960s as BankAmericard, which was issued by the Bank of America in San Francisco. To spread the card nationwide, B. of A. signed up other banks on a franchise basis. Each bank issued its own cards, set its own fees and other terms, and serviced its own customers under the BankAmericard name. Bank of America provided a clearinghouse for charge slips and merchant payments. Using a single brand with a central clearinghouse made for wide acceptance by merchants, which in turn made the cards popular with consumers.

But playing Seven Dwarves to B. of A.'s Snow White rankled the franchisee banks. At their prodding BankAmericard was spun off as a separate company and by 1977 had evolved into Visa International. Today some six thousand U.S. banks have issued 144 million Visa cards that in 1991 were used for 171 billion dollars' worth of purchases, making Visa the most popular credit card in the country. (MasterCard, with $99 billion, is #2.) But Visa remains a relatively small outfit, with just 1,200 employees in the United States. The top issuers of Visa cards (Citicorp, Chase Manhattan, and Bank of America rank 1, 2, and 3) are much bigger. A similar tale can be told about MasterCard.

What does all this mean to you, Mr. and Ms. Consumer? Simply that you shouldn't worry whether you've got Visa or MasterCard; rather, you should shop around for the bank offering the best deal on its cards. For example, many issuers charge 19.8 percent interest, but rates as low as 8 percent are available (although you need excellent credit to qualify). Bankcard Holders of America, a consumer group, will sell you a list of fifty-two no-annual-fee/low-interest issuers for $4; call 800-327-7300.

While there's not much difference between Visa and MC, there are a few distinctions in the plastic-payment racket to be aware of. Credit card versus charge card, for example. Visa and MC are credit cards—you borrow money, and the bank charges you hefty interest on your unpaid balance. If you're shrewd enough to find an issuer that charges no annual fee and rich enough to pay the bill as soon as it arrives, use of the card costs you virtually nothing. American Express, on the other hand, is a charge card—you're supposed to pay right away. AmEx makes its money by charging you an annual fee for the card. Why should anybody use a card that costs more and lets you do less? Good question. Basically it comes down to "prestige" and the fact that there's no credit limit (no stated limit, anyway) on American Express purchases.

Then there are "debit cards," where the money is taken directly out of your bank account. Debit cards are mainly a cash/check substitute; unlike credit cards, you pay now, not later. The credit limit consists of the amount of money you've got in your account. Still, debit cards are much more likely to be accepted by merchants than personal checks, and you won't invite thieves by lugging a fat bankroll. Equally important for the shopping-addicted: you won't be tempted (or able) to run up a big bill you can't pay.

The Visa Difference: The French Like It

One difference between MasterCard and Visa is that (as of a couple years ago, anyway) the stores, hotels, and restaurants I patronized in France tended to accept only the latter. I don't know if this represented a general trend throughout Europe or was characteristic just of certain regions. But as a credit card transaction is a lot simpler than fumbling with foreign currency or dealing with traveler's checks (particularly when your grasp of the language is shaky), anyone contemplating travel in Europe might consider favoring Visa over MasterCard.—David English, Somerville, Massachusetts

What does the S in the dollar sign represent? I read once that it is supposed to be a serpent. Also, what does the C in the cent sign represent?—M.J.R., U.S.A.

A *serpent*? Lord, if Florian Cajori were alive to hear such talk, it would just kill him. Professor Cajori dealt with this question definitively more than sixty years ago in *A History of Mathematical Notations*—not the ideal beach book, maybe, but one I heartily commend nonetheless.

The subject of the dollar sign was close to Professor Cajori's heart, and he could get quite indignant on the subject. As he tartly noted in his book, "About a dozen different theories [on the dollar sign's origin] have been advanced by men of imaginative minds, but not one of these would-be historians permitted himself to be hampered by the underlying facts." Among the deficient hypotheses:

1. The dollar sign was originally the letters *U* and *S* superimposed. The idea here is that the original dollar sign had two vertical lines, not one. Popular though this idea is, there is zero documentary evidence for it. Furthermore, Robert Morris, the Revolutionary War financier and the first U.S. official to use the dollar sign, made it with a single vertical stroke.
2. It's a version of the letters *IHS*, the Greek abbreviation of the name Jesus. No further comment required.
3. It was originally a *P* combined with an 8. The dollar, you'll recall, is descended from the Spanish dollar, also known as the "piece of eight" because it consisted of eight reals. Plausible, and as we shall see not that far from the truth, but still wrong.
4. The sign was inspired by the Spanish "pillar dollar," which, on one side, had two columns signifying the "pillars of Hercules" at Gibraltar. These were represented in the dollar sign by the two vertical lines, with the *S* being some sort of scroll wrapped around them.

So much for the tomfoolery; now to get serious. Professor Cajori contends that the dollar sign is an abbreviation for "pesos." Bear in mind that the Spanish dollar, also known as the *peso de 8 reales*, was the principal coin in circulation in the United States up until 1794, when we began minting our own dollars. In handwriting, "pesos" was usually abbreviated lowercase "ps," with S above and to the right of the P and with the hook on the latter written with one or two deep strokes. As time went on, the P and the S tended to get mashed together and the result was $.

The dollar sign and the PS abbreviation were used interchangeably from around 1775 until the end of the century, after which the latter faded from view. Professor Cajori backs up his argument with examples from manuscript, and I'm prepared to declare the matter settled.

As for the C in the cent sign, it seems safe to say it stands for "cent." However, you can never be too careful in this business, so I'm continuing to research the question. If there are any further developments, you'll be the first to know.

What's the origin of the word "buck," meaning a dollar?
—Anonymous, Denver, Colorado

Lots of speculation, no firm conclusions. Next time we start a language we have got to keep better notes. The leading theory at the moment is that buck comes from an old practice in poker. Evidently in the nineteenth century frontier card players were so thick they couldn't remember whose turn it was to deal from one hand to the next. So they placed a counter or token in front of the dealer du jour. This token was called a buck, since it was commonly a buck knife, whose handle was made of buck horn. When the time came for the dealer to surrender the job to someone new, he (you saw this coming) "passed the buck" to the new guy. Uh-huh.

A more plausible theory is that buck is short for buckskin, a common medium of exchange in trading with the Indians. As early as 1748 we have people writing, "Every cask of Whiskey shall be sold to you [Indians] for 5 Bucks." The transition to dollars seems only natural.

Curiously, "sawbuck," a ten-dollar bill, appears to be only indirectly related to buck. It got its name because some old ten-spots were denominated with Roman numeral Xs. The Xs looked like the X-shaped arms of the benches sawyers used to hold up logs for cutting. (Pictogrammic depiction: x-x.) The benches, which were vaguely similar to today's sawhorses, were called sawbucks.

Where did the word "dollar" come from, anyway?—Ellie Rosen, Santa Barbara, California

Finally, a colorful word-origin story that turns out to be true. In 1516 a local potentate opened a silver mine and later a mint at a locale in Bohemia called Joachimsthal (literally, "dale of Joachim"). The mint began churning out coins known as *Joachimsthalers*, soon shortened to *thalers* and called *dalers* by the Dutch. The English corrupted this to dollar and apparently began applying the word to any large silver foreign coin. In North America, for instance, English settlers referred to the Spanish piece of eight, then in wide circulation, as the Spanish dollar.

For several years after independence Americans used whatever oddball coinage they could get their hands on, Spanish dollars included. But by and by they began thinking it was time to establish their own currency. Thomas Jefferson strongly opposed using the English system and urged that the basic monetary unit be called the dollar, a term people were already familiar with. The Continental Congress said what the hell and declared the dollar the U.S. monetary unit in 1785, although no U.S. dollars were actually minted until 1794. By 1837 Washington Irving was making snide references to "the almighty dollar," and we've been slaves to the buck ever since.

Please enlighten your earth-conscious fans about the commerce in "pollution futures" at the Chicago Board of Trade. The term suggests that the pollution lobby has invented a sneaky way to poison the air at its own discretion. Don't the antipollution laws already in place preclude the creation of such "pollution rights"?—Eugene Blahut, Chicago

You're never going to make it in the PR game with that attitude, Eugene. For starters, you don't want to call them "pollution futures"; the CBOT would rather you said "clean air futures." The whole thing sounds a little Machiavellian, but therein lies the genius of it, as we shall see. Even the Environmental Defense Fund thinks pollution futures are cool.

Here's how it works. The federal Clean Air Act allows companies that reduce pollution to sell "pollution credits" to firms that are still besmirching the skies. The polluters can use the credits to avoid prosecution, having in effect purchased the right to pollute. Sounds sleazy, but actually it's pretty smart: it rewards companies that reduce their emissions at the expense of those who don't. It also greatly simplifies enforcement of the antipollution laws, since you don't get into stupid court battles with polluters who claim they just can't reduce emissions. You can't? Fine. Buy your way out of your problems.

There are a variety of pollution credit programs, most of them regional in scope. What the Chicago Board of Trade is involved in is a new national program intended to reduce sulphur dioxide emissions by coal-burning electric utilities. (SO_2 is thought to be a leading cause of acid rain.) Last year the feds selected the CBOT to hold an annual auction where utilities can buy "air emission allowances" (i.e., pollution rights).

The first auction was held March 29, 1993; 150,000 allowances sold for $21.4 million. The CBOT did it for free in the expectation that it could make money on the side by trading pollution . . . sorry, clean-air futures—that is, the right to buy a set quantity of emission allowances at a set price at a set future date. The utilities that buy and sell futures do so because they want to lock in their future revenues/expenses; the traders want to trade them because the future-contract price of the emission allowances will probably vary from the actual price, and they hope to make money on the difference. Sounds confusing, but if people can make millions selling pork-belly futures (and they have), they can do the same with pollution.

But, you object, they're trafficking in our planet's future! Well, yeah, I guess they are. But if we've learned one thing in America, it's that if people can make money on the deal, they're more likely to go along with the program. Besides, pollution futures are a game at which two can play. A Cleveland-based not-for-profit organization, the National Healthy Air License Exchange, said it planned to buy pollution allowances in order to make them too costly for businesses to use.

> *I've enclosed an ad for Infinity Reference Standard V speakers, which are described as "the embodiment of Infinity's obsession." These speakers, you will note, cost $50,000 a pair. Cecil, tell me: is there anybody out there so desperate for self-justification that they've actually plunked down $50,000 for a pair of speakers? If so, how many? Are there audiophiles who, after listening to a $5,000 pair of speaks and a $50,000 pair, can discern a difference? I always thought there was a threshold of sound beyond which the human ear just gives up. Maybe they sell themselves into slavery so their dogs can enjoy the finest in high fidelity entertainment.—Jim G., Cockeysville, Maryland*

Brace yourself, *acushla*. Not only do people buy these speakers, there's a *three-month waiting list* to get them. And they wonder where defense contractors got the idea to charge $600 for a toilet seat. Since the IRS-V was first introduced in late 1987, some fifteen to twenty sets have been sold. (This column was written in 1989.) Only two dealers in the country handle them, one in New York, the other in California. (Palo Alto, actually. Must be all those students.)

Why would anybody spend so much? God knows. As one observer has noted, speakers make a terrible status symbol. You can't wear them, eat them, or park them out front of the house. Then again, you can't crank up your Rolex and peel the first three layers of skin off your face, either, so I guess it just depends on what you're into.

As to whether you can hear the difference $45,000 (or in this columnist's case, $49,780) makes—well, Cecil can, of course. Cecil has ears so sensitive he can hear the clouds scrape. The question is whether it's worth paying all that money for what is really a trivial improvement.

After a certain point, as you rightly note, quality becomes a pretty ethereal thing. IRS-Vs have a frequency response of 15 to 45,000 cycles per second, far beyond the range of human hearing. This "may seem excessive," the company's sales literature notes, "but research indicates that overtones in [the high] region can affect the overtones we hear." Gotcha. Audio reviewers speak in awed tones of the speakers' "extension," "resolution," and "transparency," which doesn't convey much to the layman, but what it boils down to is this: the individual voices and instruments are very distinct, the illusion of live music is excellent, and the bass will rattle your kidneys.

Why do the speakers cost $50,000? Mostly, I suspect, because Infinity management has to keep up the payments on their Beamers, but partly also because the speakers are just so complex. You get four 7¼-foot speaker columns, two each for the right and left channels, containing a total of 108 separate speakers—seventy-two tweeters (treble), twenty-four midrange, and twelve woofers (bass).

Of these, only the bass speakers are your conventional cones; the others are "electromagnetic induction" speakers, which look something like heating grates. Each bass speaker column contains its own heavy-duty amplifier. You also get servo-controls, accelerometers, and nondiffracting enclosures. Computer-optimized passive crossovers utilizing optimal-Q chokes. Monster cable! Solen caps! All hand-finished in beautiful Brazilian rosewood. Everything is handmade, for that matter; that's why the three-month wait.

Needless to say, these are not speakers you want to hook up to some cheesy squeakbox you got from Radio Shack. It's expected you'll probably spend another fifty to one hundred grand for additional amps (two required) and other components, not to mention modifications to your house. You'll probably want a specially engineered room for maximum listening pleasure. You may want to reinforce the floor, since these babies weigh 1,500 pounds all told, and you'll also need to run in heavy wiring, since the bass speakers alone draw 2,000 watts per channel.

Too much trouble? Too much money? No prob. Twelve thou will get you a comparatively lightweight IRS Beta system, and if you're really caught short this month, you might even settle for the Gamma or Delta systems, $7,000 and $5,500 respectively. Unless you invite me over (and I'm not the kind to make a fuss), probably nobody will be able to tell the difference.

And Now, If You're Looking to Spend Some *Real* Money

You recently addressed a reader's question on the Infinity Reference Standard V speakers, priced at $50,000 per pair. The reader seemed to feel that these were the most expensive speakers he had ever heard of, and I thought you might not be aware of the Wilson Audio WAMM speakers, list price $80,000 per pair. These are custom-made speakers; they start making them when you place the order (and fork over the cash, I suppose, or at least a substantial deposit). They are supposed to be simply awesome, and I'm sure we are thinking they'd better be. Second, IRS-Vs are handled by Excalibur Audio in Alexandria, Virginia, and until recently you could just walk in off the street and audition a pair with no warning to the store. I did it. I spent 30 minutes alone with those monsters! Yes, it was amazing.

Also, how about that Goldmund Turntable for $15,000, not including phono cartridge, to go with your WAMMs? And some $100 per foot Kimble Kable to hook it all up with?—Gary Broyhill, Washington, D.C.

Recently a friend and I got into a debate over the price of stamps in the United States. I was complaining that the price of a stamp in this country was too high, and talk of a price increase next year I found too odious to contemplate. My companion, who hails from the continent, claimed that we Americans are spoiled, and that the 29-cent stamp was probably the cheapest letter stamp in the world, and most assuredly in Europe. We would appreciate it if you could enlighten us as to which countries give the best bang for the postal buck. A six-pack of Molson is at stake here.—Robert

A six-pack? You louse, make it a case, preferably of some deserving American brand. Your friend is right. Excluding countries that subsidize their postal services, the United States has the lowest rates for standard-size letters of any industrial country (or at least any of the twenty industrial countries I was able to dig up rates for). Letter rates for our two principal economic competitors, Japan and Germany, are more than twice as high. Americans also pay lower overall taxes than most of the developed world, and yet persist in moaning about the crushing cost of government. Herewith a list of comparative letter rates, starting with most expensive (exchange rates as of September 2, 1993):

1. Germany, 60 cents (1 mark)
2. Japan, 59 cents (62 yen)
3. Denmark, 55 cents (3.75 krone)
4. Switzerland, 55 cents (80 centimes)
5. Austria, 47 cents (5.5 schillings)
6. Norway, 46 cents (3.3 krone)
7. Ireland, 45 cents (32 pence)
8. Italy, 44 cents (700 lire)
9. France, 43 cents (2.5 French francs)
10. Netherlands, 43 cents (.80 guilder)
11. Belgium, 42 cents (15 Belgian francs)
12. United Kingdom, 36 cents (24 pence)
13. Finland, 35 cents (2.10 markka)
14. Sweden, 35 cents (2.9 krona)
15. Canada, 35 cents (42 Canadian cents plus—get this—7 percent goods and services tax)
16. Australia, 30 cents (45 Australian cents)
17. United States, 29 cents

Letter rates in the following countries are government-subsidized:

18. Greece, 26 cents (60 drachma)
19. Portugal, 22 cents (38 escudos)
20. Spain, 20 cents (27 pesetas); in-city letters are even cheaper at 13 cents (17 pesetas). Sounds great, but since subsidies are paid out of taxes, we may be sure the Spanish public pays one way or another.

Why are U.S. rates lower? Economies of scale have something to do with it, of course. European countries typically also have much higher labor costs. Postal work is considered a prestige job in much of Europe, and workers there undergo extensive training and enjoy many perks—including, believe it or not, postal worker resorts.

Do European countries get better service for the money? Not

necessarily. Germany used to promise overnight service to any domestic address, but since reunification has not consistently been able to deliver on this. Generally speaking, though, service, in most northern European countries at least, is excellent. Considering what it costs, it ought to be. Kwitcherbitchen.

Chapter 7

Oops

I am enclosing a copy of a recent column in Parade *magazine by Marilyn vos Savant, who supposedly is listed in the "Guinness Book of World Records Hall of Fame" for "highest IQ." A writer asks Marilyn for an answer to the following riddle:*

"If a hen and a half can lay an egg and a half in a day and a half, how many hens does it take to lay six eggs in six days?"

Marilyn answers as follows:

"My father loved this one, too, but I didn't get it then, and I don't get it now. What's the problem? Is 'one hen' too obvious? If a hen

and a half can lay an egg and a half, etc., that means a hen can lay an egg in a day. And if just one hen lays one egg a day for six days, we'd have six eggs right there, wouldn't we?"

I'm quite sure this is incorrect and that the answer is one and a half hens. What do you think? I've enclosed a copy of my solution.
—Margo Carraher-Sommer, Chester, Virginia

"Think" is not the operative term here, Margo. Cecil knows. What he knows in this instance is that you're right and Marilyn is wrong. If you'll permit me to adapt your solution a bit, we can put the basic proposition this way:

1½ hens × 1½ days × rate per hen per day = 1½ eggs

We convert the fractions thus:

¾ hens × ¾ days × rate per hen per day = ¾ eggs

To get rid of the fractions, Marilyn vos Savant presumably multiplies both sides by ⅔ to get:

1 hen × 1 day × rate per hen per day = 1 egg

Rate per hen per day = 1 egg

As a moment's study will make clear, however, Marilyn has done her algebra wrong. If you multiply both sides by ⅔ what you really get is:

1 hen × ¾ days × rate per hen per day = 1 egg

¾ rate per hen per day = 1 egg

Rate per hen per day = ⅔ egg

In other words, a hen lays an egg every day and a half, or four eggs in six days. If you want six eggs in six days, therefore, you need one and a half hens (your answer), not one (Marilyn's answer). And no excuses about how half a hen can't lay anything; we're talking *science* here. Marilyn vos Savant, by way of contrast, is talking off the top of her head.

Ha!

In Marilyn vos Savant's "Ask Marilyn" column in the July 1, 1990, *Parade* magazine, a reader gives essentially the answer above, to which Ms. Savant replies:

Good catch, you guys! Those of you who said "one and a half hens" are right, and my "one hen" is wrong. . . . And here I'd always assumed this was one of those "How much wood would a woodchuck chuck?" kind of tongue twisters! It's actually a logic puzzle.

Round 2

I was perversely flipping through the Parade *section of my Sunday newspaper when I stumbled upon Marilyn vos Savant's "Ask Marilyn" column. Even more perversely, I read it. It wasn't a total loss, though, because it appears she made another mistake, even worse than the one you pointed out in a very entertaining column a few months ago. Here's the question:*

Suppose you're on a game show and you're given the choice of three doors: Behind one door is a car; behind the others, goats. You pick a door, say #1, and the host, who knows what's behind the doors, opens another door, say #3, which has a goat. He then says to you, "Do you want to pick Door #2?" Is it to your advantage to switch your choice?

ANSWER: Yes; you should switch. The first door has a one-third chance of winning, but the second door has a two-thirds chance. Here's a good way to visualize what happened. Suppose there are a *million* doors, and you pick Door #1. Then the host, who knows what's behind the doors and will always avoid the one with the prize, opens them all except Door #777,777. You'd switch to that door pretty fast, wouldn't you?

Correct me if I'm wrong, Cecil, but aren't the odds equal for the remaining doors—one in two?—Michael Grice, Madison
P.S.: If the questions she answers are any indication of the intellect of the general population, this country is in a lot of trouble..

This is getting ridiculous. You're perfectly correct. If there are three doors your chance of picking the right one are one in three. Knock one out of contention and the chances of either of the remaining doors being the right one are equal: one in two. This business about a million doors is a bit of pretzel logic that maybe only somebody with the world's highest IQ (according to *Guinness*, anyway) can properly appreciate. *Parade*'s editors really ought to read the copy before they put it in the magazine.

Cecil 1, Marilyn 1

I certainly won't be the only one to catch your latest error, but the perverse joy I get pointing it out offsets the small chance this letter has of being printed. I refer to your answer to Michael Grice's question about the game-show conundrum—one prize, three doors, you pick Door #1, the host opens Door #3 to reveal no prize. Should you switch to the remaining door or stick with your original choice? You agreed with Grice that the odds of winning are equal for both—one in two. Wrong! The easiest route to the truth is to notice that resolving never to switch is equivalent to not having the option to switch, in which case, I'm sure you'll agree, the odds of winning remain one in three. Switching, therefore, has a two-thirds chance at the prize.

Your mistake was not realizing that opening Door #3 tells you more about Door #2 than about the door you originally picked. The reason for this is subtle. The host, in picking Door #3, does not choose from the full set of doors but rather from the subset of doors you did not pick. Each subset's probability of winning does not change, but the probability for a particular door in the second subset does. If you don't get it find a friend who looks like Monty Hall and play twenty rounds. It will soon become obvious which strategy wins most often.—Robert E. Johanson, Chicago

Not so fast, amigo. I'll admit I wasn't paying much attention when I wrote that column, assumed this was another instance of carelessness on Marilyn vos Savant's part, and fell into a sucker's trap. But now that I've had a chance to study the matter, it's apparent there is a subtlety that eluded you as well.

First, though, I feel obliged to eat some crow. The "common sense" answer, the one I gave, is that if you've got two doors and one prize, the chances of picking the right door are fifty-fifty. Given certain key assumptions, which we'll discuss below, this is wrong.

Why? A different example will make it clear. Suppose our task is to pick the ace of spades from a deck of cards. We select one card.

The chance we got the right one is one in fifty-two. Now the dealer takes the remaining fifty-one cards, looks at them, and turns over fifty, none of which is the ace of spades. One card remains. Should you pick it? Of course. Why? Because (1) the chances were fifty-one in fifty-two that the ace was in the dealer's stack, and (2) the dealer then *systematically eliminated all (or most) of the wrong choices*. The chances are overwhelming—fifty-one out of fifty-two, in fact—that the single remaining card is the ace of spades.

Which brings me to the subtlety I mentioned earlier. Your analysis of the game-show question is correct, Bobo, only if we make several assumptions: (1) Monty Hall knows which door conceals the prize, (2) he only opens doors that do NOT conceal the prize, and (3) *he always opens a door*. Assumptions #1 and #2 are reasonable; #3 is not.

Monty Hall is not stupid. He knows, empirically at least, that if he *always* opens one of the doors without a prize behind it, the odds greatly favor contestants who switch to the remaining door. He also knows the contestants (or at least the highly vocal studio audience) will tumble to this eventually. To make the game more interesting, therefore, a reasonable strategy for him would be to open a door *only when the contestant has guessed right in the first place*. In that case the contestant would be a fool to change his pick.

But that's absurd, you say. If Monty only opened a door when the contestant had chosen correctly in the first place, no one would ever switch. Exactly—so it's likely Monty adds one last twist. Most of the time he only opens a door when the contestant has chosen correctly—*but not always*. In other words, he tries to bluff the contestants, then counterbluff them.

This strategy changes the odds dramatically. In fact, it can be shown that if Monty always opens a door when the contestant is right and half the time when he's wrong—a perfectly rational approach—over the long haul the odds of the prize being behind Door #1 versus Door #2 are fifty-fifty.

The lesson here is that probability isn't the cut-and-dried science you might assume from high school math class. Instead it involves a lot of educated guesses about human behavior. I'll admit I jumped to an unwarranted conclusion on this one. Don't be too sure you haven't done the same.

The Last You'll Ever Have to Read About This

To beat the dead horse of Monty Hall's game-show problem: Marilyn was wrong, and you were right the first time.—Eric Dynamic, Berkeley, California

You really blew it. As any fool can plainly see, when the game-show host opens a door you did not pick and then gives you a chance to change your pick, he is starting a new game. It makes no difference whether you stay or switch, the odds are fifty-fifty.—Emerson Kamarose, San Jose, California

Suppose our task is to pick the ace of spades from a deck of cards. We select one card. The chance we got the ace of spades is one in fifty-two. Now the dealer takes the remaining fifty-one cards. At this point his odds are fifty-one in fifty-two. If he turns over one card which is not the ace of spades our odds are now one in fifty-one, his are fifty in fifty-one. After fifty wrong cards our odds are one in two, his are one in two. The idea that his odds remain fifty-one in fifty-two as more and more cards in his hand prove wrong is just plain crazy.—John Ratnaswamy, Chicago; similarly from Greg, Madison;

Stuart Silverman, Chicago; Frank Mirack, Arlington, Virginia; Dave Franklin, Boston; many others

Give it up, gang. It was bad enough that I screwed this up. But you guys have had the benefit of my miraculously lucid explanation of the correct answer! Since you won't listen to reason, all I can tell you is to play the game and see what happens. One writer says he played his buddy using the faulty logic in my first column and got skunked out of the price of dinner. Several other doubters wrote computer programs that, to their surprise, showed they were wrong and Marilyn vos Savant was right.

A friend of mine did suggest another way of thinking about the problem that may help clarify things. Suppose we have the three doors again, one concealing the prize. You pick Door #1. Now you're offered this choice: open Door #1, or open Door #2 *and* Door #3. In the latter case you keep the prize if it's behind either door. You'd rather have a two-in-three shot at the prize than one-in-three, wouldn't you? If you think about it, the original problem offers you basically the same choice. Monty is saying in effect: you can keep your one door or you can have the other two doors, one of which (a nonprize door) I'll open for you. Still don't get it? Then at least have the sense to keep quiet about it.

Other correspondents have passed along some interesting variations on the problem. Here's a couple from Jordan Drachman of Stanford, California:

- There is a card in a hat. It is either the ace of spades or the king of spades, with equal probability. You take another identical ace of spades and throw it into the hat. You then choose a card at random from the hat. You see it is an ace. What are the odds the original card in the hat was an ace? (Answer: 2/3.)
- There is a family with two children. You have been told this family has a daughter. What are the odds they also have a son, assuming the biological odds of having a male or female child are equal? (Answer: 2/3.)

Finally, this one from a friend. Suppose we have a lottery with 10,000 "scratch-off-the-dot" tickets. The prize: a car. Ten thousand people buy the tickets, including you. 9,998 scratch off the dots on their tickets and find the message YOU LOSE. Should you offer big money to the remaining ticketholder to exchange tickets with you? (Answer: hey, after all this drill, *you* figure it out.)

So I Lied—*This* Is the Last You'll Ever Have to Read About This (I Hope)

The answers to the logic questions submitted by Jordan Drachman were illogical. In the first problem he says there is an equal chance the card placed in a hat is either an ace of spades or a king of spades. An ace of spades is then added. Now a card is drawn from the hat—an ace of spades. Drachman asks what the odds are that the original card was an ace. Drawing a card does not affect the odds for the original card. They remain one in two that it was an ace, not two in three as stated.

In the second problem we are told a couple has two children, one of them a girl. Drachman then asks what the odds are the other child is a boy, assuming the biological odds of having a male or female child are equal. His answer: two in three. How can the gender of one child affect the gender of another? It can't. The answer is one in two.—Adam Martin and Anna Davlantes, Evanston, Illinois

In a recent column you asked, "Suppose we have a lottery with 10,000 'scratch-off-the-dot' tickets. The prize: a car. Ten thousand people buy the tickets, including you. 9,998 scratch off the dots on their tickets and find the message YOU LOSE. Should you offer big money to the remaining ticketholder to exchange tickets with you?"

If you think the answer is "yes," you are wrong. If you think the answer is "no," then you are intentionally misleading your readers.— Jim Balter, Los Angeles

Do you think I could possibly screw this up twice in a row? Of course I could. But not this time. Cecil is well aware the answer to the lottery question is "no"—if there are only two tickets left, they have equal odds of being the winner. The difference between this and the Monty Hall question is that we're assuming Monty *knows* where the prize is and uses that information to select a nonprize

door to open, whereas in the lottery example the fac
9,998 tickets are losers is a matter of chance. I put
the end of a line of dissimilar questions as a goof—not very
but old habits die hard.

The answers given to Jordan Drachman's questions—two in three
in both cases—were correct. The odds of the original card being an
ace were one in two before it was placed in the hat. We are now trying to determine what card was actually chosen based on subsequent
events. Here are the possibilities:

1. The original card in the hat was an ace. You threw in an ace and
   then picked the *original* ace.
2. The original card in the hat was an ace. You threw in an ace and
   then picked the *second* ace.
3. The original card was a king. You threw in an ace. You then picked
   the ace.

In two of three cases, the original card was an ace. Q.E.D.

The second question is much the same. The possible gender combinations for two children are:

1. Child A is female and Child B is male.
2. Child A is female and Child B is female.
3. Child A is male and Child B is female.
4. Child A is male and Child B is male.

We know one child is female, eliminating choice #4. In two of the
remaining three cases, the female child's sibling is male. Q.E.D.

Granted, the question is subtle. Consider: we are to be visited by
the two kids just described, at least one of whom is a girl. It's a matter of chance who arrives first. The first child enters—a girl. The
second knocks. What are the odds it's a boy? Answer: one in two.
Paradoxical but true. (Thanks to Len Ragozin of New York City.)

Cecil is happy to say he has identified the apparent originator of
the Monty Hall question, Steve Selvin, a UCal–Berkeley prof (cf.
American Statistician, February 1975). Cecil is happy because he can
now track Steve down and have him assassinated, as he richly deserves for all the grief he has caused. Hey, just kidding, doc. But
next time you have a brainstorm, do us a favor and keep it to yourself.

The following geometry problem has haunted me for thirty years. Every math teacher, Ph.D., engineer, etc., I've shown it to was stumped. Now it's your turn. Given any triangle ABC, extend the baseline and bisect the interior and exterior angles at A and B. Extend these four new lines until they intersect at D and E. Prove DCE is a straight line. (It looks straight, but no one can prove it.) How about it?—John Ricketts, Madison

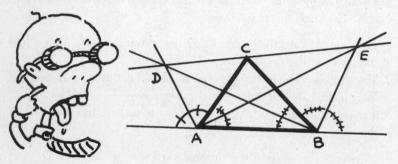

We ordinarily don't truck with pure (as opposed to applied) mathematics in this column, but since Cecil's stock in the nation's math departments has pretty much gone into the tank after the recent Monty Hall debacle, the time has come to show a little inductive flash. (Sure, it's the testosterone talking, but you ought to see the abuse I got.) This one was made easier by a handy geometrical fact that, being a master of suspense, I will conceal until later. First the proof:

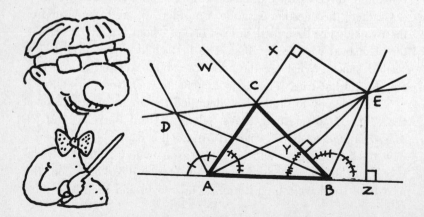

1. Extend AC and BC. Put W on BC as shown. Draw segments EX, EY, and EZ perpendicular to AC, CB, and AB.
2. Triangles EBY and EBZ are congruent (i.e., equal) because of the angle-angle-side theorem. Proof: angle EYB = EZB (both 90), angle EBY = EBZ (given), segment BE = BE.
3. Therefore segments EY and EZ are congruent.
4. Triangles AEX and AEZ are congruent. Proof: same reasoning as step 2.
5. Therefore segments EZ and EX are congruent.
6. Since EY = EZ and EZ = EX, EY = EX.
7. Triangles ECX and ECY are congruent because of the hypotenuse-leg theorem. Proof: they are both right triangles; hypotenuse CE = CE; EY = EX (step 6).
8. Therefore angle XCE = YCE.
9. Angle WCD = ACD. Proof: proceed as in steps 1–8.
10. Angle ACD + DCW + WCX = angle ACX = 180 (whole is sum of parts; angle ACX lies on a straight line).
11. Angle WCA = XCB (vertical angles).
12. Angle XCE = DCA (both are half of equal angles).
13. Angle DCW + WCX + XCE = 180 (substitution).
14. Angle DCE = 180 (whole is sum of parts). Q.E.D.

You're now thinking one of two things: (1) who cares? or (2) damn, Cecil sure is smart. Well, don't be too impressed. I knew the feet of the altitudes of any triangle DEF form a triangle ABC whose angles the altitudes bisect. What's more, circles centered on D, E, and F can be drawn such that each is tangent to the lines containing the sides of ABC. (Another tritangent circle can be centered on the point where the altitudes of DEF cross.) Given that, the rest is obvious.

Since this column was originally published I've gotten a half dozen letters from people who think the preceding is inelegant (!) and offer what they regard as a superior alternative. While the proofs vary in the details, they have one common feature: at some point in the proceedings they talk about "triangle ADE" and/or "triangle BDE." In the context of the proof, the implicit assumption is that points D, C, and E lie on one side of this triangle—that they are colinear, in other words. Sorry, folks, but that's what you're supposed to *prove*.

Marilyn vos Savant recently answered the following question in her column in Parade magazine:

"Suppose you make $10,000 a year. Your boss offers you a choice: you can have a $1,000 raise (not a bonus) at the end of each year, or you can have a $300 raise at the end of each six months. Which do you choose?" Marilyn says you should choose the $300 raise. "At the end of one year," she says, "you'd be ahead $300, at the end of three years, $700; and at the end of five years, $1,100."

Could you please double-check Marilyn's answer? I don't see how she comes up with these numbers.—Name Withheld, Novato, California

I shouldn't do this, but I can't resist. Not that you're going to catch me saying Marilyn vos Savant is wrong again. On the contrary, her response is 100 percent correct. It's just not necessarily the answer to the question she was asked.

Given the question as stated, many people would interpret a $300 raise to mean a $300 increase in annual salary—that is, after six months your salary would rise from $10,000 to $10,300 per year. In your first year you'd made $10,150—$5,000 the first six months, $5,150 the second. Under that interpretation there's no way a semi-annual $300 raise would beat out an annual $1,000 raise.

But that's not what Marilyn has in mind. She interprets the question this way: would you rather have your $10,000 annual salary increased $1,000 each year or your $5,000 half-year salary increased $300 every six months?

Put that way, the correct choice is the $300 raise. In the first six months you'd make $5,000, the second six months $5,300, the third six months $5,600, and so on. A semiannual *raise* of $300 is an annual *increase* of $600, and if you have two such increases per year your annualized salary hike is $1,200. Under that scenario Marilyn's right in saying you'd be $700 per year ahead after three years and $1,100 after five years. The difficulty here is that the question is ambiguous. So let's not blame Marilyn vos Savant, but rather the befuddled soul who wrote the original letter. It's a strategy that usually works for me.

Two questions. First, does it bug you when people write you questions on bar napkins, like I am? Second, as we leave a stoplight in our car and look at the wheels of the car next to us, we notice that when the RPMS reach a certain point we get the optical illusion of reverse rotation. What causes this?—J.R. Newman, Washington, D.C.

After seventeen years of mystery mail, J.R., believe me, the only letters that bug me are the ones that smell, bubble, or tick. I'll tell you one thing, though—if you notice the reverse-rotation phenomenon looking out your window, you're a lot more pixilated than I thought. Reverse rotation usually only shows up when you're watching a movie.

Basically what you're seeing is a strobe (i.e., stop-action) effect. A movie camera operates at twenty-four frames per second. If a wheel is turning at some multiple of twenty-four revolutions per second, the spokes will be in the exact same position every time the shutter opens. Ergo, the wheel will appear to be motionless (though possibly blurred) when the movie is played back. If the wheel now begins to slow down slightly, it doesn't get a chance to rotate all the way

around to its original position before the shutter opens again. Therefore it appears to be rotating backward.

Don't get it? Then try the following demonstration, courtesy of
*Rainbows, Curve Balls & Other Wonders of the Natural World Ex-
plained* by science writer Ira Flatow. Get a hand eggbeater. While
rotating the handle, look at a TV picture through the eggbeater's
blades. (For best results, point the eggbeater at the TV and look
through the blades the long way.) When you get to thirty revolutions
per second, the speed at which a TV picture flashes, the blades will
appear to be motionless. Slow down slightly and the blades appear
to rotate backward. Fun for the whole family.

Incidentally, this is one of the few times you'll see reverse rotation
outside the movies. People tell me they've noticed it on other occasions in real life as well, but they can never recall the circumstances.
I'll concede it's a possibility, but absent some mechanism for flickering or blinking, it's damned unlikely. If you want to dispute the issue, therefore, be prepared to dish up some facts.

Facts au Jus

*You were skeptical that J.R. could see the stroboscopic illusion of
reverse rotation while looking out of his car at the wheels of other
cars. You said this illusion is usually only visible in movies. Actually,
there's nothing surprising about what he saw if the cars were illuminated by artificial lighting rather than sunlight. When powered by alternating current, gas discharge lamps (which include neon, mercury
vapor, sodium vapor, and fluorescent tubes) flicker at twice the frequency of the power line (i.e., 120 times per second on a standard
sixty-cycle line). In each cycle of current the power peaks twice (once
with positive voltage and once with negative) and twice goes to zero,
and the light output varies accordingly.*

*Though 120 flickers per second is too fast for us to perceive directly,
such lamps can produce stroboscopic effects. Mercury and sodium vapor
lamps are widely used for streetlighting, and under such lights J.R. could
easily have seen what he said he saw. The effect may be less intense
under fluorescent lights because the fluorescence does not die away completely between each half-cycle, but you may be able to see it if you play*

with a variable-speed fan lit only by fluorescent light. (I've often seen the effect with centrifuges in fluorescently lit labs.) Incandescent bulbs have very little flicker because the filament doesn't cool off much in 1/120th of a second.—Barry Gehm, Ph.D., Chicago

"Fluorescently lit labs"? Such language. Nonetheless, Cecil is prepared to concede you're right, not because you're a Ph.D.—hey, we all God's chillun roun' here—but because he and Mrs. Adams spent a hair-raising hour driving like maniacs on the expressways trying to find out if the phenomenon in question actually occurs. Alas (for me), it does.

To tell you the truth, Mrs. Adams raised the possibility of reverse rotation being caused by flickering streetlights prior to the publication of the original column. But I blithely dismissed the idea on the grounds that what most people think is reverse rotation is really just reflections off the hubcaps from passing streetlights. Indeed, having done the research, I remain convinced that nine times out of ten that's what they *are* seeing. The tenth time, though, no question they're observing a genuine strobe effect.

For best results, check out a car with dark cutouts (bolt holes, whatever) spaced around the rim of the hubcaps—that way you won't be deceived by reflections. On a car with wheels twenty-two inches in diameter and having eight cutouts per wheel, the cutouts will appear stationary at fifty-nine MPH. If the car slows down slightly, the cutouts will appear to rotate slowly backward.

Incidentally, I got a dozen letters on this topic in a single mail. You guys are such wankers. At the Straight Dope, however, we don't let mere ego get in the way of the facts.

I've heard the following expression from people all over the country and on television. It makes absolutely no sense: "That's the exception that proves the rule."

Is this a bastardization of some other phrase? If not, what does it mean?—Lorraine N., East Weymouth, Massachusetts

Don't you get it? The whole *point* of this saying is that it doesn't make sense. It's what you say to confound your enemies when your argument has been shot out from under you by some pesky counterexample. From the point of view of advancing the debate it's about one jump ahead of "yo mama," but it beats standing there with your mouth open.

To be sure, a few scholarly types have tried to make excuses for "The exception proves the rule," as the quotation books usually phrase it. They say it comes from the medieval Latin aphorism *Exceptio probat regulam*. *Probat* means "prove" in the sense of "test," as in "proving ground," or "The proof is in the pudding." So "The exception proves the rule" means that a close look at exceptions helps us determine a rule's validity.

If Latinists understand it that way, however, they're pretty much alone. I've looked up citations of this saying dating back to 1664, and in every case it was used in the brain-dead manner we're accustomed to today—that is, to suggest that non-conforming cases, by the mere fact of their existence, somehow confirm or support a generalization. Obviously they do nothing of the kind. We like to think proverbs become proverbial because they're true; this one is an exception. It certainly doesn't prove the rule.

Exceptional Stupidity

I was surprised to see the question in your column about the exception proving the rule because I had always assumed the saying came from the "rule" that "there's an exception to every rule." Thus the mere existence of an exception to a rule proves the validity of the rule. No?—V.M., Berkeley, California

No. If all it takes for a rule to be valid is that it have an exception, *every* rule would be valid—except, of course, rules without exceptions. Obviously not an argument you want to take very far.

Exceptional Stupidity, Part Two

Your reply to the question, "What does 'That's the exception that proves the rule' mean?" was not quite right. The quote refers to a lo-

gician's axiom: that which can never be false can likewise never be true. If a statement cannot be admitted ever to be false, then it is a concealed tautology, i.e., a dogma. An instance of a proposition's not-being-the-case serves to affirm its existential validity, assuming it does not commit a violation of the rules of logic. Both logical validity AND existential verification are required for one to justly assert that such-and-such is true.—Max L., Santa Barbara, California

You're talking about "falsifiability," Max. If no conceivable evidence could prove a given statement false, then the statement is meaningless. For example, if a psychic comes out with predictions so vague they can't possibly be proven wrong, then the predictions are baloney. Note, however, that contrary evidence merely has to be *conceivable*. If contrary evidence *actually exists*, the statement is more than falsifiable, it's false. To put it as clearly as I can, THE EXISTENCE OF AN EXCEPTION DOES NOT VALIDATE THE FREAKING RULE! Quite the opposite. But anybody who can sling around phrases like "existential validity" deserves credit for trying.

Part Three and Counting

Okay, okay, I acknowledge your general brilliance, but I can't stand it another minute. The appropriate provenance of the saying "It's the exception that proves the rule" is psychology, not logic. You can have a rule without an exception, but you can't have an exception without a rule. Therefore, if something appears to be an exception, that indicates that a rule must exist. If you reflexively think of something as an exception, then you can infer that you've already, perhaps unconsciously, postulated a rule. Perceptually, the exception throws the rule into relief. It's analogous to "It's turning on the light that proves you were in the dark." Read it as, "It's the [recognition of an] exception that proves the [existence of a] rule." Geez, it's just a saying, and not a bad one at that.—Kyle Gann, Lewisburg, Pennsylvania

What is this, proverb as Rorschach test? Everybody I've heard from has a different take on this. There is nothing in the literature or common experience to support your farfetched interpretation.

The Last Word on Exceptions

I hate to have to correct Cecil Adams, but the business about "the exception proves the rule" in the latest Straight Dope seems way wide of the mark. The proverb's meaning must be expounded not in the context of natural or psychological law but of civil law. Alan Bliss, in A Dictionary of Words and Phrases in Current English, *has the following to say about the origin of this phrase:* "Exception probat regulam [Lat.], the exception proves the rule. A legal maxim of which the complete text is: exceptio probat [or (con)firmat] regulam in casibus non exceptis—'the fact that certain exceptions are made (in a legal document) confirms that the rule is valid in all other cases.'"

The application is this. Suppose a law is stated in such a way as to include an exception, e.g., "Parking is prohibited on this street from 7:00 A.M. to 7:00 P.M., Sundays and holidays excepted." The explicit mention of the exception means that NO other exceptions are to be inferred. Thus we should take the Latin verb probare *in the maxim to have the sense of "to increase the force of."—Hugh Miller, Chicago*

Hmm. It grieves me to say this, but you're right. While the interpretation I gave, namely, that the exception *tests* the rule, has a long history (it dates back at least to 1893), I'll concede that your take on it is the original sense of the proverb.

That said, your example could use a little work. We need something that better conveys the import of this ancient maxim. I have just the thing—an illustration from the Roman orator Cicero, sometimes cited as the source of the legal doctrine in question.

Cicero was defending one Bilbo. (No relation to Frodo.) Bilbo was a non-Roman who was accused of having been illegally granted Roman citizenship. The prosecutor argued that treaties with some non-Roman peoples explicitly prohibited them from becoming Roman citizens. The treaty with Bilbo's homeboys had no such clause, but the prosecutor suggested one should be inferred.

Nonsense, said Cicero. *"Quod si exceptio facit ne liceat, ubi non sit exceptum . . ."* Oops, I keep forgetting how rusty folks are on subjunctives. Cicero said, If you prohibit something in certain cases, you imply that the rest of the time it's permitted. To put it another way, the explicit statement of an exception proves that a rule to the contrary prevails otherwise.

You can see where an argument like this would come in handy in traffic court. What's more, it's basically what Kyle Gann was arguing in his letter, although his "psychological" angle obscured matters a bit. Accordingly I withdraw my unkinder remarks.

Still, whatever the original significance of the proverb, we should recognize that its many latter-day interpretations have taken on a life of their own. Since there is not much chance of stamping these out en masse, we may as well resign ourselves to trying to boost the sensible interpretations and suppress the rest. Here it seems to me that the interpretation I initially favored, that the exception tests the rule, comes off pretty well.

I am delighted to find ammunition for this view in H. W. Fowler's respected *Dictionary of Modern English Usage* (1965), which distinguishes five possible senses of "The exception proves the rule." Sense #1 is the legal (i.e., your) interpretation; senses #3, #4, and #5 are various common constructions of the saying, which Fowler regards as more or less slipshod. But he thinks more highly of sense #2, which we may state this way: an apparent exception to a rule may serve on closer examination to strengthen it. By way of example he writes,

> We have concluded by induction that Jones the critic, who never writes a kindly notice, lacks the faculty of appreciation. One day a warm eulogy of an anonymous novel appears over his signature; we see that this exception destroys our induction. Later it comes out that the anonymous novelist is Jones himself; our conviction that he lacks the faculty of appreciation is all the stronger for the apparent exception when once we have found out that, being *self*-appreciation, it is outside the scope of the rule— which, however, we now modify to exclude it, saying that he lacks the faculty of appreciating *others*.... These kinds of exception ... prove the rule not when they are seen to be exceptions, but when they have been shown to be either

outside of or reconcilable with the principle they seem to contradict.

This is not far removed from "the exception tests the rule." Under the somewhat embarrassing circumstances, that's about the best I can expect.

Sex Education

So how do porcupines mate? My zoologist roommates give me the unsatisfying explanation that they put their needles down during the act. But I'm convinced that even with needles down, mating for male porcupines must be a very painful experience.—Jean François Tremblay, Montreal, Quebec

Well, one account of porcupine romance (in *North American Porcupine*, Uldis Roze, 1989) does begin this way: "Somewhere ahead, a porcupine is screaming." However, it's not what you think. The screaming porcupine is a female letting an ardent male know she's not in the mood. Male porcupines may give vent to the occasional scream as well, but it's from frustration, not pain: the female is only sexually receptive eight to twelve hours per year.

Porcupine sex is not the exercise in S&M you might imagine, but it does have its kinky aspects. I quote from Roze: "Perhaps the strangest aspect of the interaction is male urine-hosing of the female. The male approaches on his hind legs and tail, grunting in a low tone. His penis springs erect. He then becomes a urine cannon, squirting high-pressure jets of urine at the female. Everything suggests the urine is fired by ejaculation, not released by normal bladder pressure. . . . In less than a minute, a female may be thoroughly wetted from nose to tail."

So much for foreplay. If the female decides now is the time, she hoists up her rump a bit and raises her tail, the underside of which is quill-less, and curves it up over her back, covering the quills thereon and exposing her genitalia. The male then approaches in a gingerly manner from the rear, walking on his hind legs and taking care to touch nothing with his forepaws but the safe part of the tail. The relevant apparatus having been lined up, docking occurs, followed by "violent orgasm" as the male unloads a year's worth of jism. The act lasts two to five minutes and may be repeated several times during the half-day window of opportunity.

All in all it makes me think that maybe my first time during college wasn't so bad. But the porcupines probably like it just fine, Ms. Porcupine especially. As our author notes, "The female cannot be raped." If she doesn't like the looks of one of her suitors, a swipe with her tail will cool his ardor fast.

It is also worth noting that the tip of the porcupine penis is covered with small spines or bumps, something humans can duplicate only through the use of certain exotic brands of prophylactic. "Undoubtedly the structures add something to the female's sensation during coitus," it says here, "but it is not known whether they help induce orgasm." Maybe not. But I find it interesting that once things get rolling the female is insatiable and will mate until the male is sexually exhausted.

The real problem for a male porcupine is not getting intimate with the female but surviving the bar fights with his male rivals beforehand. Researcher Roze reports coming upon the scene of an interporcupine slugfest where three males had fought it out for the favors of one female. The ground was littered with nearly 1,500 quills, and a few more could be seen in the nose of the apparent victor. How much easier to be a male human, where all you have to do to ensure reproductive success is buy a Mercedes.

Are there animal venereal diseases? Pet care books don't have much to say on the subject. Can you help? I've got to know.—Animal Lover, Dallas

Keep your hands off that collie, you deve. I can't claim to have made much of a study of the matter, but Kit Schwartz, author of *The Male Member* (1985), reports as follows:

"Venereal disease appears to be a rarity in all wild species. Not so fortunate are domestic animals, especially those given artificial insemination [or worse]. It is presumed that animals in the wild are protected because the VD organisms are not in constant transmission (VD cells are short-lived or frail until they multiply in the protection of a body) due, in part, to harem-style mating and the female having a briefer sexual time span." More than you need to know, if you ask me.

Maybe So, but Here's Some More Anyway

Recently you wrote that venereal diseases are rare in wild species. However, they do exist in almost all domestic species, and some of these maladies are quite odd in their nature and presentation.

Dogs can transmit TVT, or transmissible venereal tumor. They can also transmit disease-causing bacteria such as Brucella canis, *which frequently localizes in the canine prostate or other regions of the male canine urogenital tract.*

Horses are also susceptible to venereal diseases. People in the horse-breeding industry know of the meticulous cleaning procedures used when horses from different farms are brought together for breeding. A herpes virus specific to horses, EHV-3, causes coital exanthema. This disease is transmitted venereally and causes lesions on the penis and vulva of horses. A number of other equine diseases are also considered by some to be venereal.

Cattle are notorious for transmission of venereal diseases. A protozoal rascal called Trichomonas fetus *can cause fertility problems, abortions, and uterine infections. The organism is transmitted during coitus.*

This list is by no means complete. All domestic species that I am familiar with transmit a variety of organisms during coitus, and frequently these organisms cause urogenital disease and in some cases systemic problems, as do their counterparts in humans.—Scott Palmer, V.M.C., Carpineteria, California

Has anyone ever had sex in space? If so, how was it?—Curious in North Dallas

Guess it depends on what you mean by sex, doesn't it?

About a year ago, I asked the question "When did mankind figure out that SEX = BABIES?" (I mentioned that I'd read about the discovery being alluded to in some Abyssinian or Hittite texts.) So far I haven't seen the answer in print. What's holding things up?—Larrie Ferreiro, Alexandria, Virginia

Keep your pants on, stud. You know how much I hate reading stuff in Hittite. Besides, looking at it purely from the standpoint of global priorities, we can probably assume ignorance on the SEX = BABIES front has reached historical lows, although you never know. Some think Australian aborigines still haven't figured it out, a matter I'll return to directly, and I remember a couple high-living creatures in high school who seemed to think they were exceptions to the rule.

The general run of humankind is thought to have tumbled to the concept early in the New Stone Age, which began after 10,000 B.C. Several things may have contributed to the discovery. First, what with the invention of agriculture, looking for food did not occupy every waking moment and people had some time to contemplate the mysteries of their environment.

Second, the domestication of animals gave folks a chance to see the cycle of boink/swelling belly/birth close up. It didn't take a prehistoric Stephen Hawking to figure out if you had only girl sheep, all you wound up with was a bunch of old maid sheep, but if you threw in one or more boy sheep, you soon had baby sheep popping out all over.

Why couldn't primitive humans deduce the secret of sex just from watching their own species? Well, they could have, of course, and there's a chance some did. But the difference between humans and animals is that women are always partial to sex, whereas females of other species are in heat only during certain seasons. If you're constantly rolling in the hay and the women are constantly pregnant, the connection between the two phenomena isn't all that obvious. With animals, though, sex is infrequent and the link between intercourse and reproduction is clearer.

But some cultures—including, allegedly, Australian aborigines— never got the picture. One writer says that as late as the 1960s, "The Tully River Blacks of north Queensland believed that a woman got pregnant because she had been sitting over a fire on which she had roasted a fish given to her by the prospective father."

Whatever may be said for the Tully River crowd, aborigine ignorance is probably exaggerated. It's true most Aussie natives don't think intercourse is particularly important in making babies. They think pregnancy results from a "spirit child" migrating into the womb from a "spirit center." On the other hand, the aborigines recognize that intercourse somehow paves the way for the spirit child's arrival; they just don't think it's essential. Considering the state of sexual knowledge among some Westerners, e.g., my brother ("Whaddaya mean she's pregnant? We only did it once!"), I wouldn't be too hard on the aborigines.

A number of my karate cronies and I got into an argument recently about a question I'm sure has been bandied about men's locker rooms for years. Does sex the evening before an athletic competition decrease one's performance on the field (or in our case, in the ring)? I say this is an old wives' tale—i.e., wives tell it to avoid yet another round of boring sex. Please vindicate me. My health depends on it.— Tim P., College Park, Maryland

What kind of sex did you have in mind? If we're talking a trapeze, roller skates, and a quart bottle of Mazola, I guess I wouldn't feel too confident about facing off against Bruce Lee at dawn. Routine sex is another matter. The common view among sports medics is that sex is about as taxing as a forty-yard dash, and it takes the same time to recover from one as from the other.

Admittedly little serious research has been done on the subject. But in surveys and interviews with both professional and amateur athletes, Mirkin and Hoffman (1978) found that few refrained from sex before competing. On the contrary, some athletes claimed they'd turned in their best performances shortly after a session in the sack. There were a few dissenters, of course, and nobody is saying you can throw all caution to the winds. As the late Casey Stengel once said, "It isn't sex that wrecks these guys, it's staying up all night looking for it."

In a recent review of Thomas Laqueur's Making Sex *I read that Renaldus Columbus discovered the clitoris in 1559. I can't make sense of this. Wasn't it right under his nose the whole time, so to speak? Who discovered the penis? And who was Renaldus Columbus, anyway? Any relation to Chris?—Mark Lutton, Malden, Massachusetts*

You haven't grasped the totality of this, Mark. Renaldus was born in 1516. Can you imagine a guy who proclaims to the world his discovery of the clitoris . . . at age forty-three? Incidentally, he apparently died that same year. Too bad. They say his wife was about to broach the subject of foreplay.

But seriously. According to Thomas Laqueur, Columbus, a.k.a. Matteo Realdo Colombo, was a lecturer in surgery at the University of Padua, Italy. (Whether he was related to Christopher Columbus I don't know.) In 1559 he published a book called *De re anatomica* in which he described the "seat of woman's delight." He concluded, "Since no one has discerned these projections and their workings, if it is permissible to give names to things discovered by me, it should be called the love or sweetness of Venus."

Columbus's claim was disputed, but not because it was off the wall. On the contrary, Columbus's successor at Padua, Gabriel Fallopius (name ring any bells?), said *he* was the first to discover the clitoris. A semblance of sanity was restored when Kasper Bartholin, a seventeenth-century Danish anatomist, dismissed both claims, saying the clitoris had been widely known since the second century. By this one assumes he means "known to male anatomists." It is safe to say women had discovered it a good while before that.

Lest you think such foolishness was confined to the sixteenth century, recall Freud's bizarre claim that women had two kinds of orgasms, clitoral and vaginal—an idea not fully put to rest until the work of Masters and Johnson. More recently there was the hubbub about the Gräfenberg spot, which briefly threatened to replace the clitoris as the seat of female sexual excitement. In some ways we know more about what happened in the universe's first tenth of a second than we do about what goes on in the interval between "Your place or mine?" and deciding who sleeps on the wet spot.

Is it possible to be allergic to sex? (I'm serious—and a little bit desperate.) I've heard some women are allergic to certain hormones and this aggravates PMS. If this is true, I could be reacting to hormones just as things are getting exciting. Help!—Colinda J., Alexandria, Virginia

Nothing personal, Colinda kid, but you sound like one of the classic Dates from Hell. However, you probably don't have what you think you have.

It has long been known that some women suffer allergic reactions that coincide with their menstrual periods. In some cases this may simply be because menstruation makes them more susceptible to conventional allergens. In other cases, though, they may have "female sex hormone allergy"—that is, they've become allergic to their own sex hormones.

In extreme instances some women go into "anaphylactic shock," which can be life-threatening. On the first day of her period one woman suddenly broke out in hives and experienced a choking sensation and shortness of breath, followed by a drop in blood pressure and loss of consciousness. At the hospital doctors brought her out of it with antihistamines, but she was plenty freaked, especially when this occurred six more times over a period of ten months. Although drugs seemed to prevent the problem, she decided to take no chances and had a hysterectomy, which cured her once and for all.

It was never determined precisely what chemical the woman was reacting to; on the first day of a woman's period her sex hormone levels typically are low. But doctors suspect some women are reacting to the sex hormone progesterone. In one study of four women who suffered milder forms of anaphylaxis, two experienced marked improvement when given hormone-suppressing drugs. The big drawback (or maybe not, depending on how you look at it) was that menstruation also stopped.

Interesting as all this no doubt is, Colinda, it probably has no relevance to you. Female sex hormone allergy is generally related to your menstrual period, not to sex. Possibly what you've got is an allergy to semen. This is usually described as rare, but enough reports have accumulated in the literature to make me think it's more common than is widely believed.

The prototypical case was a thirty-year-old woman who believed she had an "allergy to men." This had become progressively worse over the years. The first time she'd had sex she experienced general itching plus irritation and swelling of the genitals. A few years later after having intercourse three times in one night she noticed itching and swelling of the right eye, which subsided over a twelve-hour period. Finally one night, about ten minutes after intercourse, she got hives, felt faint, had difficulty breathing, and found her eyelids had swollen severely. She was taken to a hospital emergency room and given a shot of some unspecified drug, whereupon the reaction began to diminish. She subsequently suffered a couple additional episodes, but noticed they never occurred when the man used a condom. (At the risk of sounding like I'm trying out for the "Geraldo" show, I note she had no adverse reaction when she swallowed semen.) Skin testing confirmed that she was allergic to something in seminal fluid, although precisely what remains to be determined.

Adverse (or at least odd) reactions to sex don't necessarily involve allergies. You may recall our correspondence some years ago with a woman who always sneezed following orgasm; I've since read a report of a man with a similar complaint. It's possible this is caused by tickling in the nose due to engorgement of the "erectile tissue," which swells at the same time erectile tissue elsewhere in the body swells, if you catch my drift.

One important note: all the above occur *after* sex. If your problem, whatever it may be, occurs "just as things are getting exciting," i.e., prior to orgasm, then I'm not sure what you've got. (Sexist thought: it doesn't involve "headaches," does it?) If it's as troubling as you suggest, find yourself a good allergist.

Can you tell me why the "missionary position" is called the "missionary position"? If the woman gets on top, is that the heathen position? Is there a difference between the Lutheran missionary position, the Methodist missionary position, and for that matter the Zoroastrian missionary position?—Victor M. Cassidy, Chicago

Victor, you're so juvenile. Learn to be serious, like me. The legend behind "missionary position" is this: early European missionaries discovered that native peoples, while going about the business of propagating the species, often used unorthodox positions—positions that people today spend thousands of dollars on Kama Sutra sex therapy to learn. (Okay, I exaggerate: the alternative position usually mentioned in this connection is the so-called dorsal or dog-style position, in which the man approaches from the rear.)

Shocked, the missionaries declared that only the couple-facing/man-on-top position was acceptable before the Lord. How the missionaries became apprised of what position the natives were using I don't know, but I suppose if it becomes apparent that everybody else in the village is having a lot more fun than you are, you make it your business to find out why.

That's the legend, at least. It may not be true. The earliest citation for "missionary position" in the *Oxford English Dictionary* is from 1969, and the Random House Unabridged says the term first showed up circa 1965–70. In other words, it may have been invented by sixties hipsters who looked down upon the uncool Presbyterian proselytizers of an earlier age. In any case the missionary position was not some Anglo invention; surveys suggest it is, and no doubt always has been, a common sexual position in most of the world.

Come-on Lines for the '90s

Having read the Straight Dope on the missionary position (what about the emissionary position, Cecil?), I thought the Teeming Millions would like to know that a more elegant word for the dorsal position exists and that a gentleman desiring to initiate intercourse with his lady pal need not embarrass them both by saying, "Let's do it doggy-style, Babs." Instead he can purr (with foreplayful huskiness), "Barbara, my dove, let us retrocopulate." No question about it, there are amazing delights to be discovered in a good unabridged dictionary.—David English, Somerville, Massachusetts

Thanks, Dave. I bet you're a riot on dates.

My skin has usually been pretty clear, even through my adolescence. But now I'm twenty-five, and recently I've been breaking out a lot. I also have been having a lot of sex for a couple of months straight. Is there some weird kind of hormone thing that's doing this to me? I thought sex was supposed to cure your pimples.—Marty Tyler, New York

What the hey, Jack, you're getting parallel on a regular basis and you're bitching about zits? Some of the cases I hear from are so desperate for love they wouldn't complain if they turned orange. Be that as it may, you're not the only one to wonder about the acne/lust connection. A couple related propositions you'll hear debated in locker rooms include: (1) having sex regularly makes your beard grow faster, and (2) the more "virile" you are, whatever that means, the

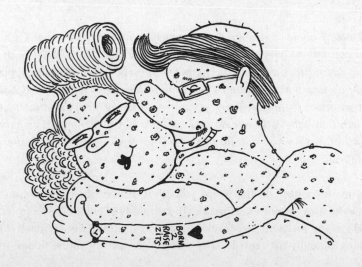

faster your hair falls out—obviously a notion that appeals to balding relics such as myself.

In the broadest sense no one doubts there's a relationship between male sex hormones and the state of your skin and hair. Eunuchs, after all, don't go bald, don't grow beards, and don't get acne. But whether sexual exercise per se will put hair on your chest (or on your palms, for that matter) nobody really knows, several shelves' worth of research papers notwithstanding.

We don't even know if sex raises the level of sex hormones in your blood. A couple attempts to answer the seemingly straightforward question, "Does masturbation increase blood testosterone levels?" (hey, it's all for science) have produced opposite results. The apparent problem: not enough participants in the studies to produce a statistically reliable sample. Next time I'd advise the researchers to visit a freshman male dorm.

Even if sex does increase hormone production, nobody's sure if that means it'll crater your face or chrome your dome. The best one recent survey of the field could do was, "We conclude that the relations between sex hormones and characters of hair and skin are very complicated and require further investigation." A committee will soon be formed. In the meantime, enjoy your lively sex life while it lasts. Soon you'll break up or get married, either way getting ample opportunity to do a baseline comparison.

I heard about a strange sexual practice the other day that I hope you can tell me more about. It seems a boy was found dead with a rope around his neck, but he hadn't purposely killed himself. Apparently he was masturbating at the time of his death and hanged himself in order to heighten the sexual sensation. The radio announcer called it an autoerotic suicide and said it is not uncommon. I've never heard of it. Can you tell me more?—Desiree Blough, Santa Barbara, California

Time for a walk on the weird side, kids. Autoerotic asphyxiation—"suicide" is a misnomer, since death is usually accidental—is, in fact, fairly common. One researcher estimates there are at least fifty deaths annually nationwide. The victims are mostly young males; evidently if you live long enough to become an old male you start getting a partner to help you, although it's quite dangerous even then.

Autoerotic asphyxiation arose out of the observation that men executed by hanging often got an erection and sometimes ejaculated. It's described in detail in De Sade's *Justine* and is mentioned in Beckett's *Waiting for Godot*. Why it works is unclear. The simplest explanation is that lack of oxygen causes lightheadedness, reducing inhibitions and enhancing the sexual experience. Masochistic fantasics, castration anxiety, and other psychological factors no doubt also play a role.

The problem is that it's easy to go too far. As little as seven pounds of pressure will collapse the carotid artery, producing unconsciousness within seconds. Many victims are bondage freaks, and their elaborate bindings make self-rescue difficult.

Needless to say, this is not something you should try at home. Judging from the photos—hey, it's my job—not only do you end up dead, you look real stupid when they find you. I mention this on the theory that if fear of death won't stop somebody, maybe fear of embarrassment will.

Read All About It

For those who feel they must know more about autoerotic asphyxiation, you might try to find a copy of *The Breathless Orgasm: A Lovemap Biography of Asphyxiophilia* by John Money, Gordon Wainwright, and David Hingsburger (1991). The first part of the book is the story of an "asphyxiophile" who lived to tell about it.

When I was back in tenth grade I did this term paper on Thomas Jefferson and I seem to remember coming by something that said he'd had a dozen or so children by one of his slaves, who was named Sally or something like that. What's the Straight Dope on this, Cecil? Is this a major cover-up conspiracy?—Kool Moe Steve, Washington, D.C.

If TJ's sex life was the subject of a cover-up, Kool Moe, it was an amazingly inept one, considering that even tenth-graders seem to know all the details. Truth is, Jefferson's alleged liaison with the mulatto slave Sally Hemings has received enormous publicity, starting with scandal-sheet broadsides by Jefferson's enemies in 1802, during his first term as president. The matter was given its fullest airing in the late Fawn Brodie's *Thomas Jefferson: An Intimate Biography* (1974), which says that the relationship lasted thirty-eight years. The most lurid stories have a daughter of Jefferson and Hemings being sold into prostitution in a New Orleans slave market for $1,000, a tale that made the rounds in abolitionist circles for many years.

The public, ever willing to believe the worst, seems to have had no trouble accepting that one of the founders of the republic was a secret sleaze. But historians aren't so sure. Jefferson did own an attractive slave named Sally Hemings, and there were a lot of mulatto kids at Monticello, some of whom bore a resemblance to Jefferson. But many of these were the work of Jefferson's randy relatives. For example, his father-in-law, John Wayles, kept Sally's mother, Betty, as a concubine for twelve years, siring Sally and five other children. Jefferson also had a couple oversexed nephews, but we'll get back to them in a moment.

The belief that Jefferson fathered children by Sally Hemings rests chiefly on two sources, both dubious. In 1802 James T. Callender, a hard-drinking pamphleteer who had done some work for Jefferson and his allies, was rebuffed in his attempt to secure a government job and promptly went to work for Jefferson's opponents. He published every scandalous rumor he could find about his former patron, including the Hemings story, none of which he bothered to verify. Jefferson chose not to dignify the charges with public comment, but he denied any hanky-panky in a letter to an associate.

Then in 1873 an Ohio newspaper published an interview with a former slave named Madison Hemings, who claimed to be one of Jefferson's five children by Sally Hemings. Another former Monticello slave backed up Madison's story but admitted he did not "positively know" Jefferson was the father. As a rival newspaper editor dryly noted, "[Madison] was no doubt present at the time of accouchement [birth], but his extreme youth would prevent him from knowing all the facts connected with that important event." The editor also noted that it was common for slave mothers to claim illustrious fathers for their children.

And that's about it for solid evidence. Fawn Brodie went on to find sexual significance in the way Jefferson remodeled Monticello and his use of the words "mulatto" and "corruption" and so on in his writings, and she muttered darkly about mysterious missing letters. But one can use the same sort of evidence to prove Elvis is still alive.

The indications that Jefferson did *not* father Hemings's children are more persuasive. His grandson and granddaughter and his former overseer all believed Hemings's children had been sired by Jefferson's nephews, Peter and Samuel Carr. Two of Hemings's children were born *after* the initial scandal broke, while Jefferson was still president, a display of brazenness that would have made even Gary Hart blanch. Jefferson's family would surely have known about (and disapproved of) a thirty-eight-year dalliance with a slave, yet their relations with him remained warm and loving. In a correspondence amounting to eighteen thousand letters, he never mentions Hemings once. If the two had any sort of relationship, there is damned little sign of it. For more, see *The Jefferson Scandals* by Virginius Dabney.

As a lad I went to the same repressive boarding school that made George Bush what he is today. As a student I believed, as did we all, that the school authorities were mixing potassium nitrate, or saltpeter, into our food to control our sexual appetites. (The food itself controlled our regular appetites.) Is this true? Was it legal? Would it have had any lasting effect on me? I shudder to think what happened to poor George.—John Daniel, Santa Barbara, California

The official word is that potassium nitrate (KNO_3), more commonly employed as an ingredient in gunpowder, has no therapeutic value as an anaphrodisiac, contrary to legend. Cecil, of course, believes this. Still, when you look at what the stuff *does* do, you can see where the idea got started. Saltpeter can cause relaxation of involuntary muscle fiber (for which reason it's used to treat asthma), and it's occasionally prescribed to lower body temperature in cases of fever. From there it's not much of a leap to think that "niter," as it was called in the old days, might cure "sexual fever," and in fact a few doctors urged it for that purpose centuries ago.

From what I can tell the idea wasn't taken too seriously, but apparently sailors in the British navy leapt to conclusions when they learned that potassium nitrate was being used to preserve the meat used aboard their ships. Ever since, the inmates of almost any large all-male institution, ranging from boarding schools to the army, have been convinced that the higher-ups were slipping the stuff into the mashed potatoes (or whatever) to cool the jets of the rank and file. During the world wars, for example, it was widely believed that government-issue cigarettes were soaked in saltpeter.

The truth is that even the most tyrannical general wouldn't inflict the stuff on his men if he expected them to be of any use—too many side effects. Among other things, potassium nitrate can cause gastroenteritis (violent stomachache), high blood pressure, anemia, kidney disease, and general weakness and torpor. It also has an alarmingly depressive effect on the heart. Too strong a dose and not only would you not be able to get it up, chances are you wouldn't be able to get up, period. All in all, there's still no substitute for the cold shower.

Everyone knows that nowadays artificial insemination is used to breed everything from cattle and horses to rhinos, gorillas, and humans. I know how they get sperm from humans, but how do they get it from bulls and male gorillas? Do they show them dirty heifer pic-

tures? Gorilla porn? Do they use blowup female rhino dolls? The
mind boggles.—S. J. Cowdery, Dallas

Go boggle on your own time, pal. In keeping with the Straight
Dope tradition of brutal frankness, however, I may as well tell you
that perhaps the most common method of sperm collection involves
an artificial vagina. I had thought to edify the Teeming Millions with
a do-it-yourself version of this technique taken from an animal
breeding manual, but on second thought it's too icky for words. Suffice it to say it involves a 2¾ inch automobile radiator hose 18 inches
long, a 30-by-30-inch automobile inner tube, and a family-size bottle
of Vaseline. An entirely different method, it says here, is "rectal mas-
sage of the ampulla." They even show pictures, for Chrissake. Just
be thankful I'm doing this job and not you.

Notes from the Gutter

Regarding collecting semen from bulls for artificial insemination, I
used to work at a vet clinic where we did fertility checks on bulls. We
used an apparatus known as an electro-ejaculator that was basically
the size of a man's arm. You inserted it into the rectum (of the bull,
silly) and turned it on to achieve the desired results. Not a pretty pic-
ture, but I swear it's true.—Chris Voorhees, Studio City, California

I heard aphids are born pregnant. Is this true? If so, how does it
work?—Lillian Wentworth, Silver Spring, Maryland

You think your life is miserable, cucumber, just be glad you're not an
aphid. Not only are they born pregnant, they're pregnant without benefit of sex. Not that sex with an aphid sounds like much of a treat. Two
things are at work here: *parthenogenesis* and *paedogenesis*.

Parthenogenesis, also known as virgin birth, is rare in humans
(one known case) but common in insects. The baby bugs, all of
which are female, develop from single cells in Mom's body. The advantage of this is that reproduction is very quick—none of this flowers and perfume jive. This helps when you've got as many natural
enemies as aphids have.

Paedogenesis—pregnancy in the young—speeds up the process even more. "Although the young are not born until the aphid has reached the adult stage," it says here, "their development may begin before she is born while she is still in the ducts of the grandparental generation." Aphids can give birth ten days after having been born themselves. The baby showers must be murder.

A Question

In your recent discussion of virgin birth, you said there was "one known case" among humans. Aren't you going to tell us about the one known case?—Alison True, Chicago

I suppose I could, Alison. But it's been pretty well publicized.

Who gets the most pleasure out of sex—the man or the woman? According to Tiresias, a prophet in Greek mythology, the woman gets nine times more pleasure than the man. Please, say it ain't so!—Sean Sherman, Montreal, Quebec

I've got some good news and some bad news, Sean buddy. But first one ground rule: we're going to confine this discussion to the physiological experience of orgasm. The more subjective aspects of sex, important though they may be, are too difficult for us scientists to quantify. Now for the good news: your basic run-of-the-mill male and female orgasms are pretty similar. Kinsey (1953) in particular took pains to emphasize that "the anatomic structures which are most essential to sexual response and orgasm are nearly identical in the human female and male" and that "orgasm in the female matches orgasm of the male in every physiologic detail except for the fact that it occurs without ejaculation." I would venture to say this jibes with most folks' everyday experience.

Okay, now the bad news (for men, I mean). Masters and Johnson (1966), while conceding that male and female orgasms were usually pretty comparable, noted two important differences. The first is well known: women can have multiple orgasms without having to rest in between, as men do. This occurs in 10 to 15 percent of women regardless of age. Young men can have multiple orgasms within ten minutes or so, but this ability drops off sharply after age thirty.

The second difference has been less publicized: women are capable of *sustained* orgasm, called *status orgasmus*. These orgasms may start with a two-to-four-second "spastic contraction" and last twenty to sixty seconds all told—and if that isn't nine times the pleasure, it's definitely in the ballpark. Masters and Johnson published the chart for one woman who experienced a forty-three-second orgasm in which one can count at least twenty-two successive contractions.

Depressed? Hey, it gets worse. Status orgasmus is usually the result of self-stimulation, but a woman can also experience it at the hands (or whatever) of a suitably skilled lover. Which means that not only can't *you* have the ultimate O, if *she* doesn't have one, it's *your damn fault*. You want to give up and join the monastery, Cecil will understand.

What can you tell us about vacuum cleaner wounds to the penis? This malady apparently afflicts an informational underclass who think that a vacuum cleaner can simulate fellatio.—Inquiring Mind, Chicago

Got those midwinter blues, kids? Cecil has just the thing to brighten up your dull lives. Several cases of "penile injuries from vacuum cleaners" were reported about ten years ago in the *British Medical Journal*. The injury reports are classic:

"*Case 1*—A 60-year-old man said that he was changing the plug of his Hoover Dustette vacuum cleaner in the nude while his wife was out shopping. It 'turned itself on' and caught his penis, causing tears around the external meatus. . . . Multiple lacerations of the glans [were] repaired with catgut.

"*Case 2*—A 65-year-old railway signalman was in his signal box when he bent down to pick up his tools and 'caught his penis in a Hoover Dustette, which happened to be switched on.' He suffered extensive lacerations to the glans.

"*Case 3*—A 49-year-old man was vacuuming his friend's staircase in a loose-fitting dressing gown, when, intending to switch the machine off, he leaned across to reach the plug; 'at that moment his dressing gown became undone and his penis was sucked into the vacuum cleaner.' "

I think it is very unfair of you to suggest that these tragic victims were involved in unnatural acts. Here they were, just trying to keep things tidy, when they were attacked by a treacherous appliance. The real fault lies with the Hoover company for manufacturing such a dangerous product. But even the doctors are snickering, the cads. The report quoted above concludes, "The Hoover Dustette [has] fan blades about 15 cm from the inlet. The present patients may well have thought that the penis would be clear of the fan but were driven to new lengths by the novelty of the experience and came to grief." New lengths, indeed. Just wait till it happens to *you*.

What is the purpose of a hymen in a woman? Ever since the painfulness of my own being broken during my first sexual intercourse, I've tried to find this out. Several gynecologists I asked simply shrugged; they never even wondered about such a thing. (Needless to say, they were men!) I once had a teacher at college who postulated that the hymen was some sort of genetic aberration that had been re-inforced once men discovered it. The idea was that the girls who had a hymen were the ones chosen as brides, since they could prove they were virgins, a valuable asset when dealing with a patriarchal culture that must be certain that a woman's children were really her hus-band's, not some previous lover's. (In some societies it was customary on the morning after the wedding night to hang out the bedsheet to show the hymen's blood.) The women with hymens passed them on to their daughters, while those without weren't chosen as brides and didn't reproduce as frequently. So hymens became the common thing. Any truth to this theory?—Nancy J., Montreal, Quebec

I feel a professional duty to state the matter as simply and clearly as I can, Nance. I don't know. What's more, anybody who tells you he (or she) does know lies like a dog. Figuring out what this or that anatomical feature is "for" is an academic parlor game whose chief product is a lot of untestable hypotheses and the occasional talk-show booking. But it ain't science.

Most writers on the evolution of sex are mum regarding the pur-

pose of the hymen, but occasionally you'll get somebody who'll take a flier—your teacher, for example, or the indefatigable Desmond Morris. In *The Naked Ape* Morris writes: "[A] feature . . . that appears to be unique to our species is the retention of the hymen or maidenhead in the female. In lower mammals it occurs [only during development of the embryo]. Its persistence [in humans] means that the first copulation in the life of the female will meet with some difficulty. . . . By making the first copulation attempt difficult and even painful, the hymen ensures that it will not be indulged in lightly. [Young males are inclined to have sex without making any long-term commitment.] But if young females were to go so far without pair-formation, they might very well find themselves pregnant and heading straight toward a parental situation with no partner to accompany them. By putting a partial brake on this trend in the female, the hymen demands that she shall have already developed a deep emotional involvement before taking the final step, an involvement strong enough to take the initial physical discomfort in its stride."

Just one problem: Morris to the contrary notwithstanding, retention of the hymen is not unique to humans. It occurs in horses, whales, moles, mole rats, hyenas, and perhaps other animals. (In the great fin whale, in fact, the hymen is not completely destroyed until childbirth.) Why? We haven't got a clue. "Such adaptations [i.e., retention of the hymen] are explicable only if the male of the species finds it to his advantage to seek a virgin," Bettyann Kevles observes in *Female of the Species* (1986). "But there is no evidence that mammal males seek inexperienced females, and no evidence that females with this peculiar anatomical feature remain monogamous. . . . In whales, one can explain the resealing of the vagina as a means of keeping water out of the reproductive organs."

Not the world's most satisfying answer, I agree. But we don't even know why women have orgasms. Morris's preposterous theory: orgasm keeps women on their backs afterward, grinning with satisfaction, whereas if they were up and about right off the bat, the semen and with it their chances of reproductive success would dribble down their legs. Sounds like something I'd make up. But the difference is, I'd wink.

*I recently celebrated my thirtieth birthday and am in the initial
stages of what I hope will be a serious and long-lasting relationship.
My dilemma is this: I've never been told the story of "the birds and
the bees." I've traveled around the world and am not an inexperienced person, but this missing piece of information may be the reason
I haven't, up till now, been truly successful in love. Please give me the
Straight Dope on the origin of the phrase "the birds and the bees"
and the details of the act(s) as it (or they) relate to man.—M. Harris,
Washington, D.C.*

Don't feel bad. Nobody explained it to me, either, and I must say I
made quite an impression that first night with the honey and feathers.
But now I'm hip. The significance of the birds and bees isn't what they
do, it's simply that they do it, "it," naturally, being a tussle in the tum-
bleweeds, or wherever it is that the lower orders engage in sex. As
such it's the perfect euphemism for a culture so prudish that even pub-
lishers of girlie magazines used to airbrush out the pubic hair.

Where exactly "the birds and the bees" originated nobody knows,
but word sleuths William and Mary Morris hint that it may have
been inspired by words like these from the poet Samuel Coleridge:
"All nature seems at work. . . . The bees are stirring—birds are on
the wing . . . and I the while, the sole unbusy thing, not honey make,
nor pair, nor build, nor sing." Making honey, pairing . . . yes, we can
definitely tell what Sam had on his mind.

The Morrises offer the theory that schools in years past taught
about sex by "telling how birds do it and how bees do it and trusting
that the youngsters would get the message by indirection." Right.
Luckily for the perpetuation of the species, there's always been
Louie in the schoolyard to explain how things really worked.

*Since you dealt so thoroughly with gerbil stuffing a few years back,
I know you are the man to answer this question. There is a rumor going around about that frozen Stone Age man they found in the glacier
between Austria and Italy in September 1991. What I have heard is
that scientists found traces of semen in the man's anus. I know this is
sticky territory, but is this rumor true? I haven't seen this mentioned*

in any AP news bulletins.—*Wayne L. Wilson, Chapel Hill, North Carolina*

Nothing like a good cheeseball question to brighten up a dull day. The following report, which supposedly originated in a Boston weekly called *In*, was posted on computer bulletin boards last fall: *"Se non e vero, e ben trovato."* ("If it isn't true, it's a good story"—the headline, I assume.)

"Otztal Valley, Italy—The mainstream media reported widely on 'Otzi,' the 5,477-year-old Stone Age man found mummified in a melting glacier high in the Italian Tyrolean Alps. The U.S. media did not, however, share a gripping detail that was reported in Italy, Austria, Switzerland, and elsewhere: there was sperm in Otzi's anal canal. 'The Tyrolean scholars have not given this little detail any special significance,' according to *Lambda Nachrichten*, the magazine of Homosexual Initiative Vienna, Austria's leading gay organization, 'but there can only be one explanation: Otzi had sex with another man in the Alps!

" 'The tight-assed Tyrolean scholars were uncomfortable even having to acknowledge it,' *Lambda* said, 'but Otzi is the first known homosexual man that enjoyed being [made a receptacle of lust]. . . . Otzi was the passive partner—of this there is absolutely no doubt. . . . The sperm was carbon dated.' . . . According to the Zurich, Switzerland, newspaper *Blick*: 'Since the homosexual innuendo has made the rounds, politicians in the North and South Tyrol regions suddenly have less interest in poor Otzi. And in Otztal they're afraid they're going to end up being called "Homo Valley." ' "

The headline pretty much says it all. Other dubious details include Otzi's absurdly exact age (what did they do, find his driver's license?) and the fact that the initials of Homosexual Initiative Vienna are HIV. But the real problem is this: judging from the photos, Otzi has no anus. His entire crotch, including penis and testicles, is gone, presumably having been eaten by scavengers shortly after his demise.

The rumor isn't a U.S. invention, though. Through the miracle of the Internet, hero of science Philipp Keller of Zurich, Switzerland, sent us a translation of a recent article in the German magazine *Der Spiegel* revealing that in Europe all manner of wild stories are swirling around Otzi. In addition to the semen rumor, German TV journalist Michael Heim claims in a new book that Otzi's body is suspiciously well preserved and must be a fraud. A recent article in *Nature* doesn't go that far but says there are many unanswered questions and criticizes the slow pace of research. And, of course, there's the woman who's writing a book saying she's Otzi's reincarnation.

Rumors have flourished largely because of the silence from the scientists investigating Otzi. Research was held up for over a year because of a dispute between Italy and Austria on ownership of the body. (It was found a few yards from the border.) That was resolved about three months ago, and examination of the body is now proceeding. But the one hundred scientists from seven countries who are working on the project are contractually bound to secrecy; the University of Innsbruck, where the work is being conducted, wants to make sure it gets the money from the book and photo rights to defray research costs. An official account is supposed to hit the streets this fall. We can't wait to hear what they really found in Otzi's nether regions, or what's left of them. As one of Cecil's screwball correspondents remarks, "What would be even more bizarre is if the semen is found to be, say, only two years old."

Getting to the Bottom, You Should Pardon the Expression, of Otzi the Gay Caveman

Enclosed please find an article I wrote last October for the Washington Blade *that will give you the inside story on Otzi. I'm amused to see that an April Fools' joke like this can survive for years.—Aras van Hertum, Washington, D.C.*

To quote from Aras's story:

"In its April 1 issue, an Austrian gay magazine ran a story that said traces of semen had been found in the anus of a stone age man, whose well-preserved remains had been discovered in the Alps. He was, said the magazine, the 'first known gay man who enjoyed being . . .' "—well, no need to be vulgar.

"The article was apparently an April Fools' joke, but half a year later, the story continues to circulate among gays around the world as fact rather than fiction. . . . Only days after the Austrian gay magazine *Lambda Nachrichten* published its joke that scientists had attempted to cover up the discovery of semen traces in Otzi's anal canal, the 'story' was picked up and published as fact by three daily newspapers in Europe—one in Switzerland and two in Austria. . . .

"The Chicago-based Outlines News Service, which supplies a large number of U.S. and foreign gay papers with national and international gay news, published the story on September 2 after obtaining copies of the reports in the European dailies. Several subscribers . . . immediately ran the report. . . . After contacting *Lambda Nachrichten* and discovering the report had been an April Fools' joke, Outlines on September 8 sent out a correction. But by then, the story of the 'world's first known bottom' had left the pages of gay papers to assume a life of its own."

Glad we could get that cleared up. Still, questions remain. Remember that Otzi's otherwise intact corpse is missing its privy part. I can't say more now, but don't be surprised if you hear they're checking around Otzi's neighborhood for a six-thousand-year-old Hoover Dustette.

What exactly is a "merkin"? Ever since the word was thrust into my consciousness it's been tormenting me. My Oxford English Dictionary *defines it as the "female pudendum," which seems a trifle sedate, given the listed quote of 1714, "This put a strange Whim in his Head; which was, to get the hairy circle of her Merkin. . . . This he dry'd well and comb'd out, and then return'd to the Cardinal, telling him, he had brought Saint Peter's Beard."*

And it's downhill from there. The OED *"b" definition says a merkin is "counterfeit hair for women's privy parts," and another dictionary calls it a "pubic hair wig." Sorry, but these explanations defy understanding. I mean, I've heard of niche markets, but this is ridiculous. My own interest in the word isn't just academic, as I'd like to make use of the fine quote of 1680, "Or wear some stinking Merkin for a Beard," but I want to make damn sure I know what the original item was.—Andrew Scheinman, Los Angeles*

Cecil doesn't have the most reputable sources for this kind of thing. In fact, I blush to admit, I have been fishing for tips once again on the Internet. I do not want to give the impression I spend all my time on the Internet, but in the right hands it is a wondrous tool, and in the wrong hands it is an even better one. Here's what turned up so far:

- A merkin is somebody who lives in Merika. (Har!)
- They used to shave off all the pubic hair as a cure for syphilis, so the well-to-do used wigs.
- Before penicillin was around to ease the lives of the promiscuous, these were used to cover up any sores prostitutes may have obtained in the line of duty.
- They used to treat the syphilitic with mercury, which caused baldness.
- The merkin is for women with no pubic hair. Some people don't develop hair down there, and this can be embarrassing.
- In days of old a common problem was lice. One of the ways people dealt with this was to shave all the hair off their bodies, including arms, legs, and pubes. Wigs became very popular. Pubic wigs caught on slowly, starting among the kinkier set, but eventually became halfway respectable.
- A merkin is a crotch wig for both men and women and is usually worn on the outside. Have you ever seen a Scot in full regalia? That little fur "purse" in front is a merkin.
- In a country of mainly dark-haired people, a prostitute may wear a blond merkin to be unusual and therefore more desirable. (Got this from a dictionary of sex.)
- One of the more recent uses is to allow exotic dancers to comply with local laws prohibiting full nudity. They wear what amounts to a flesh-colored panty with hair on the front, appearing to the patrons of the establishment to disrobe completely without actually doing so.
- In a sci-fi story by John Varley called something like "The Barbie Murders," a group of women gives up individuality (and sex) and undergoes surgery to become perfect nonsexual beings resembling Barbie dolls. This involves losing genitals, pubic hair, etc. One Barbie goes back to being a woman for a night, painting on nipples and using a merkin.

Fascinating, ja? Erudite answers from around the globe, and not one of them duplicates another. Also, one is still left with a nagging question: who's a merkin supposed to fool? By the time you get to the level of intimacy where somebody is going to see whether you have pubic hair or not, your range of observation, as we might say, is such that a wig is not going to make for a very convincing masquerade, strippers possibly excepted. VOICE FROM THE NET: Yeah, but during the period when merkins were popular, the degree of intimacy among the upper class was low even during sex. ME: What's that supposed to mean, you had your valet do it for you? You sent it in by mail? Clearly more investigation needs to be done.

Real Scotsmen Carry Purses

Despite what that imbecile on the Internet may have told you, the "fur purse" in front of a Scot's kilt is not a merkin but a sporran. It is simply a pouch and has no sexual significance.— Anonymous

Keep On Merkin

The topic of merkins came up a while ago in a mailing list of word fans on the IBM internal network, and a participant told of going to a bar that offered prizes to amateur nude dancers. There were a lot of rules; some made sense (no touching the customers), some didn't (pubic hair required). A woman in the party considered going up, but she shaved herself; however, the management provided merkins. She said they looked like little mustaches. The whole scene was a little too weird for her, so she decided not to dance.—Philip Cohen, White Plains, New York

Thank you for sharing that with us, Philip. I will have you know that Cecil recently conspired to give his good buddy Charlie the architect a merkin for his birthday, something for which, Charlie's girlfriend assured me, he had developed a desperate craving ever since having read about merkins in this column some months ago.

Since the local sex-toy shop was fresh out (and yes, we thought of the Merkin-tile Exchange joke, too), we decided to improvise by presenting him with a large industrial mop dyed a tasteful bevy of Day-Glo colors. The classiest part of the whole production, however, was the instructions. Friend Anne provided the safety tips and owner registration card ("It is imperative that we know how to reach you promptly if we should discover a safety problem that could affect you"); I added hints on operation and use. Sample:

"Confirm that merkin is the proper size before wearing. Use of an improperly sized merkin may result in paralysis or death.

"On first use your merkin may be stiff and difficult to attach properly. Do not be embarrassed to ask for assistance. For best results we recommend that four persons be recruited for this purpose—one to grasp either leg, one to apply the merkin, and one to act as lookout.

"Once the merkin is in place, it should be appropriately lubricated using light sewing machine oil, petroleum jelly, #2 fuel oil, or I Can't Believe It's Not Butter when on sale at Safeway. Do not use so much lubricant that it dribbles in the street. Merkin should not 'squish' when in use.

"Your merkin is highly flammable. Do not use if temperature rises above 73 degrees. If merkin ignites while in use, seek assistance by running into the nearest street and shouting, 'I'M ON FIRE, GODDAMIT.' Do not panic. The number of people who die as a result of burns from a flaming merkin is surprisingly small."

We had it delivered to the office. Unfortunately, the firecracker didn't go off. But it was a birthday Charlie won't soon forget.

A Few Words

Isaac Asimov posed a puzzle in a magazine and I'm going crazy trying to figure out the answer. He said there are only four commonly used English words that end in "-dous." Two are "positive," and two are "negative." The positive ones are "tremendous" and "stupendous," and one of the negatives is "horrendous." What is the fourth word?
—Adam R., Baltimore

The late Isaac may have thought there was only one other word, but around here we figure a man's reach should exceed his grasp. I'll give you *two* words—"hazardous" and "timidous." What do you mean, timidous isn't common? Timid, timider, timidous. What could be commoner than that?

The Last Word

Re the four or five English words ending in -dous, did you forget "jeopardous"?—M. H. Carter, Jacksonville, Florida

Certainly not. To forget something you have to have heard of it in the first place, which, frankly, I hadn't, no doubt because the last cited use of jeopardous in the *Oxford English Dictionary* was in 1661. ("Yo, varlet; is the new quiz show 'What's My Linish' or

'Wheel of Fortunesque'?" "Neither, milord, it is 'Jeopardous.' ") I assure you it won't happen again.

All Right Already

Re the four or five English words ending in -dous, you forgot at least a dozen more, as the enclosed xerox from Walker's Rhyming Dictionary (1936) *clearly indicates. The words are* vanadous, molybdous, mucidous, multifidous, nefandous, frondous, decapodous, lagopodous, tylopodous, steganopodous, heteropodous, gasteropodous, isopodous, *and* ligniperdous.—*Hugh R., Department of Physics, University of Wisconsin at Madison*

... amphipodous, apodous, blizzardous, gastropodous, hybridous, iodous, nodous, octapodous, palladous, paludous, pudendous, rhodous, sauropodous, schizopodous, solipedous, splendidous, tetrapodous, voudous.—*Philip C., White Plains, New York*

Very impressive, guys. But don't expect to get invited on any long fishing trips with *me*.

My pursuit of higher education has required me to study queueing theory. I have been told that "queueing" is the only word in English that has five consecutive vowels. Can you verify this? I would have asked Bill Safire, but I am not always able to get the New York Times. *I rarely miss the Straight Dope.—Doug S., Dallas*

I like the cut of your jib, lad. However, your spelling sucks. According to my trusty *American Heritage Dictionary* (How can you not like a dictionary that illustrates "décolletage" with a picture of Marilyn Monroe?), the participle of "queue" is "queuing"—four vowels. But fear not. An alternate spelling of the verb "meeow" is "miaou"; thus we can have cats "miaouing"—count 'em, five vowels.

You slam me for giving the participle of "queue" as "queueing" (five consecutive vowels) rather than your preferred "queuing" (four vowels) without bothering to research alternate spellings? It took me four minutes to go to the Oxford English Dictionary *to find both spellings. Then there's the question of usage. A sampling of the literature in this field shows over half spell it "queueing." A retraction is in order regarding my spelling's oral habits.—Doug S., Dallas*

Damn. Another potential book sale out the window. But fortunately there are still a few who appreciate my playful wit. See below.

Your response to Doug S. regarding words with the most consecutive vowels was "the cat's miaou"! Compounding the problem of consecutive vowels in English words is the compounding of words, especially when using the alternative spelling of the prefix. If compounding is allowed, then archaeoaerie *has five consecutive vowels nested in a word which means the prehistoric nest of a bird of prey. One might get drunk on consecutive vowels while trying* archaeooenology, *the study of prehistoric wine. Would something prehistoric that is unequally elastic in different directions be termed* archaeoaeolotropic, *thereby stretching English to its six-consecutive-vowel limit?—Paul K., Madison*

P.S.: Hyphenating these words would dash my hopes of creating record words.

Very good, Paul. But one more pun and I'll have you disemvoweled. Sorry, but sometimes you gotta fight fire with fire.

Do other languages have vulgarities and obscenities that are used in conversation as they are in English? My husband worked in his youth with Italian-speaking laborers and says the worst he ever heard them say in Italian was "fangooloo." (He says that, contrary to popular impression, this means only "make a tail"; in other words, "show me your back," or "go away.")

I'm sure we've all heard of "merde," but do people speaking other languages ever say anything stronger? If so, what? In particular, does

the now-common "F-word" have a counterpart in other languages?
—Sally B., Boston

Honestly, Sally, were you raised in a convent? English obscenities are a pale shadow of the invective used in other languages. The F-word is the least of it. If there's a language that doesn't have an equivalent, I've yet to hear about it. Poles have *pierdolic*, the French *foutre* (from the Latin *futuere*), Soviet Georgians *secems* . . . you get the idea.

As for *fangooloo* (in my neighborhood we pronounced it *fongool*), I'm afraid you've heard the expurgated translation. According to Kevin Beary's *Florentine Locutions* (1991), it's properly spelled *vaffanculo*, a contraction of *va a fare in culo*, and literally means "go do [it] in the ass," i.e., bugger off, fuck off, fuck you. "Some Italians affirm that the ass referred to is that of one's interlocutor, while others assert that the orifice in question is not yours or mine or anyone's in particular, but rather the universal anus," Beary says.

Vaffanculo is merely the best known of a rich tradition of Italian oaths and imprecations, although the consensus is that Spanish is the champ in this department. Herewith a few of the more printable in-

ternational classics, culled from the pages of Reinhold Aman's *Maledicta: The International Journal of Verbal Aggression*:

> *Mecàgum les cinc llagues de Crist*, "I shit on the five wounds of Christ," Catalan. Even more bloodcurdling is *Mecàgum Déu, en la creu, en el fuster que la feu i en el fill de puta que va plantar el pi*, "I shit on God, on the cross, on the carpenter who made it, and on the son of a whore who planted the pine."
>
> *Matumbo yangu huzaa maradhi*, "My womb has born a disease," Swahili. Said by a mother to a disobedient child.
>
> *La reputísima madre que te recontra mil parió*, "The twice most whorish mother that bore you again and again one thousand times," Spanish (Argentina).
>
> *Krijg de mazelen*, "May you get the measles," Dutch.
>
> *Mabial agpi-agpi ke mabial nganswang*, "[You have] very short breasts like the breasts of a porcupine," Dinga (spoken in Zaire). Or: *Dem inear-inear*, "[You have a] greatly lined and wrinkled belly."
>
> *Melewe silöm we ie maragus*, "Your mother has yaws," Ulithian (Ulithi is a coral atoll in the Pacific). Also: *Fälfúlul silöm*, "Your mother's pubic tattooing!"
>
> *Bi damâghi bâbât rydam*, "I shit on your father's nose," Farsi (Iran). Also: *Gûz bi rîshit*, "May a fart be on your beard."

English isn't totally lacking in creative vulgarity. Sanford Margalith, writing in *Maledicta 10*, fondly recalls the southerners in his World War II artillery battalion who said things like, "I wouldn't piss on his ass if his piles were on fire." Noninsults were pretty snappy, too: after a rough night on the town one soldier said he felt like he had been "shot at and missed and shit at and hit." Clearly we don't lack potential, just ambition.

Why is the word "AMBULANCE" typically stenciled backwards on the front of an ambulance?—C.L., Washington, D.C.

There are many who will think this question is dumb, C.L., but I know you are doing the best you can. It's so when the ambulance comes up behind your car, you'll be able to read the word AMBU-LANCE the right way in your rearview mirror.

Ever since I first experienced it, I've been wondering about the expression "head over heels in love." Most people understand this to mean being flipped out with passion. But if that's so, shouldn't it be "heels over head"? "Head over heels" is the way most of us spend at least two thirds of our lives. The British say "head over ears," which makes just as little sense. Any insights into the origin and meaning of these idiotic idioms would be appreciated.—Daniel Z., Chicago

Well, now you see why they're call idioms. "Head over heels" is a corruption of "heels over head," which dates back to the fourteenth century. The British "head over ears," meanwhile, is a corruption of "over head and ears," in over one's head, deeply. The corrupted versions started appearing in the eighteenth and nineteenth centuries and have now largely supplanted the originals. But don't despair. Years ago one often heard the equally nonsensical expression "cheap at half the price." Amazingly enough, years of ridicule by word mavens have largely succeeded in stamping out this barbarism in favor of the more sensible "cheap at twice the price"—a welcome if wholly unexpected victory. Maybe "head over heels" will meet the same fate.

What is the origin of the expression "hip hip hurrah"? According to one book I've read, it derives from an abbreviation of the Latin Hierusylema Est Perdita, "Jerusalem is destroyed." Apparently, medieval anti-Semites yelled "Hep! Hep!" as they exiled or executed innocent Jews. Can this be true? Can modern expressions such as hip, hipster, hippie, and hip-hop have such an odious etymology? Say it ain't so.—Name withheld, Washington, D.C.

You're not going to believe it, but there may be a germ of truth to this bizarre story.

Hip, hippie, hipster, and presumably hip-hop all derive from hep (meaning hip, of course), which dates from the turn of the century. There are several theories where hep came from:

1. From the marching cadence "hep, two, three, four." If you were hep, you were in step with what was happening.
2. From Joe Hep, who ran a lowlife saloon in Chicago in the 1890s. (You may recall our discussion on pages 92–94 of another 1890s Chicago saloonkeeper who allegedly lent his name to the language, Mickey Finn. Eighteen-nineties Chicago saloonkeepers were obviously quite a crew.) Hep liked to hover around the local hoods while they plotted their dirty deeds and fancied himself in the know. His name was originally used ironically to refer to someone who thought he knew what was going on but didn't. The ironic sense was soon lost and *to get Joe to* or *to get hep to* simply meant to get the straight dope, so to speak (source: D. W. Maurer, *American Speech*, 1941).
3. According to a 1914 slang dictionary, "from the name of a fabulous detective who operated in Cincinnati."

Of the three explanations, #1 is probably the least absurd. Hep (or hup or hip) has long been a multipurpose exclamation. In addition to being a cadence counter it was a traditional cry used by teamsters and herders to rouse animals. Hip was used to mean something on the order of "yo" or "hey" in the eighteenth century, and folks obviously thought it made a nice kickoff for hip hip hurrah.

Now we get to the bizarre part. Anti-Semitic rioters in Europe in the nineteenth century often shouted "Hep! Hep!" while on the prowl for Jews. Mob harassment of Jews in Hamburg, Frankfurt, and other German cities in 1819, in fact, became known as the "Hep! Hep!" riots.

The origin of the expression is unclear. Some claim it derived from *Hierusylema* (also spelled *Hierosolyma*) *Est Perdita*. This theory obliges us to believe that a significant fraction of the rioters were students of Latin. Others say it came from the German *habe*, in this context apparently meaning "give." But some believe it was nothing more than the traditional herdsman's cry, perhaps used because the rioters thought Jews ought to be rounded up like animals.

Does this mean we owe hip, hippie, hip hip hurrah, and the rest to the howling of a bunch of Jew baiters? Not necessarily. Literary citations of hip hip hurrah in clearly innocent contexts date from 1818, the year before the "Hep! Hep!" riots. (I've seen nothing to convince me "Hep! Hep!" was used in the Middle Ages.) The most plausible explanation is that hip hip hurrah and "Hep! Hep!" simply have a common source, the herder's cry. Still, it's something to think about next time you're about to give someone three cheers.

What a Piece of Work Is Man (A Continuing Series)

I have discovered that on every single page in every book, magazine, newspaper, etc., the words all end at the same place on the far right. This example of uniform perfection is bugging me. How do they DO that? Can't anyone "take a walk on the wild side" and end their words one or two spaces short?—Kirsten M., San Marcos High

When I get questions like this, Kirsten, it is all I can do to suppress a sob. But then I think: cripes, *some*body has to explain these things to people. Lining everything up on the right is called *justification*. It's done because typographers think it looks nice. These days computerized typesetting equipment does it automatically by putting extra space in between the words on the line.

What's the origin of the expression "It ain't over till the fat lady sings"?—Dolly G., Oakland, California

First let's get it straight: it's "The *opera* ain't over till the fat lady sings." Amazingly, we know exactly who originated this expression and approximately when.

It was first used around 1976 in a column in the San Antonio *News-Express* by sportswriter Dan Cook. (Cook does not recall the precise date or what the column was about.) Cook, who is also a sportscaster for KENS-TV in San Antonio, repeated the line during a broadcast in April 1978 to buck up local basketball fans, dejected because the San Antonio Spurs were down three games to one in the play-offs against the Washington Bullets.

Bullets coach Dick Motta heard the broadcast and used the expression himself to caution fans against overconfidence after his team finished off the Spurs and took on Philadelphia. The phrase became the team's rallying cry as they went on to win the championship, and from there it entered the common pot of the language. Most newsies aspire to nothing grander than a Pulitzer Prize, but Cook can tell his grandkids he's in *The Concise Oxford Dictionary of Proverbs*.

What is the origin of "tit for tat"? What is tat? And where can I get some in order to get the former?—PK, Baltimore

You're a stitch, PK. "Tit for tat" is a corruption of "tip for tap," blow for blow, which first turned up in the fifteenth century. (That's "tip" as in foul tip, a light or glancing shot.)

You are really cool when it comes to blowing the cobwebs off old words and phrases and telling us what they mean. But can you do the same with some new stuff? What does "funky" really mean? I don't think your most unabridged tome will have an answer. You may have to ask Don Cornelius.—Roger K., Dallas

Thanks for the advice, son, but you're dealing with a professional. It seems clear funky originally meant smelly. The question is, smelling of what? The *Oxford English Dictionary* takes the demure view that funky meant moldy, although it notes that "funk" has often been used to mean tobacco smoke and may derive from the Latin *fumar*, to smoke. By one account funky was applied to the smoky interior of jazz clubs and the somewhat ripe smell of the denizens thereof, from there was extended to the music, and finally acquired its current meaning of "hip in a down-and-dirty sort of way." (Funk, by the way, dates back to 1623; new it's not.)

That's the family-newspaper version. A less respectable view has it that funk is "the pungent odor given off by the sexually aroused female" (*The Dictionary of the Teenage Revolution and Its Aftermath*, 1983).

One last thing: funk in the sense of fear or panic, e.g., "He was in a blue funk," is a completely separate word deriving from the Flemish *fonck*, fear.

You Say It's Funky, I Say It Stinks

Re the origins of "funky": In Flash of the Spirit, *his brilliant exploration of the sacred in African art, music, and dance, anthropologist/ art historian Robert Farris Thompson proposes an alternative etymology for funky that also illuminates the word's longtime association with "smelly":*

"The slang term 'funky' . . . seems to derive from the Ki-Kongo lufuki, bad body odor. . . . Both jazzmen and Bakongo use funky and lufuki to praise persons for the integrity of their art, for having 'worked out' to achieve their aims. . . . This Kongo sign of exertion is identified with the positive energy of a person. Hence 'funk' in American jazz parlance can mean earthiness, a return to fundamentals."

This by no means negates the "sexually aroused female" theory of the word's origin, for the odor of a woman in heat is symbolic of "positive energy" in its most primitive form.—Cree M., New York

It seems to me that "shameful" and "shameless" basically mean the same thing, yet one is "full" and the other is "less." How is this possible?—Katherine C., Van Nuys, California

Shameful and shameless *don't* mean the same thing. A shameful act is one that ought to inspire a sense of shame in its author. If said person is shameless (brazen), however, it doesn't. As one of my affronted relatives once told me, many of the questions we address in this column are shameful. Luckily, we're shameless.

The most needed new word in the English language must surely be a substitute for the "his/her" attribution, which forces you to either rewrite or use the awkward "his or her" (or, for those afraid of stirring up a feminist terrorist group, "her or his"). I am perplexed that our language is so flexible and yet no one seems to have solved this

semantic problem. Is there a genius who has done it? If not, as our resident genius, will you give us a substitute?—B.C., Virginia Beach, Virginia

The trick isn't inventing a new word, it's getting people to use it. Some eighty new terms have been proposed, the first of them in the 1850s. But none of them has made the slightest headway in popular usage.

In 1884 the composer Charles Converse proposed *thon, thons*, a contraction of "that one," with the *th* pronounced as in "they." It found its way into several unabridged dictionaries, but that was as far as it got. Other nineteenth-century proposals for he/she, his/her, him/her include *ne, nis, nim; hi, hes, hem; e, es, em; ir, iro, im*; and *ip, ips* (no, smart-mouth, the objective case wasn't *ooray*). In 1912 the Chicago superintendent of schools proposed *he'er, him'er, his'er, his'er's*. She tried to get the National Education Association to adopt it, but no go.

The rise of the modern feminist movement set off a new round of linguistic invention, with identical (i.e., no) results: *te, tes, tir; shis, shims, shim, shimself; zie* (from German *sie*), *zees, zim, zeeself*; and so on. Most of these obviously are a play on the existing pronouns, but occasionally you see something like *per, pers*, short for the gender-neutral "person." Then you get comedians like the guy in *Forbes* magazine who blended "he or she, it" to produce *h'orsh'it*.

Others, recognizing the futility of trying to invent pronouns, suggest we ought to make do with what we've got. One might say "one," for example, except that it strikes most Americans as stilted. You could try "it," as we now say of babies, but few do so with any enthusiasm.

There has been progress on one front: the use of "they," "their," "them" as third-person singular with indefinite constructions such as "anyone," "somebody," "each," "the person who," etc. This produces sentences like "Somebody has forgotten their hat," which purists find offensive. However, as sociologist Ann Bodine points out, singular "they" was in wide use by distinguished writers of English prior to the attacks of nineteenth-century grammarians, and its use in speech has persisted to the present day. Not only does it fill an obvious need, it has a precedent in "you," which long ago supplanted second-person singular "thou." Cecil will go so far as to predict that within a couple generations singular "they" in many instances will be acceptable in formal written usage.

But some gaps will undoubtedly remain. The remark "A person may find themself left high and dry" would probably pass unnoticed in conversation today, but few would say, "A doctor may find themself . . ." In such cases even the most ardent feminists fall back on the old standbys: rewrite to eliminate the pronoun, use plurals or second person, and so on.

In a personal or polemical work a writer can make "she" the default pronoun. For many years "she" was also used generically in discussions of teachers, who were predominantly women. But male teachers argued during the sixties that the "feminization of teaching" was partly responsible for the chronically low pay and were able to get the pronoun changed. Women themselves sometimes object to the use of the generic "she"—for example, in business publications that invariably refer thus to consumers.

For what it's worth, you hear less and less of the old argument that "he" (and "man," for that matter) somehow "includes" women. Common sense suggests, and studies bear out, that when you see supposedly generic masculine terms you think first of males. But let's not pretend that the elimination of such problems would mean the end of sexist speech. As writer Deborah Cameron points out, the sentence "The man went berserk and killed his neighbor's wife" is un-objectionable on its surface. But stop to think: why "his neighbor's wife" instead of "one of his neighbors"?

Two questions. Soviet authorities used to brand a person as a "cos-mopolite" in order to signify his or her lack of good Soviet citizenship. Why? What pejorative connotations did this word have in their minds? Second, they often seemed to use "hooliganism" as a specific criminal charge like theft or assault, although the term as we use it is vague, covering a host of activities. What types of crime(s) did it cover?—Jonathan L., Los Angeles

Those of us who are fastidious about these things, Jonathan, al-ways say "cosmopolitan," "cosmopolite" being a too-literal translation of the Russian *kosmopolit*. Also, you seldom see "cosmopolitan" with-out "rootless" stuck in front of it like a cheap cigar. The significance of the term is clear to any Russian. It means the Jews, and has since the beginning of the Soviet state, and probably earlier.

Kosmopolit first entered the Russian language in the 1860s, around the time Czar Alexander II first permitted some Jews to em-igrate to other parts of Russia from the Pale, the region in the west-ern part of the empire to which they had long been restricted. Many Jews took the opportunity to move to big cities like St. Petersburg, where they apparently aroused the ire of the local goyim, who re-garded them basically as roving loan sharks. Jews were also widely presumed to have extraterritorial loyalties—that is, they were thought to be Zionists, dreaming even in the nineteenth century of returning someday to Jerusalem.

The Soviet-produced *Dictionary of the Contemporary Russian Lit-erary Language* defines *kosmopolit* as "a person who does not con-sider himself as belonging to any nationality." If that's too ambiguous, the definition of *kosmopolitizm* should remove any doubts about the word's implications: "a bourgeois reactionary ideol-ogy."

Jews were persecuted off and on throughout Soviet history, nota-bly by Stalin in the thirties and again during the "Doctors' Plot" in the early fifties, which involved several Jewish doctors who allegedly plotted against the dictator's life. Officially, of course, the Soviet Union did not single out ethnic groups, hence the need for code words.

A University of Chicago professor with whom I spoke on this subject recalled that a friend of his who was Jewish was once arrested in the Soviet Union for speculating (in books, of all things). The authorities officially described the friend as "a thin, agile brunette," which presumably made the situation clear to all concerned.

Moving on to "hooliganism," you're right that the term is vague to us. It's vague to the Russians, too, and that's why Soviet authorities liked it—if they couldn't nail you for anything else, there was always hooliganism. In this respect the charge is similar to our disorderly conduct, although the penalties can be far more severe.

It should be noted that hooliganism referred strictly to common crime rather than political crime. I recall reading prior to the breakup of the U.S.S.R. about thirty Lithuanians being arrested for hooliganism following anti-Soviet demonstrations, but that was just an attempt to sweep things under the rug. The authorities undoubtedly felt it was better to be dealing with rowdies than revolutionaries. Not that it made any difference in the end.

Where did the name "Dixie" come from? And exactly what states comprise Dixie?—Leigh-Anne H., Dallas

Dixie is usually thought to include the states of the Confederacy, but where the term comes from nobody knows for sure. Here are the three leading theories:

1. Before the Civil War, the Citizens Bank of Louisiana, located in New Orleans, issued ten-dollar notes that bore the Creole/French word *dix*, ten, on one side. These notes were known as "dixies" and the south came to be known as the "land of dixies."
2. The term comes from the Dixon in "Mason-Dixon Line," the famous pre–Revolutionary War surveyors' line that separated Maryland and Pennsylvania.

3. It comes from "Dixy's land," Dixy supposedly being a kindly slave owner on Manhattan Island, of all places. Dixy's regime was supposedly so enlightened that for slaves his plantation came to symbolize earthly paradise. Sounds ridiculous, but the story was widely told in the years just after the Civil War.

The trouble with all these explanations is that there are no published citations of the word prior to the appearance of Daniel Emmett's song "Dixie" in 1859. One etymologist notes that a minstrel named Dixey performed in Philadelphia in 1856, but that's not much help. For what it's worth, the editors of the *American Heritage Dictionary*, normally reliable in these matters, come down foursquare on the side of explanation #1, on the basis of what evidence I do not know.

Then you get a few characters like the guy in the journal *American Speech* who speculates that it comes from *dixi*, Latin for "I have said [it]." This is allegedly emblematic of the take-no-guff attitude characteristic of the antebellum south. Forgive me if I decline to take sides.

Why is "colonel" pronounced "kernel"?—Listener, Ed Busch talk show, Dallas

Mainly to continue the tradition of making English as incomprehensible as possible, thereby keeping the spelling bee industry in business. (Believe me, there's millions in it.) Colonel comes from Old Italian *colonello*, commander of a column of troops, which in turn derives from *colonna*, column. The word wasn't always spelled the Italian way, though. Four hundred years ago English followed the Spanish practice and spelled it "coronel," sensibly pronounced the way it looked. Eventually this was corrupted to ker-nel, still not bad considering we're talking about the British, who pronounce "Featheringstonehaugh" "Fanshaw."

But it couldn't last. Some nameless busybody decided coronel ought to be spelled "colonel" to better reflect its Italian origin, doubtless out of the same misplaced love of precision that gave us 16½ feet to the rod and $27^{11}/_{32}$ grains to the dram. It's just the Anglo-Saxon way, I guess. How these people conquered an empire I'll never know.

There are three English words that end with -gry. Two of them are "hungry" and "angry." What's the third?—Listener, Alan B. Colmes show, WNBC radio, New York

Every time I go on the radio I know this one's bound to come up sooner or later, along with "Name an English word that contains all the vowels just once in the right order." (Answer: facetiously. Come on, you think I was born yesterday?)

I don't know that I'd put either question on a par with the search for the unified field theory, but since you insist, here's the answer: the word is "gry," meaning "one tenth of a line"—not, as one might guess in these degraded times, a unit of measurement in the drug trade, but rather part of the decimal system of linear measurement proposed by English philosopher John Locke (1632–1704). A gry was a hundredth of an inch and a thousandth of a "philosophical foot." Too bad Locke's idea didn't catch on; the thought of measuring things in philosophical feet has an ineffable poignance. The *Oxford English Dictionary* says gry is also an obsolete verb meaning "to rage or roar."

But wait. Lest you think there is only one right answer to the truly cosmic questions of life, I should advise you of the existence of "puggry" and "aggry," which also fill the bill. Puggry is an alternate spelling of "puggree," meaning either an Indian turban or a scarf wound around a sun helmet with the end hanging down in back as a shade. An aggry bead, according to my "Webster's Third," is a "variegated glass bead found buried in the earth in Ghana and England." As with many enigmatic dictionary definitions, this leaves one abubble with questions: who buried them? And why Ghana and England? Sadly, we must defer the amazing answer till some later date.

Bulletin #1 from the Teeming Millions

"ABSTEMIOUSLY" HAS THE SAME VOWEL CHARACTERIS-TICS AS "FACETIOUSLY."—STEPHEN S., BEVERLY HILLS, CALIFORNIA

Thanks for the info, Stosh, but it was hardly necessary to send it Western Union.

Bulletin #2 from the T.M.

Guess what—there is another word that fits the old "all the vowels, in order, and only once" quiz: abstentiously. Okay, so it's not in Web-ster's Ninth New Collegiate Dictionary, but does that necessarily mean it's not a word?—Joanne Schell, Denton, Texas

This is not the most rigorous approach to the question that we might have devised, Joanne, but you're in luck. The *OED* informs us that there is a word "abstentious," "characterized by abstinence; self-restraining or refraining," so we'll generously declare that abstentiously is a word, too.

You may remember the infamous Susan B. Anthony dollar, a thirteen-sided coin that bombed miserably when it was offered as a substitute for the good old greenback. There are many mysteries sur-rounding this coin, not least of which is why they decided to intro-duce it in the first place. But my question is simpler: is there a name for a thirteen-sided object—that is, besides "pariah"?—Listener, Jim Althoff show, KING radio, Seattle

Having spent a good five minutes scouring my *OED*, I fail to find one. But how's this for a free-lance effort: "triskaidekagon." (Compare "triskaidekaphobia," fear of the number thirteen.) You discover any other voids in the language, just let me know.

We Digress

You really punched my button with the letter about the Susan B. Anthony dollar. One of the biggest canards ever perpetrated by the government was the notion that the coin was "thirteen-sided." As you'll notice from the enclosed sample, it is not. The reason the "Susie" was rejected by the American people is that it is, in fact, round with milled edges—just like a quarter, with which it is easily confused. If the coin actually had a distinctive shape and color, such as that of the Hong Kong two-dollar piece or the Canadian "loony" dollar, you and I would happily be plunking Susan B. Anthony dollars into vending machines today.

My theory is that the failure of the Susan B. Anthony dollar is attributable to a conspiracy by the Department of the Treasury. I believe the males in charge wished to ensure rejection of a coin with a feminist on it and designed the Susie accordingly. Little else could explain the incompetence with which this otherwise admirable project was executed. Any comments?—Stephanie F., Washington, D.C.

I'm not about to disagree with people who send me money, Steph. But it's often difficult to distinguish malicious intent from mere stupidity. Considering that we're talking about the government here, I'd opt for the latter.

I've always wondered where the wonderful American expression "Indian giver" originated. Is an Indian giver one who (1) as an Indian gives you something and then takes it back, (2) gives things to Indi-

ans, or (3) gives away Indians? Your insight is greatly appreciated.
—Michael W., Jacksonville, Florida

This whole thing is so ironic it's an instant cure for pernicious anemia. "Indian" was once used by the white man as an all-purpose adjective signifying "bogus" or "false," owing to the supposedly low morals of the red man. Thus you had "Indian summer," false summer late in the year; "Indian corn" and "Indian tea," cheap substitutes for products the original colonists had known back in England; and "Indian giver," someone who gives you something and then takes it back.

But of course the truth is that it was the Europeans who were the real Indian givers, repeatedly promising the Indians reservations by treaty and then stealing them back once valuable farmland or minerals were found. The term has thus inadvertently become an acid commentary on the character of its inventors. I think it's poetic.

The "L" Word Raises Its Ugly Head

Your definition of "Indian giver" is incorrect, biased, and incomplete. Your answer fulfills the stereotypical desire to vent frustration and anger at the "white man," the true "Indian giver." That's unimaginative and boring, which is typical of contemporary liberals. A definition showing true imagination and sensitivity can be found in the book The Gift *by Lewis Hyde, one "white man" who looks at the world with his eyes open.—Tatiana R., Washington, D.C.*

I like that "eyes open" part, Tatiana. You should try it. Contrary to your evident belief, Hyde's book strengthens my argument, such as it was. Admittedly, I didn't mention the earliest definition of "Indian gift," namely, one made in the expectation that it will be reciprocated. Hyde rectifies this omission. He then launches into a discussion of gift-giving in primitive societies, the gist of which is that the free-and-easy tribal method of passing gifts back and forth is superior to the white man's notion of hoarding the goodies for yourself. I don't entirely buy that—competitive gift-giving in Indian cultures could be just as silly and destructive as anything the white man was capable of—but it's not out of line with what I had to say.

Making Reservations

You appear to be under the impression that Indian reservations were provided by the United States to Indians in treaties and that the whites later "took back" the reservations. In fact, in the majority of cases, reservations are areas of the tribes' own homelands, usually very small by comparison to their original territory, which the Indians kept to themselves, while giving up the balance in the treaties. In legalese, the Indians "reserved to themselves" a portion of their lands while granting the rest to the government.

While this distinction may seem like nitpicking, it is important, because most non-Indians perceive the special status of Indian tribes and their lands as gifts from the benevolent white father in Washington (at the resentful taxpayer's expense). In fact, neither their special status, which is sovereignty retained by the tribes, nor their reserved lands are gifts in any sense of the word.—Anthony C., Mill Valley, California

Point well taken. Thanks.

Who Are the Physicians of Tomorrow?

I'm afraid you've goofed again. In a recent column you wrote, "The whole thing is so ironic it's an instant cure for pernicious anemia." I'm surprised you didn't know that pernicious anemia is caused by a deficiency in a protein called intrinsic factor which carries Vitamin B_{12} to the ileum, the last segment of the small intestine, where the complex binds to a receptor and is absorbed into the blood. No amount of iron would cure it but a good shot in the arm of B_{12} would do a lot of good. Would you please set the record straight?—Larry

G., junior, Northwestern University Medical School, Evanston, Illinois

Go away, kid, you bother me.

I've got a hypothetical question. I'm building this boat. It's getting bigger and bigger. At what point does it become a ship?—Jack S., San Antonio, Texas

Well, we could get technical, I suppose. Among sailing vessels, the distinction between ships and boats is that a ship is a square-rigged craft with at least three masts, and a boat isn't. With regard to motorized craft, a ship is a large vessel intended for oceangoing or at least deepwater transport and a boat is anything else.

But that's too much to remember. Try this: ships have to be big enough to carry boats, and boats have to be small enough to be carried by ships.

There are exceptions, of course. Many commercial fishing craft, for example, are sizable oceangoing vessels, yet they're almost invariably called boats. Similarly for submarines, built by General Dynamics's Electric Boat Division. The Great Lakes are pretty deep, and one sees certain large vessels on them that to all appearances are ships, but in fact said vessels are commonly called ore boats. However, these exceptions mar the classic purity of the answer above, so we'll pay them no mind.

Another question in the same vein, which we may as well get out of the way now that we've got the blood pumping, is: *what's the difference between a hill and a mountain?* We initially looked in the 1969 Random House unabridged and learned that a hill is "a natural elevation of the earth's surface, smaller than a mountain," while a mountain is "a natural elevation of the earth's surface rising more or less abruptly to a summit, and attaining an altitude greater than that of a hill." In other words, a hill is smaller than a mountain and a mountain is taller (and steeper) than a hill. Big freaking help.

Recognizing the inadequacy of the foregoing, the editors of the Random House dictionary took another stab at the problem in their second edition (1987). Hill stays the same, but a mountain is now a natural elevation, etc., "attaining an altitude greater than 2,000 feet."

This is a commendable attempt at precision, but it runs into trouble on the very next page, where we find a list of "Notable Mountain Peaks of the World." Mount Carmel, Israel, checks in at a paltry 1,818 feet. Many of the so-called mountains in the Ozarks are similarly stunted.

Perhaps we should say that anything over two thousand feet is automatically a mountain, but peaks under two thousand feet may qualify if they (1) are steep, (2) have rocky sides, or (3) have the word "Mount" in their names. Of course, this doesn't help us out with the Black Hills of South Dakota, which reach a height of four thousand feet above the surrounding country but don't qualify for an upgrade in nomenclature. But it's the best I can do for now.

Why is pound abbreviated "lb."?—Janice, Dallas

"Lb." stands for *libra*, the basic unit of Roman weight, from which our present-day pound derives. The libra weighed a little under twelve ounces avoirdupois. Speaking of ounces, "oz." stands for the Italian *onza*, ounce, and came into use in the fifteenth century. Ounce, interestingly, comes from the Latin *uncia*, a twelfth, which is also the source of the term "inch." At one time there were twelve ounces to the pound, a usage that still survives in the system of troy weight used by jewelers and goldsmiths. Sixteen oz. to the lb. didn't arrive on the scene until the thirteenth or fourteenth century. Pound derives from the Latin *pondo*, "by weight."

Your tireless research into etymology is to be applauded. The word I want you to trace for me is "honky"; where does it come from, and how long has it been in use?—David J., Paris, France

P.S.: I love your books. The only thing wrong with living in France is that I can't get your column or barbecue potato chips.

I like a man who's got his priorities straight. Honky comes from "bohunk" and "hunky," derogatory terms for Bohemian, Hungarian, and Polish immigrants that came into use around the turn of the century. According to Robert Hendrickson, author of the *Encyclopedia of Word and Phrase Origins*, black workers in Chicago meat-packing plants picked up the term from white workers and began applying it indiscriminately to all Caucasians. Probably thought they all looked alike.

Another Source for Honky

Your source for the origin of honky only gave you half the story. Another probable etymon for honky, cited by David Dalby in his "African Element in American English" (to be found in my Rappin' and Stylin' Out: Communication in Urban Black America) *is the Wolof term* honq, *red, pink, a term frequently used to describe white men in African languages.—Tom Kochman, Professor of Communication, University of Illinois at Chicago*

What was the "Great Vowel Shift" and why did it happen? PBS's "Story of English" series never explained it satisfactorily.—Sue, Detroit, Michigan

That's because there isn't any explanation. As Robert McCrum et al. note in the book version of *The Story of English*, "Phrases like the famous 'Great Vowel Shift' [are] hardly more informative than the 'unknown land' of early cartography." What happened was that between 1350 and 1550, the period in which Middle English became modern English, vowel pronunciations changed dramatically. The Middle English long *i*, formerly pronounced like the *e* in he, shifted to *i* as in high. Middle English *hous*, pronounced "hoose," changed to the modern house. The experts say the GVS "in effect moved the long-stressed vowels forward in the mouth," but to me it just sounds like you open up your mouth more. Why it happened no one knows.

What is the official name for those little plastic thingies on the ends of shoelaces?—Katie A., Mesa, Arizona

You'll never finish the crossword if you ask these questions one at a time, Katie. The little thingies are called "aglets," an Anglo-Saxon slave is an "esne," and an East Indian tree is a "dhak." My father taught me those. He used to do the crossword puzzle in ink, bless him. Naturally I had to do him one better. I type.

Why am I having a hard time finding the word "callipygian" in the dictionary? No one I ask seems to know what it means.—Kurt Jacobsen, U.S.A.

Great word, "callipygian." Means "having shapely buttocks." As opposed to "steatopygous," or "fat-arsed." Lends that essential touch of class to your locker-room conversations. The reason you can't find it is you're looking in the wrong place. Try *Mrs. Byrne's Dictionary of Unusual, Obscure, and Preposterous Words* by Josefa Heifetz Byrne, a landmark reference work this column has often recommended in the past. Where else could you find gems like "hircine," "goatlike, especially in smell," or "hircismus," "the condition of having stinky armpits"?

We were talking about the medieval theory of the four bodily humors and noticed that "sanguine," "choleric," and "melancholy" correspond roughly in meaning with the modern English "glad," "mad," and "sad." We were wishing we knew a rhyming word for "phlegmatic." Can you think of one?—Justin Quisitive, Arlington, Massachusetts

The medieval theory of the four bodily humors, eh? Well, I guess it beats talking about what's on sale at K mart. Given that "phlegmatic" means calm, sluggish, and unemotional, I vote for glad, mad, sad, and moss-clad. What do you want, Shakespeare?

What the hell is *toejam, anyway?*—*Goofy Gholson, west suburbs, Chicago*

The grotty stuff that collects between your toes, of course. A "toejam football" is the disgusting ellipsoid that forms when you rub it with your finger. What Freudian significance it had for the Beatles (cf. "Come Together") I'd just as soon not know.

How did Fido become the more or less generic name for the family dog, when in fact there are few canines that actually answer to that moniker?—*N.D.G., Chicago*

If you'd been properly educated, N., you wouldn't have to ask this question. Then again, if you and the rest of the boomers already knew the easy stuff, this job might actually become strenuous. Fido comes from the Latin *fidus*, faithful, a fitting term for man's best friend. Or at least it was back in the days when four years of high school Latin was considered the bare minimum for a person of culture (hey, I took it). *Fidus*, of course, will be familiar to the many

readers of the *Aeneid* from the expression *fidus Achates*, faithful
Achates, Achates being the character who played Pancho to the heroic Aeneas's Cisco Kid.

*Our high school French teacher always insisted learning French
was important because it was going to become the international language of business. Now I hear English is mandatory in international
aviation, and the Chinese students in Beijing spoke English to the international media. Was our French teacher shucking us? Merde!—
Les Petites, South Boston*

Now, now. He/she probably just didn't know any better. French
teachers lead such empty lives as it is that no one has the heart to
tell them the awful truth, which is that French is a language on the
way down, not up. Once the language of diplomacy, French was used
in the royal courts of Germany, Russia, and Italy during the nineteenth century. Fifty years ago Somerset Maugham called it "the
common language of educated men" (women, too, one presumes).
But it's been in a state of decline since World War II, having long
ago been supplanted by—you guessed it—English.

English is the primary language of more than 400 million people
and the second language of hundreds of millions more. It's essential
in science, technology, economics, and finance. It's the official language of airport control towers, might as well be the official
language of computer software, and of course is vital to a perfect
comprehension of MTV, Madonna, and other pillars of modern culture. French is the primary language of maybe 114 million, including
such outposts of world commerce as Haiti, Cameroon, and Burkina
Faso, and is essential chiefly to reading menus at Le Cirque.

The French have been desperately attempting to reverse this
trend. In addition to hosting international conferences of
"Francophone" (French-speaking) nations, France as of 1986 was
spending $750 million per year to support twenty thousand French
teachers in 155 countries. It also employs language police to guard
against un-Gallic intrusions such as *le compact-disc*. But all in vain.

Not that French doesn't have its uses. *Au contraire*. It remains the
language of international pretension *par excellence*, having a certain

je ne sais quoi that appeals irresistibly to the *nouveaux riches*. Also, let's face it, *je t'aime* sounds infinitely classier than "luv ya, babe." But French is more likely to come in handy in the intimate hours after the business meeting than during.

Why is the room where TV talk-show guests wait before going on the air always called the "green room"? I've never seen one that was green.—Zsa Zsa, Los Angeles

Yeah, and for good reason; greenish hues tend to make the inhabitants look like they just died of gangrene. Legend has it that the green room, also styled greenroom or green-room, goes back to the Elizabethan era, when the actors lolled away the time between entrances on the lawn behind the theater, or "on the green." Alas, like so much else in show biz, this appears to be a crock. According to my *Oxford English Dictionary*, the earliest known usage of green room was in 1701. One plausible theory is that the green room was originally painted green to rest the aching peepers of the actors, who were bleary-eyed from the bright stage lights.

Why is there an I Street and a K Street but no J Street in Washington, D.C.? At least one other federally spawned burg, Anchorage, Alaska, uses a similar street-naming scheme also lacking J. My daughter claimed the streets were named before the invention of Js, but recanted that theory upon reaching junior high school.—John Beard, Arlington, Virginia

That's what you get for subjecting her to higher education—her first guess was a lot closer to the mark than her second. *J* is a late addition to the alphabet, having initially been introduced as an alternative form of *I*. It began to be used to signify our modern consonant *J* around 1600, but the two letters continued to be used interchangeably for years thereafter, e.g., *jngeniously, ieweller*. As late as 1820 some dictionaries still weren't alphabetizing *I* and *J* words separately.

D.C. planner Pierre L'Enfant undoubtedly didn't include a J Street because he considered *I* and *J* basically the same letter. (It certainly wasn't because he disliked the statesman John Jay, as legend has it.) A similar confusion attended the letters *U* and *V*, which were also used interchangeably. The D.C. plan included both U and V streets, but using capital *V* to indicate both *U* and *V* on buildings (e.g., VNITED STATES POST OFFICE) survived until the 1930s, no doubt in imitation of such classical inscriptions as IVLIVS CAESAR.

Letters from the Teeming Millions

Your item on the letters I, J, U, *and* V *was not the last word (and no doubt what I have to add won't be either).* J *and* V *were the consonantal forms of* I *and* U, *respectively (e.g., as in "juventus").* V *in Latin was pronounced like* W *in English, and* J *was pronounced like* Y *in English.—Stewart Colten, Arlington, Virginia*

Sorry, Stewart. According to the *Oxford English Dictionary*, U and V were used "without clear distinction in value, each of them being used to denote either the vowel *u* or the consonant *v*. The practice with regard to the employment of the two forms varied considerably, but the general tendency was to write *v* initially and *u* in other positions, regardless of phonetic considerations." The story with *I* and *J* is more complex, but the *OED* lists many instances of *J* being used as a vowel.

Where does the phrase "the dickens" come from, as in "he scared the d. out of me"? I presume this refers to Charles Dickens, but I don't get the logic.—B.L., Dallas

Presume nothing, friend. "Dickens" is thought to be a euphemism for "the devil," much as "gosh" is a sub for "God," "heck" for "hell," and "mofo" for . . . well, no point getting graphic. Some speculate that "dickens" is a short form of an earlier term "devilkin," little devil, but this has never been firmly established.

Where does the expression "Mind your P's and Q's" come from? Does it mean politeness and quietness? Also, I recently came across the phrase "a labor organizer traveling on the q.t." What does q.t. stand for?—Kimberly T., New York City

As usual, we've got theories by the bushel, facts by the milligram. The more fanciful explanations for "Mind your P's and Q's" include:

- It originated in British pubs as an abbreviation for "mind your pints and quarts." Supposedly this warned the barkeep to serve full measure, mark the customer's tab accurately, etc.
- It meant "mind your pea (jacket) and queue." Queues (pigtails) were often powdered, and the woman of the family was telling her husband to keep the cruddy kid stuff off his collar. An even dumber variation of this involved "pieds," French for "feet," and says minding your P's and Q's means combing your hair and polishing your shoes.
- P and Q stands for "prime quality." According to the *Oxford English Dictionary*, to be P and Q was a regional expression meaning "top quality." It first shows up in a bit of doggerel from 1612: "Bring in a quart of Maligo, right true: And looke, you Rogue, that it be Pee and Kew."

The simplest explanation is that the expression refers to the difficulty kids have distinguishing lower-case *p* and *q*, mirror images of each other. Mind your you-know-whats was thus a teacher's admonition to students. Plausible? Yes. Sexy? No. Such is the fate of a slave to facts.

"On the q.t.," meaning on the sly, secret, is easier. Most likely it's an abbreviation of "quiet."

More Letters from the Teeming Millions

When I took typography at the University of Iowa, I was told the expression "Mind your P's and Q's" originated with printers who set headlines using movable type. If you've ever seen old type, you know the letters are mirror images of the regular alphabet. Lower-case P's

look like Q's and vice versa. "Mind your P's and Q's" was a reminder
not to mix up the letters when putting them back in the rack after use.
Printing also gave us another expression. Individual letters were
called "sorts," and if you used up all you had of a given letter, you'd
be upset, naturally, because you were "out of sorts."—Marion E.,
Chicago

I was with you until that last turn, Marion. "Out of sorts"? Get serious.

Out of Sorts over "Out of Sorts"

I enjoy your column, but you made a mistake in suggesting that
Marion E.'s explanation of the origin of "out of sorts" was wacko.
Among my proudest possessions is a 1937 Webster's Universal Un-
abridged Dictionary. Under "sort," noun, first entry, definition
number 6 reads: "In printing, a type or character, commonly one be-
longing to a font, . . . generally in the plural and in phrases; as, out
of sorts, hard on sorts, etc." I have been told by those "in the know"
that the colloquial usage derived from the annoyance that one felt
when typesetting came to a halt because the typesetter was "out of
sorts." Do I get an A?—Jay H., Stoughton, Wisconsin

If you do, it's not going to stand for "admirable." You've fallen
prey to the common fallacy *post hoc, ergo propter hoc,* the assumption that because two things follow in sequence the first necessarily
caused the second. It's true dictionaries juxtapose the two definitions
of "out of sorts," but they don't say one inspired the other and indeed they would be foolish to do so.

If we turn to the *Oxford English Dictionary,* really the only thing
for this kind of work, we find that the first known reference to "sort"
in the sense of a character in a type font occurs in 1668. The first
known use of the expression "out of sorts," irritable, occurs in 1621.
Other seventeenth-century quotes indicate you could use "out of
sorts" to mean you were literally out of stock, caught short, broke. It
seems reasonable that this general use of "out of sorts" was the origin of the modern expression, not printing in particular.

Why do they call that thing below your jawline an Adam's apple? Relative of yours?—Mike and Dave, Chicago

You heathens, the Adam in question is everybody's relative, the ancestor of humankind. It's called an Adam's apple because of a legend that a piece of the forbidden fruit got stuck in his throat. Eve, alas, didn't know the Heimlich maneuver, and the resultant bulge has been passed down to subsequent generations as a sign of male weakness—like we need reminding. In reality the Adam's apple is "the anterior extremity of the thyroid cartilage of the larynx."

Hey, you great festering gob of knowledge, why are those bastions of suburban tankdom known as station *wagons? Is it because they're so huge and clumsy they might as well be stationary?—Julie, Washington, D.C.*

"Great festering gob of knowledge"? Lord, protect me from my admirers. Automakers borrowed the term "station wagon" from the carriage-making biz, as in horse and carriage. Station wagons, known before 1890 as depot wagons, were four-wheeled covered vehicles that you might take down to the railroad station to pick up passengers and their baggage—a service not unlike that performed by station wagons today. Some had a removable backseat and a tailgate that could be lowered to facilitate loading. Other familiar features include (1) wood sides (and for that matter, wood everything else) and (2) ungainly designs—the originals looked like orange crates on wheels. Today's boats, therefore, are the product of nigh on a century of tradition. Show some respect.

I recently changed professions, and though I refer to myself as a "dancer" or "showgirl," many people use the term "go-go dancer." No one seems to know how, why, or where "go-go" originated. What's the story?—Phoenix, Indianapolis

Glad to see you're reading the Straight Dope, Phoenix; in your line of work it probably helps to keep your mind on the higher things. "Go-go" derives from the French *à go go*, in abundance, ga-lore, a term that dates back to 1440 and may have derived from an older word *agogue*, merriment.

It found its way into our language by a route that's circuitous even for English. According to John Ciardi's *Good Words to You*, Compton Mackenzie published a novel in 1947 entitled *Whisky Galore*, about a freighter with ten thousand cases of whisky that is wrecked near a booze-starved island during World War II. The book was made into a movie of the same name in England (it was called *Tight Little Island* in its U.S. release) that, when dubbed for the French, became *Whiskey à gogo*, whiskey galore.

The movie inspired someone to open a bar in Paris (or was it Cannes? I can never remember these things) called "Whiskey a gogo," which became one of the first discotheques. Later the idea and the name were both imported to New York. One day the manager of the New York Whiskey a Go-Go took it upon himself to hire scantily clad girls to demonstrate new dances, and the go-go dancer was born.

I imagine the term stuck in part because it seemed to mean something in English. Cecil recalls the pennant-winning Chicago White Sox of 1959, known as the "go-go" White Sox because of their basepath speed, and I assume you're shaking it with equal vigor down there in Indianapolis.

My friends and I adore your column and read it every week before the festivities begin at Captain White's Oyster Bar and Clog Palace. Recently we were discussing a word we've all heard but have never seen in print. It's pronounced "skosh" (long "o"). Whenever I ask somebody to spell it, they always say, "You mean as in 'a skosh more room'?" I contend that it's not a real word but was created solely for the purpose of a jeans commercial (I'm not sure which brand). Enlighten us, Cecil, and we'll tell you what a Clog Palace is.—Julie M., Silver Spring, Maryland

One doesn't tell Cecil anything, dear; one reminds him. Cecil first heard "skosh"—you spelled it correctly—from a printer in Tucson, Arizona, who applied it to any dimension smaller than a centimeter and larger than an angstrom. This fellow had learned his trade in the navy and had picked up an abundance of off-the-wall weights and measures from his fellow craftsmen. Another example was the "glug," a liquid measure—you wanted two glugs of something, you turned the bottle upside down until it went "glug, glug."

Skosh had a slightly more respectable origin: it derived from the Japanese *sukoshi*, little. United Nations troops first picked it up during the Korean War, presumably while on R and R in Japan, and it's been part of military slang ever since.

My grandmother was named Margaret. She, and every other Margaret I know, has the nickname "Peg" or "Peggy." None of them can tell me how the two are connected or how one arose from the other. Can you?—Michael Hix, Redlands, California

Never underestimate human ingenuity. Margaret has spawned an amazing variety of names, some of which you wouldn't connect with the original in a million years. For example: Margot, Marguerita, Rita (!), Greta, Gretel, Gretchen, Marjorie (originally Margery), Margie, Maggie, Madge, May, Maisie, Daisy (!!), Maidie, Meg, and Mog. As for Peg, one historian writes, "The nicknames Mog and Meg later gave rise to the rhymed forms Pog(gy) and Peg(gy)." Can't say as I know a lot of Poggies and can't say as I want to. But you see how Grandma Margaret wound up with Peg.

Oops o' Daisy

Regarding the question about how Peggy derived from Margaret, you showed some astonishment that Daisy derived from Margaret. It is, in fact, the origin of the name. La marguerite is French for daisy. Daisy historically (until this century) has been a common diminutive of Margaret, and in the fifteenth century Marguerite d'Anjou, wife of England's Henry VI, used the daisy as her personal symbol.
An anonymous poem:

In search from A to Z they passed,
And "Marguerita" chose at last;
But thought it sound far more sweet
To call the baby "Marguerite."
When grandma saw the little pet,
She called her "darling Margaret."
Next uncle Jack and cousin Aggie
Sent cup and spoon to "little Maggie."
And grandpapa the right must beg
To call the lassie "bonnie Meg."
From "Marguerita" down to "Meg,"
And now she's simply "little Peg."

—*Eirene Varley, Austin, Texas*

Poetry always chokes me up. Just so we understand each other, I wasn't personally astonished by the Margaret/Daisy connection; when you've been on this job as long as I have, you're not astonished by anything. But I'd venture to say the average citizen wouldn't suspect a link. Contrary to what is apparently wide belief, judging from the mail, Margaret doesn't derive from the French/Spanish/Yiddish word for daisy. Margaret and marguerite do have a common source, the Latin *margarita*, pearl.

Why, when someone stops using a drug abruptly, do they call it going "cold turkey"?—Michael W., Washington, D.C.

Some say it's because heroin addicts undergoing withdrawal are so pale and covered with goose bumps that their skin looks like that of an uncooked turkey. As with most good stories, however, this appears to be crapola. "Cold turkey," which dates from 1916, is related to "talk turkey," meaning to cut the comedy and talk frankly. Similarly, when you go cold turkey, you dispense with the preliminaries and get right down to it. Why turkey rather than crested titmouse, say, is not clear, but perhaps it was because the turkey, as your standard U.S. game fowl, recalled the no-bull simplicity of frontier life.

Chapter 10

Adventures in Technology

I know this is going to sound crazy, but my Slinky (that's the Original Slinky Walking Spring Toy) has the power to turn on, turn off, and change channels on our TV set! Shortly after receiving the Slinky as a birthday gift, I was watching TV and absentmindedly tumbling the Slinky back and forth in my hands. The TV went off, then came back on a minute or two later. At first I figured our TV was on the blink. But when the TV switched itself on the next time I played with the Slinky the truth dawned. Since then, all our friends and visitors

have experienced firsthand the power of Slinky. We can turn the TV off and on and change channels. My brother was even able to adjust the volume. There is no physical contact between the Slinky and the TV. It works best from a chair about six feet from the set. Can you explain this?—Karen Schrage, Chicago

It's questions like this that give me the strength to go on. To be sure, I had heard of such things before. But most of the letters were along the lines of the following: "How come when you hold a chopstick in your teeth and pluck it, the TV screen shimmies? Nothing else shimmies." Clearly a case of heavy-metal poisoning, although whether from cadmium or Aerosmith is hard to say.

Karen's letter, however, was refreshingly rational. We called to check one vital detail: did the set have an ordinary remote control? Karen didn't know, but the set was pretty old (it had come with the apartment), and it might have had one once.

That was all we needed to know. Prior to the early 1980s, most TV remote controls communicated with the set via ultrasonic sound— sound too high-pitched for the human ear to hear. Typically these devices worked by striking a series of metal bars with a tiny hammer. There was usually an audible click, but the frequencies that actually did the job were inaudible harmonics. (You acoustics buffs will know what I'm talking about.) Obviously you don't need a remote-control box to bang metal together, although getting the right frequencies is a bit hit-and-miss.

A call to the folks at Zenith, which introduced the first ultrasonic remote control in 1956, confirmed that there had been occasional reports of kids switching channels by spilling pennies onto the floor from their piggy banks. We had also heard of people switching on TVs by jingling their keys. When Karen told us someone had turned *her* set on by jingling keys, too, we concluded the Slinky was mimicking a long-lost ultrasonic remote control.

Unfortunately for those of you who were looking forward to a pleasant evening of experimenting on your own (why stop with Slinkies—why not anvils and sledgehammers, Caribbean steel drums, samurai swords?), ultrasonic remote controls are now obsolete. They've been supplanted by infrared (invisible light) technology, which is better suited to conveying the complex digital information needed to operate today's plethora of TV controls. Nothing fun ever lasts.

When Will I Learn?

Recently you put down an anonymous writer who asked, "How come when you hold a chopstick in your teeth and pluck it, the TV screen shimmies? Nothing else shimmies." You ascribed the effect to heavy-metal poisoning. Well, Cece, I think you dismissed the question prematurely, without trying it. This effect does occur and results from a vibration of the eyes (connected to the tooth bone) at a frequency near that of the vertical scan rate on the TV, producing a visible modulation effect of shimmying, speaking vernacularly. The other objects in the visual field may appear slightly fuzzy, but they don't shimmer. Chopsticks are fine, but if you want to see the effect more clearly, vibrate your jaw or head with an electric vibrator using different speeds while viewing TV. Hope this shakes you. Find that letter and apologize.—Jim S., Dallas

I can't stand it. Every time I rummage through the circular file looking for a letter exemplifying the depths to which the Teeming Millions have sunk—believe me, you'd feel the same impulse if you had this job—I come up with somebody who's tapped into some lost truth of physics. As a matter of fact, I *did* try this silly stunt—once. But not being the kind of guy who believes in doing it with the shades drawn, I used a well-lit room, which made the effect a lot less noticeable. Having returned to the (darkened) lab, I find that, sure enough, the screen *does* shimmy. To be more precise, it looks as though it had turned into a jiggling sheet of Jell-O. Very bizarre. Had we discovered this in the sixties it might have replaced the lava lamp.

A ripple effect of this sort is characteristic of interference between two wave fronts, in this case the chopstick- (or spoon- or crunchy candy-) induced vibration in your skull and the flicker of the TV. The precise mechanism of this interference I leave to the grad students to figure out, but it happens all right.

Every so often we see a work crew dig four or five squares in a row out of the street, cover them with a marker for a day, then, surprise, fill them in with cement. What is the point of this?—David D., Chicago

Who says there has to be a point to everything? Not only would it make life tedious beyond description, this hardworking columnist would be out of a job. That said, the workers probably aren't digging those holes for grins; most likely they're employed by a local utility. Let's assume it's the gas company out looking for a leak. First they check the obvious places where gas collects, like catch basins and manholes. If this proves unavailing, they drive a steel bar into the pavement to see if gas has percolated through the soil. Still nothing? Time to get serious and dig a series of two-by-two-foot holes along the route of the gas main, paying particular attention to joints and connections. The leak having been found, the crew digs a bigger hole, makes the necessary repair, and moves off to snarl traffic somewhere else.

Is it true refrigerating batteries will extend shelf life? If so, why does a cold car battery cause slower starts? The answer will help me sleep better.—Kevin C., Alexandria, Virginia

Whatever it takes, dude. Refrigerating batteries extends shelf life because batteries produce electricity through a chemical reaction. Heat speeds up any reaction while cold slows it down. Freeze your Diehard and you'll extend its life because the juice won't leak away—but it'll also make those volts a little tough to use right away. That accounts for the belief occasionally voiced by mechanics that if a battery is left on the garage floor for an extended period the concrete will "suck out the electricity." It does nothing of the kind, but a cold floor will substantially reduce a battery's output. The cure: warm it (the battery) up.

Jill and I walk every day on our lunch hour, so we see a lot of street and sidewalk repairing going on. What we'd like to know is,

Why do they put lines in cement sidewalks? They pour and smooth out a perfectly good sidewalk, then they draw lines in it. We remember the saying when we were kids, "Step on a crack, break your mother's back"—do we have sadistic city employees?—Lorraine and Jill, Santa Barbara, California

Cecil was sure this was going to be another one of those "I dunno, we've always done it that way" questions, which have been turning up with dismaying regularity lately. But it turns out there's a good reason for the lines. Not that cement contractors necessarily know what it is, of course. Many of them have the idea that the lines allow the concrete to expand and contract with changes in temperature—not true, strictly speaking.

Concrete does expand and contract, and for that reason expansion joints, typically some sort of compressible fiberboard, are put in every forty feet or so. But the lines you're talking about, which are called "contraction joints," serve another, admittedly related, purpose. Concrete normally shrinks a bit as it dries, resulting in unsightly cracks. Cement finishers put in contraction joints so that when the concrete does crack, it'll do so at the joints, where the slab is thinnest, rather than just any old place. That way it won't look so bad. Of course, a lot of times it cracks any old place regardless of what the cement finishers do, but hey, they tried.

Do you know anything about broadcast power? This has nothing to do with radio or TV. As I understand it, broadcast power involves turning electricity into a signal which is transmitted and then converted back into electricity by a special device fitted to any common appliance. I saw a demonstration of this in college about twelve years ago, when a visiting artist was using these devices in his kinetic sculptures. Could broadcast power be used for nonpolluting electric vehicles? Do you know of any experts who could speak knowledgeably on this subject who would not be biased in favor of the oil companies?—Rodney F., Madison

You've been spending too much time reading *Popular Science*, Flash. True broadcast power would involve incredible waste and probably kill everybody besides. Scientists nowadays worry about the possible injurious effects of the electric fields around wires—imagine what might happen if the juice was just poured into the air.

Most likely you heard something about the satellite power system (SPS), one of the wilder ideas to float around the federal bureaucracy in the late seventies. The plan was to build a giant array of solar cells the size of Manhattan in orbit around the earth, beam the collected solar power via microwave to a giant receiving dish on earth, convert it into standard juice, and feed it into the regular power system.

Several government agencies looked into SPS and concluded it was as crazy as it sounded. The complete system would cost $3 trillion, roughly the size of the gross national product and many times what we spend on conventional power technology. A mere demonstration project might cost $40 to $100 billion. The National Research Council declared that further study was pointless and the project died a quiet death. Proponents haven't totally given up; one brainstorm they had was to build a solar-cell factory in the low-gravity environment of the moon to save on rocket-fuel costs. (Supposedly this would save money over shipping parts from the earth.) Very ingenious, boys. Now go play outside.

Broadcast Power, Take Two

Your reply to Rodney F. concerning broadcast power was, if you'll forgive the pun, "off the beam." I think what Rodney was referring to was not the SPS/microwave downlink system, but rather Nikola Tesla's broadcast power system.

Best known for the insights that put the alternating current system associated with Westinghouse on a working basis, Tesla was a brilliant experimenter in electricity. He devised a system for broadcasting electrical power in the first decade of this century that, among other things, could (and did) light lightbulbs at a distance of twenty-five miles without their being connected by wires to a source of electricity. His broadcast power system indisputably worked, both in Colorado and Long Island—but only for Tesla. No one has been able to

duplicate this effect, even working from Tesla's notes; like many ge-
niuses, he seems not to have bothered to write things down that,
while "obvious" to him, were in fact quantum leaps of knowledge.

With Tesla's death we lost a man whose brilliance in many ways
surpassed that of Edison and Steinmetz. Scientists today are still
combing his notes and journals looking for new insights into physics
and electricity. But because of his reputation as a crackpot genius,
Tesla's proven power transmission system has never been explored.
It's a shame when official perceptions get in the way of pro-
gress.—R.J., Stamford, Connecticut

Cecil is well acquainted with the inventor of the Tesla coil, an
artificial-lightning device familiar to anyone who's ever been to a
high school science fair. But he had forgotten about Tesla's global
ambitions for his invention. Just as well. Tesla's broadcast power
scheme was even wilder than the satellite power system.

The peak of Tesla's career came in his early thirties, when he sold
his alternating-current patents to George Westinghouse for big
bucks. (He later got cuffed out of part of it.) He also did pioneering
work in radio and other fields. But thereafter he frittered away his
genius and hundreds of thousands of dollars of other people's money
on one harebrained scheme after another. Broadcast power was one
such idea.

You considerably overstate the success of this project. Tesla did
build a giant Tesla coil in Colorado Springs in an effort to broadcast
power across the globe. The coil could generate extremely high voltages and emit huge lightninglike sparks from a big copper ball atop
a tall tower. Tesla's idea was that the earth was aquiver with electrical energy, like a taut violin string. If one plucked the string at any
point, the vibrations would be transmitted throughout its length.
Same with the globe. The giant coil was to be Tesla's bow.

In his first test of the coil Tesla burned out a generator at the Colorado Springs electrical plant. Later there were reports that he managed to light two hundred incandescent bulbs at a distance of
twenty-six miles. But this was never confirmed, and it is damned
hard to believe. (Tesla coils, in my experience, can illuminate *fluores-*
cent bulbs, but usually at a distance of only a few feet.) Tesla never
published a thorough description of his work, and electrical engi-

neers scratch their heads when told of his ideas today. Even if the thing worked, it's hard to see how you'd avoid wasting huge amounts of energy.

Tesla later moved his operations to Long Island. With $150,000 from J. P. Morgan, he set about building an even larger coil. But the machine was never completed, and in 1905 the project was abandoned. Virtually everything he worked on after this time met with a similar fate. By the 1930s he was reduced to making wild pronouncements about death rays and feeding the pigeons near his hotel room. He died alone in 1943.

Many people excuse Tesla's failures by saying he was too far ahead of his time. I doubt it. His understanding of the medium in which he worked was primitive. He refused to accept the complex nature of the atom and for years denied Einstein's theories. His problems arose largely from the fact that he was an eccentric who was unable to work with other people, and the increasing unreality of his ideas shows it. Broadcast power is Exhibit A.

How do they make helium? Think about it. It's an inert gas that doesn't combine with anything else, so there can't be helium mines filled with helium ore. The only place I've ever heard of where you can find a lot of helium is the sun, where it's created by fusion. Fusion is prohibitively expensive on earth, yet somehow commercial helium is cheap enough that they can fill toy balloons with it. What's the deal?—Bob Y., Evanston, Illinois

Come now, Bob, everybody knows fusion isn't the *only* way to make helium. It's also a by-product of radioactive decay. (The "alpha particles" emitted by some radioactive materials are actually helium atoms minus the electrons.) To get helium all you have to do is find yourself a planet full of uranium and thorium and the like, wait ten jillion years, and presto, you're up to your ankles in the stuff. The helium on the earth's surface drifts off into space, but underground a lot of it collects in pockets of natural gas, particularly in the gas fields of the southwestern United States. Liquefy the natural gas and filter out impurities and what's left will float a dirigible, cool a nuclear reactor, or make the strongest man sound like a chipmunk. Definitely one of nature's noble gases.

Recently I was watching the season premiere of "Against the Law" (Fox TV) when a character mentioned that he had almost blown up his dad by sticking a potato up his car's tailpipe. Naturally I thought back to Beverly Hills Cop, where Eddie Murphy foiled the bumbling cops by putting a banana up their tailpipe. Does this really work? If so, why is it not more of a problem, especially in big cities where roving packs of thugs beat the tar out of people for fun? Seems like blowing up a car would have more comic value. Must the potato be cooked? Will any sizable fruit or vegetable (say, eggplant) do? I'd test on my own car, but it already dances on the thin line between minimal functioning and moribundity.—Patrick O., Alexandria, Virginia

Television writers are a plague. Stuffing a potato or anything short of a hand grenade up a car's tailpipe won't make it blow up. But it will make it impossible for the engine to "breathe." When a car's cylinders move up and down, they pull fuel and air in and push exhaust gases out. If the tailpipe is blocked, the exhaust can't go anywhere and stays put in the cylinders, preventing fresh stuff from entering. No fresh stuff = no combustion = no transportation. It also means no unintended explosions, which may be why street gangs haven't picked up on it. Thank God.

Blowing It Out Your Tailpipe

Your reply to Patrick O. regarding the potato-in-the-tailpipe trick was, at best, only partially correct. When I was a mere sprat, my older brother and I heard rumors concerning the effects of a potato lodged in the tailpipe. Being good little experimentalists, we naturally had to determine the truth. So a choice spud from Mom's stash went into our retired neighbor's tailpipe (that is to say, his car's tailpipe), to await his next trip to the store.

The car neither exploded nor became immobilized. (Perhaps one of those wimpy imports people drive today would've conked, but this

was the fifties, when men were men and American cars kicked butt.)
Instead, enough pressure was built up to eject the potato at high
speed. Fortunately, our neighbor's driveway sloped up from the
street, so the potato impacted asphalt within a few feet. Judging by
the mashed potatoes left on the pavement, that tuber was traveling
fast enough to take somebody's head off.

Pleased to be of service, keep up the good work.—G. Hall, Ala-
meda, California

It is all very well to talk about potato theory, G. But it's only
through the efforts of bold pioneers such as you and your brother
that real advances in potato science are made. Thanks for your con-
tribution.

Blowing It Out Your Tailpipe, Part Two

Many years ago, when I was young and lived in a city far, far
away, I was tempted to retaliate against my neighbor's Miata. Cast-
ing about for an innocuous form of annoyance, I chanced upon the
old potato-in-the-tailpipe trick. Finding, like G. Hall, that one potato
tended to be expelled from the tailpipe, I didn't quit. Rather, I just
mashed four of the suckers in there. Success! Four was too much even
for a Miata. Just trying to help those of a vengeful bent amongst your
readers. Sign me . . .—"Spuds" McKenzie, Washington, D.C.

Just proves the old saying, Spuds: if at first you don't succeed, get
a bigger hammer.

Why do the spouters on some water fountains produce two streams
of water that merge into one before reaching your parched lips? Why
not just one stream to start with?—Steven Palkovitz, Alexandria, Vir-
ginia

In an age when you can't even fix your Chevy without having to
fool with microchips, Cecil is always cheered by examples of low-

tech ingenuity. The twin-stream water fountain is a perfect example. But first we need to put things in proper historical perspective. Let me quote from a brochure for Halsey Taylor water fountains, one of the leading names in the industry:

In 1896, Halsey W. Taylor lost his father to an outbreak of typhoid fever caused by a contaminated water supply. This personal tragedy led the young Halsey Taylor to dedicate his life to providing a safe, sanitary drink of water in public places. . . . The historic Double Bubbler™ projector [spouter] was designed by Halsey Taylor himself, and still ranks as the most important innovation in the industry's history. It projects two separate streams of water, which converge to provide an abundant "pyramid" of water at the apex of the stream. This gives the user a fuller, more satisfying drink.

The folks at Halsey Taylor are being polite here. What they mean is that the Double Bubbler enables you to take in more water and less air when you drink. As a result, you don't burp. Think of all the delicate social negotiations you've been involved in that have gone awry because of an ill-timed eructation (that's "belch" for you dropouts). Had you been drinking from a Double Bubbler, that fat contract (job, babe, whatever) might have been yours.

The Double Bubbler serves other purposes as well. You get less spraying, presumably because the water slows down when the two streams merge. The double streams also act as a sort of pressure regulator. If the water pressure is unusually strong one day, a single-stream fountain might give the unwary sipper a shot in the eye. When the twin streams of the Double Bubbler meet, however, their upward momentums tend to cancel out no matter how high the pressure gets.

One last thing. You know how kids like to hold their thumbs over the bubbler to make the water spray all over the room? Halsey Taylor has a way to deal with that, too. Its fountains have an "antisquirt groove" consisting of a slot cut through the bubbler head just below the tip. If some wisenheimer puts his thumb over the tip to try to make the fountain squirt, the water merely dribbles harmlessly out the sides through the antisquirt groove—a drag if you're a rambunctious sixth-grader, but a gift from God if you're anybody else.

Little Squirts

This is how we sixth-grade wisenheimers in Dallas public school got around the "antisquirt groove" in Halsey Taylor water fountains. We just stretched the skin between thumb and forefinger flat and slipped it in the groove. Squirt-a-rama!—Jim Thompson, Dallas

The history of warfare is the eternal struggle between offensive and defensive capabilities. I'm sure strategists at Halsey Taylor will read your comments with interest.

How come water towers are always elevated, while petroleum tanks are on the ground?—T.R. Sayers

Because water towers are a cheap, reliable way of generating enough pressure to get the water into your house—not an issue with petroleum tanks. If you didn't have towers you'd have to use pumps, and buying enough pumps to meet peak demand would be prohibitively expensive for most towns. Towers simplify matters. You pump water up at a steady rate and gravity does all the work getting it down. Since the pressure is a function of the height of the column of water inside the tower, and since the height of that column doesn't diminish appreciably until the tank is virtually empty, the pressure stays steady regardless of fluctuations in supply and/or demand.

Why don't freight trains have cabooses anymore?—George, Dallas

Don't need 'em, and besides, it's cheaper this way. There used to be two guys in the caboose: the conductor and a brakeman. The conductor did paperwork, the brakeman threw switches, and they both watched for "hotboxes" (overheated freight car wheel bearings). They also radioed useful tidbits of information about the train (e.g., there's been a little accident) to the engineer. Today virtually all mainline switch-throwing is done electrically from the central office, roller bearings have eliminated most hotboxes and trackside infrared sensors catch the rest, the conductor can do his paperwork in the locomotive, and the useful tidbits of information are provided to the engineer by a soulless machine (see below). So it's curtains for the caboose.

What you see instead on the end of the train is a gizmo called an "end-of-train device" (ETD) that (1) senses motion, (2) monitors the pressure in the air brake line, and (3) automatically radios its findings to a receiving unit in the locomotive. Unlike car brakes, train brakes are released by increasing (not decreasing) the pressure in the brake line. This can take a while in a mile-long freight. When the engineer wants to start the train, she pumps air into the brake line until the rear-end gauge reaches a certain level. That tells her all the brakes throughout the train have been released and she can give that puppy some gas.

The motion detector, as you might surmise, lets the engineer know when the back of the train is moving. The significance of this will not be apparent until I let you in on a key fact from my vast storehouse of railroad lore: you can't start a whole freight train at once. Too much inertia. Instead, you start have to start it one car at a time, taking advantage of the slack in the couplers that connect the cars.

Before starting, all the cars in a freight train are bunched up behind the locomotive. When the engineer opens the throttle, the locomotive starts moving solo until the slack in the first set of couplers runs out, whereupon the first car in the train starts with a jerk. An instant later the slack in the next set of couplers runs out and the second car jolts into motion, and so it continues all the way back through the train. Eventually the last car starts moving and the motion detector signals the engineer, who can then lay on some serious horses. (If you pressed the pedal to the metal too soon, you might start the last car with too much of a jerk and break the coupler.) If more people knew stuff like this, the country would be a lot better off.

The questions you deal with in your column are usually pretty cosmic, but maybe as a change of pace you wouldn't mind taking a whack at the following shallow topics: (1) What are those red or orange balloon things you see on high-voltage utility wires when you're driving out in the country? I've heard several theories, but none seems to hold up under critical examination. (2) Is there any rhyme or reason to the assignment of area codes? Why aren't numerically sequential codes given to geographically adjacent areas? When I call Mom in area code 414 (eastern Wisconsin) but get San Francisco (415), it seems like a plot to separate me from more of my money. —John R., Madison

Johnny, Johnny, Johnny. (Kinda Garboesque, ain't it?) The telephone company is your *friend*. One of the reasons area codes are assigned the way they are is precisely to *prevent* you from dialing the wrong code by mistake. But let's take your questions in order.

(1) The "balloon things" are aircraft warning markers intended to prevent some joker in a Piper Cub from clotheslining himself. You see them near airports with a lot of general aviation traffic—i.e., low-flying small planes—or else in areas where they do crop dusting. Typically the markers are fiberglass spheres tricked out in some high-visibility color, but occasionally you see

other designs as well. They've definitely inspired their share of carrot-brained theorizing. I knew a guy who said the purpose of the balloons was to "scare away the birds." Tragic evidence of the impact of the thinning ozone layer.

(2) The assignment of area codes may seem random or even malevolent to you, John, but this merely reflects your troubled inner being. Actually it's pretty sensible. The North American Numbering Plan, of which the area codes are a part, was worked out in the late 1940s to ensure standardized numbering nationwide, helping to make direct-dial long distance possible. (Prior to that time you had to go through an operator.)

On the rotary-dial phones then in use, dialing a nine took a lot longer than dialing a one, which tied up expensive switching equipment. So AT&T assigned "low dial pull" numbers to the markets with the most telephones and thus presumably the highest number of incoming long-distance calls. New York got 212, Chicago 312, L.A. 213, Detroit 313, Dallas 214, and so on.

Some area codes aren't so easy to explain. Boston got 617 while comparatively rural western Massachusettes got 413; Washington, D.C., got 202. (Zero, remember, has the highest dial pull of all.) Whether these anomalies represented some smoldering vendetta against the Eastern Seaboard we may never know; the people responsible have long since retired.

The issue of dial pulls became academic with the introduction of Touch-Tone phones in the early 1960s. Since then the guiding principle behind the assignment of new area codes has been to make the new number as different as possible from the adjacent old ones in order to avoid confusion. That's why the split of New York's 212 produced 718, L.A.'s 213 begat 818, and Chicago's 312 was joined by 708. The drawback of this approach is that when you do make a mistake it's a lulu, giving you San Francisco, for example, when you were trying to dial Milwaukee. But the phone company will readily delete such goofs from your bill.

As far as Ma Bell is concerned, the real problem with assigning area codes is that it's running out of numbers to assign. Originally the switching system required that the middle digit in each code be a one or a zero, which meant there were only 152 numbers available. By the early 1990s, all but a handful of these had already been spoken for. To get around this limitation, phone companies around the country have been implementing "Dial-1" service, which requires you to dial one at the start of any direct-dial long-distance call. This will permit the use of additional digits in the middle position, giving us a total of 792 potential codes, which ought to hold us for a while.

Area Codes: A Wrong Number?

Unless I'm missing something, you slipped a bit in your discussion of area codes. You said "the switching system requires that the middle digit in each code be a one or a zero, which means there are only 152 numbers available." If this, in fact, were the only constraint, there would actually be two hundred possible combinations (10 × 2 × 10). But I believe there's a further constraint: the first and third digits may not be one or zero. This leaves eight digits available for positions one and three, or 8 × 2 × 8 = 128 possible area code combinations. So where does 152 come from? And if in the future the constraint on the middle digit is eliminated, how do you figure there will be 792 potential codes?—Paul Chapin, Reston, Virginia

You want details, I'll give you details. There are eight potential digits in the first position; zero and one are ineligible. There are two potential digits in the second position and ten in the third. 8 × 2 × 10 = 160. Codes 211 through 911, eight codes in all, were reserved for special uses, e.g., 411, directory assistance. This leaves 152. (Most of the "-10" codes, such as 210, have not been assigned, but they could be. The international long-distance access code, 011, is not considered part of the area code universe by definition.) When the middle-digit constraint is eliminated, the number of potential codes will be 8 × 10 × 10 = 800 minus the eight reserved codes, or 792.

In my bedroom I have one of those cheap little extension phones—you know, the kind you get free with three rooms of carpeting for $299.95. Instead of ringing, it makes a little electronic *warble. It also makes a tenth of a warble when someone picks up the phone in another room. Now here's the thing: sometimes this tenth-of-a-warble occurs spontaneously. What's more, it seems to happen at the same time every day—about 2:00 A.M., when my wife and I are in bed. What's going on? Is someone sneaking into our house every morning to make surreptitious calls? Is someone tapping the line—someone who knocks off for coffee every night at two? Is Ma Bell, or one of her numerous offspring, checking up on us?—Mike L., Chicago*

Evidently the last, Mike, but having spent eighteen months on this godforsaken topic (honest), I'm so punchy I hesitate to say for sure. The problem was never really finding out the answer. Cecil knew, in the calm and instinctive way he knows everything, that the cause of the mystery rings was some kind of automatic line-testing program run by the phone company. The trouble was getting the phone folks to admit it. Bell spokespeople conceded they did "trunk testing" of the lines that connected their switching centers and opportunistic testing of customer lines whenever a call was put through. But they repeatedly denied there was any scheduled testing of individual phones.

I didn't believe this, but before proceeding I thought it wise to get a little independent corroboration of the phenomenon, having gotten reamed on some of these techie conspiracy reports in the past. When my minions appeared on radio talk shows, I had them ask if anyone else had experienced "ghost rings." The phone lines invariably lit up, and it wasn't ghosts on the other end. Callers said the ghost rings generally came at a fixed time, usually in the evening or early morning. Commonly there was a half ring or a full ring, occasionally a couple rings. But nobody was ever on the line.

Listeners of Eddie Schwartz's late-night gabfest on (then) WGN radio in Chicago seemed particularly interested in the topic and devoted untold hours to talking about it. Speculation on the cause always got progressively woollier as the night wore on. Many callers blamed computer hackers, who allegedly programmed their modems to dial up phone numbers in sequence looking for data banks to plunder, à la the movie *War Games*. This theory had a certain paranoid charm, but why dial the same numbers night after night?

Others guessed it was telemarketing companies: sell-by-phone outfits supposedly had their computers dial up numbers to see if any were out of service. (Nobody could explain the purpose of this.) A few screwballs said that 2:00 A.M. (or whenever) was when the wiretappers changed the batteries on their equipment.

Meanwhile, I talked with people at Ameritech, AT&T, Bell Labs, and the like. Nobody would come clean. Figuring it was time for direct action, we returned to the airwaves and rounded up two volunteers: Penny, who got chirps on her phone between 10:38 and 10:44 every evening, and Pat, an answering-service operator who logged dozens of ghost rings a night on her multiline switchboard. I reported their cases to the phone company and said, Okay, guys, here's the facts. You figure it out.

A couple weeks later a Bell spokesperson called back. Son of a gun, he said, it seems there *is* a routine customer line-testing program after all. During off-peak hours a central-office computer goes around injecting a small voltage into each line to check transmission quality. The juice is too low to trigger a ring in most phones, but apparently a few are hypersensitive. The whole thing seems to have started when the phone company began replacing its old electromechanical switching equipment with new electronic stuff. Line testing on the old system never caused problems, but obviously the new system has a couple bugs. When the phone company suspended testing, the ghost rings stopped. When it started up again, the rings returned. Case closed at last. This job can be a pain in the keester sometimes, but it has its satisfactions.

I am ten years old, and I ask my mom a lot of questions. She said to ask you because she asked you questions before and you know everything. My question is, Why do gas stations sometimes have rocks on the roof?—Owen K., Seattle

I assume you're not talking about rocks meaning boulders, but rather the layer of small stones you see not just on gas stations but on many flat roofs. Ideally the stones are river gravel, which has smooth edges and won't cut into the roof when somebody walks around on it.

Talk to ten roofing contractors and you'll get ten answers on what the gravel is for, but this seems to be the consensus:

1. *Stabilization.* In a typical tar-and-gravel roof (which, by the way, is gradually being supplanted by gravelless roof systems), you put down a layer of tar paper, then tar, and finally gravel. Tar has a low melting point. In the summer it gets pretty soft and if left to its own devices would flow to the lowest point on the roof. The stones force it to stay put.
2. *Protection.* The gravel prevents sun, hail, errant baseballs, etc., from damaging the "membrane," the all-important moisture seal created by the tar paper and tar.
3. *Ballast.* The stones keep the tar paper in place and prevent it from buckling or blowing away in a high wind.

That's all there is to it. My regards to mom.

I love to fix toasted tuna fish sandwiches, but sometimes a whole one is too much and I make one with only one slice of bread. Imagine my horror and shame recently upon realizing I'd toasted the single slice in the wrong slot of the toaster (the one not marked ONE SLICE)! I ate it anyway. What are the implications of using the wrong slot—jail, food poisoning? Why is there a ONE SLICE slot at all?—Cliff F., Springfield, Virginia.

The ONE SLICE slot is where the toaster's thermostat is. Use the other opening and you could wind up with under- or overcooked toast. If your toaster has an energy-saver feature, in which only the heating coils in the center and on one side warm up when you make one slice, things might come out half-baked.

Why do so many public buildings want you to use the revolving doors rather than the regular doors?—Seamus McC., Hoboken, New Jersey

As with many things, there are two reasons—the ostensible reason and the *real* reason. The ostensible reason is that the revolving doors

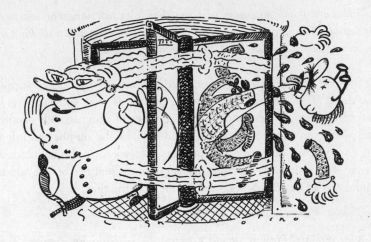

create an air trap. Since the interior of the building is never directly exposed to the outdoors, there's less chance of all that expensively heated or cooled air getting out and running up your utility bill. An alternative way of accomplishing the same thing is a vestibule, where you have to pass through two sets of doors to get inside. Another reason for revolving doors is to prevent wind from howling down (or up) the elevator shafts and stairwells and blasting out (or in) the doors due to indoor-outdoor pressure differentials.

So much for the rationalizations. The *real* reason you're told to use the revolving doors is so the real estate operators of the world can test your willingness to play ball. Do you follow directions and use the revolving door, or are you one of those independent types who insist on doing their own thing and entering through the swinging version? If the latter, be forewarned: when Donald Trump takes over, you're history.

What are those antennae you see that have a triangular platform on top of a fifty-foot pole with two or three little antennae sticking up or down on the corners?—Mark Downing, Dallas

They're for cellular telephones, the ultimate (for now) yuppie plaything. The genius of cellular, of course, is that you can divide any region into an increasingly large number of progressively smaller "cells" (the area served by a single antenna) as the number and density (no offense) of mobile-phone users increases. So the cellular antenna will ultimately become as common a feature of the urban landscape as the dandelion, and about as attractive.

Why did Mr. Phillips invent a new type of head for screws? Was he bored? Do Phillips-head screws have any advantage over the standard slot-type screw? Or was Phillips just trying to invent a market he could corner?—Roger W., Mount Pleasant, South Carolina

So many opportunities for rude puns, Roger. I must be strong. Actually, Phillips screws have many advantages, most of which I am personally acquainted with, having once had a job repairing power tools. (Cecil has had quite the varied career.) Unfortunately, none of these advantages is of much use to Joe Handyman, who typically regards Phillips screws as a first-class pain in the neck, owing to their propensity to strip out at the least provocation. But more on this directly.

To engage the cross-shaped indentation in the head of a Phillips screw you need a Phillips screwdriver, whose pointed tip makes it self-centering. This is helpful when you're using a power screwdriver, which is the reason the Phillips screw was invented: it lends itself to assembly-line screwing, so to speak.

The inventor of the Phillips screw was Henry M. Phillips, a businessman from Portland, Oregon, who obviously had a lot of time on his hands. (I learn this, incidentally, from a delightful article on the Phillips screw that appeared in the *Wall Street Journal*.) Henry knew that power screwdrivers don't work well with ordinary slot screws because (1) you waste precious seconds trying to fit the screwdriver into the damn slot; (2) once you succeed, centrifugal force tends to make the bit slide off the screw and into the workbench; and even if you avoid this, (3) when the screw gets as far in as it's going to go, the power screwdriver either stalls, strips out the screw, or starts to spin around in your hand.

A Phillips screwdriver, is a different story. Get it anywhere in the general vicinity of the screw and it engages as if by magic, and what's more, stays engaged. Furthermore, the cross-shaped indentation in the screw is so shallow that when you're done the screwdriver pops right out, before you get into trouble. Cecil found this handy fixing power tools, and back in the 1930s Henry Phillips thought the automakers would find it handy making cars. The automakers were no brighter then than now, but eventually realized the usefulness of Henry's device, and it's been with us ever since.

The only problem is, easy as they are to get in, Phillips screws can be a bitch to get back out. The screwdriver pops out too readily, stripping the screw, gouging the work, and in general transferring to Joe Handyman all the problems that were formerly the province of the assembly line. Once again, in other words, the little guy gets shafted by the dehumanizing forces of capitalism. The only solution, socialism obviously being in decline, is to buy a power screwdriver of your own. You can't beat 'em, join 'em.

Why are there green lights under escalators? Should I start believing in Escalator Trolls? Am I seeing the Otis borealis? *Or do I just have a brain tumor? Please—the Straight Dope!—John Sandel, Chicago*

I don't know about the brain tumor, John, but I do know you can't have a stomach tumor without a stomach. Escalator companies put lights under the steps near the top and bottom of the escalator in order to silhouette the edges of each step. The improved visibility is supposed to help you avoid stumbling, or worse, as the step slides against its neighbors on reaching (or leaving) the landing area. The yellow strip you see on the edge of the steps on some escalators performs a similar function. The lights are part of a code of standards for escalators devised by the American Society of Mechanical Engi-

neers and since adopted by many cities and states. As for why they're green, as opposed to, say, lavender, nobody at ASME could remember. But presumably it was to cut down on glare.

How come the United States is practically the only country in the world where household electricity is 110 volts instead of 220 volts?
—Mark, Berkeley, California

The penalty of leadership, champ. While inventors in many countries contributed to electric power technology, the United States was way out front in putting that technology to practical use. In the early days, lower voltages were the most practical for electric lights—higher voltages burned out the bulbs. So the hundreds of power plants built in the U.S. prior to 1900 adopted 110 volts (or 115 or 120 volts) as their de facto standard. Tradition has it that 110 volts was settled on because it made the bulbs of the day glow with the same brightness as a gas lamp.

Trouble was, power transmission at higher voltages was more efficient—you didn't have to use so much copper in the wires. By the time most European countries got around to making big-time investments in electricity, the engineers had figured out how to make

220-volt bulbs that wouldn't burn out so fast. So, starting in Germany around the turn of the century, they adopted the 220-volt (or 230- or 240-volt) standard. But the U.S. stayed with 110 volts (today it's officially 120 volts) because we had such a big installed base of 110-volt equipment.

But don't worry that we're stuck with a technological dinosaur. Fact is, homes with standard three-wire electrical service in most parts of the country get 240 volts. The three wires that come in from the street are 120 volts positive, zero volts (neutral), and 120 volts negative. (I know, this is alternating current, not DC, so we can't really say "120 volts positive," but don't bother me with details.)

Take the neutral and either of the other wires (the usual practice) and you've got 120 volts. But tap into your plus-120 and minus-120 and you'll get a 240-volt jolt, handy for energy-hungry appliances like air conditioners, electric stoves, and clothes dryers. The telltale sign in the fuse box is a special double-width circuit breaker that straddles the plus-120 and minus-120 bus bars. Not the most vital fact in the world, but at least next time you're poking around in there when the lights blow you'll have some idea what you're looking at.

Static

Are you going to explain to your readers that, with the three-phase wiring prevalent in the world, the two lines are only 120 degrees apart in phase, and not of opposite polarity as you stated? And that therefore tapping across them provides only 208 volts, not 240? Or do you figure nobody will miss the other 32 volts AC? And that explaining three-phase polarity isn't worth the space, justifying your fudge?—Robert Goodman, Bronx, New York

Sarcasm plays better when you have at least a general idea of what you're talking about, Robert. Three-phase power is used primarily in commercial applications, not homes. When I was an electrician's apprentice, I remember we installed it in a garment factory for use with portable electric cloth cutters. The electrical service in most U.S. homes is 240 volts single phase with a center tap, giving you the 120 volts needed for most household uses. To be fair, New

York, in this as in so many other things, is an exception. There 208 volts is the standard high-end voltage.

A few of us were discussing those booming megawatt sound systems cars have nowadays—a bane of urban existence if ever there was one. We fantasized about being able to send an electronic signal that would defeat, override, distort, or blow out an offending car stereo, without blowing up the driver unless absolutely necessary. Could this be done with available technology?—Jonathan Jensen, Baltimore

Well, there's always electromagnetic pulse, or EMP. EMP has the drawback of requiring you to detonate a nuclear bomb, which may deter the squeamish. But it does work, no small thing in an age of halfway measures.

Scientists got their first hint of EMP in 1962 after a hydrogen bomb test high over the Pacific. In Hawaii, eight hundred miles away, three hundred streetlights failed, burglar alarms rang, and circuit breakers popped on power lines. Investigators concluded that the exploding bomb had unleashed a brief but intense burst of energy that, by means of various atmospheric reactions that we need not go into here, poured a killer dose of juice into every hunk of unshielded metal for hundreds of miles around and fried the electrical and electronic devices connected thereto.

According to one writer, "A nuclear burst over the United States would produce an electromagnetic pulse that could cause widespread damage or disruption to electronic communications equipment, commercial power and telephone lines, and especially to digital computers." I know: sounds like a dream come true. Solid state electronic gear is particularly vulnerable, so if you do it right there won't be an operative boom box (or computer) in the entire state. You'll be a national hero.

Interesting sidelight: when a defecting Soviet pilot landed his supposedly high-tech MiG-25 fighter in the West some years ago, U.S. experts were amused to discover that the plane was equipped with tiny vacuum tubes rather than transistors. How primitive, they thought—but then they got to thinking, Jeez, what if those wily Russkies were using tubes, which are less vulnerable, to protect themselves against EMP? Cecil must inquire next time he visits the Kremlin.

Using electromagnetic pulse as an antinoise measure isn't without its problems. One is that while EMP itself makes for a nice surgical strike, the underlying bomb would definitely diminish the property values (although there are some who would say a little collateral damage is a small price to pay for peace and quiet). Possibly the side effects could be minimized if you were to locate the bomb according to scientific principles. I regret to say that research in this area has not been as aggressive as it might have been, but come on—you wanted a concept, you got a concept. Now all that remains is to work out the practical details.

Advances on the Anti–Boom Box Front

Your recent column about using EMP [electromagnetic pulse] to combat "boom cars" shows real forward thinking. Your tax dollars are already being applied to this problem. Federal scientists have the fix at hand. Once again, you are both ahead of and behind the curve.
—Rob Mohr, Chicago

It's a gift, babe. You enclose an article from *Aviation Week* reporting that the air force, sensitive to the boom-car phenomenon but reluctant to use nuclear weapons to combat it, is developing a new weapon that will generate EMP by nonnuclear means. "A nonnuclear EMP burst is produced by creating a magnetic field in a coil and then squeezing it by the detonation of conventional explosives," it says here. "The resulting pulse of microwave energy can carry thousands of feet and damage or upset electronic components."

The air force is retrofitting a bunch of ex-nuclear cruise missiles with EMP generators. We know they'll work, too. *Aviation Week* continues, "In early 1993, private automobiles parked about 300 meters from a U.S. EMP generator test site had their coils, alternators, electric seats and electronic engine controls accidentally disabled by the pulse." Accidentally, eh? Sure. I say somebody in the test site heard one rap song too many.

The Boom-Car Abatement Debate: Getting Ugly

A while back someone wrote asking if there wasn't some effective device to render car stereos and boom boxes inoperative when they were turned up to a certain volume. Your reply referred to something like nuclear bombs or cosmic forces or some other sad expression of comic overkill rather than taking your correspondent's question seriously and answering it accordingly. You could have advised the gentleman that several such devices have already been invented and are available on the open market. One good example is the very handy Smith and Wesson .38 caliber Police Special. For fine-tuning accuracy the five- or six-inch barrel is recommended. In a steady hand, this tool is also effective on explosively loud motorcycles with hollowed-out tailpipes instead of mufflers.—B. J. Merholz, Los Angeles

There are other solutions to the question of how to take out a boom box: (1) Pump in a signal with more wattage than the speakers' capability and kaboom! Fried boom box. (2) Stick a lightning rod on or near the stereo and let a gigawatt or more do the trick. (This can also cause an electromagnetic pulse effect.) Neither solution is without side effects: (1) If the signal can burst a speaker, it can also "pop" one's eardrums. (2) If you don't fry from the bolt of lightning your car could konk out and you could drive over a cliff or into another car. But hey, no pain, no gain.—Wayne Tracy, Malibu, California

For years I have wanted someone to design a device small enough to fit in a standard briefcase that would consist of some very large capacitors kept permanently charged by a battery. At the touch of a switch, concealed under the briefcase handle, the capacitors would put a huge surge of power into a transmitter tuned to the critical frequencies of the transistors in the offending boom box or radio. The thing would have very short range so it would not fry every radio for a mile around, just the targeted one, pretty much next to which you would have to be standing. The destructive radiation could be focused to reduce the chances of collateral damage, such as to a passing police car. Is such a device feasible?—Peter Brennan, New York

Later, champ. Right now I'm trying on the shoulder holster and practicing the proper inflection for: "Hey ... you talkin' to *me*?"

How do the television program codes for VCR Plus+ work? VCR Plus+ is a handheld device similar to a TV remote control that tells the VCR to record a target program at a specific time, channel, and duration based on a numeric code listed in TV Guide *and many newspapers. I see no pattern to these codes, which have a different meaning each month. One month "12345" may indicate a Friday night news show on Channel 2, the next month something entirely different. How can this be? There must be some sort of algorithm. Any ideas?—Frederick C. Lee, Honolulu*

Yes, there is an algorithm. If we had any sense we would leave it at that. But no, I can see you want to know what the algorithm is. Maybe you'd also like to know how to perform brain surgery with a can opener. Either way we are stretching the limit of what human

ingenuity can accomplish in a six hundred-word column. But hey, your wish is my command.

The VCR Plus+ control box, which is sold by Gemstar Development, can be set up to emulate the remote controls for your VCR and/or cable box. You punch in the number(s) for the program(s) you want to record, put a blank tape in the VCR, and leave the VCR Plus+ box pointed at the TV. At the right time VCR Plus+ beams out the proper pulses to turn on the VCR, switch to the right channel, start recording, then shut the VCR off when the show is over. VCR Plus+ can even record shows on two different cable channels when you're not home, something a VCR alone can't do.

Gemstar is cagey about its business strategy, but presumably profits from VCR Plus+ in two ways: by selling the control box to you and the TV listing codes to newspapers. Since the codes are encrypted, competitors can't bootleg the boxes and newspapers can't figure out the codes on their own.

But Gemstar didn't reckon with the nation's tireless computer geniuses. Three of them, Ken Shirriff, Curt Welch, and Andrew Kinsman, got together via the Internet computer network, broke the code (most of it, anyway), and published the result in the journal *Cryptologia* in July 1992. Somebody else used this as the basis for a VCR Plus+ encoding/decoding program that is now posted on computer bulletin boards and such (e.g., CompuServe, Zenith forum, VCRPLS.ZIP). You want to decrypt VCR Plus+ codes the easy way, get the program. For the silicon-adverse, however, here's an example of how the algorithm works, taken from the *Cryptologia* article:

1. Start with the code number 3316 from May 1991. "No-carry" multiply 3316 by the magic decoding key 68150631. (No-carry multiply means to do regular multiplication except you discard all carries.) This gives us 82324978296.
2. Truncate this to the same number of digits in 3316 (four), i.e., 8296. Take the last three digits (296), subtract 1, divide the result by 32, add 1 to get the quotient. This gives us the day of the month, 10.
3. Take the remaining digit (8), and . . . ah, it's hopeless to explain in detail. You perform this incredibly complicated routine involving numerous sums, products, and quotients plus a double-barreled

dose of modular arithmetic, squeeze the result through an if-then sieve based on the number of digits, do some more sums and products, and convert the result to binary. Take the remainder from Step 2, the month plus one times the day (that's why the codes change each month), and the "offset" (never mind) and add them modulo 32; convert the result to binary. (REMEMBER, THIS WAS YOUR IDEA.) Rearrange certain bits from the two binary numbers previously described according to a specified formula to make a new binary number, add 1 to get the channel. Rearrange other bits from the first two binary numbers according to the aforesaid formula to get still another binary number; use this as an index to a table that gives start times and durations of shows. The result, take my word for it, is a two-hour show on Channel 4 at 9:00 P.M. on May 10, 1991.

NOTE: This only works for VCR Plus+ numbers up to six digits long. Shirriff et al. haven't figured out the drill for the longer ones yet—are these guys lazy or what? My advice: give up, be a consumer, and let the damn box do it for you.

Affairs of State

I want to start my own country. My question is, How do I go about this? I assume it is illegal to buy land in an existing country and proclaim sovereignty simply by virtue of ownership. Is there any way to avoid this difficulty and either (1) buy some territory in an existing country with the intent of seceding, (2) claim some previously unclaimed (or at least not very heavily guarded) land, (3) settle an area that had not existed earlier (e.g., a volcanic island), or (4) find some other way to realize my dream of founding a nation where all people are truly equal, the state respects individual rights, and free pizza delivery is constitutionally guaranteed? The fate of a nation rests on your answer.—James Hyder, Columbia, Maryland

I'm used to it, James. There are several schools of thought on what it takes to establish an independent state. One is that you're a nation if other countries recognize you as such. This approach has a certain practical appeal, but from a philosophical standpoint it eats. It suggests the minimum number of nations you can have is two, so each can recognize the other. More important, it denies reality: if you look like a nation and act like a nation, why should nonrecognition by a bunch of foreigners prevent you from actually *being* a nation?

Okay, but what constitutes looking and acting like a nation? Opinions differ, but some suggest there are four conditions:

1. *Defined territory.* In other words, a nomadic tribe with no fixed address cannot constitute a sovereign state. My advice: get yourself some stakes and string, put in a border crossing and a video store, and bingo, you're covered.
2. *Permanent population.* Here's where you get into trouble, Jimbo. In theory the authorities don't have any problem with small-population states, presumably including the one-man variety, but somebody always has to mind the store. Your problem is, the second you go to visit Mom in Poughkeepsie, the population drops to zero and there goes your country. Maybe you and Mrs. Hyder can just take separate vacations so there's always somebody around to baby-sit.
3. *Government.* They're a drag but you have to have one. No prob, though—you can vest all sovereign authority in yourself. People will call you excellency and maybe you can get Moammar Gadhafi to lend you one of his hats.
4. *Capacity to enter into relations with other states.* Cleopatra, Queen of the Nile, had a rather literal idea of how to go about this, but you needn't go to that extreme. Basically the question is: are you in charge—i.e., do you exercise supreme bosshood over your chunk of real estate and thereby have authority to negotiate on an equal basis with other sovereign states? If not, did you ever? (This is the sleeper clause that lets conquered nations, e.g., the Lithuanians prior to the breakup of the Soviet Union, claim sovereignty.)

Seems to me you're on pretty weak ground in this department, so your best bet may be to outfit yourself and a couple buddies with AK-47s and nuclear bombs and see if you can fend off the local panjandrums for a few years. (And don't leave the premises to go to the bathroom, either; see #2 above.) If you can manage it, *I'll* recognize your sovereignty, and that's basically the ball game. A chore? Sure, but nobody ever said being a country was a bowl of cherries.

A Country of One's Own: A Follow-up

Regarding my column on how to start your own country, a reader has chastised me for not mentioning the 1984 book by that title written by Erwin Strauss and distributed by Loompanics Unlimited, an outfit that also peddles such gems as *Human Sacrifice in History and Today* and *Ragnar's Guide to Home and Recreational Use of High Explosives*. Strauss describes successful new countries such as Sealand, founded in the sixties by former pirate radio operator Paddy Roy "Prince Roy" Bates on an abandoned antiaircraft platform off the coast of England. He also mentions the smallest country in existence, the Sovereign Military Order of Malta, whose realm consists of one building in Rome. So there's hope for you would-be potentates.

Strauss describes five routes to nationhood:

1. *Traditional sovereignty.* This is the approach I mentioned in my column. You need territory, people, and a government, and you have to defend it against all comers. Strauss takes this pretty seriously. Readers who do likewise may wish to obtain his other book, *Basement Nukes*, priced to move at $8.95 (no kidding). If that sounds a bit drastic, you might check out another book from Loompanics, *Uninhabited Ocean Islands*, by Jon Fisher.

2. *Ship under flag of convenience.* Register your tub with a see-no-evil outfit like Liberia (well, maybe not Liberia these days, but you know what I mean), and for all practical purposes you're independent, and mobile, too. Not exactly sovereignty, but maybe close enough.

3. *Litigation.* Sue the bastards and make them recognize you, or at least let you alone. It worked for Roy Bates in England, but I wouldn't try it in Iraq.

4. *"Vonu."* A coined term basically meaning "out of sight, out of mind." Slip off into the forest where the government can't find you and establish your own society. The favored region for this seems to be the Pacific Northwest. Fine if you can stand the giant slugs.

5. *Model country.* That's model as in "pretend." Declare your bungalow a sovereign state, issue stamps, fly your own flag—the "real" government won't care so long as you pay your taxes and otherwise cooperate with your oppressors. Maybe not as spiritually satisfying as traditional sovereignty, but you might live longer. Hunger to know more? Write Loompanics Unlimited, PO Box 1197, Port Townsend, WA 98368.

While watching a recent World War II documentary, I noticed the U.S. flag with forty-eight stars in a 6 × 8 matrix. Of course now we have fifty stars, with alternating rows of five and six. This raises several questions. When we add a state, who makes the decision on how the stars will be arranged? Is there a Senate subcommittee on star arrangement? Or is it done by some bureaucratic pencil pusher— another example of the American public having no say in matters of national importance? Finally, if the District of Columbia becomes a state, how the heck would one arrange the stars? Isn't this the real reason D.C. will never become a state?—Mark Thornquist, Seattle

Could be; I always thought that fear-of-Jesse-Jackson-as-U.S.-senator stuff was a smoke screen. Fortunately, I have solved the problem. But first some facts.

The general appearance of the flag—thirteen stripes, a star for each state, etc.—was set by Congress in 1818. The star arrangement, however, is up to the president. The deliberations within the Eisenhower administration on this burning issue prior to the admission of Alaska and Hawaii were cloaked in secrecy. So we don't know if Ike convened a late-night cabinet meeting, consulted experts in the science of tesselation (mosaic pattern arrangement), or just worked it out himself with David's blocks. No matter; in the end, it was a completely arbitrary exercise of presidential power.

Undemocratic? Sure, but if you'd seen the cockeyed suggestions sent in by the public, you'd say it was just as well. Stars in star patterns, stars spelling out U.S.A.—one shudders. In fact, until relatively recent times, half-arsed star arrangement has been something of a national curse. At the Battle of Guilford Court House in North Carolina in 1781, American troops carried a banner with thirteen stars in a dweebish arrangement of two rows of four, one row of three, and the remaining two stars shoehorned in one above the other on the far right. Worse, the flag had alternating red-and-*blue* stripes, with blue eight-pointed stars arranged on a white field. Not surprisingly, the troops obliged to fight under this pathetic rag got massacred. I'd have been too embarrassed even to show up.

Things did not improve as time went on. The thirty-one-star flag that Commodore Matthew Perry sailed into Tokyo harbor with in 1853 had five vertical columns of five plus one dippy-looking column of six crammed in on the extreme left. Even stranger was the thirty-three-star flag that flew over Fort Sumter at the start of the Civil War in 1861 (actually there were thirty-four states at the time—they weren't big on details then). It had an indescribable mess of stars that can only be attributed to hallucinogenic molds in the hardtack.

Luckily, today we've got people like me to keep things on a professional basis. A fifty-one-star flag? No prob. When President Quayle calls in 1997, I'll tell him to make it six rows with alternating rows of nine and eight. For fifty-two stars try eight rows, alternating six and seven, and for fifty-three, seven rows, alternating eight and seven. That takes care of D.C. and Puerto Rico and leaves us a spare for emergencies. *Semper paratus,* that's me.

Vexed

By the way, Cecil, the expert to consult on flag design wouldn't be a tesselationist but a vexillologist—a flag scientist.—Peter T. Daniels, Chicago

Peter, haven't you ever heard of getting the right guy for the right job? If we wanted to exchange idle gossip about flags, or discuss flag lore, or tell flag jokes, a vexillologist would be fine. When it comes to star arrangement, however, you want an expert in two-dimensional patterns—a tesselationist.

While trying to figure out why our troops are in Saudi Arabia recently, I looked up the Kuwait–Saudi Arabia–Iraq area in my 1966 atlas. I found two large areas along the border called "neutral zones." What does this term mean? Do Romulans live there? Do the zones have any relevance to the current conflict?—D. Davis, Chicago

Time to get a new atlas, sport. One of the neutral zones was divvied up in 1969 between the countries adjoining it, Kuwait and Saudi Arabia. But the other one, between Saudi Arabia and Iraq, is still there. I notice the CNN weatherdroids mention it with the same matter-of-fact tone they use to refer to Cleveland, as though you ac-

tually have some clue what they're talking about. Unless you're the kind of person who knows that before 1932 Saudi Arabia was called "the Kingdom of the Hijaz and of the Nejd and its Dependencies" (*I* knew, of course), 'tain't likely.

The neutral zones date back to 1922. The father of modern Saudi Arabia, Abd al-Aziz ibn Abd al-Rahman ibn Saud Al Faysal, known to the west as Ibn Saud, had managed to consolidate much of the central Arabian peninsula under his rule. To keep the peace, the British—then the dominant foreign power in the region—called the local potentates in to settle on national boundaries.

Fixed boundaries at the time weren't a big Arab priority. The desert nomads were organized along feudal lines, with local tribes proclaiming their loyalty to one or another overlord. The territory of said overlord basically consisted of whatever his tribes happened to be camped on at the moment. Since the tribes moved around a lot, the situation was pretty fluid.

The British weren't about to put up with that kind of bush-league attitude and insisted on fixed boundaries or else, their main concern being simplicity of administration. This led to considerable wrangling with the Arab leaders, since almost any boundary was likely to cut some tribe off from its traditional grazing lands or water sources. Another problem was that some of the nomads were fickle and

quarrelsome. Once the borders were firmed up, any vengeful ex-
cursion across national frontiers might well be regarded as an act
of war.

To avoid these problems while still getting their freaking borders,
the British finally convinced the relevant parties that there should be
two neutral zones, one between Saudi Arabia and Iraq, the other between Saudi Arabia and Kuwait, the latter bordering the gulf coast.
(The Saudi-Iraqi zone was mainly the domain of a troublesome tribe
called the Zafir.) As spelled out in the Protocol of Uqayr, no government could build fortifications or station troops in or near the zones,
or near the border generally.

Border disputes continued for many years thereafter, but the neutral zones endured until oil was discovered under the one between
Kuwait and Saudi Arabia. By and by the Kuwaitis and Saudis decided to hell with the nomads, let's divide this sucker up. To date
this has not occurred with the Saudi-Iraq zone, although I imagine
it'll happen eventually. But right now those most concerned have
other things on their minds.

Drawing the Line

*Your recent column on the neutral zones of the Arabian peninsula
said the Iraq-Saudi zone was still in existence. On the contrary, the
zone was divided in 1981. This was done to stabilize the border after
the Iranian revolution and the outbreak of the Iraq-Iran War "im-
pelled Saudi Arabia and Iraq to seek closer relations," according to
one book on the subject.—Richard Jones, Washington, D.C.*

I was afraid somebody was going to bring this up. Strictly speaking you're right—the zone was divided by treaty between Iraq and
Saudi Arabia on December 26, 1981. For unknown reasons, however,
the treaty was never filed with the United Nations and nobody outside Iraq and Saudi Arabia was officially notified or shown the text
giving the new map coordinates. So legally speaking the U.S. government has to act as though the neutral zone still exists. Practically
speaking, though, it's well aware that it doesn't.

The Office of the Geographer at the U.S. State Department, which provides the official word on international boundaries for all U.S. government maps, continues to show the diamond-shaped neutral zone with a line running through the middle and the words "de facto boundary as shown on official Iraqi and Saudi maps (alignment approximate)." Similar notes appear on U.S. maps showing the rest of the Saudi-Iraq border (which was basically straightened) and the Iraq-Jordan border (which was made more crooked). The de facto borders are believed to be accurate within 150 meters, or perhaps a city block—no big deal to you and me, but to government cartographers used to pinpoint precision, a constant thorn.

Iraq's borders are by no means the only ones up in the air. According to maps I got from the state department's Bureau of Intelligence and Research (amazing what you can find out these days with a little pull and a fax machine), the boundaries between Saudi Arabia and its neighbors Yemen, Oman, the United Arab Emirates, and Qatar are either in dispute, undefined, or defined but undisclosed. If you want to stay out of trouble next time you visit the Arabian peninsula, don't take any long walks in the desert.

I recently moved from Minnesota to Washington, D.C. Not only did I leave behind ten thousand lakes, it seems I left the United States as well. No, I'm not talking about the drive for District statehood. I'm wondering why my new home, Virginia, is called a commonwealth instead of a state. Is there a difference between Virginia—and the commonwealths of Massachusetts, Pennsylvania, and Kentucky—and the commonwealth of Puerto Rico? If there's no legal difference, how come Puerto Rico doesn't get a star on the U.S. flag?—Tim Walker, Washington, D.C.

Oh, fine, Timsy, stir up the revolutionaries. Fact is, in this country we've got commonwealths and then we've got commonwealths. Old-style CWs, including VA, MA, PA, and KY, harken back to a seventeenth-century notion of the state (generic, not U.S.) as common enterprise—you know, all for one, one for all, that kind of stuff.

The proto-Virginians at Jamestown referred to their undertaking as a commonwealth virtually from the day the colony was founded in 1607. A few decades later in England "the Commonwealth" came to mean the period of Puritan rule under the Cromwells, 1649–1660. The big-C Commonwealth having collapsed, the notion of a little-C commonwealth assumed a distinctly antimonarchical cast and "commonwealthmen" became ardent republicans.

For that reason, as well as the original idea of common enterprise, the term commonwealth commended itself to rad (well, semirad) Massachusetts statesman John Adams. Adams must have been a good persuader; the folks who walked into the Bay State's constitutional convention in 1780 styled themselves "the Delegates of the People of the State of Massachusetts-Bay" but came out carrying "the Constitution of the Commonwealth of Massachusetts."

Later "commonwealth" evolved to mean a voluntary association of colonies or nations. Thus in 1900 we had the Commonwealth of Australia, a collection of former colonies amalgamated into a nation, and later the British Commonwealth (now merely the Commonwealth, to avoid the imperialist taint), an association of former British subject states.

It was apparently the latter brand of commonwealth that Washington brain trusters had in mind when they pondered the future of Puerto Rico in the 1940s. "Commonwealth" status was the perfect have-your-cake-and-eat-it-too compromise, signifying that Puerto Rico was sort of independent but not really, and sort of a state but not really that either. Don't worry about the Old Dominion (i.e., Virginia), though. Legally the old-style commonwealths are indistinguishable from states, and from the standpoint of terminological coolness you've got states beat by a mile.

Has anyone ever made a study of the comparative heights of winners and losers in elections, and if so, what were the results?—Wistfully, Eli "Shorty" Pindsey, Chicago

Well, being a dwarf sure didn't help that little Greek fella in 1988. And no question everybody in politics *thinks* being tall is an advantage. Five-foot-nine-and-a-half-inch Jimmy Carter's handlers went to great lengths to prevent him from having to stand next to 6'1" Gerald Ford during the 1976 presidential debates.

But the data on this question is notoriously flaky. U of Chicago

statistics professor William Kruskal, who used to keep track of this sort of thing in his spare time, says he never found anybody whose height estimates could be relied upon, particularly when it came to the heights of the losers in earlier elections.

That caveat aside, various sources do claim that the taller candidate usually wins. For example, in *Language on Vacation* (1965), word and number buff Dmitri Borgmann claimed that in the nineteen U.S. presidential elections between 1888 and 1960, the taller candidate won the popular vote all but once, when 6′2″ Franklin Roosevelt beat 6′2½″ Wendell Willkie in 1940. In 1888 5′11″ Grover Cleveland beat 5′6″ Benjamin Harrison at the polls but was cuffed in the electoral college, and in 1896 and 1900 both candidates were the same height.

In his 1982 book *Too Small, Too Tall* psychologist John Gillis presents similar results: in the twenty-one presidential elections from 1904 to 1984, the taller candidate won 80 percent of the time. What's more, he says, in the whole history of the Republic, only two presidents—Harrison and James Madison (5′4″)—were appreciably shorter than the average height in their day.

We glean further insight on this issue from a delightful book called *The Height of Your Life* (1980) by Ralph Keyes (5′7.62″). Keyes notes that a survey of the U.S. Senate in 1866 found the average height of the members to be 5′10½″, well above average for men at the time. Keyes's own survey of twenty-seven senators found the average height had risen to 6′0.33″, 3.33″ taller than the average American male. A similar survey of thirty-one governors found the average height to be 6′0.46″.

So, case closed, right? Not so fast. Consider an alternative theory of presidential electoral success—the Longer Name Hypothesis, which is also discussed in the Borgmann book. Of the twenty-two elections between 1876 and 1960, the candidate with more letters in his last name won the popular vote twenty times.

In two cases, Tilden-Hayes in 1876 and Cleveland-Harrison in 1888, the longer-named winners of the popular vote lost in the electoral college. In 1916 Wilson and Hughes had the same number of letters in their names, so the voters obviously chose on the basis of the issues. The only time the longer-named candidate lost the popular vote was in 1908, when Taft whomped Bryan. However, Taft weighed more than 300 pounds and probably attracted votes by force of gravity alone.

The situation has been somewhat muddied in the seven presidential elections since 1960, with only one victory for the long-named candidate, five defeats, and one case in which both candidates had names of equal length. This just shows you the difficulty of doing good science in the face of an uncooperative fact situation. As far as I'm concerned, the Longer Name Hypothesis remains at least as persuasive as the Longer Body Hypothesis. Until scientific measurements can be adduced for *all* dimensions of the presidential person (something that can surely be expected any day in light of the Thomas-Hill hearings), I think we must admit the question remains open.

Picking Presidents: A New Paradigm

I read with interest your article discussing the Longer Body (Greater Height) and Longer Name hypotheses in predicting the outcome of American presidential elections. To help you further with the political education of your readers, I would like to share a rule which correctly predicts every election since the modern American politico-economic system began under FDR: a president with an unusual first name always alternates with a president with a common first name— Franklin, Harry, Dwight, John, Lyndon, Richard, Gerald, Jimmy, Ronald, George.

Ignore the occasional nitpicker who does not think Gerald is all that unusual a name, and you have a powerful analytical tool. While either John (Kennedy) or Richard (Nixon) could have followed Dwight (Eisenhower), and George (Bush) and Michael (Dukakis) both had a chance after Ronald, Adlai Stevenson could no more unseat Dwight than Hubert (Humphrey) could succeed Lyndon.

The acid test of any theory, of course, is in predicting the future. To put it on the line: neither Paul (Tsongas) nor Bill (Clinton) nor Tom (Harkin) nor Jerry (Brown) nor Dick (Gephardt) nor, for that matter, Pat (Buchanan) has a prayer of replacing George. Mario (Cuomo) or Jesse (Jackson) could, but they may want to wait until 1996, when the Republicans will be stuck with Dan (Quayle), Jack (Kemp), or Dick (Cheney). Pierre Du Pont would be their only hope, unless he pursues the chimera of populism by insisting on being called Pete.—Juozas Algimantas Kazlas (a common name, but only in Lithuania), New York

Not to give anybody ideas, Joe. But if Mario and Jesse have opted out, there's always (blush) Cecil. Time having passed, I am also obliged to note that Bill did defeat George. Maybe we could just start calling him Wilhelm.

Is there some rumor about George Bush's alleged marital infidelities that I'm supposed to know about but don't? I keep seeing these veiled references in places like Newsweek's "Conventional Wisdom Watch," but no details. Please, help me get hip. Half the time I don't even get "Doonesbury" these days.—Elizabeth A. Clarke, Chicago

I know the feeling. If you're not wired into the media gossipnet (and even I take a week or two off occasionally just to detox), getting through the trendier magazines is like trying to read code. The rumor you're supposed to know about refers to one Jennifer (with a J, not G) Fitzgerald, a sixtyish longtime aide to Bush. Described as domineering, she was unpopular with coworkers but could do no wrong in her boss's eyes. This led some to conclude that the two had something going, although you could use the same reasoning to prove Bush had an affair with John Sununu.

The rumor had been circulating since the early eighties and occasionally surfaced in the papers, most notably (and explicitly) in a story in the *L.A. Weekly* during the 1988 presidential campaign. A few days later the stock market dropped forty-three points on rumors that the *Washington Post* was about to do a similar exposé. The actual evidence for the alleged liaison was laughably thin: anonymous secondhand accounts, mysterious daylong disappearances during 1978–79, that kind of thing. Fitzgerald denied the story; Bush, on one of the few occasions reporters had the nerve to ask him about it, said, "I don't respond to rumors." Personally, I won't be satisfied until we get lab tests and a televised hearing. For a fuller discussion (no additional facts, but an amusing account of mainstream media squirming on the subject), see the November 15, 1988, *Village Voice*.

What is the purpose of underground nuclear testing? Do governments actually learn something from these explosions? Or is it just a deranged form of political muscle-flexing?—Dave Hines, Chicago

What, you think nuclear weaponry is a mature (I use the word loosely) technology? Well, it isn't, and considering the untold billions we've spent on nuclear weapons research since 1980, it better not be. The purpose of underground nuclear testing is to (1) help build better bombs, (2) test the old models to see if they still work, and (3) see what happens to something if you drop an atom bomb on it. The United States is thought to have conducted more than nine hundred nuclear tests since 1945, all but ten of them at the Nevada Test Site, a vast federal reserve about one hundred miles north of Las Vegas. These tests have helped make nuclear weapons the sophisticated, reliable instruments of destruction they are today.

Many people are surprised to learn that serious nuclear weapons research is still underway. What's the point, if we've already got enough bombs to destroy the world several times over? This thought is so naive. Strategic planners assume that most of our nuclear weapons won't survive a first strike and we'll have to wreak what havoc we can with what remains. Thus the search for better bombs.

This is not necessarily a bad thing. Early nuclear weapons were big and dumb. The idea basically was to get them within fireball distance of a major city, industrial complex, or military facility, on the theory that if you obliterated every work of man for ten miles around you were bound to take out a few targets of military significance. Strategic planners finally realized this was a waste of good neutrons and ever since have been trying to build bombs and warheads capable of being delivered more efficiently.

For example, one project being considered in the late eighties was the strategic earth penetration warhead, or EPW. These "are designed to penetrate some tens of feet underground before detonating," says my bomb guide. "The principle underlying EPWs is that a warhead exploded underground couples more of its energy to the earth than does one exploded in the air or on the earth's surface, creating more ground shock per kiloton of explosive yield." Perfecting one of these babies will require tests, as will such *Star Wars* fantasies as nuclear-pumped X-ray lasers, should they ever be built.

Another reason for nuclear testing is to make sure that bombs already in service will work. In 1981, the government became concerned that model W80 warheads, which had been deployed the previous year, would fail at low temperatures. You can imagine the reaction if we nuked our enemies one frosty morning only to have the stupid things drop like rocks into somebody's kitchen without further result. As a consequence of testing, the problem was headed off at the pass.

In another case in the early sixties, scientists switched the chemical explosive on the W52 warhead because it was prone to premature detonation. (Chemical explosions are used in atom bombs to trigger the nuclear ones.) But an underground test revealed that the new chemical explosive resulted in a distressingly low-wattage atomic blast. Designers came up with a fix, did another test, and were pleased to find that the desired lethality could now be achieved.

So there you go. A nasty business, I agree. But the bomb jockeys say, and it's hard to argue with them, that if you're going to have nukes, they might as well work.

What's Bad About Bombs

You are usually so hip that I checked your naive repetition of the excuses for bomb testing five times before I was sure it was not satire. Let's get two points out of the way first: (1) There is no known case of a nuclear bomb being tested and not going "boom." The likelihood of a nuclear warhead failing is almost nil. (2) The purpose of nuclear weapons is to threaten *to use them. Combine these and the scenario that weapons tests are supposedly preventing runs like this: "Ten percent of the weapons with which the Yankee dogs are threatening us haven't been tested. Our scientists are convinced there is one chance in a thousand they won't work. If we attack now, 10 percent of our cities have one chance in a thousand of surviving until U.S. satellites redirect the last sub-based warheads. I suggest we attack now!"*

You mention the danger of most of our nuclear weapons not surviving a first strike. The CIS (née U.S.S.R.) could put up a credible first strike against American ground *forces. They haven't up to now, and it is hard to figure why we need to test any weapons against the likelihood of them doing so with decreased armaments, decreased motivation, and increased complexity in command and control. For that matter, we have a sufficient threat in telling them we will suspend all aid to any country attacking us with nuclear forces.*

The fact is, we have a bomb-testing bureaucracy because we once needed to test bombs; we now test bombs because the bureaucracy wants to have a purpose.—Frank Palmer, Chicago

"We will suspend all aid to any country attacking us with nuclear forces?" Tell me, Frank, what do the other Martians think about this?

As for your specific gripes: (1) The fear is not that our nuclear bombs won't go boom but that they won't make a big enough boom. We covered this in the original column. (2) Loss of confidence in the nuclear arsenal is cumulative. If we arrived at a point someday that none of the active warheads had been tested, the credibility of our nuclear deterrent would be significantly reduced. (3) I agree the CIS does not pose much of a threat and that the nuclear arsenals of both countries should be dismantled. Pending that happy day, however, it'd be foolish to go to all the expense of maintaining nuclear weapons without being sure they'll work.

Are Social Security numbers "recycled"? If not, then why is my number lower than my (older) boyfriend's? If you add the current population (now about 250 million) to the number of Americans who have died since 1935 (when Social Security began), wouldn't the resulting number exceed nine digits in an S.S. number, proving my little theory about recycling? Okay, Cecil, tell me I'm full of blarney, but what do the numbers represent?—Lisa W., New York

Cecil wishes he could tell you Social Security numbers were as fraught with meaning as the driver's license numbers issued by some states, which encode everything but your IQ, but no such luck. Prior to 1973, the first three digits indicated the state of the issuing Social Security office. Since 1973, the first three digits "are determined by the ZIP code of the mailing address shown on the application for a Social Security number," the feds inform me. But it's still basically done by states. The remaining digits are simply a serial number. To date recycling hasn't been necessary, but more on this in a moment.

So you can make sure they didn't screw up and give you a wrong number with God knows what ghastly consequences for your retirement, here's how the numbers are assigned:

001-003 NH	237-246 NC	756-753 TN	501-502 ND	530, 680 NV
004-007 ME	681-690 ″	416-424 AL	503-504 SD	531-539 WA
008-009 VT	247-251 SC	425-428 MS	505-508 NE	540-544 OR
010-034 MA	654-658 ″	587-588 ″	509-515 KS	545-573 CA
035-039 RI	252-260 GA	752-755 ″	516-517 MT	602-626 ″
040-049 CT	667-675 ″	429-432 AR	518-519 ID	574 AK
050-134 NY	261-267 FL	676-679 ″	520 WY	575-576 HI
135-158 NJ	589-595 ″	433-439 LA	521-524 CO	750-751 ″
159-211 PA	268-302 OH	659-665 ″	650-653 ″	577-579 DC
212-220 MD	303-317 IN	440-448 OK	525, 585 NM	580 VI
221-222 DE	318-361 IL	449-467 TX	648-649 ″	580-584 PR
223-231 VA	362-386 MI	627-645 ″	526-527 AZ	596-599 ″
691-699 ″	387-399 WI	486-477 MN	600-601 ″	586 GU
232-236 WV	400-407 KY	478-485 IA	528-529 VT	586 AS
232 NC	408-415 TN	486-500 MO	646, 647 ″	

Some states were assigned additional numbers due to population growth. Numbers that show up for more than one state were reassigned or cover several small localities. Until 1963, workers covered under the Railroad Retirement Act, which predated Social Security, were given numbers between 700 and 728. The Philippines prior to independence had 586. You're fascinated, I'm sure.

The question one might ask is: why should a Social Security number mean anything—why not just make it a straight serial number? No reason, from what I can gather; it's mainly a holdover from the old days. Before 1973, Social Security numbers were issued by local field offices. To prevent duplication, states were allocated blocks of numbers. In 1973, number issuance was centralized at Social Security Administration HQ in Baltimore. The feds could easily have switched to the straight serial method at this point but didn't, apparently out of a primordial bureaucratic instinct that once a system, always a system.

No big deal, I guess, except that the numbers will run out faster than they might have otherwise—that is, as soon as the last block of a million numbers is allocated and the first state begins to run dry. Happily for us, this is yet another looming crisis we can fob off on our grandchildren. About 360 million Social Security numbers have been issued to date, 211 million of which are "active," i.e., the holders are still breathing. Since there are about a billion possible numbers (actually 999 million, since nobody seems to want the 000 series), we'll be halfway into the next century before it's time to panic. At the moment Social Security masterminds aren't sweating it—their most pressing concern isn't running out of numbers, it's running out of money.

Our Days Are Numbered

Cecil, you're a hopeless romantic. Sure, it makes sense that if only 360 million people have ever had nine-digit Social Security numbers, it'll take 639 million more before we run out. But when did logic ever have anything to do with the federal government? One major use of Social Security numbers is for taxpayer and employer identification— and what with corporations, trusts, partnerships, not-for-profits, and various other obscure business enterprises, there are a lot more tax-payers and employers than Social Security registrants. So what's the REAL Straight Dope? Is D(uplication)-Day right around the corner?—Harry Doakes, Portland, Oregon

Don't be a mope. Only people can get Social Security numbers, not corporations. When businesses file taxes they have to use what is variously known as a taxpayer or employer ID number. Like the S.S. number, it has nine digits, but it's grouped differently—00-0000000 versus 000-00-0000. You may say a hyphen is a pretty frail bulwark against national chaos should a significant fraction of taxpayer ID numbers duplicate Social Security numbers (as indeed has probably occurred), but the folks at the Social Security Administration basically say, Hey, not our problem—we don't issue taxpayer ID numbers, the IRS does. A pretty cavalier attitude, but look at the bright side: they might accidentally send you the tax refund check for IBM.

One more thing. It occurs to me I may have been too hasty in describing the last six digits of the Social Security number as "simply a serial number." Whatever may be said about Uncle Sam being logical, nothing involving the federal government is simple.

The fourth and fifth digits of the S.S. number are what's known as the "group number." For reasons that are perverse even by government standards, S.S. numbers for a given state are issued in this order: first all those having odd group code numbers from 01 to 09, then even numbers from 10 to 98, then even from 02 to 08, and finally odd numbers from 11 to 99. According to one of my less reputable sources, all numbers issued before 1965 are either odd numbers between 01 and 09 or even numbers between 10 and 98.

I'm told the purpose of this rigamarole is so that some sharp-eyed sleuth at S.S. HQ can look at a Social Security number and say, "Ha! Group number 99 from the state of Maine! We haven't issued them yet—this number is a fake!" Seems to me it would be just as easy to look the thing up in the Big Book of Issued Numbers, but I guess if you're a federal bureaucrat you have to cook up schemes like this to justify your appropriation.

Why does Queen Elizabeth carry a purse, and what could she possibly have in it? I took an informal poll at work and got these results:

3 people said she carried carfare.

2 people said she carried identification.

5 people said she carried makeup.

1 person said she carried nothing at all; it was like a security blanket. I hope you can help.—Jimmy Perez, Santa Barbara, California

Maybe I never told you this, J.P., but years ago Elizabeth and I used to double-date (she loved Roller Derby). The subject of purses,

unfortunately, never came up. Now, of course, she won't give me the time of day, the snob. No problem, sez I, I'll just call up the embassy in D.C., the better to save on the transatlantic tolls. You've heard about the fabled British sense of humor? It's a fraud. Total noncooperation. "Look, bub," I tell this sniffy lackey, "here in America we believe in freedom of information." But still no dice.

Diplomatic channels having proved unavailing, I call up Buckingham Palace (no small achievement in an era when all the phone companies hate each other). The queen continues to stonewall. A press aide tells me (and believe me, how these people can breathe with their noses at that angle I'll never know) that she carries items "of a personal nature," but not money. Pressed further, she said you'd find what you'd expect to find in a woman's purse. This being the nineties, I blanch to think what I'd expect to find in a woman's purse. Let's give her the benefit of the doubt and assume it's puppy biscuits for the corgis.

More on the Royal Bag ... Uh, Purse

As anyone who reads Majesty *magazine knows, the Queen carries a comb, a handkerchief, a small gold compact, and a tube of lipstick in her handbag. However, you were somewhat misled by Buckingham Palace. The Queen does carry money on Sundays—a folded note of unknown denomination which she discreetly places in the collection plate.*

Mr. Perez was also partially correct: Her Majesty does use her handbag as a security blanket. She carries it with her throughout the day as she moves from one room of the palace to another. She is rarely photographed without a handbag. All tables and her desk at Buckingham Palace and other royal residences are equipped with special hooks on which the Queen may hang her ubiquitous handbag. Finally, the Queen never uses a shoulder bag or clutch bag as these make shaking hands and accepting flowers awkward.

I could go on to discuss the Queen's hats, but perhaps that would be a bit much.—Elizabeth Giangrego, Chicago

Adolf Hitler spoke of the empire he was trying to build as the Third Reich. What were Reichs One and Two?—Wilberforce, Blue Mounds, Wisconsin

According to a fascinating tome called *The Hitler Fact Book* by Thomas Fuchs (like I say, I get the most amazing stuff in the mail), "The first Reich was the Holy Roman Empire of the Middle Ages; the second, the one established by Bismarck and ended by Germany's defeat in 1918." The term was a favorite of Hitler's propaganda minister, Joseph Goebbels. Hitler himself wasn't that crazy about it, Fuchs notes; he outlawed the term at the beginning of World War II and referred to his realm merely as the Reich.

Another Nazi term, "Thousand Year Reich," supposedly had its origin in a remark by Hitler following the purge of June 1934, when he had many of his onetime supporters murdered. Hitler said the victims had been plotting a revolt and promised there would be no more such strife for a thousand years.

Why are Communists so attached to the color red? Why did the anti-Communists call themselves "whites"?—Robert Feinstein, St. Lambert, Quebec

You want the facts on a question like this, Robert, you have to go straight to the source, in this case the *Great Soviet Encyclopedia*. From this formidable work we learn that "popular uprisings occurred under red banners as early as the eighth century (the Red Banner rebellion in Iran) and in the 16th (the Great Peasant War in Germany) and 17th centuries." The Iranian thing is reaching a bit, but let us be kind.

The encyclopedia goes on: "The people of France fought under red banners against the king's rule in July 1792. With the revolt of June 5–6, 1832, in Paris, the red banner became a symbol of the blood spilled by the people and thus the banner of revolution, and after the Paris Commune of 1871 it became the banner of [specifically] proletarian revolution." The red banner was first flown in Russia in 1861 and became the Soviet flag in 1918.

The Whites, counterrevolutionaries who fought the Reds in the period 1918–1920, took their name from the White Guards, a Finnish police force organized in 1906 to fight subversives. "The origin of the term 'White Guards' is connected with the traditional symbolism of the color white as the color of the supporters of 'legitimate' law and order," the *GSE* notes. It wasn't just in the Old West that the alleged good guys (or at any rate the forces of the establishment) wore white hats.

The East Is Red

Regarding why the Russians like the color red: the Russian words for "red" and "beautiful" are almost identical. They both stem from the same concept in archaic Russian. To the pre–twelfth-century savages who settled in what is now Great Russia (around the Volga, between White Russia and the Ural Mountains), redness and beauty were one; red was a kind of superlative ideal. Modern Russian retains the idea of red being beautiful. The site we know in English as Red Square, a focal point in Moscow, is literally translated as "beautiful place." I'm not sure if this is why the Bolsheviks adopted red as their official color, but subsconsciously it may have had something to do with it.—Gail Burke, Chicago

Could be; I'll ask Boris next time he drops by. The word for "red" is *krasnaia* (or some reasonable phonetic equivalent), that for "beautiful" *kracivaya*.

How did "left" and "right" come to represent the ends of the political spectrum that they do?—Lisa Martinovic, Lafayette, California

The *Oxford English Dictionary* explains it this way: "This use originated in the French National Assembly of 1789, in which the nobles as a body took the position of honour on the President's right, and the Third Estate sat on his left. The significance of these positions, which was at first merely ceremonial, soon became political."

Why can't Prince Rainier become a king? You will probably find this question really stupid, but no one can tell me.—L. Cord, New York

If you've been reading this column long, L., you know that stupid is not a major disqualifier, questionwise. But this one's a lot smarter than some. The short answer is that the male heads of the ruling Grimaldi family have styled themselves princes for something like seven hundred years, and it would be a little presumptuous for Prince Rainier to give himself a promotion now. The long answer is that "prince" is the title traditionally given to the head of a vassal state, that is, one under the protection of and hence subordinate to a larger and more powerful ruler.

That pretty much describes the case with Monaco. Except for interludes with Spain and Sardinia, it's been under the thumb of neighboring France . . . well, that's the wrong way to put it. Let's say France guarantees its independence. During the French Revolution France welshed on the deal and annexed the 0.7-square-mile country, but Monaco regained its independence following the fall of Napoleon.

Today Monaco is a sovereign state but as a practical matter remains so at the sufferance of France. It has only a token military. It uses French currency, the official language is French (although there is a Monégasque dialect), and France supplies the gas, water, and electricity. When France is peeved, as happened in the early sixties when Monaco became a haven for rich folks trying to evade French taxes, the Grimaldis perspire. (Rainier does, that is. Grace glowed.)

The solution then was to close a few tax loopholes. The bigger deal long-term is a 1918 treaty with France—if the Grimaldis don't produce an heir, Monaco becomes an "autonomous state under the protection of France." (Probable translation: everybody pays French taxes.) It's only a guess, but if Rainier suddenly started taking on kingly airs, Monaco might find itself incorporated into its larger neighbor a little sooner than expected.

Some Insight into the Origin of the Conflict in Bosnia-Herzegovina

As a Welsh-American, I am deeply offended by your use of the ethnic slur "welshed." What is your factual basis for stereotyping Welsh people as a race who fail to honor their obligations? You owe the people of Wales an immediate apology.—Malcolm Solomon, Palo Alto, California

Okay, I apologize. Next time I'll say they "malcolmed" on the deal.

You are the only person that can clear this up once and for all. What exactly is the Bilderberg Group? There have been accusations on "The Larry King Show" that it is some kind of secret organization that has a lot of influence in shaping world events today and in the past. According to one caller, Bill Clinton was at one of their meetings a few years ago. Is any of this true? What's the deal?—J. D. Levine, Mount Royal, Quebec

Here we go again. The Bilderbergers are another of those discussion groups for world leaders that have become a target of right wing crazy people. They're a little more secretive than most. You may remember we had a similar question a while back about the Trilateral Commission, which also sponsors meetings of international big shots. I was delighted to discover that this supposedly secret nerve center of the one-world conspiracy was listed in the New York phone book.

Not so the Bilderbergers, and there wasn't much about them in the clip file either. No problem. I figured, Hey, all these guys must hang out together, I'll call up my buds at the Trilateral Commission and ask for the Bilderbergers' number. Sure enough, while they're not all members of the same bowling league (the Bilderberg folks are headquartered in Amsterdam, so they couldn't get together on Wednesday nights), they do have some contact. In short order I'd gotten the number of a fellow named Charles in

New York who does administrative and consulting work for the Bilderbergers.

Turns out there isn't really a Bilderberg "group" (although there is a thirty-or-so-member steering committee), just an annual Bilderberg meeting, so named because it was first held in May 1954 in the Bilderberg Hotel in Oosterbeek, Holland. Why Holland? Well, it was the tulips, surely, but also the fact that the thing was organized by Prince Bernhard of the Netherlands, a devout internationalist who wanted to get selected leaders from Europe and North America together on a regular basis to talk about global problems. (The Japanese weren't and aren't invited; one of the reasons for the Trilateral Commission, in fact, was to cut the Japanese in on the world conspiracy action.) Typically there are about one hundred attendees; apart from the core group, it's usually different people from government, business, and labor each time. Bill Clinton made the cut a couple years ago.

What do they talk about at Bilderberg meetings? Deep stuff, although from the standpoint of riveting your attention I don't know that it ranks up there with the NCAA finals. Charles was kind enough to send an old press release for the 1992 meeting in Evian, France, which lists such ponderous topics as Prospects for the Former Soviet Republics, What Should Be Done for Eastern Europe, and Whither the United States?

Then again, I've never actually been to a meeting, my invite having been swallowed up by the same postal black hole that got my MacArthur genius grant, so for all I know it's a front and what they really do is sit around in their skivvies and swap dirty jokes. Be that as it may, such luminaries as George Ball have written warmly about the experience.

All this internationalism has earned the enduring wrath of the America-first element, notably the ultrarightist Liberty Lobby, which goes after the Bilderbergers periodically in its newspaper *The Spotlight*. (Other targets include the Federal Reserve, the electoral college, and Social Security.) Prior to the fall of Communism, the idea that international cooperation might lead to a one-world state run by the Bolsheviks had the necessary few molecules of plausibility to give even sensible people the occasional twinge. Now it all just seems quaint.

Why does a lieutenant general outrank a major general while a major outranks a lieutenant?—Bob Spertus, Berkeley, California

This question has gnawed at me for years, Bob. As near as I can make out, here's the deal: in your modern army (modern defined as dating from the 1500s onward), you've got three basic units: your company, commanded by a captain; your regiment, commanded by a colonel; and your army or division, commanded by (ultimately) the sovereign. In the past as today, the individuals who actually held these lofty posts, sovereign included, were often no-talent nebbishes, whose principal qualification was that they had clout, noble blood, or some unsavory combination of the two. Lest the army be massacred, those behind the scenes maneuvered to have "lieutenants" (deputies) appointed to assist the nominal commanders. These lieutenants, lieutenant colonels, and lieutenant generals did much of the actual decision making.

To help them with the scut work of war, the lieutenants turned to parties known as "sergeants major." You had a low-level sergeant major who kept the grunts in line, a regimental sergeant major who got the companies organized for battle, and a sergeant major general, who helped get the army in battle order. For simplicity, the regimental sergeant major eventually became a major and the sergeant major general became a major general. I'm oversimplifying to beat the band, you realize. But the point is, major-somethings (or something-majors) have always been outranked by lieutenant-whatevers.

I and a number of my friends were raised Jewish. In different Sunday and Hebrew schools, we all heard myths that Hitler was Jewish, and some said that his heritage, not the impending allied victory, caused him to commit suicide. One stubborn boy insists that Hitler's father was at least half Jewish and that young Adolf hated his father, causing him to translate his hatred into mass slaughter as an adult. Secular teachers, history books, and encyclopedias make no mention of Hitler having any Jewish blood. I hope you, Cecil the all-knowing, can set the record straight.—Anonymous, Dallas

Wish I could oblige, bubeleh. But while Hitler probably didn't have any Jewish blood, it can't be completely ruled out. Hitler's fa-

ther was illegitimate and to this day there is some question about who his grandfather was. Throughout his career he was dogged by rumors about his pedigree, some of them circulated by his fellow Nazis. In 1933 the London *Daily Mirror* published a picture of a gravestone in a Jewish cemetery in Bucharest inscribed with some Hebrew characters and the name Adolf Hitler. It's now known the Bucharest Hitler could not have been grandfather to our Adolf, but Hitler was sufficiently worried about the whole business that, according to the historian John Toland, he had the Nazi law defining Jewishness written to exclude Jesus Christ and himself.

Here's what we know: Hitler's paternal grandmother, Maria Schicklgruber, gave birth to Alois, Hitler's father, in 1837. She was forty-two and unmarried at the time and apparently never revealed the father's identity. Five years later she married Johann Georg Hiedler or Hitler (spelling was a bit casual in those days). But Alois kept the surname Schicklgruber until he was thirty-nine years old.

In 1876 a new baptismal certificate was issued declaring that Alois's stepfather, J. G. Hiedler, was in fact his real father. By this time both Maria and J.G. were dead. Why the name change so late in the day nobody really knows, but there is speculation that Alois did it so he could come into an inheritance. At any rate, few researchers today believe J.G. was really Alois's father.

Now for the weird stuff. After the war Hitler's former lawyer, Hans Frank, claimed that Adolf told him in 1930 that one of his relatives was trying to blackmail him by threatening to reveal his alleged Jewish ancestry. Hitler asked Frank to find out the facts. Frank says he determined that at the time Maria Schicklgruber gave birth to Alois, she was working as a household cook in the town of Graz. Her employers were a Jewish family named Frankenberger, who had a nineteen-year-old son. The son, according to Frank, was Alois's father and Hitler's grandfather—which would make the man who inspired the Holocaust one-quarter Jewish.

Frank's allegations have vexed historians ever since. The distinguished Hitler scholar Werner Maser was so irritated he claimed Frank made the whole thing up. Others think Frank was telling the truth but that the research he did for Hitler was faulty. It turns out that all Jews had been expelled from Graz in the fifteen century and were not allowed to return until the 1860s; what's more, so far as can be determined, Maria Schicklgruber never lived in Graz. Frank's source for the Frankenberger yarn was a distant relation of Hitler's, who supposedly had letters exchanged by the Frankenbergers and Maria Schicklgruber. (It's claimed they gave her child support.) But neither the relative nor the letters have ever surfaced, and chances are it's all a crock.

So who really was Hitler's grandfather? Werner Maser thinks it was the brother of his legal grandfather, one Johann Nepomuk Hiedler. But that's not all. J. Nepomuk was also the grandfather of Klara Poelzl, Hitler's mom. In other words, J.N. was both Adolf's paternal grandfather and his maternal great-grandfather. I'm not about to tell you any of this was the proximate cause of Hitler's persecution of the Jews, his suicide, or anything else. Still, if you believe Maser, not only was Hitler twisted, so was his family tree.

Why do they call it Latin America? It always sounded like Spanish to me.—Smartass, Miami

Well, you're one jump ahead of the late, great Dan Quayle, who, if memory serves, thought Latin Americans spoke Latin. Actually it's called Latin America because the countries of the New World from

Mexico on south speak languages descended from Latin—namely Spanish, Portuguese, and French.

Quayle: Not That Stupid

Okay, Quayle bashing is fun, even if a little dated. But I'm shocked that you of all people would perpetuate the myth of Quayle supposedly saying that Latin Americans spoke Latin. He never said it! It was a Jay Leno joke!—Paul Vander Woude, Chicago

Actually, according to Charles Halevi, who researched this for a Chicago journalists' newsletter, the joke was introduced to the nation by Representative Claudine Schneider (R., Rhode Island). I'm told she lifted it from the Hexagon Show, a political revue that raises money for Washington-area charities. (This from George D. Krumbhaar, who says he was both Claudine's chief of staff and in the show at the time.)

Many publications reported the joke as fact during late April and early May 1989, including *Newsweek*, which is where I saw it. Serves me right for believing what I read in the mainstream press.

Is it true that there has never been a war between two democracies, excluding civil wars? One part of my extended brain trust, a highly unreliable source, claims that this is a natural fact, Jack, and I have not yet thought of an instance in which one democracy declared war against another democracy. In a quandary, we resolved to consult the Dope, and now refer this question to your esteemed self. Prithee, O ocean of fathomless learning, we sincerely and earnestly entreat you to [additional fawning verbiage deleted].—J.S., Berkeley, California

Don't gush, lad, it doesn't leave room for the cartoon. Cecil does not dispute the general proposition that war between democracies is rare. Common sense suggests that embarking upon a military adventure is simpler for a king or dictator than it is for a head of government answerable to a parliament. But proponents of this idea argue that a war between democracies has *never* occurred. One arrives at this comforting conclusion chiefly by setting up the rules to exclude all the nonconforming cases.

The most egregious omission is civil wars, which account for a high percentage of the world's violent conflicts—159 of 575 wars between 1816 and 1980, by one count. The spectacle of the American Civil War, in which two popularly elected governments engaged in four years of brutal slaughter, refutes the naive notion that citizens will not vote for politicians who send them off to die. Clearly they will if they think the stakes are high enough.

Okay, you say, but at least democracies won't get into wars with one another for purposes of foreign aggrandizement. Here we get into the issue of what constitutes a democracy. The United States and Britain fought in the War of 1812; Britain at the time had a parliament and a prime minister. So did imperial Germany prior to World War I. Advocates of the peaceful-democracy school account for these cases by saying that neither Britain in 1812 nor Germany in 1914 were *liberal* democracies. The definition of liberal varies with the teller, but the simplest formulation, proposed by Dean Babst, who first advanced the peaceful-democracies idea in 1972, is that "If a hereditary ruler, such as a king, can choose the prime minister or president, then the country is not considered to have an elective government." This takes both Britain and Germany out of the picture for the period in question. That's fair enough in the case of Germany, where responsibility for the war can be laid pretty clearly at the feet of Kaiser Bill and the Junkers. But the War of 1812 was largely the work of the War Hawks in the democratically elected U.S. Congress.

The more basic objection to excluding all but liberal democracies is that throughout most of history the number of such democracies has been small. According to political scientist Michael Doyle, there were only thirteen liberal democracies prior to 1900, and just twenty-nine between 1900 and 1945—and many of those didn't last. Doyle counts forty-nine liberal democracies as of 1983; setting aside the confusing instance of Israel vs. Lebanon, none has fought another since 1945. But it may be argued that this merely reflected the postwar Pax Americana.

One would like to believe democracy = peace, of course, but if we look at the big picture we find little to persuade us that it is a sure thing. Nazi Germany was not a democracy after 1933, but the Nazis had dominated the democratically chosen Reichstag. The United States and France conducted wars of great savagery in Vietnam and Algeria. The United States helped topple the elected Allende regime in Chile, with murderous consequences for the Chilean people.

One can easily make the case that what prevents war between democracies is not their liberal scruples but their wealth, coupled with the recognition that war would mean economic ruin. If we look down the list of wars over the last fifty years we see that in almost all cases one or both of the belligerents was poor. We now have a proliferation of poor democracies in the wake of communism's collapse. Will they refrain from attacking one another, as their authoritarian or totalitarian predecessors did not? One considers India vs. Pakistan, Russia vs. Ukraine. Clearly the notion that democracies will not make war on one another now faces its great test.

While scanning the shortwave radio bands recently, I discovered a station broadcasting five-digit numbers in Spanish. Each number was repeated twice before a new one was broadcast. It was a little strange, but I figured I had stumbled onto the Cuban Lotto numbers station. Then last night I picked up a similar broadcast in English. It lasted about twenty-five minutes, then ended abruptly. A fellow shortwave enthusiast says these "numbers stations" are a big mystery and may somehow be tied into the CIA or drug smuggling! The FCC and CIA were no help, so I turn to you.—Michael P., Chicago

It's spies, likely. There are dozens of "numbers stations," some of which have been in business for decades, yet no government or private agency has ever acknowledged them. The stations broadcast in a variety of formats (three, four, and five digits, etc.) in languages ranging from English and Spanish to Czech, Korean, and Serbo-Croatian. The voice is often female and its unchanging inflection suggests that it may be machine-generated, like those wrong-number recordings used by the phone company.

At least some of the numbers stations are broadcasting coded messages. The messages have a definite beginning and end, start with an indication of how many number groups the message will contain, repeat each group carefully, and use standard-sized code groups (i.e., four or five digits), a universal feature of modern cryptography.

David Wise's book *The Spy Who Got Away* (1988), about a CIA defector, offers the following insight into how the codes (or at least some of them) work:

> A former CIA case officer with long experience in Moscow explained that . . . "a transmitter is set up in Germany or even at [CIA] headquarters in Langley [Virginia]. The agent knows that at certain times on certain nights you will transmit to him, normally in five digit code groups. He is given a [one-time pad, or OTP], of which only one other copy exists, which the sender has."
>
> The pages of a one-time pad consist of different, random five-digit groups of numbers that are used to encipher messages with the aid of a matrix, or number grid, that can be read much like the coordinates of a road map. Each page is destroyed after use. Since only one other copy of the pad exists, the code is unbreakable. The agent uses his copy of the one-time pad to decipher the message.
>
> The old Moscow hand explained what happens next. "The OTP is on edible paper. Once he deciphers the message, he tears the pages out, burns them, flushes them down the toilet, or eats them—however he's been instructed. You can use [this] voice link to confirm or change a meeting." He paused and smiled. "Sometimes we would broadcast code groups just to make the Soviets think we had a lot of assets even if we didn't."

Interestingly, the volume of coded message traffic doesn't seem to have dropped appreciably with the end of the cold war. I suppose that only makes sense: even if you were running fewer spies than you used to, you'd keep the code numbers booming out at the same rate so as not to clue the bad guys should you have the need to expand your agent roster in the future.

It's reasonable to assume other folks besides the CIA are broadcasting code groups, too. But nobody will say publicly (1) exactly who's doing it, (2) whether private parties are involved (some suspect drug traffickers because so many messages are in Spanish), (3) where the stations are located (because of atmospheric reflection, direction-finding is difficult), (4) how many of the messages are real and how many are dummies intended to lull eavesdroppers, (5) who the intended recipients are (they can't *all* be Cuban agents in the United States), and, of course (6) what the messages say.

Clearly the time has come for a courageous subset of the Teeming Millions to get jobs with the world's national security agencies, find out the whole story, and then betray their respective fatherlands by clueing us in on the secret(s). (I'd do it, but I'm tied up this week.) If they catch you, of course, you'll probably get the chair, but hey, you can't make an omelet without breaking some eggs. For more details on number stations, see *Big Secrets* by William Poundstone (1983).

Weird Science

*Can operatic sopranos really break glasses with their high notes?
What note does the trick? How come they don't break windows and
eyeglasses and whatnot at the same time? Can women do this better
than men? Can I learn how? Or have I been the victim of an elaborate hoax?—Vox Clamantis, Chicago*

I dunno—you ever buy whole-life insurance? Now *there* was a
hoax. Shattering glasses, on the other hand, is entirely legit. Italian

opera singers Enrico Caruso and Beniamino Gigli are said to have managed it, and I seem to remember Ella Fitzgerald doing it once in a Memorex commercial.

The technique is simple. First you find somebody with perfect pitch and leather lungs. Then get a crystal glass and tap it with a spoon to determine its natural frequency of vibration (this varies with the glass). Next have the singer let loose with precisely the same note. When he or she is dead-on pitchwise, the glass will commence to resonate, i.e., vibrate. Then turn up the V. Bingo, instant ground glass.

What we have here is a graphic demonstration of *forced oscillation resonance*. If something has a natural rate of vibration, pump in more energy of the same rate and with luck the thing will vibrate so bad it'll self-destruct. It's like giving somebody on a swing a good shove at the top of every arc—soon they'll reach escape velocity and soon after that they'll be picking vertebrae out of their sinuses.

Breaking glasses, however, is strictly light entertainment. For real forced oscillation action you want a suspension bridge. In 1831 troops crossing a suspension bridge near Manchester, England, supposedly marched in time to the bridge's sway. Boy, did they get a surprise. Ever since soldiers have been told to break step when crossing bridges. The same fate befell the Tacoma Narrows suspension bridge in Washington state on November 7, 1940, only it wasn't soldiers that caused it to collapse, it was the wind.

Back to the home front. Crystal is more vulnerable than ordinary glass because it has more internal structure, which allows waves to propagate. (Take my word for it.) But you can annihilate damn near anything given enough volume. One physicist, obviously one of your classic Roommates from Hell, claims he inadvertently shattered a glass lampshade while playing the clarinet.

Think of the possibilities. Most of us don't have the pipes to break glasses by sheer voice power, but we all have clarinets, don't we? Unfortunately, none of the standard physics cookbooks gives a detailed glass-bustin' recipe. Too bad. A fascinating classroom demonstration like this would surely convince many young people to give up MTV and devote their lives to science.

Shattering Myths

In the matter of glass-shattering vocalism, Cecil seems to have been led astray by Günter Grass's fictional tin drummer, Oskar. In fact, there is no authentic record of glass being broken by the unamplified human voice. Dorothy Caruso categorically denied rumors that her late husband had accomplished the feat; a fortiori it was beyond Gigli's comparatively feeble instrument. Practically speaking, there are reasons to believe the thing impossible, and without going into technical detail, the following are among them: (1) Glass is simply much too strong. Try shattering a wineglass in your (gloved) fingers. Not easy. Now imagine doing the same with the puny little bands of your vocal cords. (2) Coupling acoustic energy from larynx-to-air-to-glass is highly inefficient due to large impedance mismatches; by contrast, marching troops couple very efficiently to bridge platforms. (3) In glass-shattering attempts, resonance or no resonance, the glass structure finds other ways to dissipate energy short of fracturing. Remember the playground swing in which successive small but well-timed swings sent your sister sailing higher and higher? And the tales of going "over the top" when the process went critical? Alas! It never happened, because other dynamic processes supervened ("Gee, Mom, we were just playing") before the longed-for loop could occur.
—*Timon, Dallas*

A fortiori? Supervened? Boy, I see I wasn't the only one to get a Word-A-Day calendar for Christmas. As for glasses, let's clarify one thing: it is certainly possible to shatter glasses with the *amplified* human voice. The folks at the Memtek company in Fort Worth, Texas, which makes Memorex recording tape, do it all the time for sales demonstrations and whatnot. (You'll remember that Memorex used to run those TV commercials showing Ella Fitzgerald and others breaking glasses with their voices.)

What's more, they do it pretty much the way I described: they go out and get a drinking glass with high lead content, tunk it with a rubber mallet to make it ring, then read the frequency on an analyzer. Then they get a singer to sing the same note (typically F above middle C), amplify it to maybe ninety-two, ninety-four decibels, and with luck you get glass shrapnellini. Memorex technicians using a strobe have found that prior to the break the sound causes the rim of the glass to deflect as much as a quarter inch. (I get this from Rick Needham, engineering manager, lest you think I am making this up.)

Your beef is that I suggested this could be done with the *un*amplified human voice. I'll grant I haven't been able to turn up a documented instance of this, but it seems subsidiary to my main point, which is that you can shatter glasses with sound, and furthermore that the human voice, which can generate a relatively pure tone, is well suited to this purpose. Furthermore, none of the technical people I spoke to about this seemed to think doing it by voice alone was completely impossible. Admittedly, ninety-plus decibels is pretty damn loud, but one of the reasons that Memtek folks crank it up that much is that they're using an inexpensive ($7) glass rather than fine crystal, which is more fragile. So let's not be so negative, Timsy. It's the can-do attitude that has made this country great.

Bridge Crash News Flash!

In his recent treatise on whether singers can break glasses with their voices, Cecil mentioned "forced oscillation resonance," in which an external force amplifies the natural vibration of an object, sometimes with destructive results. As an example he cited the 1940 collapse of the Tacoma Narrows bridge. The usual explanation for this disaster is that the wind gusted (to be precise, "generated a train of vortices") in perfect synch with the bridge's natural rate of bounce, causing its demise.

Reader Wilbur Pan has alerted us to a recent report in *Science News* questioning this widely held view. Mathematicians Joseph McKenna and Alan Lazer doubt that a storm could produce the perfectly timed winds required. They're working on a "nonlinear" model of bridge behavior they hope will provide a better explanation. The main problem apparently is that when the roadway of a lightly constructed suspension bridge flexes, the cables supporting it go slack, introducing an element of unpredictability in which small causes (i.e., the wind) produce big results (i.e., a collapsing bridge). They hope to have the mathematical model describing this effect finished in five years—not the most aggressive schedule in the world, but apparently this is government work. You'll read about it here first.

Have you ever gotten your fingers stuck to a metal ice-cube tray in the freezer? They won't come loose until you run warm water over them. Similarly, I've heard you're in big trouble if you put your tongue on a cold flagpole in the winter. Yet you can eat a totally frozen Popsicle without injury. What makes human flesh stick to some frozen stuff and not others?—Mike Jones, Chicago

Applying your tongue to a flagpole is definitely asking for it, Michael, especially if the daddy flagpole finds out. The reason flesh sticks to metal is that the moisture on your skin freezes on contact, bonding it to the metal. Your tongue doesn't stick to a Popsicle (for long, anyway) because the Popsicle warms up too fast. Metal is an efficient conductor of heat and can easily disperse the warmth from your fingertips, but ice isn't and can't. The surface of the Popsicle melts almost instantly when you lick it, whereas you have to warm up half the ice-cube tray before the surface under your fingertips

Signorino

rises above freezing. That's one reason plastic trays have become such a popular substitute.

Why do stars twinkle?—Ben Schwalb, Laurel, Maryland

Ben, you amateur, stars don't "twinkle." They exhibit "stellar scintillation." The Pentagon isn't going to fund a damn twinkle study. Whatever you call it, it's caused by turbulence in the atmosphere, which in turn is caused by convection—clumps of warm air rising through colder stuff. Air will refract (bend) light a varying amount depending on its temperature.

You can see this in exaggerated form in the waves, or striae, that ripple above a radiator, a sunbaked highway, or some other heated surface. Because of the bending, sometimes you see more starlight, sometimes less—twinkling in action. The planets and the moon don't scintillate (as much, anyway) because their apparent size is so much larger that a little atmospheric refraction doesn't greatly alter the amount of light that reaches the eye.

What do the letters PA stand for? I know some, we'll say, amateur chemists who concoct all sorts of things and consistently have to check the PA to get it right. But none seems to know what PA stands for or why it's such an important factor. The makers of the "Strong Dope" have let me down, so I turn to you, the writer of the Straight Dope.—Duncan Staggs, San Antonio, Texas

P.S.: Could you mail me a reply? I'd send you a stamp, but I'm in jail awaiting transfer to the Texas Department of Corrections. If you can't, put it in the next book and I'll read it depending on which of us (the book or me) is out first.

Too bad about prison, Dunc, but I *told* you to get that census form in on time. I imagine what your friends are referring to is not PA but pH, a measure of the acidity or alkalinity of a solution. The pH scale ranges from 0 to 14, 0 being highly acidic, 14 highly alkaline, and 7 neutral. Maintaining a proper level of acidity is important in many chemical processes, and while my experience in home-brew drug manufacture is limited, I imagine it's important there, too.

The pH scale was invented in 1909 by one S. P. L. Sorenson and stands for the exponential *power* (originally German *Potenz*) of *h*ydrogen ion concentration. Hydrogen ions are the positively charged particles that make acids acidic. They like to mix it up with other molecules, so the more of them you have, the more potent the acid. For the record—I know this is going to sound like high school chemistry, but I feel obliged to be thorough—a pH of 1 means you've got 10^{-1} moles of hydrogen ions per liter, or one tenth of a mole; a pH of 14 means you've got 10^{-14} of a mole, or one hundred-trillionth. What's a mole, you inquire? Science talk for "monstrous gobs of," of course. Don't ask silly questions.

Now We Now Why They Call It The Texas Department of Corrections

In reference to the question you answered from Mr. Duncan Staggs concerning what PA means, you are wrong. Mr. Staggs most likely is asking about PA as it relates to the manufacture of methamphetamine. PA stands for lead acetate. Trust me, I know.—Speedy from Irving, Texas

Far be it from me to tell large gentlemen with prison records they're mistaken about their terminology, but Dunc said his buds "consistently have to check the PA to get it right," which sounds like the litmus-paper pH test. Also, the chemical notation for lead acetate is $Pb(C_2H_3O_2)_2 \cdot 3H_2O$, not PA.

Why don't magnets stick to aluminum?—Les, Los Angeles

It all has to do with electron shells. In a column of general circulation, however, it is always risky to jump straight into a discussion of electron shells. Better we should edge into this.

First some facts. Fact #1: magnets only stick to other magnets. Fact #2: big magnets are made up of jillions of tiny magnets. Fact #3: so are the metals the magnets stick to, notably iron, nickel, and cobalt, which are called ferromagnetic materials. The difference is that in the big magnets the tiny magnets are organized, i.e., they're all lined up with their north poles in one direction and their south poles in the opposite direction. In an ordinary ferromagnetic material, the tiny magnets are scattered every which way and their magnetic fields cancel each other out, so no magnetism overall.

But suppose we enterprisingly place a ferromagnetic material in a strong magnetic field. *Voilà*, the formerly scrambled atoms line up parallel with one another. The material as a whole becomes magnetized and sticks to the magnet. Aluminum doesn't contain tiny magnets, so there's nothing to get organized and nothing for the big magnet to stick to.

Certain restless intellects out there may now be wondering: what's with this tiny magnet crap, anyway? That's where the electron shells come in. As you may have guessed by now, the tiny magnets we're talking about are individual atoms. Some atoms, such as those in iron, have individual magnetic fields, while others, such as those in aluminum, do not. It all has to do with the electrons.

Electrons may be thought of as spinning, much as the earth does. They spin one way, they develop a magnetic field with north on top and south on the bottom; they spin the opposite way, they develop a magnetic field with north on the bottom and south on top. For convenience, we call the two directions of spin positive and negative.

Most atoms, such as those in aluminum, have half their electrons spinning in one direction and half in the opposite direction. That means the magnetic fields of the individual electrons cancel each other out. But in the ferromagnetic materials, things are different. Take a gander at the third subshell of the M shell of iron, for example. (A shell is an electron's orbit. Electrons are rigidly organized into layers of shells, with so many electrons per shell.) What a wacky sight! We find five electrons with a positive spin and one with a negative spin. This gives the iron atom a pronounced magnetic field. You get those iron atoms lined up, you've got yourself a magnet.

Then we get into a little matter requiring a discussion of quantum mechanics. (What's that, you're sorry you asked? Too late now.) Certain non-ferromagnetic materials, such as chromium and manganese, also have uneven numbers of positive- and negative-spinning electrons in their inner electron shells. Each atom of these substances is magnetic, but the substance as a whole is not. Why? Well, in chromium and manganese, each atom with "up" magnetism is paired with an atom of "down" magnetism, cancelling out the magnetism of the substance as a whole. In iron, however, all the atomic magnets point in the same direction, so it does (or can) have magnetism overall.

What keeps all the iron atoms pointed in the same direction? It's a quantum mechanical effect known as "exchange interaction." The details of this are still being debated, but one plausible interpretation goes like this: let's say the inner shell or "local" electrons of iron Atom A are spinning in such a way that they have "up" magnetism. The local electrons cause the nearby loose electrons floating around in the metal (the "conduction" electrons) to have opposite or "down" magnetism. The conduction electrons in turn cause the local electrons of neighboring iron Atom B to have "up" magnetism. Result: all the atomic magnets point up and the iron is potentially magnetic.

Why are chromium, manganese, et al. different? It turns out manganese and chromium atoms are so close together that the local electrons of Atom A force the local electrons of neighboring Atom B to orient themselves in the opposite direction, without any intervening conduction electrons entering into the picture. Thus each "up" atom is paired with a "down" atom, and the material has no magnetism overall.

That's all pretty clear, right? Well, maybe not. But it's about as clear as stuff like this ever gets.

In Science *magazine a while back an article about the latest attempts to calculate pi to the umpteen zillionth decimal place made a passing reference to a curious Oklahoma law. It said Oklahoma legislators had passed a law making pi equal to 3.0. I also remember Robert Heinlein in one of his novels mentioning that Tennessee had passed a similar law. Did either of these states ever pass such a law? Are they still on the books? What are the penalties if I proclaim that pi equals 3.14159 . . . ?—Wulf Losee, Andover, Connecticut*

Cecil had heard this story, too, only the state in question was Kansas, leading him to believe the whole thing was made up by big-city sharpies having a little fun at the expense of the rustics. However, with the help of Joseph Madachy, editor of the *Journal of Recreational Mathematics*, I've learned the story does have a germ of truth to it.

It happened in Indiana. Although the attempt to legislate pi was ultimately unsuccessful, it did come pretty close. In 1897 Representative T. I. Record of Posey County introduced House Bill #246 in the Indiana House of Representatives. The bill, based on the work of a physician and amateur mathematician named Edward J. Goodwin (Edwin in some accounts), suggests not one but three numbers for pi, among them 3.2, as we shall see. The punishment for unbelievers I have not been able to learn, but I place no credence in the rumor that you had to spend the rest of your natural life in Indiana.

Just as people today have a hard time accepting the idea that the speed of light is the speed limit of the universe, Goodwin and Record apparently couldn't handle the fact that pi was not a rational number. "Since the rule in present use [presumably pi equals 3.14159 . . .] fails to work . . . , it should be discarded as wholly wanting and misleading in the practical applications," the bill declared. Instead, mathematically inclined Hoosiers could take their pick among the following formulae:

1. The ratio of the diameter of a circle to its circumference is 5/4 to 4. In other words, pi equals 16/5 or 3.2.
2. The area of a circle equals the area of a square whose side is 1/4 the circumference of the circle. Working this out algebraically, we see that pi must be equal to 4.
3. The ratio of the length of a ninety-degree arc to the length of a segment connecting the arc's two end points is 8 to 7. This gives us pi equal to the square root of $2 \times 16/7$, or about 3.23.

There may have been other values for pi as well; the bill was so confusingly written that it's impossible to tell exactly what Goodwin was getting at. Mathematician David Singmaster says he found six different values in the bill, plus three more in Goodwin's other writings and comments, for a total of nine.

Lord knows how all this was supposedly to clarify pi or anything else, but as we shall see, they do things a little differently in Indiana. Bill #246 was initially sent to the Committee on Swamp Lands. The committee deliberated gravely on the question, decided it was not the appropriate body to consider such a measure, and turned it over to the Committee on Education. This committee gave the bill a "pass" recommendation and sent it on to the full House, which approved it unanimously, 67 to 0.

In the state Senate, the bill was referred to the Committee on Temperance. (One begins to suspect it was silly season in the Indiana legislature at the time.) It passed first reading, but that's as far as it got. According to *The Penguin Dictionary of Curious and Interesting Numbers*, the bill "was held up before a second reading due to the intervention of C. A. Waldo, a professor of mathematics [at Purdue] who happened to be passing through." Waldo, describing the experience later, wrote, "A member [of the legislature] then showed the writer [i.e., Waldo] a copy of the bill just passed and asked him if he would like an introduction to the learned doctor, its author. He declined the courtesy with thanks, remarking that he was acquainted with as many crazy people as he cared to know."

The bill was postponed indefinitely and died a quiet death. According to a local newspaper, however, "Although the bill was not acted on favorably no one who spoke against it intimated that there was anything wrong with the theories it advances. All of the Senators who spoke on the bill admitted that they were ignorant of the merits of the proposition. It was simply regarded as not being a subject for legislation." Whatever the motive, Indiana legislators saved themselves from being made any more of a laughingstock than they already were.

The Wisdom of Solomon: Not What It's Cracked Up to Be

Your response to the question about attempts to legislate pi suggests not only that your scholarship is weak but that you are a heathen. When King Solomon constructed the Temple of Jerusalem, the Second Book of Chronicles, chapter 4, verses 2 and 5, tells us:

"Then he made the Sea [a big tub] of cast bronze, ten cubits from one brim to the other; it was completely round. Its height was five cubits and a line of thirty cubits measured its circumference. It was a handbreadth thick; and its brim was shaped like the brim of a cup.... It contained three thousand baths."

The ratio of thirty cubits for the circumference to ten cubits for the diameter "from one brim to the other" of the "completely round" circle gives the value of pi as being exactly 3. Perhaps reliance on the Word of God motivated the Indiana legislators you trashed. You should have checked with the ultimate reference.—H.K.S., Springfield, Virginia

Some of the mail I get is unbelievable. As I attempted to point out, the Indiana legislature did not consider making pi equal to 3, but rather to 3.2, 4, or approximately 3.23, depending on which formula you used. Neither the text of the bill nor any of the commentaries regarding it refer to the Bible. Perhaps Kansas or one of the other states mentioned was the one that attempted to legislate a pi of biblical proportions.

Interesting you should bring this up, though. In 150 A.D. a Hebrew rabbi and scholar named Nehemiah attempted to explain away the anomaly in Chronicles by saying that the diameter of the tub was ten cubits from outer rim to outer rim, whereas the thirty-cubit circumference was measured around the *inner* rim. In other words, the difference between the biblical notion of pi and the actual value may be accounted for by the *width of the tub's walls*. A stretch, sure, but ingenious just the same. Next time I get into a mathematical jam (not that I ever have before, of course), I'm going to pray to the spirit of Nehemiah.

As kids we were taught in art class that the primary colors were red, blue, and yellow. By mixing these primary colors, we were told, we could come up with any color of the rainbow. Experiment seemed to bear this out.

Now that we are older and in the age of video, we have been told that color TV monitors use red, blue, and green as primary colors. The obvious questions are, How do you mix red, green, and blue to get yellow? And why can't I replicate the feat with my daughter's crayons?—Kevin May, Plano, Texas

When I was a little sprite this bugged me, too, so I asked Mr. Grayson the science teacher about it. His response was to bring in

a power drill with a red, green, and blue color wheel attached to the tip. When he pulled the trigger the colors on the spinning wheel merged into a sort of light gray. Nobody in class had the faintest idea what this was supposed to prove. However, it did have the effect of making Mr. Grayson, a bespectacled, slightly bucktoothed fellow, look like Flash Gordon on acid, so we considered it an afternoon well spent.

It was only later that the significance of the color wheel demonstration dawned on me. It turns out there are two ways of creating colors: the *additive* method and the *subtractive* method.

When using the additive method, the primary colors are red, blue, and green. The more additive primaries you add, the lighter the resultant color. Mix all three and you get white.

The subtractive primaries are red, blue, and yellow—to be exact, magenta, cyan (light blue), and yellow. These are the colors that, together with black, are used in color printing. The more subtractive primaries you mix, the darker the color. Mix all three and you get black (okay, brown, but with kindergarten paints you can't expect miracles). Color TVs make use of the additive principle, while the pigments in paints and crayons are subtractive.

Additive colors are easy to demonstrate on a color computer monitor equipped with a color-control program. How do we make yellow? By adding full-strength red and full-strength green. Adding two-thirds-strength blue gives us a lighter (not darker) yellow. Full-strength blue, red, and green produce bright white—a counterintuitive result, if you learned your color-mixing skills in kindergarten. But it only stands to reason that the more light you shed on something, the brighter (that is, closer to white) it gets.

Proceeding with our experiments we fill out the additive color-mixing chart as follows:

> Green + red = yellow
> Green + blue = cyan (light blue)
> Red + blue = magenta
> Red + blue + green = white

Next we turn to subtractive colors. As the name suggests, these work by subtracting certain colors from white light and reflecting the rest, like so:

Pigment	Absorbs	Reflects
Yellow	Blue	Red, green
Cyan	Red	Green, blue
Magenta	Green	Red, blue
Blue	Red, green	Blue
Red	Blue, green	Red
Green	Blue, red	Green

If white light strikes yellow paint, the paint absorbs blue and reflects red and green. Then the additive principle takes over—red and green combine to make yellow.

Now mix cyan and yellow paint. The cyan pigment absorbs red light; the yellow pigment absorbs blue light. What's left is green, the color you see.

How do you know whether it's additives or subtractives you're dealing with? 'Tain't easy. Spotlights, TV electron guns, and spinning color discs are additive; pigments, filters, and *stationary* color discs are subtractive. Confused? Who isn't these days? But perhaps at least you understand the apparent paradox of a TV making light colors from dark ones.

What is the opposite of absolute zero? I can accept the idea that there's a coldest possible temperature, but I like my limits in pairs. Is there a limit to how hot things can get? If so, what is it and why is it?—Mark Stewart, Chicago

There is a limit, sort of, but it's so inconceivably large that nobody but high-energy physicists talks about it (although as I think about it absolute zero doesn't exactly qualify as breakfast table conversation either). The highest possible temperature, called the Planck temperature, is equal to 10^{32} degrees Kelvin. For comparison, the center of the sun bubbles along at 15×10^6 degrees K (15 million degrees); silicon can be created by fusion at 10^9 degrees K (1 billion degrees). In short, the Planck temperature is very toasty indeed.

Absolute zero is easier to understand than the Planck temperature. What we perceive as heat is a function of motion. The colder something gets, the less internal motion or vibration its molecules exhibit. At absolute zero—that is, zero degrees Kelvin or –460 degrees Fahrenheit—molecular motion virtually stops. At that point whatever the molecules are a part of is as cold as it's going to get.

There's more latitude in the opposite direction. The faster molecules move, the hotter they get. At 10^{10} degrees K electrons approach the speed of light, but they also become more massive, so their temperature can continue to rise. At 10^{32} degrees K such staggering densities obtain that greater temperature would cause each particle of matter to become its own black hole and the usual understanding of space and time would collapse. Ergo, the Planck temperature is as hot as things can get. Or at least it's the highest temp conceivable in present theory. There's a chance when a quantum theory of gravity is worked out we may find even higher temperatures are possible. The prospect, I have to tell you, leaves me cold.

Visa cards are printed with little holographic doves as forgery protection, and I've seen similar holographic images printed on things no thicker than a piece of construction paper. Soon there will be chocolate bars with holographic decorations etched on the surface (this according to Scientific American*). How are these little holographic* *pictures made and how do they fool the eye into seeing depth where there really is none?—Susannah Faulhaber, Alameda, California*

As is often the case with technical subjects, Susannah, we are presented with an unfortunate choice: an explanation that is accurate but incomprehensible or comprehensible but wrong. Being a journalist and therefore shameless, we naturally opt for the latter. What follows is the Ollie North explanation of holography: it might get you past a congressional committee, but don't try it on your Ph.D. board.

A reflection hologram, the kind found on a credit card, is a high-tech version of those plastic novelty pictures we used to buy at the dimestore—the kind where the image changes when you tilt it. The hologram's surface is an emulsion that can be thought of as consisting of many tiny facets, each containing a fraction of a larger image. As you look at the hologram you see a set of facets that together constitutes one perspective of the holographed scene. As you tilt the hologram, a different set of facets comes into view showing the scene from a slightly different perspective. The changing perspective creates the illusion of three dimensions.

Simple, no? Okay, now for a Jack Anderson–like expose of the many lies and omissions in the preceding.

L&O #1. There aren't really any tiny facets. Actually what you've got is a set of quasihyperboloidal interference fringes. Interference fringes reflect a percentage of the light that strikes them. Amounts to the same thing as tiny facets, but they look a lot different, and, from the standpoint of conceptual grabbiness, they're strictly from hunger.

L&O #2. The change of perspective isn't the only thing that creates the 3-D effect. There's also parallax shift. Your eyes, being two inches apart, look at the scene from slightly different angles and thus see two different sets of "facets." Your brain combines the two images to create one scene with the illusion of depth, just as with a stereoscopic viewer.

L&O #3. I didn't tell you anything about lasers, wave fronts, or coherent light. Do I hear anybody complaining? I didn't think so. However, for those who absolutely must know, I should say that lasers are essential to creating holograms because they're the only known way to create the requisite interference fringes. Memorize the preceding sentence and mutter it under your breath next time your precocious eight-year-old starts to quiz you too closely on the subject. We may not explain everything in this column, but we give you enough to get by.

Why is it that when traveling in a car with the air conditioning on, with the vent blowing directly on you, the "breeze" goes off you for a few seconds when you turn the corner? Is air subject to inertia?
—T. Cichock, Arlington, Texas

Get hep, T.—of course it is. We can demonstrate this by means of the following experiment. Take a balloon filled with helium along next time you're out for a drive and put it on the passenger's side. Now SWERVE LEFT TO AVOID THAT OLD LADY, YOU ID-IOT! Sorry, just trying to make a point. Normally when you turn sharply left, everything in the car is thrown to the right. When we swerved left just now, however, the helium balloon was thrown to the left, the opposite of what you'd expect.

How can this be? Credit the inertia of the air. When you swerved left, the air, like everything else in the car, wanted to keep going straight, so it got crammed into the right (passenger) side. The heavy air forced the light helium balloon out of the way, and the only place for said balloon to go was left. Interesting, no? Well, maybe it's not up there with "Monday Night Football." But the kids will love it.

I was looking in the mirror the other day without wearing my glasses, which I occasionally use because I'm nearsighted. I noticed that things that were far away, even when reflected in the mirror, were blurry. When I put my glasses on and looked in the mirror again, everything was in focus. I found this strange. I thought every-thing should have been in focus without my glasses because the mir-ror was close to my eyes and so (I thought) were the reflections. I guess that's why people don't use mirrors for vision correction, huh?—Kirsten Munson, Santa Barbara, California

You got it, babe. The reflection is out of focus, even though you're close to the mirror, because you're *not looking at the mirror*. You're looking at the image *in* the mirror, a different matter entirely.

You can prove this by a simple experiment. Look at a mirror from a distance of six to twelve inches. With your glasses off, focus as best you can on some distant object reflected in the mirror—say, a bathroom towel on the wall behind you. No doubt the image of the towel is pretty fuzzy, and not just because you haven't cleaned the lint screen on the dryer. Now look at something on the *surface* of the mirror, such as a dust speck. You'll observe that (1) it requires a noticeable effort to adjust your eyes—in other words, you're refocusing—but that when all is said and done (2) the speck, unlike the towel, is in reasonably sharp focus. This clearly demonstrates (to me, anyway) that when you look at a reflection in the mirror, you're not looking at the mirror's surface.

So what are you looking at? For purposes of focusing, at the object itself (in this example, the towel). Without going into the technical details, the image of the towel in the mirror is out of focus for the same reason that the towel is out of focus when you look at it directly. In both cases the light travels more or less the same distance from the object to your eyes; the fact that in one instance it bounces off the mirror en route is irrelevant. Unless you want me to get out my giant model of the exposed human eye—and it *is* looking a little bloodshot—I say we leave it at that.

What is the effing difference between a constellation and a galaxy? My understanding of the cosmos is at stake.—G-Man, Montreal, Quebec

Get a grip, ace. A constellation is an *apparent* cluster of stars (that is, they look close together to us easily deceived sods on earth), while a galaxy is a *real* cluster of stars, i.e., a bunch of stars that actually are (in astronomical terms) close together. The stars in many constellations are actually quite distant from one another, but we don't realize it because when we look at the stars we can't perceive depth. Never caused us to think less of John Wayne, so why should we hold it against the Big Dipper? I'll tell you why: because the Big Dipper *isn't* a constellation. It's an *asterism*, which sounds like something you might want to dab with Preparation H but actually signifies a star cluster within a constellation, Ursa Major (the Great Bear) in the case of the Big Dipper. Ain't this column educational?

Where does the candle wax go?—Dave, Vanessa, Jill, Susannah, and everyone else we know

Where do you think it goes? It burns, just like the logs in a fireplace. You evidently have the idea that candle wax is only there to hold the wick upright. On the contrary, the wax is the fuel for the flame, the wick being merely the conduit, drawing melted wax up by capillary attraction. Rapid oxidation (burning, for you civilians) scrambles the constituent elements of the wax and they recombine to produce, among other things, carbon dioxide and water vapor, which drift off into the void.

Many people find the fact that burning produces water surprising. They shouldn't. The great British scientist Michael Faraday used to give an annual lecture on the "chemical history of a candle" in which he would hold a flask full of ice above a candle flame. After a short time the flask would be covered with droplets of water, most of it newly manufactured by the burning candle. They say Faraday used to pack the house for this demonstration. How fortunate to live in an age when you didn't have to compete with music videos.

How come archaeological ruins are always underground? Think about it. Why isn't everything right on the surface? Where does this dirt come from that keeps burying the past? Is the earth getting thicker and thicker, like the trunk of a tree? Doesn't make sense to me.—Nig Lipscomb, Chicago

Actually, Nig—and listen, you really should do something about that nickname—I like to think the earth is getting slightly *less* thick each year, owing to my selfless educational ministry. Physically, on the other hand, the earth *is* getting a bit thicker, since it picks up more than ten thousand tons of meteorite dust a year. But that's not why ruins are buried.

Archaeologists have to dig for lots of little reasons and one big reason. Sometimes the stuff they're looking for was buried to start with, as in the case of graves and rubbish pits. Sites that are abandoned for a long time become overgrown with vegetation that gradually decays and builds up a layer of topsoil. Places located in valleys may get covered by erosion from nearby hillsides. Occasionally a site gets buried because of some natural disaster, such as a flood or the eruption that buried Pompeii. The great Egyptian temple at Abu Simbel (the one with the giant seated figures carved into a cliff) was partly buried by drifting desert sand. The same thing happened to the Sphinx—for centuries all that was visible was the head. The Roman port of Ostia was also engulfed in sand, which accounts for the remarkable state of preservation in which modern excavators found it.

The major reason archaeologists have to dig, however, has to do with the peculiarities of human settlement. Towns don't get built just anywhere; they're usually located near water, transportation routes, fertile land, etc. A good location may be deserted once in a while due to war or disease, but generally it's soon reoccupied. In the ancient world many places were continuously inhabited for thousands of years, being finally abandoned only after some change in external circumstances—say, deteriorating farming conditions or one malaria outbreak too many.

Then we get to the matter of (ahem) shoddy home construction. You may think this problem only dates back to the invention of aluminum siding, but not so. In many parts of the world, Mesopotamia (modern Iraq) for one, the principal building materials were mud or mud brick, neither of which was very durable. When a mud house collapsed, as it inevitably did sooner or later, the owner went off to find more hospitable quarters and rain reduced what was left to a flat pile of mush. Eventually some mope scrounged up more mud and built a new house on top of the old one.

Meanwhile, trash and sewage were piling up in the streets. After a few centuries of this the prevailing grade rose to such an extent that the town wound up sitting on an artificial hill or mound. Wholesale destruction due to war or fire obviously accelerated things.

If and when the site was finally abandoned, natural forces gradually reduced it to an odd bump on the landscape. It might even be farmed, since it was basically just a big mud pile. Archaeologists have learned to look for these mounds (called *tells* in the Middle East), which have concealed what's left of places like Troy, Babylon, and the biblical city of Nineveh. They have to dig especially deep to find things like temples, because these generally were kept free of trash and in good repair, meaning that their grade did not rise with the surrounding city. Many temples, in fact, were semiburied even in ancient times.

Cities built of more durable materials like stone or fired brick are usually not completely buried. The monuments of Rome, for example, have always been visible, even though prior to the start of serious archaeological work some were half buried due to siltation, plant overgrowth, trash accumulation, and so on. The real problem was medieval and Renaissance contractors carting away parts of old buildings to use in putting up their own. (That's what happened to most of the Colosseum.)

In some cases, not just in Rome, buildings were completely razed and new structures built on the old foundations, providing yet another lode of artifacts for researchers to dig through—a fact that must give us pause, given the sorry state of many modern basements. God knows what future archaeologists are going to make of the 5 million old egg cartons my mother-in-law's got. Clean up that mess today, lest you make us look bad in the eyes of scientists yet unborn.

How come all the bad ozone that shows up during pollution alerts doesn't float up to replenish the good ozone that's disappearing from the ozone layer? Where does the bad ozone go? If we sawed off L.A. and floated it down to the Antarctic would we solve all our problems? Conversely, during the next ozone alert, could we break into a warehouse full of old chlorofluorocarbon-laden hair spray and clear the air?—Russ and Larry, Chicago

Further proof, boys, that the difference between a Nobel Prize winner and a lunatic is a fine line indeed. Your ideas as proposed are a bit over the edge, but something not too far removed from them has been seriously proposed. More on that later. First, however, let's get one thing straight: you can't literally use bad ozone to replenish the good ozone.

The problem with ozone is that it's unstable: it breaks down in a few minutes, long before it can float much of anywhere. Ozone is created and destroyed continuously as a result of the sun acting on oxygen in the presence of pollution (in the lower atmosphere) or on oxygen alone (in the upper atmosphere). Lower-atmosphere ozone, hereinafter called local ozone, decomposes once it gets beyond the cities that spawn it and never reaches the upper atmosphere.

But suppose it miraculously became possible to transport a couple cities' worth of ozone to the Antarctic, where there's a "hole" (actually a thin spot) in the ozone layer. Our troubles still wouldn't be over. The amount of ozone generated by urban pollution, while it seems like a lot to us, is trivial compared to the ozone hole, which extends over roughly all of Antarctica. Another problem is that vertical mixing between the troposphere (where we and our ozone-laden cities are) and the stratosphere (where the ozone layer is) is poor.

Still, it might not matter that local ozone never gets to the upper atmosphere. Some scientists think it might do us some good just hanging out near the ground. The importance of ozone is that it blocks ultraviolet radiation that causes skin cancer. It's more convenient if the ozone is in the upper atmosphere, but the process will still work if the ozone is near the ground. It's just that the stuff then also irritates your throat. In addition, local ozone is quite variable, so the UV protection it provides isn't as reliable as what you get from the upper-atmosphere variety. But hey, these days you take what you get.

Now for your last question. Could we get rid of excess local ozone by spraying the air with chlorofluorocarbons (CFCs), the leading cause of ozone depletion in the upper atmosphere? Nice try, but no. CFCs as such don't destroy ozone; the dirty work is done by chlorine, a CFC breakdown product. CFCs don't break down until they reach the stratosphere (unlike ozone, they're quite durable), where ultraviolet radiation causes them to release the fatal gas.

There's more to it than that, though. In most of the world free chlorine recombines quickly into relatively harmless compounds like hydrochloric acid and chlorine nitrate. The exception is the Antarctic. There the bitter cold (even colder than the Arctic) causes ice clouds to form in the stratosphere, something that rarely happens elsewhere around the globe. These clouds enable the free chlorine to survive long enough to attack the ozone, which is why the ozone hole is over the South Pole and not North America. What makes the problem so bad is that when chlorine destroys ozone, it's not itself destroyed—it remains free to kill again. A little chlorine can thus do major damage.

Still, your idea of spraying yet more stuff in the atmosphere to solve our pollution problems—what we might call the air freshener approach—may not be as nuts as it sounds. Ralph Cicerone, a professor of geosciences at the University of California at Irvine, has suggested spraying fifty thousand tons of propane or ethane over the South Pole early each winter. The resultant chemical reaction, he wrote in a 1991 article in *Science* magazine, would temporarily neutralize the ozone hole. It would also cost a zillion bucks. But if things keep up like they have, we may yet have to do it.

Is the earth getting heavier or lighter? After all, we've littered the cosmos with a lot of NASA stuff, which should shave off a few pounds, along with vapor escaping from the atmosphere. On the other hand, there's a lot more people and meteorites around than there was in 8011 B.C. What do you think?—Edward M. Smith, Jr., Los Angeles

Puny humanoid, you think the pitiful efforts of mankind have appreciably altered the mass of the earth, reliably estimated at 6 sextillion, 588 quintillion tons? (And man, if you don't think it wasn't a bitch getting that puppy on the scale. . . .) If so, shed your illusions. It's believed the earth gains anywhere from several dozen to several hundred tons *per day* due to meteorites and meteoritic dust—ten thousand to one hundred thousand tons a year. (Sorry, but estimates vary widely.) This far exceeds any losses. The weight of the *people*, on the other hand, has increased the mass of the earth by zero, for the obvious reason that we are but dust, and unto dust we shall return. To put it another way, human cells are merely rearrangements of the compounds previously found (i.e., before we ate them) in plant cells and animal cells. Net change pound-wise, nada.

This has bugged me all my life: why do wet things look darker than dry things?—Kathleen H., Brookline, Massachusetts

We'll take this in stages, Kathleen. Stop me when you can't take any more. (1) Talk-show-on-commercial-radio version: because when something is wet, light bounces around inside it more (as opposed to merely bouncing off the surface) before being reflected back to the eye. The more the light bounces, the more of it gets absorbed, the less reaches the eye and the darker the object appears.

This is fine for most purposes, but sometimes I have to escalate to (2) the talk-show-on-PBS version, which goes on to add that the reason the light bounces more is that the moisture increases the average scattering angle of the light particles. When the photons strike the surface of the wet material most of them bounce forward and hence deeper into the stuff rather than backward toward the eye.

At this point I'm sometimes tempted to launch into (3) the Ph.D.-thesis version, which comes complete with wavelengths, angstroms, and electron shells, but invariably the host's eyes start to glaze over and I find myself swiftly segueing into the latest on Rocky and Bullwinkle. Being the world's smartest human is all very well, but even I know when to quit.

Long ago I noticed that the bubbles in clear carbonated beverages seem to stream from fixed spots on the bottom and sides of the glass containing them. Boiling water seems to behave in a similar way.

What's so special about these spots?—David Peterson, Washington, D.C.

They've got a fancy name, for starters. As we discussed on pages 111–112, the places from which the bubbles stream are known as *nucleation sites*. They're microscopic defects or bits of crud on the glass. When water is changing phase (e.g., boiling, condensing, freezing), it needs a place where the vapor bubbles, droplets, crystals, or whatever can congregate until they're big enough to survive. That's what nucleation sites provide. Snowflakes and raindrops, for instance, typically form around dust motes. When water reaches the boiling point, the scratches in the container provide havens where microscopic bubbles can collect long enough to become big bubbles.

The carbon dioxide bubbles in beer and soft drinks work the same way. Before you uncap the bottle, the pressure inside keeps all the CO_2 in solution. After uncorking, the reduced pressure enables the gas to slowly boil away, which is where the nucleation sites come in handy. If you want to see some serious bubble action, try sprinkling salt in your beer. The salt provides numerous nucleation sites, producing not only a fascinating demonstration of physics, but pots of fun besides.

I read recently that two supercomputer manufacturers were in a contest to determine who could calculate pi to the most digits. My simple question, simple for you at least, is, What data do they input to begin these calculations? Every schoolchild knows that pi is the ratio of a circle's circumference to its diameter. Obviously mathematicians do not draw a circle and then measure out the circumference with increasingly tiny rulers. But what do they do instead?—Maxwell Stephens, Washington, D.C.

Dreaming up "algorithms" (techie talk for "methods") to compute pi has occupied the world's great minds for more than two millennia. Low creatures such as ourselves may think: jeez, somebody should buy these guys a book of crossword puzzles. But that's because we fail to appreciate the mathematical beauty of the thing. The ancient Greeks used a simple method: you draw polygons (e.g., hexagons) around a circle with a diameter of one—one hexagon inside the circle, one out. Calculate the perimeter of the polygons (which is pretty straightforward), take an average, and you get a rough idea of pi. Use polygons with more sides and your approximation of pi gets closer and closer. The mathematician Archimedes got as far as ninety-six sides, calculating that pi was between 3.1408 and 3.1428.

Today mathematicians use far more sophisticated algorithms involving converging infinite series. A converging infinite series is a mathematical sequence that approaches (but never actually reaches) a target number called a *limit*. For example, the limit of the series $1 + \frac{1}{2} + \frac{1}{4} + \frac{1}{8} + \ldots$ is 2.

Long ago it was realized that certain infinite series converge on fractions or reciprocals of pi. For example, in 1671 mathematician Gottfried Leibniz discovered that the series $1 - \frac{1}{3} + \frac{1}{5} - \frac{1}{7} + \ldots$ converges on pi/4. This may seem strange—I mean, what do fractions have to do with the circumference of a circle?—but take my word for it, it happens.

The discovery of ever more "efficient" infinite series—that is, that converge on pi faster for each term you add—coupled with the development of bigger and better computers has made it possible to calculate pi to thousands, millions, and now billions of decimal places. Cecil, knowing his readers' love of higher mathematics, would be pleased to reprint one of these magic pi recipes in full, but there isn't room, and besides, I gave up Greek subscripts for Lent.

Why compute one billion digits? God knows. As one learned treatise notes, "Thirty-nine places of pi suffice for computing the circumference of a circle girdling the known universe with an error no greater than the radius of a hydrogen atom." One pi-wars participant rationalizes by saying once you get beyond a billion digits subtle patterns may begin to emerge in the numbers, but give me a break. The real reason, many feel, is "because it's there." So childish. Thank God the rest of us have put such foolishness behind us.

Show Some Respect

Most of Cecil Adams's comments on the pi calculation were reasonable, but the last few sentences were not. Gregory Chudnovsky is one of the people doing these calculations, and he is the wisest man I know. Adversity can lead to deep growth. He got myasthenia gravis when he was ten or twelve and has spent the last twenty-five years in bed or a wheelchair. The KGB worked the family over in their usual way before they were allowed to leave Kiev about twelve years ago. He was the one mathematician in the first group of MacArthur fellows and the best of all the mathematics appointments. As Herbert Robbins once said, Gregory seems to have come directly from a Dostoievski novel.

There are serious questions about what "random" is, and David and Gregory Chudnovsky care about it. Their pi calculations are concerned with this, and with certain deep problems in transcendental number theory. The right way for Cecil to have answered the letter would have been to say the people who do these calculations know why they're doing it but Cecil doesn't. Even the Straight Dope doesn't have all the answers.—Richard Askey, Department of Mathematics, University of Wisconsin at Madison

Well, excuse *me*. However, see below.

Thanks to Cecil Adams for the beaut on calculating pi to umpteen decimal places. Absurd though it is, I can think of one good reason why some computer guys may do it: they may need some standard, endless task with which to calibrate their computer's speed.

It's even more absurd that the "learned treatise" Cecil quoted said, "Thirty-nine places of pi suffice for computing the circumference of a circle girdling the known universe with an error no greater than the radius of a hydrogen atom." Actually, only thirty-five places are required. Here's why: a reasonable value for the radius of the universe is 2×10^{34} angstroms. That's just 20 billion years (the time since the Big Bang) times the speed of light (the upper limit on the rate of expansion). Since pi equals the circumference divided by twice the radius, the uncertainty in pi equals the uncertainty in the circumference (one half angstrom, the radius of a hydrogen atom) divided by twice the radius. That's $\frac{1}{2}/(2[2 \times 10^{34}])$ or $1/(8 \times 10^{34})$ or about 10^{-35}. Knowing pi to thirty-nine decimal places would nearly suffice for computing the circumference of a circle enclosing the known universe with *an error no greater than the nucleus of a hydrogen atom, and that's a whole lot smaller than the entire atom. I'm sure you'd want to get a thing like that straight.—Dr. Neil Basescu, Madison*

I knew that, of course. But I always like it better when you guys figure things out for yourselves.

If a match is lit in an atmosphere like earth's but outside of gravity's pull, will it suffocate? Will it snuff out from its own gases faster than if it had a steady earthbound updraft to refresh it with more oxygen? I heard the space-shuttle astronauts were doing tests with fire in microgravity. I missed reading any results so all I can do is guess: it snuffs. My earthist rivals insist fire will burn in zero Gs; some say heat rising will start a draft which in turn ventilates the reaction. I immediately ask: which way is up? Duh!—John Inkman, Hodgkins, Illinois

It is just this kind of restless curiosity, John, that is at the heart of all great science. They've been doing a lot of fire experiments on the space shuttle lately, and while the official line is that they're trying to advance the frontiers of knowledge, etc., one suspects the scientists just want to know, among other things, whether a flame would smother in its own smoke.

As it turns out, a match is not the ideal experimental medium for this purpose. The head may contain oxidizers and whatnot that would queer the results. What you really want is a candle. The space-shuttle astronauts brought a couple along on a mission in 1992 and lit them inside a sealed chamber having an earth-type atmosphere. (This is not something you would want to do in the open space-shuttle cabin, where for obvious reasons an exposed flame is on a par with leaving the front door ajar.) One candle burned for about two minutes, the other for twenty seconds. Then—here's the vindication you've been waiting for—they snuffed. The flames were weak, spherical, and pure blue.

As you realized and your earthist friends obviously didn't, in a zero-gravity environment you don't have convection. Convection is the familiar process whereby heated air over a candle flame rises, carrying smoke and waste gases with it. Cool, oxygen-rich air rushes in to replace the departing warm air and in the process keeps the flame going. Convection works in normal gravity because warm air is less dense and thus lighter than cool air and so rises above it. But in a weightless environment the exhaust gases basically hang around the candle flame until all the oxygen in the immediate vicinity is exhausted, at which point the flame goes out.

So there's your basic answer. Now for the hedging. It turns out that with a little tweaking you can get stuff to burn in zero Gs just fine. If there's the slightest breeze, as opposed to dead still air, enough oxygen gets through to sustain combustion. Pump in 35 to 50 percent oxygen instead of the earth-normal 21 percent and you'll get a self-sustaining flame even in still air. Adjust the air flow just so and you can get some weak flames to burn longer in zero Gs than they would on earth, where too-hearty convection currents can cause a flame to blow itself out. Dunno that it's worth spending $6 jillion a year on the space program to find this all out, but it's nice to have the definitive word.

Chapter **13**

Grab Bag

Did Neil Armstrong muff his historic line or didn't he? When I along with half a billion others witnessed the first human step on the moon on July 20, 1969, I swear I heard Armstrong say, "That's one small step for man, one giant leap for mankind." What he meant to say, of course, was "one small step for a man." In leaving out the "a," he destroyed the sense of the statement and in essence said, "One small step for humans, one giant leap for humans."

Okay, so we all make mistakes. Every encyclopedia I've consulted, however, corrects the error. In recent years I've even heard recordings of his famous line—purportedly from the original tape—that also include the "a," making sense of the statement. Did NASA or someone else doctor up the tape to save Armstrong's (and the U.S.'s) face in the eyes of posterity? Or am I going loony?—James Hulin, Madison

Can the lame puns, James, the honor of the nation is at stake. Fortunately, the latest in miracle technology has been brought to bear on the question. But let's take it from the top.

Most earwitnesses to the event, including newspaper reporters, thought Armstrong said, "one small step for man." At least that's the way the *New York Times*, the *Washington Post*, and the *Los Angeles Times* (among others) reported it. Armstrong, however, has always maintained that he said "*a* man," and most encyclopedias have played along. But the skeptics have been, well, skeptical. Come on, would you admit it if you'd traveled a quarter million miles only to blow *your* big line?

Enter Al Reinert, the mad Texan. Al spent years prowling through NASA's vaults digging up forgotten lunar film footage to make what is said to be the muthah space movie of all time, *For All Mankind*, now in limited release. (Check it out next time it comes through— the visuals are said to be unbelievable.) After finding the original quarter-inch audiotape used to record Armstrong's words in a Fort Worth warehouse, Al and friends used a digital synthesizer to clean up the radio static so they could use it on the sound track. (Perhaps the cleaned-up version is what you heard.) This makes it perfectly clear that what Neil said was . . .

Well, to tell you the truth, we still don't know what he said. According to Reinert, "Cleaning it up does not truly answer the question. He did not clearly say 'a man.' But there's definitely a beat there. It's open to interpretation—maybe he was in the middle of a step when he said it. . . . I'm prepared to give him the benefit of the doubt." Armstrong, for his part, is willing to concede he may have mumbled.

My feeling is, Why persecute the guy? As reporters were once urged to do with the tortured syntax of the late Chicago Mayor Richard J. Daley: don't write what he said, write what he meant. "A man" it is.

Is there such a thing as "cow tipping"? I have two friends, both sons of farmers. One says it can be done and is great sport. The other says no way. Do cows sleep standing up? Can they be tipped? I suppose this will take some late-night research.—Robert Schreur, Baltimore

Don't look at me, pal. Fortunately for the cause of science, not all researchers are handicapped by an instinct for survival. It appears there really is a rural pastime called cow tipping, which is favored by likkered-up country kiddies with nothing better to do on a Saturday night. (One presumes the sheep were busy.) The cow is easy prey for pranksters since it's one of a number of critters (the horse is another) that sleeps standing up with its knees locked.

I recently discussed the fine points of cow tipping with a reformed ex-tipper named Robin, who had done it (once) as a student. Robin attended Albion College in Michigan, a school so snooty it's said the students read *The Preppie Handbook* without realizing it was satirical. Despite their pretensions, however, Albionians were mad for cow tipping.

The usual modus operandi, or at least the approach followed by Robin and company, was to get tanked at some frat party and then drive out with a half dozen of your most brainless friends to some nearby farmer's field. While Robin and the others watched from a safe distance, the two most daring lunatics took off their shoes, climbed over the fence, snuck up on a dozing cow, pushed, and then ran like hell.

Watching a cow tip over apparently is the sort of Zen experience that only those with higher consciousness or a couple six-packs can properly appreciate. Remember that film snippet from the TV show "Laugh-In" where the guy riding the tiny tricycle suddenly falls over? Same idea. Once down, the cow woke up, got pissed, scrambled up, and rousted out the rest of the herd, resulting in pandemonium. Sounds like a hoot.

Farmers aren't crazy about cow tipping because the cow might get hurt. There's also a chance one of the idiot students might get killed, so at least there's one bright spot. Happily for the cows, tipping is the sort of thing even the most desperate only feel compelled to do once, and most people never feel compelled to do at all. Obviously the dairy industry's public education program ("Please, No Tipping") has finally paid off.

A Contrary View: Cows Are Lousy Tippers

Regarding cow tipping, your friend Robin tells lies. If a sleeping cow could be tipped over by some tanked-up frat rat, she could be tipped over by the wind. Mother Nature is not so easily outsmarted. Cows weigh from less than a thousand pounds to around two thousand pounds, and they have a low center of gravity. Tipping a cow would be like toppling a low-built piece of concrete statuary. It would not be a tip-and-run situation; it would be a challenge, and old Bossy is not going to just stand there and cooperate. Methinks Robin made

up the whole story so you wouldn't know he and his fellow frat rats really were looking for the sheep.—*Marty Murphy, Chicago*

You have been misinformed about the fabled practice of cow tipping. I spent a year working on a dairy farm where I participated in countless 3:30 A.M. milkings and observed over three hundred sleeping cows a day. Cows sleep lying down, not standing up.—Mitchell Bellman, Montreal, Quebec

Despite popular belief, horses do not go into a deep sleep standing up like cows. Horses go into something of a catnap in which they lock their knees, bow their heads, and leave their eyes open. In order to really sleep, they must do so lying down. For this reason and the fact that they have exceptional hearing, it is almost impossible to sneak up on a horse. It is also dangerous because some will turn and kick before they run. So please tell your readers not to try "horse tipping."— Terese Hernandez, Chicago

When you're out on the front lines of science like myself, you learn to expect days like this. On the one hand, we have various profound theoretical and philosophical reasons why cow tipping is impossible; on the other, somebody who claims to have seen it done.

I checked back with Robin (who is female, incidentally). She sticks with her story. To review: one night after a boozy party at Albion College in Michigan in either the fall of 1980 or the spring of 1981, Robin drove with a carload of other kids out to a field where a bunch of sleeping cows were standing. Whilst she and the others watched from behind a fence (guesstimated distance: the width of a football field), two freshman boys crept up on a likely cow and gave it a shove, as a consequence whereof the cow tipped over. Kind of limited entertainment value, but I guess at Albion it's either that or watch the milk curdle.

Notwithstanding the foregoing, knowledgeable people I checked with (a couple farmers, an animal science expert) claim cow tipping can't happen. Apart from their sheer size (1,200 pounds is typical), cows do not fall into a deep sleep while standing the way horses do (more on this below); rather, they simply doze while chewing their cud. They are easily startled, making it difficult to sneak up on them.

Robin believes the two freshman boys were reasonably stealthy in sneaking up on the cow in question, which may not have been full-grown. She admits that given the darkness and the distance, it's conceivable there was some furtive funny business—tripping the cow with a rope or some such thing. But she can recall no definite evidence that this occurred and has no doubt that the cow did fall over.

Robin has forgotten who her fellow tippers were, making her story impossible to corroborate, but she gives every sign of sincerity. Either she hallucinated the whole thing or cow tipping is possible under some conditions. I invite further reports from, you should pardon the expression, the field.

Given the inconclusive state of the cow-tipping debate, I am pleased to make the following definite statement regarding Ms. Hernandez's claim about horses' sleeping habits: it's R-O-N-G *wrong*. Horses routinely fall into deep sleep while standing up—which is not to say they can't be startled awake. Some can go for many days without lying down, though most recline for at least a short time each day. One researcher (Winchester, 1943) has claimed that horses use less energy while standing than lying down—for one thing, it's easier to breathe. Sounds good to me, brother. Next case.

"Star Trek" episodes often refer to the "star date." What exactly is a "star date"? How does it equate to our calendar? Or is it merely sitcom disinformation?—Evan Williams, Austin, Texas

Details are for guys who get paid by the hour, sport. Star dates were among hundreds of unexplained terms thrown into "Star Trek" by scriptwriters whose main objectives were plausibility, a space-poetical ring, and getting done by deadline.

The dates in the original show (1966–69) were of the form 0000.0 and were assigned pretty much at random, the producers merely keeping a list to avoid duplication. The numbers meant nothing at first, but eventually it was agreed the units were roughly equivalent to earth days and the decimals were tenths thereof.

In "Star Trek: The Next Generation" things are more systematic. One production staffer is "keeper of the star dates" and parcels them out to the episode writers to avoid mix-ups. The numbers are of the form 40000.0, sometimes with two decimal places. The initial 4 was assigned arbitrarily, the second digit refers to the season, and the remaining three usually progress from low to high as the season progresses. But everybody is still pretty vague on what the numbers mean in the context of the show.

Not that star dates don't have a rationale. Something of the sort would certainly be required on an actual starship. We know from the theory of relativity that time is local, not universal. When a starship approaches the speed of light, time aboard it slows down from the perspective of us here on earth but continues to hum along at the usual rate for the passengers. Trying to use earth time aboard the *Enterprise* would require abruptly speeding up the calendar every time Kirk had Scotty pour on the ions. Better to use "ship time," that is, time as measured on the ship's own clocks. Ship date 1000.5 would mean noon (.5) on day 1000, presumably the thousandth day since the launching of the ship. "Ship date" doesn't sound as snappy as "star date," which falsely suggests there is some universal "star time" (although see below), but I suppose we can allow for a little dramatic license.

Trouble is, star dates don't follow this logical scheme. During the original series star dates ranged from 1312.4 to 5943.7—a span of 4,600 days, or about twelve and a half years. We know from the opening voice-over that the *Enterprise* was on a five-year mission.

This means either that (1) Kirk and friends were running up some serious overtime, (2) there's more to star dates than meets the eye, or (3) nobody in the show gave the matter a moment's thought.

The real answer is obvious, but Bjo Trimble's *Star Trek Concordance* (1976), written with some input from producer Gene Roddenberry, gamely attempts to account for things by saying star dates are "a function not only of time but of a ship's position in the galaxy and its velocity." How mere mortals could cope with a time-keeping system of such breathtaking complexity is not explained.

Another problem is that several episodes in the original series took place only a star date or two apart, even though they seemingly cram in a lot more than twenty-four hours' worth of action. For example, "What Little Girls Are Made Of" begins on 2712.4, "Miri" on 2713.5, and "Dagger of the Mind" on 2715.1. The *Concordance* ventures the explanation that "warp drive distorts time." This suggests two things: first, star time is universal and not local (in fact, the current assumption is that star dates are not peculiar to a given ship but are standard throughout the Federation), and second, inertial (e.g., earth) time would pass more slowly than ship time, the opposite of what Einstein told us actually occurs. Bjo cheerfully concedes this is a little feeble but says it was the best they could do to make the "theory" fit the numbers in the show. I say they should have admitted Kirk was sniffing dilithium crystals while making entries in the log.

One flub left Bjo no choice. The episode "Spock's Brain" starts on 5431.4, but in midshow the date is inexplicably given as 4351.5. "The horror of having Spock's brain stolen does strange things to his friends' minds," she notes dryly. "Among other mistakes, the wrong star date is entered in the log."

Does every fur coat you see represent an animal who lived or died miserably? It's hard to believe they trap coyotes or foxes, for example, and then leave them to die slowly and painfully. I've heard that farm-bred animals such as minks are kept in tiny cages until they are killed for their coats. Is this true?—Lauren Giles, Chicago

I've spent the last week trying to nail down the facts on this, without spectacular success. Not having the time to make personal in-

spections, I am forced to rely on word from the fur industry on the one hand and the animal-rights crowd on the other, each of which regards the other as a bunch of lying scum. But it seems safe to draw the following conclusions.

The broad answers to your questions are that (1) yes, at least some of the animals die slowly and painfully, although how many, how slowly, and how painfully is a matter of debate, and (2) yes, farm-bred minks are kept in small if not tiny cages until killed for their coats.

Are they miserable? Some sure are. The folks at Friends of Animals, an antifur group, sent Cecil a video of life on a fur farm. There are some horrifying scenes. Animals, some of them with large open sores, pace neurotically in cages. A pup hobbles around with what appears to be a broken leg bone protruding through the flesh. The bodies of several mink are scattered in the dirt; narrator Sally Struthers informs us in a quivering voice that they died of heat stroke.

Fur-industry spokespeople say fur farms aren't like that and that farm operators have an economic incentive to keep their animals healthy. No doubt there is some truth in this. But fur farming is geared to mass production, and it's hard to believe operators are going to lavish a lot of time on the occasional injured or distressed animal. Not that that's the heart of the argument for animal-rights advocates. They say the fact that humans exploit animals at all is the real crime. We'll get back to this in a moment.

Trapping, for those troubled by the thought of animals cooped up in cages all their lives, has the advantage that the critters roam free until caught. But the end isn't pretty—a blow or a bullet to the head, suffocation, etc. Snares (nooses, basically) can cause strangulation or amputation of a limb; even the trappers' association frowns on them. Then there's the famous (or infamous) leghold trap, which according to the trappers simply immobilizes animals until they can be found and dispatched, typically within twenty-four hours. Antifur activists say baloney, leghold traps seriously injure animals, who may suffer for days until the trapper makes his rounds. Another common type of trap is the conibear, which kills the animal by crushing its skull—instantly in theory, but Cecil is willing to believe there's a considerable gap between theory and practice. Whatever really happens out there, we're not talking about taking old Bowser to the vet to be put to sleep. It may or may not be fast, but it's definitely violent.

Then again, they didn't put out silken cushions before offing the cow (steer, whatever) that went into that hamburger you just ate, either. If you wear leather shoes, partake of miracle drugs that involved animal research, or even use no-pest strips, you may be sure that animals were killed, sometimes painfully, in your behalf. Hard-core animals-rights activists denounce this; the fur folks, and for that matter medical researchers and some conservationists, say get a life—nature is cruel; our first responsibility is to our own kind, our second to preserve species, not individuals. Cecil, like any good liberal, opposes the gratuitous destruction of life. But as concerns the exploitation of animals by humans in principle, he is of the view that the means must be considered in light of the ends and, equally important, the alternatives. In the case of furs worn by the wealthy, the ends are frivolous. I don't try to squish turtles when driving the back roads, either. But I do wear leather shoes, and plan to.

The enclosed ad describes something called The Strecker Memo-
randum, *a video that purports to show that AIDS is a man-made disease. This sounds like the usual AIDS-conspiracy mumbo jumbo, but
it's so well documented it's made me wonder. Can you get to the bottom of it?*—Edna Welthorpe

Cecil is reluctant to spend too much time on this, because it
seems so obviously nuts, but I've gotten a few letters about it and
hey, we live to serve. There are two main alternative AIDS theories,
as we might call them: the Strecker AIDS theory and the Duesberg
risk-group theory. The Strecker theory, which is the wilder of the
two, is the work of Robert Strecker, an L.A. gastroenterologist. He
claims that "AIDS was a disease that was requested, manufactured,
and deployed and does exactly what it was intended to do," i.e., it's
a weapon of germ warfare.

Strecker says scientists cooked up AIDS around 1972 from something called "bovine visna virus." He guesses that smallpox vaccine
made from the lesions of BVV-infected cattle was injected into humans in Africa, where it transmuted into AIDS. One item of evidence in support of Strecker's theory is a quote from the July 1,
1969 *Congressional Record* in which a physician mentions a
government-sponsored research project that would create a "syn-
thetic biological agent . . . for which no natural immunity would have
been acquired."

Strecker's work has been expanded on by others. Among the
claims (I rely here mainly on a 1990 story in *Essence*): (1) AIDS was
invented by the CIA or (2) the Russians. (3) It was manufactured at
the U.S. Army biological research center in Fort Detrick, Maryland.
(4) It has something to do with Agent Orange. (5) It was intended to
wipe out black people; gays were a pilot test. Crack cocaine also was
invented to kill blacks.

Mainstream AIDS scientists say Strecker's a kook. From a micro-
biological standpoint, AIDS bears little resemblance to bovine visna
virus; it bears a lot of resemblance to simian immunodeficiency virus
(SIV), from which AIDS is widely thought to have naturally evolved.
There may have been some proto-AIDS cases substantially predating
1972. And frankly, inventing a fatal disease that singles out minori-

ties, gays, and drug abusers would require the CIA/Russians/U.S. Army to be a lot smarter a lot earlier in the day than there is any evidence of them ever being.

The Duesberg risk-group theory, which we may as well cover while we're on the subject, isn't quite as bizarre. Peter Duesberg, a respected (until now) virologist at UCal–Berkeley, says human immunodeficiency virus (HIV) doesn't cause AIDS, as is otherwise almost universally believed. Instead, AIDS is caused by a general weakening of the immune system due to drug abuse, disease, parasites, malnutrition (in Africa), etc. Evidence: U.S. AIDS patients don't get the same opportunistic diseases that African AIDS patients do; predictions of a sharp upswing in heterosexual U.S. AIDS cases have not come true; the HIV virus isn't especially virulent and is suppressed by the immune system, etc.

Duesberg's ideas, like Strecker's, are dismissed by mainstream AIDS researchers. They sensibly argue that people without HIV don't get AIDS (although a couple apparent exceptions have turned up), while most of those with HIV do get it. Also, drug abuse, parasites, malnutrition, and so on have been around for a long time, but nobody came down with AIDS until HIV showed up.

Still, Duesberg isn't a paranoid conspiracy theorist like most of those in the Strecker crowd. A few scientists think he may be on to something; more than a hundred have joined the Group for the Scientific Reappraisal of the HIV/AIDS Hypothesis. There have been efforts to portray the guy as a latter-day Galileo, scorned but maybe right. Cecil, Lord knows, isn't about to dismiss a fellow contrarian out of hand. But I wouldn't bet the mortgage money on him either.

I can't understand why this wouldn't be a cure for someone infected with HIV, the AIDS virus: put them in one of those plastic bubbles like they use for people with genetic immunological deficiencies. No germs, no opportunistic infections, no AIDS, right?—Bob Kernell

If only it were that simple. There are a couple problems with your idea: first, AIDS is quite capable of killing you all by itself, without any help from opportunistic infections. It can directly infect the brain and the gut, producing such syndromes as HIV encephalopathy, also known as AIDS dementia (symptoms: loss of memory, alertness, balance, and vision; weakness), and HIV wasting syndrome, where you simply waste away. (Opportunistic infections may also contribute to this.)

The other problem is that AIDS makes you vulnerable to germs that are already in your body. For example, there's toxoplasmosis, which people sometimes get when they eat undercooked meat or come in contact with cat feces. In normal adults toxo produces mild symptoms (swollen lymph nodes, fatigue). But it remains in the brain and muscles, and if you subsequently get AIDS it can lead to encephalitis and eventually abscesses in the brain, causing headaches, seizures, and convulsions.

Then there's cytomegalovirus. Kids and mothers of small children often get it, since it's passed in the urine. In normal adults it produces monolike symptoms (fever, sore throat). But it, too, remains in the body and in an AIDS patient can infect the retina, causing blindness.

I could go on, but it's too depressing. If you get HIV, doctors will try to determine what infections you already have and do what they can to prevent you from getting anything else. (If you don't already have toxo they'll tell you not to change any cat litter boxes, for example.) But this merely prolongs the inevitable. So far as is now known, AIDS will kill everyone who contracts it.

Please provide some honest, realistic odds on a 100 percent heterosexual male contracting AIDS from a female by engaging in "traditional" (i.e., nonanal) intercourse—and I'm talking one-in-??? numbers. I am led to believe that a very low percentage of U.S. AIDS patients are women, and most of those are prostitutes or intravenous drug users. Assuming one exercises reasonable discretion in one's choice of partners, the risk of infection has got to be slim. But I'm so confused by the subject I trust no one but you.— Paranoid, Dallas

You want numbers, numbers it is. According to a report by researchers Norman Hearst and Stephen Hulley in the *Journal of the American Medical Association*, the odds of a heterosexual becoming infected with AIDS after one episode of penile-vaginal intercourse with someone in a non-high-risk group without a condom are one in 5 million. With a condom it's even safer—one in 50 million. Just to put this in perspective, the chances of someone in your family getting injured next year in a bubble bath are 1 in 1.3 million (source: *The Odds on Virtually Everything*, 1980). You're in much greater danger of being struck by lightning (1 in 600,000), having your house bombed (1 in 290,000), or being murdered (1 in 11,000).

The numbers get a lot worse if you engage in "high-risk behavior": having sexual intercourse or sharing needles with a member of a high-risk group, e.g., a gay or bisexual male or IV drug user from a major metro area, or a hemophiliac. The chances of getting AIDS from one such encounter range from 1 in 10,000 using a condom to 1 in 1,000 unprotected. Even if your partner tests negative for human immunodeficiency virus (HIV), the chances of infection from a high-risk person are still relatively high—1 in 50,000 without a condom. That's because the tests aren't foolproof. HIV doesn't show up in blood tests until ten weeks after you become contagious.

From there on out, statistically speaking, things deteriorate pretty fast. If your partner is HIV positive, your chances of getting AIDS after one night are 1 in 5,000 with a condom, 1 in 500 without. Have sex with an HIV-positive partner five hundred times using condoms and your chances escalate to 1 in 11. Skip the gift wrap and they're 2 in 3.

A couple points: these odds apply equally to men and women. Although there's reason to believe male-to-female AIDS transmission happens more often than female-to-male, the amount of difference is unknown. Also, the numbers involve some guesswork. The authors admit they could be off by a factor of ten in either direction. Still, one message comes through loud and clear: by far the best thing you can do to avoid AIDS is to be picky about your partners. Use of condoms reduces your risk by a factor of ten, sleeping only with people who test negative reduces it by a factor of five to fifty, but avoiding high-risk partners reduces it by a factor of five thousand. Asking for a résumé may not be romantic, but it beats Kaposi's sarcoma.

This is important! What are the Roman numerals for 1990? Possible solutions: (1) MXM, (2) MCMXC, or the cumbersome (3) MDCCCCLXXXX. Help!—Anonymous, Chicago

This *is* urgent. Even now sweaty movie moguls are surely wondering: what the hell are we going to do about the date at the end of the credits? Well, much as I'd like to cash in selling Roman-numeral consulting services to Hollywood, this time you guys are on your own. There is not now nor has there ever been any universally accepted method of styling Roman numerals. For that matter, it's only been in the last few hundred years that there's been any general agreement on what symbols stand for which quantities.

In school, for instance, you may have learned that the Romans used M for 1,000 because it stood for the Latin *mille*, thousand. Wrong on two counts: many authorities think it's only coincidence that the number M happened to look like the letter M (ditto for C = 100—it's unlikely C stood for *centum*, hundred). In any case, as often as not, the Romans indicated 1,000 not with M but either the lazy-8 infinity symbol or else something along the lines of CIↃ —that is, a vertical stroke framed by exaggerated parentheses.

Grade-school teachers often tell their students that the Romans adopted the so-called subtractive principle, i.e., IV = 5 − 1 = 4, in order to save themselves the trouble of chiseling extra strokes in the stone. But it turns out the subtractive system was used only sporadically by the ancient Romans and their medieval successors and never in a systematic way. Comb through old documents and inscriptions and you'll find such erratic usages as LXL, 90; XXCIII, 83; LXXIIX, 78; and even IIIIX, 6. A popular German arithmetic textbook published in 1524 gives 99 as XCIX, but even today you'll find some people who'll hold out for IC.

So where does this leave us? Well, if we are truly desperate for moral guidance, we may turn to the world of computers. Cecil happens to have a desktop publishing program known as Xerox Ventura Publisher, an amazing bit of software that I believe was used originally to torture heretics during the Inquisition. Among other things it will convert numbers up to 9,999 into Roman numerals for use as page numbers.

Punching in 1990, we come up with MCMXC, an unsurprising

376 · RETURN OF THE STRAIGHT DOPE

and somehow comforting result. But if we then try 1999, we get MIM. Why MIM for 1999 and not MXM for 1990? Lord knows. Worse, if we enter 9,999 we get what appears to be IZ. I have scoured my reference books in vain for any indication that Z was ever used for 10,000, which moves me to write the whole thing off as the product of malicious computer geekery, an impression that actually trying to *use* Ventura will certainly strengthen.

No doubt all this numerological uncertainty is distressing. But look on the bright side: it also gives us a strange and terrible freedom. You can use any damn notation for 1990 you want to, and no one will be able to say you're wrong. It may not give you the same rush as dancing on the Berlin Wall, but in post-Reagan America you make do with what you get.

Pretty soon we'll be starting a new decade (since, as all educated people realize, decades start with a one, not a zero). This got me wondering. A.D. 1991 means "in the year of our Lord 1991." When did this system start? I assume that after Christ was crucified, it wasn't just a matter of people saying, "Truly, he was the Son of God. Better renumber the calendar." What numbering system did Christ's contemporaries use?—Rob Rodi, Chicago

Good question, Robster, but first let me congratulate you on getting the facts straight on the new decade not starting until the end of 1990. When I pointed this out last New Year's, one woman cried out in anguish, "My God, you mean it's still the eighties?" She had my sympathy, but facts is facts.

The Christian system of year numbering was invented in what we now know as A.D. 525 by a monk named Dionysius Exiguus, who had been asked by the pope to work out a better way to figure when Easter occurred. There was probably a simpler way of doing this than renumbering the entire calendar, but I guess Dionysius got a little carried away. Surprisingly, considering the distinguished nature of the honoree, it took a while before the Anno Domini ("in the year of the Lord") method caught on. The popes didn't use it routinely until the tenth century A.D., and the Greeks didn't come around until the fourteenth century.

One defect of the calendar is that Dionysius miscalculated the date of Christ's birth. The somewhat incongruous result was that by modern calculation Christ was born about 4 B.C.—meaning Before Christ, of course. But we all make mistakes.

In Christ's time the Romans numbered their years *arburbe condita*, from the founding of the city [of Rome]. Christ was born circa 750 A.U.C. Other systems of reckoning were also used from time to time. One of the odder ones, in common use during the Middle Ages, was called the *indiction*. It was a rotating fifteen-year cycle; you got to fifteen, you started over again at one. No doubt this bespeaks a rather static conception of history—none of this modern idea of progress, you know. But at least they weren't bothered by people getting nostalgic for the sixties.

Battle of the Decades

It is extremely disappointing to find you spouting the line that the "0" year is the end of the decade. So let's get this straight: there is no such thing as "starting a new decade"—a decade is any ten years, and you can define it from May 25, 1985, to May 24, 1995, if you so desire. The "80s," however, is that decade every century during which the numeral "8" appears next-to-last in the year number. So don't try to be so much more clever than the rest of us all the time, okay?
—Kenny Mostern, Oakland, California

I try not to be, Kenny, but sometimes it just happens. I assume we're agreed the next century starts on January 1, 2001, not January 1, 2000. (If not, there's no point continuing.) Call me wacky, but it seems only reasonable that the start of the new century and the start of the new decade ought to coincide. Granted there's no harm done if they don't. No harm if your socks don't match, either. But some people it bothers. Sorry if I'm such a fussbudget.

Battle of the Decades, Part Two

Cecil, you fell into an ignorant trap trying to claim the nineties won't start until 1991. Let's take it from the top. The first decade A.D.

started in the year 1; the second began in year 11. Time marched on. People acknowledged that the fifth century, the fifth set of one hundred years since 1 A.D., began in 401 A.D., the eleventh century in 1001, etc. But one day somebody started talking about, oh, the "1300s." Linguistically, this is a very different term from "fourteenth century." It refers to the set of a hundred years designated 1300 to 1399. The 1300s include the year 1300, even though 1300 is the last year of the thirteenth century. Complicated, but I'm sure you can understand the foolishness of trying to claim 1300 isn't in the 1300s.

The same reasoning applies to decades. I will grant you that the two-hundredth decade A.D. will not begin until 1991. But "decade" refers to a ten-year period. Any ten-year period. Webster's New Collegiate Dictionary defines the sixties as "the years 60 to 69 in a lifetime or century." If someone tells you they live in New York "in the East Sixties," you wouldn't expect them to live on Seventieth Street, would you? The nineties (and the 1900s) will end as the year 2000 begins. But the twentieth century will still have a year to go.—John Cork, Los Angeles

Oh, piffle. There's no point being a columnist if you can't be obstinate in the face of all logic. If you're determined to stick to this silly idea that "the eighties" means all the years with eighty-something in their names, be my guest.

And Now Back to the Battle of the *Centuries*

Your bland assumption that no intelligent being could possibly believe anything but that the second millennium of our era will begin on January 1, 2001, sent me into such a froth that I simply had to reply. Hence the enclosed.—Chris Breyer, El Cerrito, California

Fun's fun, Chris, but a man's got to draw the line somewhere. The essay you enclose draws an analogy between the calendar and a mathematical number line. The starting point on the number line is zero; therefore, you opine, the starting point on the calendar should be the year zero. If that's so, one hundred years will have elapsed on

December 31 of the year 99 and twenty centuries will have gone by on December 31, 1999, making January 1, 2000, the start of the second millennium.

This argument is appealing but stupid. As we discussed in my first book, *The Straight Dope* (which appeared ten years ago, for Pete's sake), the first year in the calendar is not zero but 1. The first century concludes December 31 in the year 100, the second millennium finishes up December 31, 2000, and the next century and millennium start January 1, 2001.

There is a host of logical counterarguments to be raised against the number line analogy, but never mind them. We need merely point to the example of history. On September 22, 1792, French revolutionaries declared a republic and, in the interest of doing a thorough job sweeping out the old, decided to restart the calendar. Did they call the first year of their grand social experiment "the year zero"? Don't be silly. They proclaimed that "henceforth all public acts shall bear the date of the first year of the French Republic," Year I for short. Year I was followed by Year II, Year II by Year III—you see the pattern. I hope (but doubt) this will settle the question once and for all.

I understand the new Comiskey Park recently constructed in Chicago is the only baseball stadium in the major leagues with home plate in the northwest corner, rather than the southwest. Why are all ballparks oriented this way? Don't the owners of the White Sox care that they have the only exception?—Jerry, Chicago

Some White Sox fans at the time worked themselves into a real lather over this. A letter in the *Chicago Sun-Times* began, "Am I the last 'right field is the sun field in baseball' American living in America? Left field will be the sun field in the new White Sox stadium [due to the orientation of home plate]. All the current geniuses creating this new stadium are ignoring tradition. I am appalled and shocked," blah, blah, blah.

I should explain that right field is the "sun field" in most major-league ballparks because the right fielder must look into the sun when catching fly balls during afternoon games. This is one reason (though not the most important one) that most clubs put a stronger defensive player in right field than in left. Making *left* field the sun field, some purists claim, will throw off the game's subtle balances, create havoc in the outfield, and, to hear some tell it, hasten the decline of the West.

This is absurd. For one thing, not all major-league ball fields have home plate in the southwest. Southwest admittedly is common (at least fourteen of twenty-two outdoor parks). But several parks have home plate in the northwest, including County Stadium in Milwaukee, for God's sake, which is only ninety miles from Chicago. Other northwest parks (as near as I can make out—the records on this topic are dismal, and the people at the ballparks have a pretty vague sense of direction) include Arlington Stadium in Texas, Three Rivers Stadium in Pittsburgh, and Busch Stadium in Saint Louis.

The reason home plate is oriented the way it is, in any case, has nothing to do with the outfielders. It's meant to help the batter. If the plate were on the *east* side of the ballpark, the batter would be facing west, meaning he'd have the afternoon sun in his eyes. Not only would his batting average suffer, he might fail to duck next time a wild pitch came screaming toward his noggin. Putting home in the southwest or northwest corner eliminates this problem.

It's also the reason left-handed pitchers are called "southpaws." Because a lefty has to pitch in a generally westerly direction, his throwing arm is toward the south. This is as true in the new Comiskey as it was in the old. In sum, White Sox fans needn't get too excited about the ballpark. Better they should reserve their panic for the team.

Voice from the Grandstand

You are way out in left field regarding the origin of "southpaw." If you consult Paul Dickson's Dictionary of Baseball, *in which he gives me credit for many of the entries, you will find that the term is cited before any ballgrounds were constructed according to the direction of the sun. The story that the pitcher's left arm was on the south side of the slab is fanciful. No extra charge for the Straight Dope I'm giving you.—David Shulman, New York*

Cecil is not ready to admit he was wrong—Cecil would sooner have his nails pulled out by pliers—but he'll concede the situation is more complex than he first let on. According to the *Oxford English Dictionary*, the first recorded use of southpaw was in 1848 to describe a boxer's left-handed punch. This is long before the start of professional baseball and only a few years after baseball was supposedly invented in 1839. (Actually, of course, the game's origins go back much earlier.)

Fatal though this might seem to your ordinary argument, Cecil is no ordinary guy. Obviously there were no professional-baseball stadiums in 1848. But it is reasonable to suppose that any game involving pitching and batting usually would have the batter's spot oriented toward the west, even for sandlot games, for the reasons already stated. Historians agree such games have been played for centuries, long before the establishment of modern baseball. This is ample time for the term southpaw to have gotten anchored in the sporting lexicon and for me simultaneously to wiggle off the hook. So there.

I just received a letter from a friend of mine in France, and it occurred to me that he had purchased his stamps there in France. Why then did the U.S. Postal Service bother to deliver the letter? What's in it for them? How does this intercountry mailing business work, anyhow?—Ray Balestri, Dallas

Once upon a time there was an elegantly simple answer to this question. Not today. After twenty years of well-intended tinkering, international mail has overtaken assembling Christmas toys on the complexity index and it's breathing down the neck of setting the clock on your VCR. So brace yourself.

First the easy part. Cheap, efficient international mail was one of the great achievements of the Victorian era. Previously, trying to get a letter delivered overseas had been an accounting nightmare. In calculating postage, hapless users had to figure in the local rate in their home country, the rate paid for ship transport ("sea postage"), the rate paid to each country that handled the letter en route ("transit fees"), and finally the domestic postage in the destination country.

Postage could vary widely depending on the route by which you sent a letter—from five cents to $1.02 per half ounce from the United States to Australia, for instance. Detailed accounts had to be kept for each mail shipment so that everybody who got his mitts on it in transit would be sure to get his proper share. We had separate postal treaties with every country, and everybody figured things differently—by the ounce, by the gram, by the German *loth*, by the sheet. Predictably, the mail was slow and the rates were exorbitant.

Fed up with this, the U.S. called for an international postal congress, which was held in 1863. This led to the creation of the Universal Postal Union, which established a few straightforward principles: (1) There should be a more or less uniform flat rate to mail a letter anywhere in the world, (2) postal authorities should give equal treatment to foreign and domestic mail, and (3) each country should keep all the money it collected for international postage.

The rationale for Item #3 was ingenious. Reformers argued that each letter begot a reply. If each country had as much outgoing mail as incoming, the international postage it took in would cover the cost of delivering foreign mail.

The new system worked fine for quite a while. Postal rates dropped, international mail boomed, prosperity reigned. But by and by grumbling arose, partly because the nature of the mails had changed. One-way commercial mail such as periodicals came to account for a much larger portion of mail volume than letters. Countries like the U.S. became net exporters of mail. Since we kept the postage, poor nations griped that they had to deliver our mail essentially for free.

So in 1969 the UPU decided on a new system. If we sent India one hundred thousand kilograms of mail per year and they sent us eighty thousand, we'd pay them a fee for the twenty-thousand-kilogram difference. These fees were called terminal dues.

That opened the door to a long round of rate tweaking. Since terminal dues were originally charged strictly by weight, bulky periodicals incurred huge costs while letters, which required just as much handling, got off dirt cheap. After complaints by the U.S. and other nations, the UPU devised a new "threshold" system, which was implemented in 1991. It set separate letter and periodical rates for countries we sent at least 150 tons of mail to annually. For countries with less mail, the old flat rate was kept. Meanwhile, we negotiated a separate terminal dues formula with thirteen European countries that included a rate per piece plus a rate per kilogram. We have yet another arrangement with Canada.

And you ain't seen nothin' yet. European countries want to make the system even more complicated, for reasons I can't bring myself to go into. Wily bulk mailers are shipping out mail via the under-150-ton countries to take advantage of cheap rates, which will probably call for some additional rate response.

In short, the international mail system is beginning to approach the complexity it had prior to 1863. At the moment we've got two UPU formulas, a European formula, and a Canadian formula. More formulas are in the works. We still pay transit fees, too. Happily, consumers haven't been affected much—so far. Though its own accounting is getting knottier by the year, the U.S. Postal Service inflicts only three basic international rates on users: one for Canada, one for Mexico, and one for everywhere else. But we could yet wind up with separate rates for every foreign destination.

After doing my monthly bills I happened to notice all the envelopes provided by my creditors had two sets of bar codes printed on them. The ones at the top were all the same except for a "business reply" envelope, which was slightly different. The ones at the bottom were all different—maybe ZIP codes. What's the deal? If we are picking up the postage, what do the companies get out of it? If it's to ease mail sorting and keep the price of postage down, I guess it hasn't worked.—Mark Cnota, Chicago

Where is our faith in progress, Mark? Bar-code sorting costs one-fifth as much as older mechanical sorting ($3 versus $15 per thousand pieces) and less than one-eleventh as much as hand sorting ($35 per thousand). By 1995 the postal service hopes to be using bar codes on virtually all mail, resulting in a savings of $5 billion per year. In light of this it may seem strange to you that mail rates are going up, but that's because you don't understand the intricacies of postal economics. Join the crowd.

Business reply mail and "courtesy reply" mail (a company sends you a preaddressed envelope but you have to put the stamp on it) usually have two kinds of marks on them. There's the bar code on the bottom, which is nothing more than the nine-digit ZIP code in machine-readable form, and the "facing identification mark" (FIM), which is five or six vertical lines at the top. The FIM tells the first sorting machine the mail goes through, the "facer canceler," to shunt the letter aside for special handling.

There are three different FIMs: one for business reply mail pre-bar-coded by the mailer (this earns the cheapest postage rate), one for non-pre-bar-coded BRM (meaning the post office has to put the codes on after accepting the mail for delivery), and one for courtesy reply mail. Businesses precode courtesy reply envelopes, which are usually used for bill payments, so the mail will get to them faster and they can deposit the checks sooner. They may earn only a few cents' extra interest per item, but multiply that by a few million checks per year and we're talking serious money.

Chances are you're seeing bar codes on an increasingly large fraction of the mail you receive. The bar codes are put on by the PO using optical character recognition (OCR) equipment. This reads the typewritten address, looks up the proper nine-digit ZIP code (if missing) in the PO's vast address database, and prints it in bar-code form on the envelope. All subsequent sorting is done by relatively inexpensive bar-code readers.

Soon you'll see even more bar codes. In 1993 the postal service began offering discounts to mass mailers to induce them to pre-bar-code all their big mailings. By 1995 the PO hopes 40 percent of all mail will be pre-bar-coded by the mailer, 40 percent will be coded by the postal service with OCR machines, and the remaining 20 percent—hand-addressed envelopes and the like—will be bar-coded by clerks viewing the envelope on video.

Awesome, no? Hey, wait till you hear about eleven-digit ZIP codes, already in use in some areas. In theory every addressable location in the nation could have its own private ZIP code, although I gather the day when ZIP codes get as specific as phone numbers is still a ways off. Don't worry, eleven-digit ZIPs, known as Advanced Bar Codes, or ABCs, are strictly for the use of mass mailers and the postal service; the only hint you and I will have of their existence is that the strip of bar coding on our mail will have gotten longer. Seems pretty complicated, I know, but if you're the postal service and you're competing with fax machines, cellular phones, and Federal Express, you need every technological edge you can get.

I've been hearing advertisements on the radio for years now urging us to "name a star for a loved one" by sending $35 to the International Star Registry. Is this outfit for real? If I send my $35, will there be a legitimate star in the actual sky named for me? And will this name be internationally recognized forever?—Eric Lundberg, Chicago

Two guesses. Read the International Star Registry brochure carefully and you'll find that all they promise to do is "register" a star in the name of your choice. This means they write it down in a book. Needless to say, you can get this done for a lot less than $35. I, for one, will do it for a double sawbuck, and think of you often when I spend your cash on my next Caribbean cruise.

Unfortunately, no matter whom you pay your money to, the only way your star will be "internationally recognized" is if you tell it to your brother-in-law in Tobago. The only accepted authority on star naming is the International Astronomical Union, which has no connection with the International Star Registry or any other such outfit. The IAU calls attempts to exploit the general ignorance on this subject a "deplorable commercial trick."

The thing that gives (or used to give—see below) the International Star Registry an ersatz aura of respectability is the claim that they're going to put your star name in a book they're going to register with (drumroll) "the copyright office of the Library of Congress in the United States of America." As any fool knows, or ought to, you can copyright just about anything if you fill out a form and pay the fee. Copyright merely protects the rights of authors; it doesn't mean the government vouches for what's in the books.

In 1985 the copyright office issued a statement disavowing any connection with star registry services. It refused to grant copyright to a reel of microfilm submitted by ISR, although it did so later when the list was resubmitted in a different format. Library officials also pressured ISR to stop mentioning the L. of C. in the firm's promotions. ISR agreed, but a brochure the firm sent me a while back shows a sample star registration certificate in which "Library of Congress" still figures prominently. An ISR spokesperson says I got an old brochure. Uh-huh.

Should you mail in $35, what you'll get is the aforementioned certificate and a star map with your star ringed in red. One lucky recipient of such a map, who happened to be an amateur astronomer, found that it had been copied from a standard star atlas. But even though "his" star was located on the map about where the star catalogs said it was supposed to be, it didn't appear in the atlas because it was too faint. Puzzled, he examined the map under a magnifying glass. The star with the circle around it turned out to be an inkspot.

Enclosed for your enjoyment is a bottle of "Doctor Bronner's 18-in-1 Pure Castile Soap," which you can get at any health food store. The soap is great, but you'll note the label is crammed with weird religious ravings. What's the poop, Scoop? Is Doctor B. really a "master chemist and Essene rabbi"? What's the story behind his company, All-One-God-Faith, Inc.? And—this one is urgent, Cece— how about the unusual birth control method Dr. B. recommends? Should I throw out my diaphragm and stock up on lemons and Vaseline?—Sourpuss, Chicago

Not unless you like unusually gooey lemonade. As you can probably tell from the copy (can you imagine a slogan like "Eternal Father, Eternal One! Exceptions eternally? Absolute none!" on the side of a Tide box?), "Dr." Emanuel H. Bronner is inhabiting a different plane of being from the rest of us. So don't take anything he says too literally.

Bronner is an eighty-five-year-old (as of 1993) German immigrant who hangs out in Escondido, California. He's not an M.D. or strictly speaking a rabbi, but he claims he's got the equivalent of a Ph.D. in chemistry, which I guess makes him a master chemist. He's also not your average soap maker. Whereas Messrs. Procter and Gamble dream (well, dreamt) of enzymes and long-chain fatty acids, Bronner dreams of world peace.

Bronner wants to convince mankind of the virtues of the "All-One-God-Faith," which, together with the "Moral ABC," his answer to the Ten Commandments, will unite the human race. The details of this can be a bit hard to follow. For example: "Replace half-true Socialist-fluoride poison & tax-slavery with full-truth, work-speech-press & profitsharing Socialaction! All-One! So, help build 4 billion Hannibal wind-power plants, charging 96 billion battery-banks, powering every car-factory-farm-home-monorail & pump, watering Babylon-roof-gardens & 800 billion Israel-Milorganite fruit trees, guarded by Swiss 6000 year Universal Military Training," etc.

Talking to the doc on the phone is the audio equivalent of reading one of his labels. He can be pretty linear when he wants to be, but eventually always veers off into a rap about the Essene rabbis and whatnot, delivered in a nutty-professor German accent. Believe me, it's an experience.

Bronner has had an eventful life. The son of a Jewish German soap maker, he emigrated to the United States and pleaded with his father to do the same when the Nazis came to power. The old man refused. One day Bronner got a postcard with the words, "You were right.—Your loving father." He never heard from his parents again.

Initially settling in the Midwest, Bronner married the illegitimate daughter of a nun, who eventually became suicidal and died in a mental hospital. (He says she was tortured by the hospital guards.) He also began devising his plan for world peace. Fittingly, he took to the soapbox to promote it. One of his listeners, Fred Walcher, was so inspired that in 1945 he had himself crucified in Chicago in order to publicize the plan. (He survived.)

Later Bronner was arrested while trying to promote his plan at the University of Chicago and was committed to a mental hospital. He escaped three times, finally fleeing to California in 1947. He's been there cranking out soap and soap labels ever since.

Despite his eccentricities, Dr. Bronner has built his soap company into a prosperous concern, mostly by sheer force of personality. In the early days he would set up a table at health food conventions. If a dealer strayed within ten feet, Bronner would pounce and not let go until he'd gotten an order.

But things didn't really take off until he was discovered by the counterculture during the sixties. With the aid of his sons, Jim and Ralph, who handle production and sales, he currently sells some 400,000 gallons of liquid soap and 600,000 pounds of bar soap a year. He says he's now worth $6 million—not bad, he notes dryly, for somebody who's supposedly nuts.

Bronner's birth control method involves using lemon juice and Vaseline as a spermicide. While it's true the high acidity in lemon juice will kill sperm, doctors say it could also cause your insides to become irritated or burned. Besides, Vaseline isn't water soluble. You'd be clogging up your insides and wreaking God knows what kind of havoc. With all respect to Bronner, I'd advise sticking to diaphragms.

I hope you'll be able to solve the mystery behind eelskin wallets and their supposed ability to demagnetize my automatic bank teller card, rendering it completely useless. After going through four new plastic cards in as many weeks, I complained to the bank and was told that I was either (1) exposing them to excessive heat, water, or microwaves, (2) scratching them, or (3) keeping them in an eelskin purse or wallet. When I answered affirmatively about the eelskin, I was told it's demagnetizing the black strip on the back of the card. When I asked how eelskin could do this, the only response was, We don't know, it just happens. I have asked others with eelskin wallets and they've been told similar tales. What goes on?—V.W., Tempe, Arizona

Cecil has been working his little heart out on this for six months now, and though he does not have the final answer, he thought it wise to give an interim report so as to avert national panic. I have checked with my banker friends (believe me, the success of the Straight Dope books has elevated me to a whole new social stratum), and they confirm that stories about eelskin wallets are widespread in the industry. No doubt this is in large part because of press reports. Actual evidence, however, is skimpy and anecdotal.

Numerous explanations for the phenomenon have been offered. Some say the creatures used to make the wallets are electric eels and that sufficient electric charge survives the tanning and manufacturing process to sabotage teller cards. Others say that an iron compound is used during tanning that remains in the leather and is capable of retaining a charge, possibly produced by static electricity resulting from friction in, say, a hip pocket.

A variation on the preceding is that the wallets pick up a charge during shipping. It's known that a ship traveling through water generates its own magnetic field. Some speculate that during the long sea voyage from factories in the Far East this field leaves an electrical imprint on the ship's eelskin cargo.

The simplest explanation, however, which Cecil must say he greatly favors, is that many eelskin wallets have magnetic clasps. Since eelskin is thinner than cowhide, the clasp comes in closer contact with the wallet's contents, conceivably to the point that it might demagnetize a teller card.

We decided this was another job for the Straight Dope Science Advisory Board. We called up our buddy Henry, a banker of experience and breeding. He advised us that he had purchased two eelskin wallets during a recent junket to the Virgin Islands, one with, one without magnetic clasp. Entering immediately into the spirit of things, he crammed them full of teller cards and placed them in a "magnetically neutral environment" (Henry loves this scientific jargon), which turned out to be the top of his bedroom bureau. Fifteen days later he tested the cards. All worked perfectly.

Quickly regrouping, we tried again. Mrs. Adams bought me two eelskin wallets for my own. Retail value: $22, completely bankrupting the Straight Dope Research & Entertainment Fund. (Donations gratefully accepted.) The wallets were dyed a hideous red. Forget the eelskin, I exclaimed, the color alone will demagnetize the cards. I loaded the wallets with cards and stashed them in strategic locales on my person, then went about my daily routine, testing the cards every few days. No dice. It got to the point that the magnetic clasp on one wallet made a noticeable dent on the black strip on the back of one of the cards—but it still worked.

Meanwhile, a worried manager for a major wallet-making concern called to see how things were progressing. (No kidding.) I comforted him as best I could. A woman told me that when she bought an eelskin wallet her teller cards *stopped* getting demagnetized—obviously a case of deep and troubled vibes.

I am now at the point where I believe the whole phenomenon is a case of mass hysteria, like cattle mutilations or Cyndi Lauper. However, I am willing to give it one more shot. If you have an eelskin wallet that consistently demagnetizes teller cards and you're willing to lend it to us temporarily (heh-heh), notify us pronto. Otherwise we'll declare this ridiculous matter closed.

The Eelskin Wallet Mystery . . . Solved!

Cecil read with interest recent declarations in the newspapers that the famous eelskin wallet controversy, discussed in this column some months ago, had at last been solved. (The wallets had been blamed for demagnetizing automatic bank teller cards.) Unfortunately, the newspapers, with their unerring instinct for the meaningless, managed to omit such details as what exactly the solution was, technically speaking. So I called up Katie Jarman, the assistant vice president at the Bank of America in San Francisco who was credited with solving the mystery, to determine the facts. To my delight, I discovered that Katie, in the great tradition of Straight Dope Home Science, had undertaken an experimental regimen that would have done this column proud.

After a sudden rash of complaints about bad cards from eelskin-wallet owners, Katie and her colleagues examined the magnetic stripe on several failed cards and found that magnetic information had in fact been erased. They further noted that most of the complainers were women who used eelskin wallets with large magnetic clasps. As an experiment, Katie ran a variety of magnetic items over some test cards. Sometimes the cards became demagnetized, sometimes not. But when she ran an eelskin-wallet clasp over the cards, they *always* became demagnetized, even at a distance of two inches. A call to the fellow who owned the patent on the special donut-shaped magnet used on eelskin wallets confirmed that the magnet was unusually strong. (Why you need a heavy-duty magnet on an eelskin wallet is not clear to me, but hey, not my problem.)

Katie and company then ran a variety of eelskin products that *didn't* have magnetic clasps over the test cards. (Her boss, a sucker for kitsch, had picked up a boatload of souvenirs during a trip to Korea.) All the cards continued to operate normally. Conclusion: it's the clasp, not the eelskin itself, that does the demagnetizing. (The eel in question, by the way, is the hagfish, not an electric eel.) The Bank of America now advises its customers to keep their teller cards in a separate place to avoid demagnetization.

Meanwhile, eelskin-wallet makers are scrambling to save their hides, so to speak. Katie says at least one company has come out with a polyester clasp. But for some it's too late. Two companies reportedly have already gone belly-up. Then again, they knew the business was a little fishy going in.

Department of Indispensable Clarifications

Far be it from me to question you, but in your discussion of eelskin wallets, you mentioned that the "eelskin" in question was actually the skin of the hagfish. Hagfish are agnathans, or jawless fishes, and thus barely related to eels at all. I've had the "honor" of having to care for live hagfish for a zoology class. If you've ever seen one you know it exudes gobs and gobs of disgusting mucus and can turn a whole tank full of water into a tank full of slime in minutes. What I would like to know is (a) how come the companies call them "eelskin" wallets instead of "hagfish" wallets, and (b) what do they do with all that slime?—Karen Moody, College Park, Maryland

Why do people feel compelled to tell me things like this? My feeling is, if it's long, squirmy, and unconnected to a higher vertebrate, it's an eel. As for the wallet companies' choice of terminology—listen, would *you* want to be called a "hagfish"?

How do they know with any degree of certainty that no two snowflakes are alike? When I took statistics I was taught that to draw a valid conclusion one had to take a representative sample of the entire population. But considering the impossibly large number of flakes in a single snowfall, let alone that have ever fallen, how could snowologists have possibly taken a sample large enough to conclude that no two are alike?—Leslie B. Turner, San Pedro, California

They didn't, of course. Chances are, in fact, that there are lots of duplicates. What the snowologists really mean is that your chance of *finding* duplicates is virtually zero. It's been calculated that in a volume of snow two feet square by ten inches deep there are roughly one million flakes. Multiply that by the millions of square miles that are covered by snow each year (nearly one fourth of the earth's land surface), and then multiply that by the billions of winters that have occurred since the dawn of time, and it's obvious we're talking unimaginable googols of flakes. Some of these are surely repeats.

On the other hand, a single snow crystal contains perhaps 100 million molecules, which can be arranged in a gigajillion different ways. By contrast, the number of flakes that have ever been photographed in the history of snow research amounts to a few tens of thousands. So it seems pretty safe to say nobody's ever going to get documentary evidence of duplication. Still, it could happen, and what's more, Leslie, it could happen to *you*. The way I figure, any-

body who could dream up a question like this has got to have a lot
of time on his hands. Get out and get looking.

We Encounter a Little Problem

*Considering some of the dope you dish out, I'd expect your mis-
takes to be equally spectacular, and you've certainly outdone yourself
this time. The mind (mine, anyway) boggles at the magnitude of error
in your recent dissertation on snowflakes in which you said that over
the history of the earth there have been "unimaginable googols of
flakes." A googol is one followed by one hundred zeroes (10^{100}). My
calculations show that since the earth was formed 4 billion years ago,
the estimated number of flakes (not counting you and me and your
other readers) is only about 10^{28}. That leaves a difference of 10^{72}.*

*Let's try to get a handle on the size of that error. The difference be-
tween the diameter of a carbon atom's nucleus and the diameter of
the known universe is about forty orders of magnitude. That still
leaves about thirty-two orders of magnitude to sweep under the rug,
or about the difference between a carbon atom and the Milky Way.
To put it another way, the number of protons, neutrons, and electrons
in the known universe is much less than one googol. You've exceeded
that by a margin of unimaginable to the unimaginable power. I knew
you could do it, Cecil. Congratulations.—Josef D. Prall, Carrollton,
Texas*

I knew some smart-ass was going to call me on this. I am well
aware that the number of snowflakes falls short of a googol by a considerable margin. However, swept up in a fit of literary
grandiosity—I mean, come on, how often do you get to use a word
like "googol" in a sentence?—I decided to fudge it. I'm so embarrassed. Incidentally, by my calculations, the number of flakes is actually about 10^{30}, a difference of 10^2 from your figure. (You goofed up
the multiplication for the number of square feet in a square mile,
judging from your work sheet.)

Another Little Problem

I am a senior electrical engineering student at Northwestern University. Regarding the number of snowflakes that have fallen since the dawn of time, I have no problem with Josef Prall's point that there have been 10^{28} to 10^{30}, as opposed to your estimate of a googol (10^{100}). However, I feel compelled to point out that the difference between the two amounts is not 10^{72}. Obviously neither Prall nor you learned manipulation of exponents correctly in high school. 10^3 (or 1,000) minus 10^2 (100) doesn't equal 10^1 (10), it equals 9 times 10^2, or 900. Likewise, 10^{100} minus 10^{28} isn't 10^{72}, it's $10^{28}(10^{72} - 1)$ or $10^{28}(10^{71} \times 9.999 \ldots)$ or $9.999 \ldots \times 10^{99}$. Get it straight.—Janet M. Kim, Evanston, Illinois

I hate senior electrical engineering students. Whatever his other failings, I think it is reasonably clear from his letter that Josef Prall knows 10^{100} minus 10^{28} doesn't equal 10^{72}. He was using—certainly I was using—the expression "a difference of $10^{\text{so-and-so}}$" as a shorthand way of saying "a difference of so-and-so orders of magnitude." This may seem a bit careless, but in today's fast-paced world, every microsecond counts.

Vindication!

Some months ago, Straight Dope fiends will recall, this column struck a mighty blow for truth and freedom by attacking the belief that no two snowflakes are alike, a superstition that has blighted the lives of millions. Not having time to inspect all the world's snowflakes (besides, I lost the tweezers), Cecil relied instead on the crushing logic of mathematics, arguing that so many flakes had fallen since the dawn of time that there were bound to be a few duplicates.

Naturally, many scoffed. One peanut-brain called to say he knew for sure no two snowflakes were alike because he had heard it on "Nova." There was also the unfortunate business with the googols, which we won't go into here. My defense in all cases was couched strictly in theoretical terms, since I did not expect any actual cases of twin flakes to turn up (although I must say the cast of characters in those Doublemint commercials certainly came close).

I was therefore pleasantly surprised to read in the bulletin of the American Meteorological Society that matching snow crystals were recently discovered by Nancy Knight of the National Center for Atmospheric Research. The crystals in question admittedly aren't flakes in the usual sense but rather hollow hexagonal prisms. They are also not absolutely identical, but come on, if you insist on getting down to the molecular level, nothing's identical. They're close enough for me, and further proof that not only is this column at the cutting edge of science, but that sometimes we have to wait for the cutting edge to catch up.

Jumpin' Jack and Lazy Jim, twins, emerge from a fancy restaurant only to find all the valets have split and a heavy rainstorm lies between them and their car, one hundred yards away. Jumpin' Jack bets Lazy Jim that if he runs and Jim walks, he will arrive at the car not only faster but drier. Jim accepts the bet, arguing that Jack's broad chest will run into more raindrops than will hit Jim on the top of his slow-moving but small head. Who wins the bet? If distance and rain

density are important to figuring the answer, please provide us with
a handy wallet chart so we may know when to be nimble and when
not. Meanwhile, I'll place my bet with Jack.—Ryan Kuhn, Chicago

You're obviously a sensible young man, which is more than I can
say for some of the people who have looked into this. According to
Discover magazine, Alessandro De Angelis, a physicist at the University of Udine, Italy, calculated some years ago that "a sprinter racing along at 22.4 miles an hour does get less wet, but only 10
percent less wet, than a hasty stroller (6.7 miles an hour)." Conclusion: running isn't worth the trouble.

I haven't been able to find the original paper, if any, on which this
report was based, so I don't know how De Angelis arrived at his conclusion. Not that it matters. Neither theory nor experiment (mine)
bears out his crackbrain view. Running through the rain will keep
you a lot drier (not just 10 percent drier) than walking.

First the theory. We divide the raindrops hitting you into two cat-
egories: (1) head drops, which fall from above and would hit you
even if you were standing still, and (2) chest drops, which you run/
walk into and which wouldn't hit you if you were standing still. We
can all agree that the number of head drops is strictly a function of
how long you're out in the rain; if you run, fewer head drops. The
question is whether the allegedly larger number of chest drops you
get when running outweighs the definitely larger number of head
drops you get while walking.

Not to keep you in suspense, the answer is no. If we ignore aerodynamic effects, we can show mathematically (but won't) that while you'll
collect many fewer head drops running rather than walking, you'll get
exactly the same number of chest drops, regardless of the speed at
which you travel. Bottom line: you'll be a lot wetter if you walk.

But wait, you say. What about those pesky aerodynamic effects?
The requisite math is a bit daunting, but never fear. Heedless of his
delicate health or his already low reputation with the neighbors,
your columnist spent a recent rainy Saturday running down the
street like an idiot brandishing pieces of red construction paper
clipped to cardboard, the better to snag and count raindrops. Methodology: three trials of two runs each over a fixed distance, once run-

ning, once walking. Winds: calm. Angle of attack of paper relative to ground: forty-five degrees. Results:

Trial #1. Running, 15 seconds to run course; 213 drops. Walking, 40 seconds; couldn't count drops, paper soaked. Shortened course.

Trial #2. Running, 7 seconds; 131 drops. Walking, 20 seconds; 216 drops.

Trial #3. Running, 7 seconds; 147 drops. Walking, 17 seconds; 221 drops.

So there you are. The differences are larger than the numbers suggest because many drops on the "walking" papers dried before I could count them. My guess is that the number of drops is exactly proportional. If you're out twice as long, you get twice as wet.

One obvious caveat. If enough rain falls on you, whether because of the intensity of the rainfall or the distance you have to travel, eventually you'll be thoroughly soaked. After that it doesn't matter whether you run or walk; you're as wet as you're going to get. So the preceding applies only to relatively short sprints through less-than-torrential downpours. Sorry, no wallet charts. My advice: always run; if nothing else you could use the exercise.

You Can Fool Some of the People Some of the Time . . .

I enjoyed your column about whether we get less wet running or walking in the rain. I was particularly impressed with your initiative in collecting data. Regrettably, some tests of statistical significance I performed on the data you supplied seem to poop the party. [Two pages of incomprehensible mathematical symbols follow.] I know your data look convincing to the untrained eye, but to a statistician they smack of the problem of small numbers. Next time invest in a few extra sheets of construction paper and improve your significance level.—Catherine Hagen, Montreal, Quebec

Your argument, Catherine, is that two trials isn't a large enough sample to base any firm conclusions on. Cecil knows this. Cecil also knows that if he doesn't get his column in on time, a chancy proposition under the best of circumstances, he may eventually be informed the time has come for him to get a real job. So he takes certain shortcuts. But your point is well taken. Next time I need somebody to dash through the drink a few dozen times, I'll give you a call.

You are my last resort. In the TV series "The Flintstones," what was Barney Rubble's job? We all know that Fred worked at the quarry, but Barney's job was never directly referred to, except in a couple episodes where he worked as a TV repossessor or a short-order chef, after having been fired from his regular (unknown) job. Please help!—Nancy B., Chicago

I love this gig. Where else would I get the chance to be on the front lines of journalism, tracking down the questions all America is buzzing about? Actually, Barney's occupation was left up in the air in the early years of the series, which ran 166 episodes from 1960 through 1966. The folks at Hanna-Barbera, the studio that created the series, say Barney was a TV repossessor in one episode and a geological engineer in another—not your typical white-collar career path, but hey, it's the cartoons. They don't recall him being a short-order cook but admit it's possible. In later years Barney settled into a more comfortable existence working with Fred at the quarry. In one episode he was even made Fred's boss by Mr. Slate, the head honcho.

The problem with settling questions like this is that TV continuity ain't what it could be. In one episode, for example, Mr. Slate's first name was George and in another it was Sam. Once his company was called the Slate Rock and Gravel Company and another time Bedrock Quarry and Gravel. A little disconcerting, especially for hardcore "Flintstones" viewers, whose grip on reality has to be pretty shaky to start with. I'm sure the people at Hanna-Barbera are suitably chastened and won't let it happen again.

I've been listening to Don McLean sing "American Pie" for twenty years now and I still don't know what the hell he's talking about. I know, I know, the "day the music died" is a reference to the Buddy

Holly/Ritchie Valens/Big Bopper plane crash, but the rest of the song seems to be chock full of musical symbolism that I've never been able to decipher. There are clear references to the Byrds (". . . eight miles high and fallin' fast . . .") and the Rolling Stones (". . . Jack Flash sat on a candlestick . . ."), but the song also mentions the "King and Queen," the "Jester" (I've heard this is either Mick Jagger or Bob Dylan), a "girl who sang the blues" (Janis Joplin?), and the Devil himself. I've heard there is an answer key that explains all the symbols. Is there? Even if there isn't, can you give me a line on who's who and what's what in this mediocre but firmly-entrenched-in-my-mind piece of music?—Scott McGough, Baltimore

Now, now, Scott. If you can't clarify the confused, certainly the pinnacle of literary achievement in my mind, history (e.g., the towering rep of James Joyce) instructs us that your next best bet is to obfuscate the obvious. Don McLean has never issued an "answer key" for "American Pie," undoubtedly on the theory that as long as you can keep 'em guessing, your legend will never die.

He's probably right. Still, he's dropped a few hints. Straight Dope musicologist Stefan Daystrom taped the following intro from Casey Kasem's "American Top 40" radio show circa January 1972: "A few days ago we phoned Don McLean for a little help in interpreting his great hit 'American Pie.' He was pretty reluctant to give us a straight interpretation of his work; he'd rather let it speak for itself. But he explained some of the specific references that he makes. The most important one is the death of rockabilly singer Buddy Holly in 1959; for McLean, that's when the music died. The court jester he refers to is Bob Dylan. The Stones and the flames in the sky refer to the concert at Altamont, California. And McLean goes on, painting his picture," blah blah, segue to record.

Not much to go on, but at least it rules out the Christ imagery. For the rest we turn to the song's legion of free-lance interpreters, whose thoughts were most recently compiled by Rich Kulawiec into a file that I plucked from the Internet. (I *love* the Internet.) No room to reprint all the lyrics, which you probably haven't been able to forget anyway, but herewith the high points:

February made me shiver: Holly's plane crashed February 3, 1959.

Them good ole boys were . . . singing, "This'll be the day that I die":
Holly's hit "That'll Be the Day" had a similar line. *The Jester sang
for the King and Queen in a coat he borrowed from James Dean*: ID
of K and Q obscure. Elvis and Connie Francis (or Little Richard)?
John and Jackie Kennedy? Or Queen Elizabeth and consort, for
whom Dylan apparently did play once? Dean's coat is the famous
red windbreaker he wore in *Rebel Without a Cause*; Dylan wore a
similar one on "The Freewheeling Bob Dylan" album cover. *With the
Jester on the sidelines in a cast*: On July 29, 1966 Dylan had a mo-
torcycle accident that kept him laid up for nine months. *While sergeants played a marching tune*: The Beatles' "Sergeant Pepper's
Lonely Hearts Club Band."

*And as I watched him on the stage / My hands were clenched in
fists of rage / No angel born in hell / Could break that Satan's spell
/ And as the flames climbed high into the night*: Mick Jagger,
Altamont. *I met a girl who sang the blues / And I asked her for some
happy news / But she just smiled and turned away*: Janis Joplin OD'd
October 4, 1970. *The three men I admire most/ The Father, Son, and
Holy Ghost / They caught the last train for the coast*: Major mystery.
Holly, Bopper, Valens? Hank Williams, Elvis, Holly? JFK, RFK,
M. L. King? The literal tripartite deity? As for the coast, could be
the departure of the music biz for California. Or it simply rhymes,
a big determinant of plot direction in pop music lyrics (which may
also explain "drove my Chevy to the levee"). Best I can do for now.
Just don't ask me to explain "Stairway to Heaven."

The Last Word (Probably) on "American Pie"

*As you can imagine, over the years I have been asked many times
to discuss and explain my song "American Pie." I have never discussed the lyrics, but have admitted to the Holly reference in the
opening stanzas. I dedicated the album* American Pie *to Buddy Holly
as well in order to connect the entire statement to Holly in hopes of
bringing about an interest in him, which subsequently did occur.*

*This brings me to my point. Casey Kasem never spoke to me and
none of the references he confirms my making were made by me. You*

will find many "interpretations" of my lyrics but none of them by me. Isn't this fun?

Sorry to leave you all on your own like this but long ago I realized that songwriters should make their statements and move on, maintaining a dignified silence.—Don McLean, Castine, Maine

14

Feedback

I was amused to read your comments and reader reaction concerning slugs in More of the Straight Dope. *If you thought these terrestrial pulmonate gastropods were disgusting before, get a load of the following, from* Cascade Olympic Natural History *by Daniel Mathews:*

"Banana slugs are notorious for chewing off their penises to conclude mating (both partners chew), probably because their unusually large organs are more difficult for them to withdraw than to regenerate later. . . . To make themselves recognizable, the species have evolved a bizarre assortment of palpable structures—sharp little jabbing needles, delicately branched sperm packets, and overdeveloped penises, all with dimensions peculiar to the species. Banana slug penises are large, but nothing like those of one rare race in the Alps— 32½-inch tumescences dangling from 6-inch slugs.—N.S., Mercer Island, Washington

Thanks, N. You can't imagine how knowing this enriches my life.

Thanks for quoting me twice in More of the Straight Dope. *I notice you discuss the alleged practice of gerbil stuffing. [The gerbil is* supposedly inserted in the keester for purposes of sexual stimulation.] *Have you found any evidence yet that this has ever actually occurred? I ask because the compilers of* News of the Weird *include a*

*list of "items recovered from the rectums of patients" (page 157 of
their book) that includes "a live, shaved, declawed gerbil." I included
this in a list of ten urban-legend-related items I found in their book
in a column I wrote about NOTW, which elicited two nasty, defensive, insecure letters from Chuck Shepherd, its originator. He says the
list was summarized from a 1987 issue of the journal* Surgery *so it
cannot be a legend. You and I and everybody else know that the story
has circulated since 1982 at least. It doesn't stop being a legend if
somebody tries it, as witnessed by the recent attribution in vicious rumors of gerbil stuffing to Richard Gere.*

*If there's a firsthand medical report of gerbilling, I'm surprised that
some doctor hasn't sent me a copy by now; ye gods, they send me
copies of articles on exploding patients, relative's cadavers, bugs in
the ear, hairballs, and virtually everything else of medical interest I've
ever mentioned. If you know anything more than what's in your book,
I'd appreciate your sharing it.—Jan Brunvand, University of Utah,
Salt Lake City*

Sorry if this seems like writers kaffeeklatsching around the water
cooler, folks, but we world-famous columnists must keep in touch.
Mr. Brunvand, of course, is the legendary investigator of "urban legends," whose books include *The Vanishing Hitchhiker*, *The Choking
Doberman*, and most recently *The Baby Train*.

As for Chuck Shepherd, he's either pulling our leg or someone's
pulling his. The *Surgery* article he's apparently referring to appeared
not in 1987 but 1986. Entitled "Rectal foreign bodies: Case reports
and a comprehensive review of the world's literature," it describes
"approximately 700 identified objects recovered from approximately
200 patients." The list includes everything from turnips to ice
picks—but no gerbils or any other critter.

I have also gone through the biological abstracts and the Medline
computer database. There is an abundant literature on rectal foreign
bodies in general, but nothing on gerbils. It is inconceivable to me that
a doctor with firsthand knowledge of this bizarre practice would fail to
write it up pronto, if only because of the public health implications.

The indication in *News of the Weird* that the gerbil was recovered
alive strongly suggests the report is bogus; by the time the victim got
to the emergency room the gerbil would surely have been asphyxi-

ated. The one solid lead I thought I had on a case of gerbil-stuffing back in 1986 evaporated on further inquiry. I won't say it's never happened in this nutty world, but I have yet to see proof. I doubt Chuck Shepherd has, either.

The News: Not *That* Weird

You are correct (as usual) [about gerbil-stuffing]. *I made a transcribing error.—Chuck Shepherd, Deadfromtheneckup, Inc., Washington, D.C.*

Confession is good for the soul, Chuck. But let me get this straight: are you saying that including "a live, shaved, declawed gerbil" on a list of "items recovered from the rectums of patients" was a *transcribing* error? If so, you really gotta work on that handwriting.

A Clarification

Your smart-ass comments reside on safer ground when you do your traditional serious research first than when you infer among several meanings of words. I made a transcribing error in the following sense: I received the Surgery *article reprint, along with a cover letter describing the rectal inventory in the article but also mentioning the gerbil story. In the course of committing the information to the paragraphs that I use to construct my columns and books, I misattributed the gerbil story as appearing in the article when in fact it only appeared in the cover letter. I was careless, and I freely and unconditionally acknowledged my error. I was disappointed to find out that a man whose work I so admire would so casually and gratuitously imply either insincerity or comical incompetence to me when I was so obviously attempting to be humble to you in my note.—Chuck Shepherd, News of the Weird, Washington, D.C.*

Oh, Chuck, cool out. If you hadn't been so cryptic in your first letter, you wouldn't have given me the chance for such an obvious (and shameless) cheap shot.

Contrary to your column of some years ago [More of the Straight Dope, *page 329*], *there is authority that a marriage performed by a ship's captain on the high seas is valid. In* Fisher v. Fisher *in 1929 the New York Court of Appeals (the state's highest court) held that "in the absence of any such law which condemned the marriage . . ." such a marriage was valid. The court also reasoned that Congress "had recognized that on board a ship at sea . . . there is . . . a law of marriage," because Congress had enacted a statute requiring a vessel's master to keep a logbook recording every marriage taking place on board. (There is still such a statute.)* Fisher *is still reported as good law in* Corpus Juris Secundum, *although other authorities are to the contrary.—John Ratnaswamy, Chicago*

Oh, God, not *Fisher v. Fisher*. The case is one of those freaks that crop up frequently in marriage law and make it impossible to offer any sweeping statement, about ships' captains or anything else, without having it studded through with asterisks and qualifications.

Let's start with the one rock of certainty in this discussion: no state has enacted a statute explicitly authorizing ships' captains to solemnize marriages. However, in ruling on the validity of such mar-

riages, the courts have waffled. On the one hand, there is a long-standing legal presumption that if two people think they got married, they did get married, even if the proceeding by which this was accomplished was suspect. On the other hand, judges have also felt, Jeez, we can't let just *anybody* solemnize marriages, we gotta have rules.

This ambivalence has resulted in decisions on both sides of the fence. In *Fisher v. Fisher* the court ruled a marriage by a ship's captain valid; in an 1898 case in California, *Norman v. Norman*, the court ruled the opposite. It's important to note that in *Fisher* the court did not specifically single out ships' captains (as opposed to say, mailmen) as having the power to perform marriages; rather it ruled that, absent a statute to the contrary, and subject to certain other conditions, an exchange of vows between consenting parties constituted a valid marriage—as I read it, whether there was an officiant or not. In other words, marriage by ship's captain, or by anybody other than a recognized minister, J.P., etc., was a type of common-law marriage.

There are still some states that recognize common-law marriage. Typically all that's necessary is that the parties (1) be legally free to marry (e.g., no undissolved prior marriages), (2) properly consent, (3) "cohabit" (do it), (4) live together, and (5) let the neighbors think they're married. (Contrary to common belief, it is not necessary that the couple live together for seven years.)

What's *not* required are the services of a minister. So while you're correct in saying "There is authority that a marriage performed by a ship's captain on the high seas is valid," captains don't have any special powers in this regard. A close reading of *Fisher* suggests the ceremony might as well have been performed by a waiter.

Granted the issue isn't as clear as it might be. The family-law experts I spoke with scoffed at the idea that courts in the 1990s would recognize marriages by ships' captains on a non-common-law basis. (That is, unless the captain had been granted the right under the laws of a foreign country, in which case recognition would be granted as a matter of course.) But you never know. There has been at least one case in which the court recognized a marriage performed by a "minister" who had gotten his credentials by mail order from the Universal Life Church. By comparison to such patent flakery, ships' captains seem like the soul of rectitude. If only somebody would submit themselves for a test case (you single, John?), we could get this cleared up once and for all.

Keyboard Scam Exposed!

You and others have commented on the received "history" of the QWERTY [i.e., conventional] typewriter keyboard design and remarked on the supposed superiority of the Dvorak keyboard, which puts all the vowels in the "home row" and slightly favors the right hand [The Straight Dope, page 249]. The time has come to put this myth to rest. Enclosed is an article from the Journal of Law and Economics. *Enjoy.—Scott Koslow, Assistant Professor of Marketing, University of Texas at Dallas*

Okay, doc, you got me dead to rights. The origin of the QWERTY keyboard, so named because that's what the top row of letter keys spells out, is one of those oft-told tales about how we got stuck with an oddball standard because of a shortsighted decision by some mope(s) in the dawning days of a new technology.

According to legend, the seemingly random layout of today's keyboards has its origins in the limitations of the first typewriters. The early machines were crude and prone to jamming if you typed too fast. The QWERTY keyboard was designed to place the most commonly used letters on the opposite sides of the keyboard, making jamming mechanically less likely. Legend has it that the QWERTY keyboard was also made intentionally clumsy (only one vowel in the home row, for instance) in order to slow down typists and further reduce the possibility of jamming.

Within a relatively short time, of course, typewriter engineering had improved sufficiently that jamming was no longer a major concern. But by then, the story goes, people were used to the QWERTY keyboard and we've been stuck with it ever since, even in the face of allegedly superior alternatives such as the Dvorak keyboard. Advocates say research proves the Dvorak is easy to learn and makes typing faster and more accurate. But it's never made much headway because of the crushing power of standards, even stupid ones.

Baloney, say the authors of the article you enclose, S. J. Liebowitz and Stephen Margolis. They point out that (1) the research demonstrating the superiority of the Dvorak keyboard is sparse and methodologically suspect, (2) a sizable body of work suggests that in fact the Dvorak offers little practical advantage over the QWERTY, (3) at least one study indicates that placing commonly used keys far apart, as with the QWERTY, actually speeds typing, since you frequently alternate hands, and (4) the QWERTY keyboard did not become a standard overnight but beat out several competing keyboards over a period of years. Thus it may be fairly said to represent the considered choice of the marketplace. It saddens me to know I helped to perpetuate the myth of Dvorak superiority, but I will sleep better at night knowing I have rectified matters at last.

On page eleven of your book The Straight Dope, *you mention that Russian scientists are trying to clone a mammoth from preserved cells. Sorry, but this story originated as an April Fools' joke in* Technology Review *magazine, published at MIT. A student in the science writing class submitted a convincing but entirely bogus account of the first successful mammoth cloning. This supposedly produced two male "mammontelephases"—hybrid animals that were half mammoth, half elephant. The* TR *editors were tickled and ran the piece in their April 1984 issue.*

Despite a multitude of clues, e.g., the comical name given to the Russian in charge of the project ("Dr. Sverbighooze Nikhiphorovich Yasmilov"), the silly cartoon accompanying the piece, and, most obvious of all, the April 1 dateline, the story was picked up by the Chicago Tribune *and sent out via its syndicate service. It eventually appeared in* Family Weekly, *a Sunday supplement carried in over 350 U.S. newspapers.* Technology Review *and MIT spokespersons were then obliged to explain the concept of April Fools' Day to baffled journalists from around the world.*

MIT students have a long history of pranks. In 1968 they carried buckets of snow to a shower stall in a dorm and called the Boston Herald Traveler. *They told the reporter that steam from a hot shower had mixed with cold air coming in an open window to produce snow. The story made page one and was picked up by a wire service. Then*

there was that stunt at the Harvard-Yale game in 1982 . . .—Brian Leibowitz, Cambridge, Massachusetts

I'll admit the *Chicago Tribune* isn't exactly run by Einsteins, Brian, but let's not be so quick to dismiss this cloning stuff. A specimen of the woolly mammoth really was discovered in Siberia in 1977. In 1980 Soviet scientists said they were trying to clone a live animal from the preserved cells, but a year later they conceded the attempt had been a failure. The grain of truth is what made the *Technology Review* spoof so convincing.

Joe Newman Update

The Teeming Millions will recall our discussion some years ago of the eccentric inventor Joseph Newman of Mississippi, who claimed he had invented a machine that produced more energy than it consumed—a perpetual motion machine, in other words. The United States refused to grant Newman a patent, saying perpetual motion machines were impossible. He sued but lost his case when a scientific analysis revealed that his machine produced far less energy than it consumed. Newman was ticked, of course, and claimed he was robbed by bureaucrats too stupid to comprehend his genius.

Now a Straight Dope reader in Mississippi sends word that Joe is in the news again. According to the *Mississippi Press*, Newman says he was ordered by God to marry both his thirty-year-old secretary and her eight-year-old daughter. Newman complied—God presided over the ceremony—and happily notified the world in a twelve-page press release. (One copy was sent to the Ayatollah Khomeini.)

The only problem—well, maybe not the *only* problem—is that Newman was already married to a third woman. Authorities promptly removed the eight-year-old from Joe's home, though he says he has not consummated the marriage. Newman, who once ran for president on God's instructions, angrily declared that this shabby treatment was going to get God really PO'ed: "I wouldn't be a bit surprised if this does not result that God will place misery upon the State of Mississippi. . . . I can see the handwriting on the wall and the people of Mississippi had better wake up."

Clearly this is one wild and crazy guy. Hope nobody out there invested too much money in his machine.

Eating It Raw: An Update

Readers who recall Cecil's discussion some years back of the hazards of eating raw fish will be fascinated by a recent report in the *New England Journal of Medicine*. It seems a twenty-four-year-old student with a pain in his right side underwent surgery for appendicitis. His appendix was found to be normal, but surgeons were startled to see a *ten-inch pinkish-red worm* crawl out of the guy's body. Turned out to be a *Eustrongylides*, a parasite normally found in fish-eating birds. The victim, obviously not a regular reader of the Straight Dope, said he ate sushi and sashimi once a month. My feeling is, if you must eat this stuff, work it over pretty good first with a rock.

A *Small* Rock

Re the ten-inch post-sushi stomach worm, enclosed is a page from a recent Nutrition Action Healthletter. *Turns out the Sushi Worm from Hell was "only" about one and a half inches long. Some comfort.* —Junu Kim, Chicago

It seems the editors of *Nutrition Action*, from which I got this horrifying item, multiplied instead of dividing when converting from the metric. I am surrounded by schmucks.

Re pre-Charmin toilet paper substitutes (cf. More of the Straight Dope, *pages 373–377)—my parents tell me peach season was considered a real treat in the old days because the semisoft paper each peach was wrapped in was far preferable to the Sears catalog or a corncob.—Chris V., Studio City, California*

*In the discussion in your book on human penis length [*More of the Straight Dope, *pages 193–194], you stated, "Specimens as long as 13 inches (when erect) . . . have been reported." Well, records are made to be broken—or in the case of the enclosed photos, pulverized. This gent beats the old mark by a good five inches. If you think the photos are retouched, altered, or in any way exaggerated, videotapes of this guy in action are readily available through commercial suppliers.— Roger Jackson, West Bend, Wisconsin*

I ask you, is the Straight Dope in the vanguard of knowledge or what? The fellow in the picture, which I got in maybe 1990, is none other than the legendary Long Dong Silver, the guy made famous during the Anita Hill–Clarence Thomas hearings. Though no official measurements are supplied—pornmongers have no grasp of science—eighteen inches appears to be in the ballpark. In some of the photos L.D. is accompanied by the usual well-endowed maiden, who is gazing at his member with an expression of . . . well, it's hard to say whether it's interest or horror. But I wouldn't want this guy gazing down at *me.*

Re: the question about average penis sizes, I was reminded of an almost certainly apocryphal anecdote. Seems that in the latter part of the cold war Russia was allowed some limited trade with the U.S., and some nameless institution ordered fifty thousand condoms from an American plant (located in Texas, I like to think). The order specified that the condoms were to be eleven inches long. The Americans scratched their heads, called the Russians to verify the measurement, and were rudely told that the order was correct, all of the condoms should be 11 inches long. So the Americans proceeded to fill the order and shipped the Russians fifty thousand eleven-inch condoms—in boxes labeled "medium." Heh heh heh.—Craig Becker, Austin, Texas

Another Triumph for Animal Rights!

Readers of *More of the Straight Dope* know that despite slurs to the contrary, humans aren't the only mammals capable of seeing in color. Extensive research has demonstrated that cats are physiologically capable of perceiving color as well—they just aren't very adept at it, being creatures of the night. Now comes new research indicating that dogs can see in color, too.

Three scientists at the University of California at Santa Barbara adopted the traditional strategy of trying to tempt the dogs with food. The menu, frankly, could have stood some improvement: would *you* cooperate with people whose idea of a reward was a cheese-and-beef-flavored pellet? Nonetheless, the researchers found three mutts who were sufficiently desperate to play along. They showed the dogs three screens lit up from behind with colored lights—two of one color, the third of a different color. The mutts got the pellet if they poked the odd-colored screen with their noses.

The dogs had no difficulty distinguishing colors at the opposite ends of the visible spectrum, such as red and blue, and they proved to be demons with blues in general, quickly learning to differentiate blue from violet. But they bombed at other colors, confusing greenish-yellow, orange, and red.

The researchers concluded that dogs suffer from a type of color blindedness that in humans is called *deuteranopia*. Normal humans have three types of color receptors for red, green, and blue. Deuter-anopes lack the green receptor and thus (apparently) can't tell a lemon from a lime—or, for that matter, a red traffic light from a green one. One more reason to put your foot down next time the pooch says he wants to drive.

I suppose I'm not the first to inform you that, the introduction to More of the Straight Dope *to the contrary, Oscar Wilde and Max Beerbohm were quite well acquainted. Beerbohm apparently admired Wilde's work, but not his character.—Gretchen S., Jefferson, Louisiana*

Damn. Another great one-liner ruined by the facts.

On pages 239–240 of More of the Straight Dope *you give two versions of the origin of the word "Yucatan." Enclosed are photocopies of a third version, from the chronicler Bernal Dias del Castillo, who went on the first European expedition to the area in 1517. Dias criticized Gomara for numerous inaccuracies in the latter's account of the conquest. The following is my translation of the relevant passage.*

[It is 1517. The Spanish governor in Cuba, Diego Velázquez, is interviewing two Indians whom the soldiers had captured in Mexico and brought back to Cuba.]

"And in this way [by signs] they demonstrated the mounds where they put the plants from whose roots is made the cassava bread, called on the island of Cuba yuca *[yucca], and the Indians said* tlati *for the soil in which they planted them: in [such a] manner that* yuca *with* tlati *means Yucatan, and to [interpret] this the Spanish who were with Velázquez said to [him], 'Sir, these Indians say that your land is called Yucatlan.' And thus it acquired this name, which in their language is not called this way."*

Also, on page ninety-one you made a casual statement that if we burn clean natural gas for fuel we won't have a problem with the greenhouse effect. On the contrary, all hydrocarbons, including natu-

ral gas, yield carbon dioxide upon combustion. Carbon dioxide is a major contributor to the greenhouse effect. Lloyd Bentsen made the same mistake in the 1988 vice-presidential debate, so you're in esteemed company [cough].—Bill H., Blacksburg, Virginia

Guess that's the last time Lloyd will ever trust *me* to write the briefing book.

With regard to how much wood a woodchuck could chuck, etc. [More of the Straight Dope, page 83], I am happy to say that science marches on, and the quaint but oh-so-unscientific answer you gave has been replaced with a modern one. See the enclosed article in The Wall Street Journal.—*Randy B., Los Angeles*

The article reports on the work of New York state wildlife expert Richard Thomas, who found that a woodchuck could (and does) chuck around thirty-five cubic feet of dirt in the course of digging a burrow. Thomas reasoned that if a woodchuck could chuck wood, he would chuck an amount equivalent to the weight of the dirt, or seven hundred pounds. We are pleased to know this, of course. But it sure isn't easy to fit into a snappy verse.

Of course the Corinthians wrote back [More of the Straight Dope, page 86]. Internal evidence shows that what we call "I Corinthians" is at least Paul's second letter—cf. I Cor. 5:9ff., which refers to a previous effort, evidently largely misunderstood. Scholars think that II Cor. 6:14–7:1, patently an insertion that interrupts the flow of Paul's thought, may well be a fragment of this lost "first letter."
More to the point, some scholars have theorized (admittedly in an attempt to save Paul from some of the epistle's more sexist attitudes) that much of I Corinthians is Paul's quoting of a Corinthian letter, with his own reply appended. The mention of "reports" in I Cor. 5:1 hints at this. The best example is chapter 14, where vv. 33b–35 represent "quoting" from the Corinthian letter and vv. 36–40 are Paul's

liberal reply. Take it for what it's worth.—David T., M.A. (Oxon.), Montgomery, Alabama

This is very interesting, David. But I'll bet Mary and Ted, the ones who asked whether the Corinthians ever wrote back, are glad they didn't pop their little joke on *you.*

At the end of the first question in More of the Straight Dope, *you suggest that schizophrenia refers to split- or multiple-personality disorder. As a psychology professor at Purdue I frequently must correct this error. The enclosed handout demonstrates the pervasiveness of the error and provides a corrective explanation.—David Santogrossi, West Lafayette, Indiana*

Professor Santogrossi's handout includes a photocopy of a letter to the editor he saw in *Rolling Stone* magazine:

> With regard to the Ian Hunter album [*You're Never Alone with a Schizophrenic*], shouldn't the title be *You're Never Alone When You're Schizophrenic,* as opposed to *with* a schizophrenic? If you are with a schizophrenic, you're *with* somebody—it really doesn't matter if he is schizophrenic or not. But if you *are* schizophrenic, then you're never alone. Trust me.

The letter inspired the professor to write *Rolling Stone* the following:

> The apparent intent of the title for Ian Hunter's new album, and the title revision suggested by [the letter writer] (who asks us to trust him, no less) are both in error. It is common to encounter in the media the word "schizophrenia" used as if it meant multiple or "split" personalities. While "schizo-" does derive from the Greek for "split," schizophrenia actually translates "splitting of the mind." The term refers to a form of psychosis characterized by a

severe disharmony of normal mental functions and a lack of integration among thoughts, feelings, and activities.

Multiple personality, on the other hand, is a rare and somewhat controversial category of neurotic disorder in which a person is thought to develop one or more distinct and separate secondary personalities. The secondary personality has its own consciousness unaware of the primary personality and carries out actions independent of it. In the purported cases of multiple personality in the psychological literature, there frequently is no interaction among the personalities, at least until a therapist "introduces" them to one another.

Thus, you can be alone even with multiple personalities, and you can certainly be alone if you are schizophrenic. Trust *me*.

Aspiring rock stars, letter-to-the-editor writers, and know-it-all columnists, take note.

In regards to your answer to why outhouses have half-moons on their doors [More of the Straight Dope, pages 352–383], *you are quite right about the holes being ventilators. According to the enclosed clipping, half-moons or crescents were a popular choice "'cause they're graceful and simple." This throws some doubt on your assertion that privy builders stole the idea from Al Capp.—Gary McNab, Baltimore*

You enclose a reprint of "The Specialist" (1929), a classic bit of humor by Charles (Chic) Sale. The Specialist is a country carpenter who styles himself "the champion privy builder of Sangamon County." Here are the Specialist's views on cutting the hole in the door:

"Now, about ventilators, or the designs I cut in the doors. I can give you stars, diamonds, or crescents—there ain't much choice—all give good service. A lot of people like stars, because they throw a ragged shadder. Others like crescents 'cause they're graceful and simple. Last year we was cuttin' a lot of stars; but this year people are kinda quietin' down and runnin' more to crescents. I do twinin' hearts now and then for young married couples and bunches of grapes for the newly rich. These last two designs come under the head of novelties and I don't very often suggest 'em, because it takes time and runs into money.

" 'I wouldn't take any snap judgment on her ventilators, Elmer,' I sez, because they've got a lot to do with the beauty of the structure. And don't overdo it like Doc Turner did. He wanted stars and crescents both, against my better judgment, and now he's sorry. But it's too late; 'cause when I cut 'em, they're cut. And, gentlemen, you can get mighty tired, sittin' day after day lookin' at a ventilator that ain't to you likin.' "

Hard to argue with. However, you'll recall that in my telling, the crescent ventilator had its origin in the colonial era, regarding which neither the Specialist nor Chic Sale can be regarded as an expert.

As researchers at the Florida Solar Energy Center, we have conducted an experiment that sheds some light on one of the questions in your second book, More of the Straight Dope. *The question was whether running the car air conditioner during freeway driving has less effect on fuel economy than turning the AC off and rolling down the windows, which increases drag. Our answer, which was obtained using a VW GTI under repeated testing with fairly accurate instrumentation, is contrary to that described in your book.* [Based on my experiments, I said mileage with the AC on and windows up was about the same as with AC off and windows down.] *Although rolling down the windows reduced mileage, the reduction at 67 MPH (3 percent) was not as great as that caused by running the AC (12 percent). The answer could vary depending on the automobile. One would assume that a different answer might be obtained using a very aerodynamic car with a large power plant (engine load from AC is a smaller fraction of overall power output).—Danny S. Parker, Florida Solar Energy Center, Cape Canaveral, Florida*

As scientists, Dan, we accept calmly the possibility that our results may not be replicated by other researchers. So you won't hear *us* saying you guys are lying scumbags. We note that our car had a bigger engine than yours and that we were doing our testing in Ohio in May, not (as in your case) south Florida in July. Obviously more research is called for. We'll get on it right away.

Update on Mexican Food Antidotes

In *The Straight Dope* I mentioned that milk will quench the fiery taste of Mexican and other spicy foods. I described milk as a dilutant, but it turns out there's more to it than that. According to Robert Henkin of the Taste and Smell Clinic in Washington, D.C., writing in the *Journal of the American Medical Association*, the capsaicin in hot peppers binds to nerve receptors in the mouth, causing a burning sensation. A protein in milk called casein "acts like a detergent and literally wipes or strips the capsaicin from its receptor binding site."

I Can't Stand It

Readers of *More of the Straight Dope* will recall our discussion of whether the Great Wall of China was the only man-made object on earth you could see from orbit. I said, correctly, that it wasn't. This moved a reader to reply that the Great Wall was the only man-made object on earth you could see from the moon. I said that wasn't true either; *no* man-made objects on earth were visible from the moon.

Now I see a magazine ad for the Royal Viking cruise line that features a photograph of the Great Wall with the following headline:

> IT BEGAN 400 YEARS BEFORE CHRIST.
> IT IS VISIBLE FROM MARS.

I give up.

Index

C

cabooses, why trains don't have any more, 282–283

calendar numbering, origin of modern system of, 376–377

"callipygian," 259

calories: how quantified, 97; in airline food, 145; why all cereals seem to have same number of per serving, 114–115

cancer: and fiber, 94–95; and plastic foam cups, 109–111; prevention of by spinach and other vegetables, 121

candle wax, where it goes when candle burns, 351

cannibalism, debate over extent of, 54–56

cans, how they get beer into, 114

carbonation, whether hanging spoon in champagne bottle will preserve, 121–123

carburetors, 200 MPG, feasibility of, 150–153

carotene, 120, 121

carrageenan (food additive), 97–98

Caruso, Enrico, 334, 335

cashmere, origin in Kashmir, 21

catsup vs. ketchup, 102

cattle, lack of singular gender-neutral term for, 100–101

Cayley, George (paper airplane pioneer), 19

cellular telephones, 290

cent sign, significance of C in, 178–179

century, when new one begins, 378–379

cereals, why all seem to have same number of calories per serving, 114–115

CFCs (chlorofluorocarbons), why

they can't be used to destroy local ozone excess, 354–355

champagne, whether hanging spoon in bottle of will save carbonation, 121–123

channel changing. See TV

charge cards, 177

"cheap at half the price," 241

checks. See rebate checks

chefs and white hats, 25–26

Chicago Board of Trade, 180–182

chicken. See "If a chicken and a half . . ."

children, alleged raising of by wolves, 46–47

"Chinese restaurant syndrome" (MSG-induced symptoms), 86

cholesterol, 117

chopstick, why plucking while gripped in teeth causes TV to shimmer, 272

Christmas Carol, A (Dickens novel), and emergence of modern Christmas celebration, 15

Christmas celebration, emergence of modern, during Victorian era, 14–15

CIA, and "numbers stations," 330–332

clean air futures (Chicago Board of Trade product), 180–182

clitoris, alleged discovery of in 1559, 212–214

cloning, of mammoth by Russian scientists, 408–409

cochineal, 119–120

"cold turkey," 269

coldest possible temperature, 347

"colonel," why pronounced "kernel," 250–251

color vision, in dogs, 412–413

colors, primary. See primary colors

Columbus, Renaldus, 212–213

Comiskey Park, 379–380

O

P

About the Author

Cecil Adams is the author. You got a problem with that?